Orienta
Postcolo

Y LOAN
ng Centre of
of issue

SOUTH ASIA SEMINAR SERIES

A listing of the books in this series appears at the back of this volume

University of Pennsylvania Press
NEW CULTURAL STUDIES
Joan DeJean, Carroll Smith-Rosenberg, and
Peter Stallybrass, Editors

Orientalism and the Postcolonial Predicament

Perspectives on South Asia

Edited by
Carol A. Breckenridge
and Peter van der Veer

University of Pennsylvania Press

Philadelphia

Permission is acknowledged to reprint excerpts from published material:

Georges Duby, "Histoire sociale et idéologies des sociétés," in *Faire de l'histoire: Nouveaux problèmes,* ed. Jacques le Goff and Pierre Nora. Paris: Gallimard, 1974. Also in *Constructing the Past.* Cambridge: Cambridge University Press. Translated by Sheldon Pollock.

Library of Congress Cataloging-in-Publication Data

Orientalism and the postcolonial predicament : perspectives on South Asia / edited by
    Carol A. Breckenridge and Peter van der Veer.
       p.   cm. — (South Asia seminar series) (New cultural studies)
    Papers presented at the 44th Annual South Asia Seminar held at the University of
Pennsylvania, 1988/1989.
    Includes bibliographical references and index.
    ISBN 0-8122-3168-6. — ISBN 0-8122-1436-6 (pbk.)
    1. South Asia—Study and teaching—Congresses. 2. South Asia—Foreign public
opinion, Occidental—Congresses. I. Breckenridge, Carol Appadurai, 1942–
II. Veer, Peter van der. III. South Asia Seminar (44th : 1988 : University of
Pennsylvania). IV. Series. V. Series: New cultural studies.
DS339.8.O75   1993
954—dc20   93-18290
                                        CIP

Contents

vi   Contents

Preface

The 44th Annual South Asia Seminar at the University of Pennsylvania spent the academic year 1988/1989 on the topic "Orientalism and Beyond." The present volume is the outcome of those deliberations, although some lecturers (Richard Fox, Peter Gaeffke, Wilhelm Halbfass, Barbara Metcalf, Triloki Pandey, and Gyan Prakash) are not represented here. The essays by Arjun Appadurai and David Lelyveld were not presented in the seminar series, and the essays by Nicholas Dirks and Gayatri Chakravorty Spivak depart considerably from their original presentations.

The seminar was organized by Carol A. Breckenridge, Wilhelm Halbfass, and David Ludden. Regrettably, neither of the latter was able to assist in the editing of this volume. In 1990 Carol was joined by a new colleague, Peter van der Veer, who, in addition to helping to shape the volume intellectually, has largely been responsible for seeing that deadlines were set and met and that this volume was sent off to press.

South Asia Regional Studies at the University of Pennsylvania was the first South Asia area studies program in the United States. It therefore seemed appropriate for Penn South Asianists collectively to engage in reflection on what today constitutes the reproduction of knowledge in respect to the modern countries of South Asia, which include India, Pakistan, Bangladesh, and Sri Lanka. The lecture series unveiled differences of opinion about the relationship between knowledge and power that were sometimes the subject of public debate, sometimes the cause of personal turmoil, and sometimes the topic of criticism presented in other arenas. Some participants disagreed with revisionist propositions about such foundational social formations as caste and religion. Others objected to what they regarded as an injection of ideology into scholarship and to what they saw as "orientalist-bashing." One has written that "the whole seminar seemed to be set up to defame textual scholarship and Orientalist learning" (Gaeffke 1990: 73). It is true that more voices from among the humanists studying South Asia than from among the social scientists could be found to participate in the seminar. But this was not by design. It is worth reflecting on why the reflexive voice is so difficult to find among

social scientists, particularly those in the fields of psychology and economics. The organizers were painfully aware of this absence.

In the course of the seminar year, graduate students were made privy
to the challenges that they face as heirs to the tradition of study about
South Asia that derives from colonial India and continues into the present
period. They are the beneficiaries of both the doubts and the certainties of
the late twentieth century. This volume serves as a reminder that there is a
time and a space in which to investigate the authority of received wisdom.

We thank Amy Trubek for her detailed attention to the needs of the
seminar, Karen Vorkapich for her management of the lecturers' travel arrangements, and Alan Heston for his calm and steady support. Finally,
without the commitment of Victoria Farmer neither the manuscript nor
the index would have been prepared for publication. Her thoroughness
and thoughtful reflection on some of the knotty intellectual issues in the
volume were greatly appreciated.

Carol A. Breckenridge
Peter van der Veer
Philadelphia, 1992

Reference

Gaeffke, Peter. 1990. "A Rock in the Tides of Time: Oriental Studies Then and
Now." *Academic Questions* 3, 2: 67–74.

Carol A. Breckenridge and
Peter van der Veer

Orientalism and the Postcolonial Predicament

The contemporary world is discussed by journalists, scholars, and architects as an age of "posts": the postmodern, the postnational, and the poststructural, to mention a few. Yet another "post" is invoked here: the *postcolonial*. "Post" implies that which is behind us, and the past implies periodization. We can therefore speak of the *postcolonial period* as a framing device to characterize the second half of the twentieth century. The term "postcolonial" displaces the focus on "postwar" as a historical marker for the last fifty years. "Postwar" refers of course to the period after World War II and, although the war was central to "decolonization" and the division of the postcolonial world into what came to be called the first, second, and third worlds, it is used to periodize history much less frequently in the ex-colonial world than in the metropolitan worlds of Europe and America.

To call the second half of the twentieth century postcolonial, then, is to call for a reappraisal of the way we frame contemporary world history and to emphasize the rupture in national and global relations created by the urge to forge independent nation-states first in the colonial world and now in the "second world" of Eastern Europe and the former Soviet Union. It brings to our attention the relations between colonialism and nationalism in the politics of culture in both the societies of the ex-colonizers and those of the ex-colonized.

The postcolonial predicament in which students of society and history find themselves stems from a growing awareness of the role of their academic disciplines in the reproduction of patterns of domination. For scholars who think with and about the (ex)colonial world, this awareness is strongest when applied to colonial scholarship (e.g., the recent turn to "colonial discourse") and weakest when it comes to a critique of the present and to the formulation of critical alternatives and methods for approaching the study of other world regions. In fact, the investigation of the power of colonial knowledge is, in an interesting way, often matched by a mood of impotence and irrelevance in sparse reflections on the present. Indeed, one aspect of the postcolonial predicament is that critiques of colonialism have not really led to a reflection on the evolution of knowledge that brings us into the postcolonial (or neocolonial) present.

The present volume poses the problem of knowledge and power from a historical perspective by showing the contradictory relations—intellectual, administrative, and cultural—between the (colonial) past and the (postcolonial) present. Our proposition is not so much the usual historical one, that we have to understand social and cultural processes historically, but rather that we have to rethink our methodologies and the relation between theories, methods, and the historical conditions that produced them. The postcolonial predicament has two dimensions: the first is that the colonial period has given us both the evidence and the theories that select and connect them; and, second, that decolonization does not entail immediate escape from colonial discourse. Despite all the recent talk of "third-world voices," this predicament defines both the ex-colonizer and the ex-colonized. To some extent this is tantamount to saying that we cannot escape from history, but this volume goes on to demonstrate that in the Indian subcontinent—and the study thereof—we cannot escape from a history characterized by a particular discursive formation that can be called "orientalism."

The discourse and practice of orientalism exemplifies the postcolonial predicament of South Asians and westerners alike. Western studies of South Asia in general use, explicitly or implicitly, a comparative framework in which "the West" is contrasted to "the rest." This is exemplified in studies of South Asian democracy and politics in general as a "failed experiment" in contrast to an idealized western reality (see Lele in this volume). This is also obvious in many descriptions of India's "communalism" as a "failed" nationalism (see van der Veer, in this volume). More generally, the religious nature of India's society is contrasted to the secular nature of western society. Much of this derives from the modernization and development paradigm as discussed by Lele. Clearly, we are dealing with images of the Orient that make images of the Occident possible.

At the same time that these peculiar reciprocal images of Orient and Occident proliferate, it grows increasingly clear that the problems of both the metropolis and the ex-colonies are both common and connected.

Rapid and large movements of laboring groups create and add to ethnic tensions in the United States and in Europe, thus making it difficult to distinguish the tensions of pluralism from the dread of ethnic violence. The rapid flow of high technologies such as video and laser and fiber optics make news and images instantly available across long distances. Diseases such as AIDS, problems of terrorist violence, and the rapid de-skilling of large populations now bedevil most societies in the world. Everywhere the power of nationalism is on the rise, even as states struggle to maintain civil control over their populations. These linkages and dilemmas as well as others involving economic instability, homelessness, and drug addiction make it increasingly impossible to draw a sharp line between ex-metropoles and ex-colonies. The postcolonial predicament is now constituted by an interconnected series of religious, political, economic, and social dilemmas that are global in their scope. While this volume does not engage this global dimension directly, it tries to show that orientalism provides one discursive link between the special features of the colonial period and the more globalized political and social dilemmas of the present, certainly in the case of India.

The Critique of Orientalism

The present volume derives much of its inspiration from Edward Said's stimulating publication entitled *Orientalism* (1978). Said's work deals primarily with scholarship on the Arab world and the Middle East, but much of his argument can be (and has been) applied to other regions of what has been defined as the "Orient."

Said was heir to two bodies of literature that served him as points of departure. One pertained to the place of Asia (particularly India) in the historical construction of the European *imaginaire*. The other, more critical literature called attention to the politics and ideology of orientalist projects, emphasizing their relations with the colonial expansion. Representative of the first literature is Raymond Schwab's *The Oriental Renaissance: Europe's Rediscovery of India and the East, 1680–1880* (French original 1950; English translation 1984) and representative of the second is Anwar Abdel Malek's seminal essay "Orientalism in Crisis," which in 1963 called for a careful examination of the politics of the orientalist project. It took the *reflexive turn* of the 1970s and 1980s in literary studies, anthropology, and history for a critical audience to form that could debate our own praxis as well as the practices underlying global relations more generally. Said's critique of orientalism was part of a more critical conjuncture in the 1980s that was facilitated by theoretical developments in poststructuralism, neo-Marxism, and deconstructionism and feminism, where the Enlightenment topic of subject-formation prevailed (Bhatnagar 1986).

The orientalism debate has been sharpened in relation to South Asia by scholars who have contributed to both of the above bodies of literature. Following the path opened by Schwab, the historian of Indian philosophy Wilhelm Halbfass has written a book entitled *India and Europe: An Essay in Understanding* (1988), which pursues an analytical perspective that is grounded in the philosophical concerns of India as well as Europe. And, following the more political direction taken by Malek and Said, Ronald Inden has recently published an important study entitled *Imagining India* (1990). Inden gives a critique of essentialist depictions of "Hindu" India since the Enlightenment. By recasting India's precolonial political institutions, he attempts to restore agency to its people and structures. While this is illustrated in a reconstruction of the Indian polity in the early medieval period, the bulk of Inden's book focuses on the deconstruction of essentialist categories, such as caste, the Indian mind, village India, and divine kingship. Both Inden and Halbfass restrict themselves to an analysis of orientalist ideas about India.

The present volume goes beyond such analysis by dealing explicitly with the relation between orientalist ideas and the colonial project to organize and rule Indian society. Theoretically, this volume runs parallel to Said's and Inden's work inasmuch as they have their roots in Foucault's project to unravel the multiple relations of knowledge and power in the West (e.g., Bhatnagar 1986) and in Gramsci's speculations about hegemony and resistance. These perspectives on the nature of power have more recently been connected to orientalism and concerns about the politics of representation in scholarly writing (Clifford 1988).

The present book engages Said's arguments in three ways. First, it attempts to clarify the relations between literary, anthropological, and historical understandings of South Asia on the one hand, and colonial and nationalist understandings on the other. Significant continuities can be seen in the disciplinary projects of both the colonial and the postcolonial periods. Attention is given to the historical development of these projects with all the attendant shifts and ruptures. Second, the essays here show that colonized subjects are not passively produced by hegemonic projects but are active agents whose choices and discourses are of fundamental importance in the formation of their societies. And third, some steps are taken to show the extent to which orientalism is not only constitutive of the Orient but also of the Occident and that these images cannot be divorced from the political arenas in which they are produced.

Colonial Discourse and Colonial Practice

Within the field of cultural studies, the discussions that are most germane to the issues here revolve around "colonial discourse." This term has turned critical attention to the study of the language of the historical representation of colonized peoples and, by extension, of oppressed others more generally. The discussion of otherness (e.g., Mohanty 1989) has tended to imply that others are undifferentiated and that projects that focus on difference—whether the difference of gender, race, class, or cultural otherness—have a homologous relation one to the other: race can stand in for gender; gender can stand in for class and class for the culturally distant. Positioning the third world along side race and gender in debates on otherness is worthwhile, particularly when it calls attention to the legacies of domination and repression, the multiplicity of voices, and the complexity of power that is culturally embedded in the everyday. But such accounts usually limit themselves to the study of textual rhetoric in travel accounts, biographies, and bureaucratic memoranda. Such efforts to analyze colonial discourse can have the curious effect of textualizing colonialism, and even, sometimes, of making the colonial project a largely textual one. The word discourse in this context itself shows the strain of making these texts provide evidence they do not contain.

The use of the term "discourse" in Said's work is already highly problematic. While he derives the term from Foucault, Said's usage is very different. As Aijaz Ahmad (1991: 145–46) reminds us, when Foucault uses the term discourse in dealing with a western episteme, he presumes the presence of modern state forms and institutional grids that arise between the sixteenth and eighteenth century. Said seems at points to refer to a singular, transhistorical orientalist discourse, tracing it back to ancient Greek theater, that really essentializes "the West" to a considerable extent. The challenge of orientalism is precisely the challenge of a discursive formation that has complicated extratextual and nondiscursive implications and consequences. Part of this challenge can be taken on by looking at the interpenetration of multiple colonial discourses, and another part can be addressed by asking about the kinds of brute empirical realities and the new forms of subjectivity that such colonial discourses produced. This volume takes on both these challenges. The chapters by Appadurai, Ludden, and Lelyveld show that the discourse of number, of land, and of language are deeply interconnected pieces of a complex discursive formation. These chapters, along with the chapters by Dharwadker, Pollock, and Lele, also show that colonial discourses are not only interconnected but also *productive* discourses, which create new kinds of knowledge, expression, political practice, and subjectivity.

Most important, the literature that alludes to colonial discourse typically is unable to deal with, or is unengaged by, the question of the postcolonial predicament, thus making the colonial narrative sufficient unto itself. Many of the chapters in this volume relate colonial projects of knowledge and domination to specific aspects of the postcolonial political and cultural world. Rather than suggesting a linear, historical link between colonial and postcolonial projects and discursive habits, these essays take a more complex, genealogical approach, looking for the continuities and the ruptures between these two discursive formations and placing these links within specific kinds of practice: poetic, social scientific, and administrative.

Orientalism, thus, is not just a way of thinking. It is a way of conceptualizing the landscape of the colonial world that makes it susceptible to certain kinds of management. Said's own book is long on the intellectual history side of this but short on the administrative *imaginaire* that it both obscures and facilitates. The time has come to spell out some of the links between the poetics and politics of colonial discourse and the practical projects of colonial rule. This would allow us to see postcolonial cultural practices as products not just of orientalist theory but of colonial practice.

As David Lelyveld shows in his essay on the formation of the North Indian language known as "Hindustani," the very languages that are called "native" are products of an intricate dialectic between colonial projects of knowledge and the formation of distinctive group identities. The social history of how people learn languages and how they use them is undoubtedly fraught with questions of power and authority. The fate of Hindustani can be enclosed between the dates of two lexicons—Gilchrist's, started in 1785, and All India Radio's, completed in 1945. By paying native speakers, Gilchrist attempted to create a literature for the classroom on the basis of everyday speech. There was no Indian "public" that could serve as an audience for his books and, as Lelyveld observes, it was the colonial imagination that set out to create a common language on the basis of the immense linguistic diversity of everyday speech in North India. The All India Radio lexicographers also attempted to establish a finite body of words that could constitute a language called Hindustani. Here, however, the imagined speech community had to be related not to the early construction of a common language for colonial consumption but to language as a matter of national unity.

The construction of conflicting nationalisms that led to the failure of the All India Radio project have to be related to projects of the colonial state that succeeded Gilchrist's market-oriented enterprise. The gradual formation of such knowledge-related projects receive considerable attention in this volume; they demonstrate that the "order" imposed on Indian society by the colonial state accounts for many of the postcolonial predicaments faced by the societies of South Asia today. Here all the contributors are clearly indebted to Bernard S. Cohn's seminal insights on the relation between the colonial state and colonial society (1987). Cohn's project on the sociology of colonial knowledge and its instantiation in administrative and sociological agendas is advanced here by Appadurai, Dirks, Lelyveld, and Rocher particularly.

The first step is to look at the late eighteenth century, in which an incipient colonialism under the mantle of the British East India Company could still largely be interpreted as a mercantile enterprise. Rosane Rocher notes in her contribution the importance of treatises on Hindu law in the production of orientalist knowledge. There can be no doubt that the formulation and textualization of a Hindu law (and of a Muslim law, for that matter) created a legal discourse that changed the administration of justice in Indian society in fundamental ways. The underlying assumption of Hasting's Judicial Plan was that India's cultural and religious diversity could be reduced to a dichotomy of Hindu versus Muslim law, which created a discursive framework for later colonial policy to "divide and rule" Hindus and Muslims.

Early orientalism developed alongside the European Enlightenment. This convergence of oriental and Enlightenment discourse facilitated the coalescing of important notions of modernity, citizenship, and rationality. As Halbfass (1988: 60) has shown, India came to illustrate "the theme of the eclipse and suppression of the 'natural light' through superstition and ritualism, a theme that enjoyed great popularity among thinkers of the Enlightenment." This orientalist view coincided with an indigenous Brahmanical notion of the staged deterioration of civilization to the depraved conditions of the present (*kaliyuga*).

Early orientalists looked for the "finer specimens" of Indian tradition.

Hastings found them in the first translation of the *Bhagavadgita,* which he thought, as Rocher shows, contained "many specimens of fine morality" that coincided with the principal concerns of liberal, undogmatic Anglicans. This was clearly not only a matter of taste, but also of politics. Hastings sent the *Gita,* a text without any possible governmental application, to England for publication. He sought to show British public opinion the advanced state of Indian civilization in order to thwart the attempts of the home administration of the East India Company to usher in British common law for the administration of justice in India. Rocher demonstrates that these seemingly contradictory intellectual moves provided a basis for later reformist views of what had come to be called "Hindu" religion. This orientalist intervention provided the foundation whereby the *Gita* could become the Hindu text par excellence for India's great nationalist leader, Mohandas Gandhi.

Fascinating in the orientalist pursuit of knowledge is its empiricism, rooted in the Enlightenment rubric of objective science. David Ludden argues that orientalism was conceived as a body of scientific discoveries about Indian reality, a set of "factualized" statements detached epistemologically from colonial politics. With the transformation of the British East India Company from a mercantile agency to a governing body in the late eighteenth century, empiricism came to embrace more and more aspects of Indian society and its landscape as well. Ludden shows the gradual transition from individual exploration to systematized knowledge production that accompanied the routinization of the colonial rule in the period between 1770 and 1820. This is the period in which the facticity of India's "autonomous village communities" is established as is that of "Hindu" religion and caste. All three features quickly came to be earmarked as the foundational elements of Indian society. Data were collected to construct an authoritative account of India, and in that process competitive accounts were silenced in the official record. Of course, the collection of data was not the only method employed for the construction of colonial knowledge. Theory was often shaped by political and intellectual discourse in Europe, in which the relation between India and Europe became more and more a feature of a universal history leading to Europe's modernity. As Ludden remarks, orientalism became the template for knowing an oriental Other in contradistinction to European capitalism, rationality, and modernity.

Once it had been empirically substantiated, orientalism as a body of knowledge became institutionally embedded in Indian political culture. This is clearly brought out by Arjun Appadurai's focus on number in the colonial imagination. Appadurai argues that the politics of entitlement and classification that lie behind the antireservation and communal riots of the postcolonial period have their roots in orientalism. Quoting Said, he notes that various colonial projects specialized "in the particularizing and dividing of things oriental into manageable parts" (Said 1978: 72). Appadurai highlights the quantitative, numerical side of the classification of India by the British colonial state. Numerical data were of course crucial to what Ludden has called "orientalist empiricism" as well.

Appadurai's thesis is that the cadastral project of measuring and classifying the land constitutes a rehearsal for later discourse concerning human populations and their enumeration. In effect, it "unyokes" people from the agrarian landscape, which enables the later census operation to treat castes as abstractable from their territorial context. Numerical majorities in what Appadurai calls a "pan-Indian social encyclopedia" were given prominence in the census and became the basis of the communal and caste politics of the twentieth century. What makes the cadastral project so applicable to India's human populations is the essentializing and exoticizing gaze of orientalism that makes bio-racial commonalities and differences the principle of its politics of difference. The "imagined communities" of Hindu and Muslim nationalism were produced in the colonial *imaginaire* as "enumerated communities."

Orientalist empiricism conceived its reliance on native informants as highly problematic for the establishment of "facts." This was already a problem for the *ur* orientalist Judge William Jones, who in 1784 wrote to his superior Warren Hastings that "I can no longer bear to be at the mercy of our Pundits, who deal out Hindu law as they please . . ." (see Ludden in this volume). The problem is traced in Nicholas Dirks's essay on the career and writings of the administrator Colin Mackenzie, who spent most of his time in India compiling a massive collection of documents, manuscripts, inscriptions, drawings, and other artifacts. Mackenzie did not know any Indian languages and had to rely on native assistants in his surveys. Mackenzie was exemplary in this respect; his chief interpreter, the Brahmin named Boria, commanded four Indian languages plus English. Boria recruited and trained an establishment of learned Brahmans to work for Mackenzie. Dirks demonstrates the extent to which the native assistants were instrumental in constructing colonial knowledge in this early period only to be silenced when the Mackenzie collection was accessed by the archive of the colonial state. There the voices of the natives are marginalized in a hegemonic colonial discourse.

It is not only the reliance on native informants that underlines the agency of colonized subjects in the formation of colonial discourse. One can go one step further by showing, as Sheldon Pollock does, that there are important family resemblances between precolonial Brahmanical discourse and orientalist scholarship. Pollock argues that the German orientalists took a feature of Brahmanical discourse, namely its distinction between Aryans and non-Aryans, as "civilized" and "uncivilized" respectively, and applied this distinction to their own society in their attempt to define the Jews as non-Aryan.

This interplay between indigenous and orientalist discourses of power in the formation of authoritative knowledge deserves further attention as it was manifest in Europe as well as in South Asia. A number of the essays collected here demonstrate that there were complicated links between the projects of the colonizer and the colonized. This is not the facile argument that the colonial state and colonized elites were actually hand in glove. Nor does it replicate the invitation of the subaltern group of historians to recover the voices of the Indian masses by authorizing them as the true native voices of resistance (e.g., Guha and Spivak 1988). The point is that there is neither a monolithic imperial project nor a monolithic subaltern reaction, but rather that there are different historical trajectories of contest and change with lags and disjunctures along the way. While denying the absoluteness and uni-directionality of colonial hegemony and while ascribing agency to both colonizers and colonized, there is no doubting the larger evolving picture of colonial domination that goes far beyond the individual intentions or aspirations of any of its principal actors.

Colonial sites like India need not enter cultural studies only through the lens of colonial discourse, with its implicit textual and rhetorical implications. Part of the difficulty with the "colonial discourse" mode of entry into the politics of "otherness" is that it locates the otherness of the other wholly (and even solely) in the colonial moment, thus eliding the question of pre- or noncolonial differences of consequence. In the manner noted by Fabian (1983), this approach tends to place the other in the colonial past and thus to ignore the contemporaneity of what used to be the colonial world—its current politics and its debates about modernity.

The postcolonial predicament is not the explicit topic of most of the essays in this volume, but it is the framework within which we suggest many of the essays are best read. The heritage of orientalism has affected many aspects of Indian life, ranging from the nature of vernacular fiction to the practice of modernization theory by social scientists. Of course, not all that is of consequence about the postcolonial predicament can usefully be related to orientalism. But the pervading sense that India is a land of pathological differences, that its essence is unique and unfathomable and that its populations are ungovernable, owes itself to orientalist views of some sort. What is more important is that orientalism as theory has affected a number of political and administrative practices, which have, in new forms, affected the political life of the subcontinent.

This "internal orientalism" (by analogy with Michael Hechter's (1975) "internal colonialism") is by far the most problematic feature of the postcolonial predicament. As is most clearly brought out in the chapters by Appadurai, Lele, and van der Veer, it is very difficult for both Indians and outsiders to think about India outside of orientalist habits and categories. The consequence is not simply a sort of lag, where political independence runs ahead of intellectual dependence. Rather, the very cultural basis of public life has been affected (and infected) by ideas of difference and division that have colonial and orientalist roots. Whether it is the matter of language and literature, communalism and the census, or caste and social science, orientalist theory casts its shadow over cultural politics in postcolonial India even though the specific politics of colonial domination are no longer relevant. This irony is at the heart of the "postcolonial predicament," namely that a theory of difference that was deeply interwoven with the practices of colonial control lives on in the absence of foreign rule.

Orientalism without colonialism is a headless theoretical beast, that much the harder to identify and eradicate because it has become internalized in the practices of the postcolonial state, the theories of the postcolonial intelligentsia, and the political action of postcolonial mobs. Though this volume is devoted to the analysis of orientalism in its original setting—colonial rule—it is haunted by the specter of postcolonial orientalism, no longer explicitly formulated as part of a theory of difference and of dominion, but transposed now into the very sinews of public life and group politics.

There is a crucial and peculiar link between orientalist discourse and the vitality of the public sphere in India today. By casting its master-questions in terms of what made Indians different qua Indians, and also what made differences among Indians so much more pervasive than differences elsewhere (e.g., the specter of caste), orientalist discourse gave a peculiar essentialist twist to nationalist discourse in India. It is of course the case that all nationalist discourse appeals to primordial images—of blood, of kinship, of soil, and of sexuality—in order to imbue the nation with the force of bodily self-interest. But in those colonial sites where orientalist discourse held sway, it made it impossible to conceptualize the nation in relation to any sort of civil society on the western model, since all social groups, all habits of thought, and all traditions of politics were seen as emanations of group identity and essential bodily differences. By thus linking the discourse of the nation irretrievably to the politics of biologically based group difference, orientalist discourse made it impossible to evolve a postcolonial language of politics in which the essence of Indian unity was not the master problem: the entire rhetoric of Nehru's *Discovery of India* (1946), for example, is suffused with the anguish of India's elusive, enduring, unique essence, and it was this essence that was seen as the sole possible foundation of its unity.

In thus making it impossible to separate the problem of national essence from the problem of unity, orientalist discourse laid the grounds for a political discourse in which all group differences could only be seen as dangerous separatisms. To take only a small aspect of this, it is difficult in contemporary India for a political group to constitute itself on the basis of shared interests of some sort (such as trade unions or political parties or voluntary association) without being seen, both by themselves and by others, as thinly disguised representatives of some sort of religious, caste, or sectarian interest. This essentialization and somaticization of group differences is probably the most damaging part of the orientalist bequest to postcolonial politics.

Orientalism and Nationalism

Nationalism is thus not the answer to orientalism as implied in Said's book. Rather, nationalism is the avatar of orientalism in the later colonial and postcolonial periods. As both Ludden and Appadurai argue here, one of the most lasting and fundamental of the orientalist contributions to knowledge about India was the essentialization of the Hindu-Muslim opposition and its institutionalization in political representation. Colonial discourses reified complex structures of ideas and practices and produced the "culture" both nationalism and anthropology sought. A recurring theme in these essays is the thesis that orientalism created the discursive space in which widely divergent understandings of South Asia had to be located.

Peter van der Veer probes the extent to which the anthropological understanding of culture as a bounded, integrated, and homogeneous whole shares common intellectual grounds with the nationalist search for historical continuity and cultural identity. He discusses Louis Dumont's influential essay "Nationalism and Communalism" (1970) and shows its affinity with the two-nation theory that was developed in colonial India and was so influential in the separation of Pakistan from India as a homeland for Muslims in 1947. Dumont's theory of Indian society explicitly combines Indology and sociology and is as such one of the clearest heirs of the orientalist legacy.

Orientalism has not only been influential in the construction of nationalism in South Asia, but it has also played a significant role in fortifying aspects of European nationalism. In his analysis of German Indology and its public uses during the national socialist period, Sheldon Pollock shows that in Germany orientalism helped define Semites as non-Aryan and thus as inferior. (It is noteworthy that, although German Indology was unrivaled in its scope and productivity and was thus fundamental to orientalism as a body of knowledge more generally, German Indology was largely ignored by Said, because Germany was not a colonizing state in Asia). While Pollock's argument problematizes the relation between colonialism and orientalism, Pollock makes it clear that orientalist discourse had a fundamental effect on the society that produced it in the first place, namely Germany. In the German case the colonizing project turned itself inward to produce an "internal orientalism" (discussed above) under the rubric of the master race, which was given philological legitimation through the imbrication of ideology and appropriated Indian ideals.

The deployment of orientalist discourse by national projects may be one of the most striking features of the postcolonial predicament for both the colonized and the colonizer. Nationalism, however, is not the only historical successor of colonialism. There is an interesting interface between nationalism and transnational processes. While nationalism can be seen as a discourse that defines the nation in terms of territorial boundaries, there is concurrently a constant movement of those defined as citizens outside of national boundaries. The flow of goods, persons, and information in the world system creates cultural arenas that go beyond those defined by the nation-state while undoubtedly related to them. Here again orientalism plays a role in the definition of cultural selves in diasporic confrontations with cultural alternatives. This is clear in van der Veer's description of the role of transnational Hinduism in nationalist discourse in South Asia today. But like nationalism, transnational cultural flows also move in both directions to shape the ex-colonized as well as the ex-colonizer. This has been poignantly borne out by the public debate in Britain about multiculturalism in the wake of the Rushdie affair. Being "British" became a political issue of great urgency for the English when Muslim immigrants started to assert their difference in terms of their own religious traditions rather than in the language of multiculturalism, which has been dominated by an ideology predicated on the belief and commitment to a shared secular culture that was of course "British" at its core (Asad 1990).

Powered by the complicated international diasporas of guest-workers and other disenfranchised populations, the internal racial cultural politics of both metropolis and colonies, and by the unifying rhetorics of various global fundamentalisms, the postcolonial pathologies of various colonial sites are again being globalized and retrojected into the politics of the metropolis (Appadurai and Breckenridge 1987). Thus England and France have to deal with the cultural politics of Saudi Arabia, Iran, Iraq, Pakistan, and India, as mediated through various layers of diasporic imagination and global financial linkage (Kramer 1991). Again, while the essays in this volume do not dwell on this global and transnational dimension of postcolonial politics, it is important to see that the orientalist heritage has its part to play here as well. For example, Rushdie and his critics struggle to claim the high ground on how to "read" and how to "write" Islam, as well as on the deeper question of the role of cosmopolitan artists and intellectuals in addressing topics that tread on religious and nationalist sentiments.

Modernity and Authenticity

Another side of the construction of identity and difference can be found in the cultural debate on authenticity and modernity. V. S. Naipaul, a Trinidadian Indian, has argued that Indian writers such as R. K. Narayan have difficulties with the novel as a modern literary form since they cannot shed their traditional perspective. In Naipaul's understanding it is the "view from outside" that enables the Indian in the diaspora to "see" and then write. In this argument Naipaul has adopted the orientalist perspective by drawing a sharp boundary between the traditional "inside" and the modern "outside." This assumption leads to the attribution of "authenticity" to what is seen as traditional and of "mimicry" to any effort to adopt modern practices. What he fails to see is that writing and reading in India take place in a society that has gone through a colonial transformation that makes this whole set of oppositions inappropriate. Moreover, this view fails to account for the expectations Naipaul himself has when he comes to read Indian writing.

As Vinay Dharwadker shows in his essay, the orientalist understanding of "Indian literature" is embedded in the development of European conceptualizations of what constitutes "literature" and of ways to study this category. He suggests that early orientalist studies have been in the forefront of the development of innovative conceptions in both the Enlightenment and in the romantic-nationalist traditions. Instead of situating India and its study outside of the history of western discourses, we have to realize that it is centrally located within them. At the same time, substantively, orientalism constitutes "foundational knowledge" about India that cannot be dismissed, as Dharwadker argues (see also Ludden, in this volume). Orientalism provides a totalizing discourse on literature as the expression of the cultural identity of Indian society that is recaptured, from the nineteenth century, in cultural nationalism. Ultimately, it is this discourse that enables Naipaul to understand contemporary Indian literature as the expression of India's "traditional spirit."

Similarly, the use of English—the language of the colonizers—as against that of vernacular languages of India is often seen as "unauthentic," "unIndian," "westernized," and "modern." However, English itself has been naturalized in the Indian experience, with many implications and complications, which are skillfully explored by Gayatri Chakravorty Spivak in her essay in this volume. Examining the complex pedagogic place of English literature in contemporary Indian curricula, as well as the place of English fiction as a thematic in Indian fiction, Spivak resists any form of linguistic nativism and argues instead that the teaching of English literature must be yoked to the teaching of literary and cultural expression in the mother tongues. In thus confronting English literature with its indigenous counterparts, Spivak suggests that literature be seen and constructed as "the staged battle-ground of epistemes." In making these suggestions, and embodying them in a close reading of a short story by Tagore, among other examples, Spivak does not only engage the problematic of a "Commonwealth" literature in the postcolonial setting. She also makes the sort of pedagogic proposals that resist the containment of the colonial subject within his or her mother tongue, the eternal object of scrutiny from an English viewpoint. Such containment and objectification of one set of languages by another is, of course, central to the interpretive technologies of orientalism, in which English and its literatures became the vehicles both for scrutinizing and civilizing the colonial subject.

Orientalism, History, and the Social Sciences

Among workers in the human sciences, social scientists have been particularly recalcitrant when it comes to self-reflection on their *representational* strategies in respect to the nonwestern world, and in respect to South Asia in particular. The humanities are not the only realm of scholarship that has facilitated the construction of an enfeebled, subservient, and sometimes oppositional other. Scholars in the fields of psychology, economics, and political science have launched far-reaching projects and critiques of the nonwestern world based on cultural essentialisms that have come to explain the "failure" of modernity and their modernization ventures. Recent critiques of development theory (e.g., Marglin and Marglin 1990) have paved the way for the social scientists to interact with the critique of orientalism to expose the contradictions that underlie social science theories of modernity.

Jayant Lele's essay attempts to explore some of the contradictions in the way the social sciences portray India by linking them to the changing fortunes of colonial and postcolonial capitalism and imperialism. Lele argues that the failure of Foucault (and Said) to provide this linkage has done little to reduce the power of the metanarrative of modernity, which can easily absorb a critique of its pathological consequences. By focusing not on power relations but on the power of decontextualized discourse, these authors, in Lele's view, contribute to the dominance of the ruling classes. Lele argues that within the western tradition there are critical counterpoints to the dominant discourse that can be related to crises in the political economy. An example of this is the demise of structural-functionalism that derived its dominance from the requirements of post-war political economy. In development theory, as applied to the "third world," structural-functionalism with its emphasis on means-ends rationality was infused with an evolutionist optimism. It is the crisis of Fordism in the late 1960s that has put an end to this general perspective, and Lele gives some examples of the confusion among social scientists after that. He argues forcefully that the reason for the often contingent and relativistic "explanations" given for events in India lies in an orientalist isolation of the study of the third world from critical reflection about the western social formation. In Lele's view, a critique of the orientalist nature of modernization theory may open up the possibility of a new understanding not only of India but also of the West.

Moving beyond orientalism is one of the more pressing needs of contemporary scholarly investigations. The option that has been opened by the critique of orientalism is an option to shape a critical theory of our contemporary practice. Such a project is well within the bounds of Foucault's mandate in his later work to pursue "a permanent critique of our contemporary age." Though Foucault did not ground what he meant by a "permanent" critique either methodologically or theoretically, a permanent critique can be assured by the continual return to the task of unveiling the complex contradictions of modernity and its associated academic practices.

Written by academics working mainly in North America, written in English, and laden with the terminology of western academic theory, this volume itself may not have escaped the traps and dilemmas of orientalism. To some extent, the contributors to this volume, constituting India as its subject, are open to the charge of the very same topological distinctions through which orientalism constructed its objects and colonial power constituted its domains. Indeed, all the contributors speak of "India" and "Hindus" and "Muslims," while they make considerable efforts to show the extent to which these categories have been constructed by colonialism and orientalism. The term "India" in the postcolonial period refers to a nation-state that has been constituted through the dialectics of orientalism/colonialism and nationalism. By deconstructing the categories, we certainly do not dissolve political realities. It is precisely the postcolonial predicament that both orientalism and its critique play a role in the arena in which these realities are challenged. The deconstruction of secularism, nationalism, and communalism cannot be separated from an arena in which the nature of the postcolonial state is the subject of violent confrontations.

However, there are two underlying strategies that characterize the orientalist way of looking at things. One is the tendency to constitute a particular space as inherently timeless (or confined to its past, which is much the same thing). The other is the tendency to deny the project of power that is part and parcel of the study of Others through techniques to which those who are studied have no access. In the postcolonial world in which we live, it has become impossible to avoid the many dilemmas of the present that link us with our others. Thus, one way out of the orientalist dilemma is to remain steadfastly focused on the present, seen as a historical moment that owes itself at least in part to the very heritage of orientalism that we now seek to undo. This historical consciousness of the present both as a matter of public life and as a matter of academic practice entails persistent vigilance against two dangers that this volume has tried to avoid: the study of orientalism outside its colonial framework and the study of the colonial period as if it has no relevant successor.

References

Ahmed, Aijaz. 1991. "Between Orientalism and Historicism: Anthropological Knowledge of India." *Studies in History* 7, 1: 135–63.

Appadurai, Arjun and Carol A. Breckenridge. 1987. The Making of a Transnational Culturel: The Asian Indian Diaspora in the United States. Unpublished manuscript.

Asad, Talal. 1990. "Multiculturalism and British Identity in the Wake of the Rushdie Affair." *Politics & Society* 18, 4: 455–80.

Bhatnagar, Rashmi. 1986. "Uses and Limits of Foucault: A Study of the Theme of Origins in Edward Said's 'Orientalism'." *Social Scientist* 16, 7 (July): 3–22.

Clifford, James. 1988. "On Orientalism." In *The Predicament of Culture: Twentieth-Century Ethnography, Literature, and Art*. Cambridge: Cambridge University Press, 255–76.

Cohn, Bernard S. 1987. *An Anthropologist Among the Historians and Other Essays*. Delhi and New York: Oxford University Press.

Dumont, Louis. 1970. "Nationalism and Communalism." In Dumont, *Religion, Politics and History in India: Collected Papers in Indian Sociology*. The Hague: Mouton, 89–112.

Fabian, Johannes. 1983. *Time and the Other: How Anthropology Makes Its Object*. New York: Columbia University Press.

Guha, Ranajit and Gayatri Chakravorty Spivak, eds. 1988. *Selected Subaltern Studies*. Oxford: Oxford University Press.

Halbfass, Wilhelm. 1988. *India and Europe: An Essay in Understanding*. Albany: State University of New York Press.

Hechter, Michael. 1975. *Internal Colonialism: The Celtic Fringe in British National Development, 1536–1966*. London: Routledge and Kegan Paul.

Inden, Ronald B. 1990. *Imagining India*. Oxford and Cambridge, MA: Basil Blackwell.

Kramer, Jane. 1991. "Letter from Europe." *New Yorker* (January 14): 60–75.

Malek, Anwar Abdel. 1963. "Orientalism in Crisis." *Diogenes* 44 (Winter).

Marglin, Stephen A. and Frederique Appfel Marglin, eds. 1990. *Dominating Knowledge: Development, Culture and Resistance*. Oxford: Clarendon Press.

Mohanty, S. P. 1989. "Us and Them: On the Philosophical Bases of Political Criticism." *Yale Journal of Criticism* 2, 2: 1–31.

Nehru, Jawaharlal. 1946. *The Discovery of India*. Calcutta: Signet Press; New York: John Day Company.

Said, Edward W. 1978. *Orientalism*. New York: Vintage Books.

Schwab, Raymond. 1984. *The Oriental Renaissance: Europe's Rediscovery of India and the East, 1680–1880*. New York: Columbia University Press.

Part I

The Postcolonial Predicament and Contemporary History

Peter van der Veer

1. The Foreign Hand
Orientalist Discourse in Sociology and Communalism

Introduction

Western theories of Asia reflect, to an important extent, power relations between western and Asian societies, and this connection calls for critical reflection. Altogether different is the extent to which we are ready to accept that western knowledge about the Orient in the post-Enlightenment period was, as Said (1978: 3) argues, "a systematic discourse by which Europe was able to manage—and even produce—the Orient politically, sociologically, militarily, ideologically, scientifically, and imaginatively." Such an argument portrays the production of knowledge about the Orient as an exclusively western affair. European and later American views created a reality in which the Oriental had to live, according to Said. Although we have to admit that this is a forceful vision, it is also surely a misleading one. It is itself a product of orientalism, since it neglects the important ways in which the so-called Orientals not only have shaped their own world but also the orientalist views criticized by Said. It would be a serious mistake to deny agency to the colonized in our effort to show the force of colonial discourse.

Orientalist discourse about India is based largely on a politics of difference. It focuses on the essential differences between East and West, and, within India, between castes and between religious communities. In its analysis of Indian society it relies heavily on Brahmanical discourse about caste and kingship that provides a negative counterimage for the self-perception of the "enlightened" West. It is a discourse that legitimates colonial rule, but, as we shall see, it continues to exert a considerable influence on the sociological understanding of India after Independence.

A major element in orientalist discourse about India is the essentialization of difference between Hindus and Muslims. This essentialization is certainly not a colonial invention, since it depends on essentializing features of Hindu discourses about the Muslim "other" and of Muslim discourses about the Hindu "other." In the colonial period, however, these indigenous discourses were transformed under the influence of orientalism to support the imagination of the religious community as a "nation." It is here that the metaphor of the "foreign hand" that is routinely used in India to explain the violent antagonism of Hindus and Muslims seems appropriate. Although there is no point in denying the existence of important and politically salient differences between Muslim and Hindu communities in various parts of India long before the colonial encounter, it remains important to see the discursive shift that is brought to the understanding of difference by orientalism. For our purposes, we may perhaps interpret the "foreign hand" as a metaphor that is used to express the extent to which a relatively recent discourse from outside, as it were, has come to bear on the ways Hindus and Muslims perceive one another in India.

In this chapter I do not want to trace the historical development of orientalist discourse on Hindus and Muslims, but focus rather on the way orientalist discourse is adopted in a postcolonial sociological understanding of Indian society. My main aim is to demonstrate that Louis Dumont's understanding of nationalism and communalism depends largely on orientalist discourse. I will give an analysis of a relatively short but important paper that is included as an appendix in the most recent English translation of *Homo Hierarchicus* (Dumont 1980: 314–34), in which Dumont discusses the relation between communalism and nationalism. I have chosen this paper first because of the centrality of Dumont's work in the postcolonial understanding of Indian society in general and second, because of the influence his approach has had on major contributions to the understanding of nationalism (Handler 1988; Kapferer 1988). Moreover, I hope to demonstrate that Dumont's approach to the relation of Hindus and Muslims in India shows some basic flaws that are shared by other influential approaches, such as the ethnosociology of Marriott and Inden (1977). My second aim is to show that the orientalist assumptions in Dumont's sociology of India are shared by Hindu nationalism, so that, at some points, the Dumontian analysis follows the same reasoning that we can also find in Hindu nationalist discourse. While the commonality of anthropological and nationalist representations of culture is a general problem (Spencer 1990), this is compounded in the study of South Asia by the influence of orientalism. It is a crucial aspect of the postcolonial predicament that orientalist understandings of Indian society are perpetuated both by western scholarship and by Indian political movements.

Oriental Essences

My argument is that there is an orientalist discourse on South Asia that dominates, to an important extant, theories in the social sciences that deal with such subjects as the Indian caste system and Hindu-Muslim communalism. This discourse reifies culture as an unchanging system of ideas and values that is not historically produced but that simply exists out there. Indian civilization is supposedly founded on a Hindu religious ideology, and Muslims are seen as either not belonging to that civilization and therefore not to India or as hierarchically subsumed in an inferior position within that civilization. This orientalist perception is, for example, clearly expressed in the preface to the recent volume *Indian Religion* by British anthropologists. The editors argue that Islam and Christianity, although present in India, are not Indian in a cultural sense (Burghart and Cantlie 1985: vii, xi). Such an argument presents Islam and Christianity as "foreign" elements, introduced into an indigenous Hindu culture that remain separate from that culture. This view of the separate, unchanging essences of Islam, Christianity, and Hindusim also underlies modern, communalist discourse on the nature and history of Indian society.

Why should we call such a reification of culture orientalist? In fact there is a major strand in the social sciences devoted to the symbolic analysis of cultural systems of meaning that ignores the varying historical conditions in which power (that is movements, classes, institutions) produces culture (Asad 1983). Reification is thus an aspect of some theories in the social sciences that have no particular relation with orientalism. However, in the study of South Asia there has been a strong tendency to combine the symbolic analysis of the cultural system with indological constructions of Indian civilization. This is nicely expressed in Dumont's programmatic statement from 1957 that "in our opinion, the first condition for a sound development of a Sociology of India is found in the establishment of the proper relation between it and classical Indology" (Dumont [1957] 1970: 2). By "proper relation" he means, following Marcel Mauss, that sociology and Indology have to be combined to understand that "the very existence, and influence, of the traditional, higher, sanskritic, civilisation demonstrates without question the unity of India" (1970: 4). Dumont's plea for the combination of anthropological and Indological insights has been very influential among anthropologists working on South Asia. There can be no doubt about the importance of the Indological study of Indian textual traditions even for major arguments about South Asia that conflict with Dumont's views in other respects (e.g., Marriott and Inden 1977; Marriott 1976).

There is nothing wrong with such an interdisciplinary approach to South Asia; on the contrary it is a very good thing, one would be inclined to argue. However, as Bernard Cohn has repeatedly argued in his work (e.g., Cohn 1968), Indologists have developed a view of Indian society based primarily on the study of Brahmanical traditions in Sanskrit texts from before 1200 A.D., which were interpreted in collaboration with Brahman pandits. This led to the consistent notion that Brahmans were the most important group in society. Moreover, it led to a picture of Indian society as being static, timeless and spaceless. Ancient Vedic texts and contemporary Brahmanical statements were all combined to form a consistent orientalist perspective on contemporary Indian society and culture that ignored time in the sense of historical development and space in the sense of regional differences. To the extent to which orientalism accepted time as a relevant category, it referred only to decline and degeneration from the Indo-European civilizational standards that were now inherited by their European cousins, whose colonial burden it was to redeem these impoverished members of the family. Space was only relevant in relation to the so-called Aryan-Dravidian divide, sometimes in a curious anachronistic and inverse combination with vague notions about the Islamic North and the unadulterated Hindu South that are important in contemporary Hindu nationalism.

The reification of Indian cultures as a timeless and spaceless Brahmanical Sanskrit civilization was, of course, not simply an invention of the orientalists. Orientalism did not create out of the blue a reality in which the oriental had to live, as Said has it. Orientalism feeds on an existing, dominant discourse carried by a Brahman elite. It is quite clear that groups of Brahmans all over India have, for a very long period, had a major role in Hinduism as intermediaries between the supernatural and the world that is based on their monopoly of certain ritual discourses. This role is legitimized in terms of timeless and spaceless knowledge that is called *vai-*

dik (derived from the Vedas) or *shastrik* (derived from the shastras, the law books), while other competitive types of knowledge are deemed as inferior, *laukik* (worldly) (cf. Parry 1985).

It is important, however, to realize that reference to the timeless and spaceless Vedas enabled Brahmans to legitimate practices that in reality depended largely on the historical and regional contexts in which they were produced. Moreover, localized groups of Brahmans were (and are) constantly involved in debating "orthodoxy" (cf. Appadurai 1981). The difference orientalism has made to this situation is that it created a Brahmanical discourse that came much nearer to the realization of its ideological claims. Brahmanical discourse was systematized as "Hindu Law" and "Hinduism" to the extent that in the end it no longer needed actual Brahman "spokesmen" to interpret and authorize it. The arena of debate about "correct practice" goes through a drastic change in the colonial period. The British tried to create the conditions in which Brahmanical discourse could indeed be applied irrespective of place and time. An important aspect of the transformation is that colonialism shifted the sources of power from palaces and religious shrines to colonial institutions, such as the law court, which ultimately served the needs of empire and not of local societies. In this way colonialism constructed a *shastrik* tradition that was separated from its social origins in indigenous debate and the relative power of the parties in the arena.

Dumont's proposal to combine Indology and sociology into a sociology of India has therefore an important history. The Indological study of the Sanskrit tradition has been essential to the transformation of *vaidik* discourse into an orientalist discourse on a homogeneous, unified Hindu civilization that impinged on Indian societies and cultures through the institutions of the colonial state. In fact, one can say that colonial sociology depended on this orientalist construction and that Dumont's proposal had already been realized in the colonial project to know and rule Indian societies. There is an interesting passage in Dumont's analysis of the classical Hindu text of statecraft, the *Arthashastra,* in which he argues that his ethnographic description of a South Indian subcaste shows the continuous importance of those elements of Hindu society that are stressed by the *Arthashastra* and "that cannot be attributed to mere chance" (Dumont 1970: 85). Indeed, an Indian social configuration of the 1950s, which he as a postcolonial ethnographer describes, is the product not of mere chance but of a specific orientalist discourse within a colonial history. While Dumont thinks that he finds "traditional India" in his field-work, he finds in fact the product of a colonial history. And, again, his understanding of "tradition" fits that history perfectly.

As I have argued earlier, orientalism develops a politics of difference that is inherent in Brahmanical discourse. The ideology of castes and stages of life (*varnashramadharma*) becomes a central element in the various projects of colonial knowledge (see Cohn 1968 and Appadurai in this volume). It is also the main focus of Dumont's sociology. Here I want to examine another aspect of the politics of difference, namely the essentialized difference between Hindus and Muslims.

Dumont on Communalism

I will give a brief summary of Dumont's argument about the relation between communalism and nationalism. His main contention is that to understand communalism we have to make a comparison between traditional and modern societies, since communalism is a phenomenon that combines the two. Communalism is an ideology that emphasizes the religious community as a social, political, and economic unit in antagonistic distinction from other such groups. Nationalism is an ideology that emphasizes a collectively of individuals united on the basis of their political will, common history, and common territory. The most fundamental difference between the two phenomena is the fact that a nation is not built on the common religion of a people. Nationalism thus presupposes a secularization of society that implies that religion becomes the private affair of individuals and that the political organization becomes autonomous, having its own values. In Durkheimian terms, traditional India had the holistic values of group religion (*dharma*), which regulated all spheres of life and was based on the interdependence of human species (*jati*). Modern society, on the contrary, has separate values for separate spheres of life and allows the individual to have his own religion. Indeed, the nation is conceived as a collection of individuals and the individual has become the measure of everything. Communalism in Dumont's view is Janus-faced, mixing the traditional and the modern, since it stresses group religion as well as the political will to live united in a given territory.

Dumont's understanding of communalism is based on the analysis of systems of values that are, in his theory, constitutive of society. It is therefore not surprising that in Dumont's interpretation, Hindu-Muslim communalism derives from the proposition that although Hindus and Muslims may have lived together for centuries, they developed no shared value system. The modus vivendi of the two communities in the pre-colonial period was based on the political power of the Muslims. When Muslim power was replaced by the *Pax Britannica*, communal riots could easily be provoked. Hindu and Muslim revivalism provided the middle class with an ideology to mobilize the masses in the struggle against the colonial power. In the modern era the two religious communities on the subcontinent were forced to express their heterogeneity of values in terms of separate territorial claims. Communalist ideologies were necessary for political mobilization in the anticolonial struggle, but led to the formation of two nation-states: India and Pakistan.

At first glance Dumont's argument seems very convincing, and many disinterested scholars might agree with it. Many communalist ideologues, however, might also agree with it. The idea that their value systems have led Hindus and Muslims to form entirely separate communities, and in the nineteenth and twentieth century under influence of western ideas to demand territory freed from foreign occupation, is often called the two-nation theory. The basic orientalist fallacy of this theory in both its sociological and communalist versions is that it portrays Muslim and Hindu values as reified systems. Values are in that way separated from their origin in historical practice. They become unassailable, primordial, *sanatan*, as the Hindu would say, and thus the ideological ground for communalism. The combined reifying tendencies in colonial orientalism and postcolonial sociology of values make that products of scholarship are easily assimilated as the scholarly support of communalist ideology. The positivist view of scholarship is "to get the facts right," but scholarly theories play a role in politics that may create the facts to fit the theories.

It is important to look at Dumont's argument somewhat more closely, since it illuminates some of the basic aspects of the orientalist production of knowledge. In the first place, we have to consider his opposition of the traditional and the modern. The traditional polity in India is described in terms of the Brahmanical conception of kingship. Dumont relies here on a number of Sanskrit texts and their Indological interpretation, among which the Brahmanical treatise on statecraft, the *Arthashastra*, receives special attention (see in particular Dumont 1980: 287–313). The king rules in the name of *dharma* over the "country," which is population-cum-territory (*janapada*). *Artha* is the subsistence of men, economics, and the land supplied with men, politics. *Artha* then is the politico-economic domain that is relatively autonomous but ultimately subordinated to the system of values, *dharma*, just as the political force (*danda*) of the king is subordinated to the religious authority of the Brahman priest. Traditional India is a hierarchical society, in which power is only a secondary phenomenon. The king is a protector of the caste system, but his power derives its legitimacy only from the authoritative discourse of Brahmanism. The caste system denies individuality. The individual in India renounces the world, which means caste society. Within caste society human individuality is of no consequence.

The modern polity, on the contrary, is that of the nation-state characterized by the political will of the people and by the notion of territory. The notion of kingship is thus replaced by the notion of a sovereign people and that of *dharma* by that of democracy. The people is conceptualized as a collection of individuals that rules itself according to the principles of liberty and equality. The traditional conception of people-cum-territory is replaced by that of a collection of individuals with their property. This implies that a system in which every human species (*jati*) has interconnected rights in the produce of the soil becomes replaced by a system of individual property in which land becomes marketable. Territory is thus a continuous tract of country that symbolizes the unity of individuals who own parts of the country.

In India, according to Dumont, the uneasy combination of the modern and the traditional produced that ideological hybrid, called communalism, that combines group religion and territory. Partition was therefore inevitable. This theoretical opposition of the traditional and the modern and its later conjunction, though ingenuous, is in my view not valid. It replaces the muddle of historical change by a model of ideal types and their combination. This can readily be seen when we apply Dumont's argument to what is happening in the Punjab today. The argument would be that the Sikhs combine the traditional and the modern by demanding Khalistan as a separate territory for their religious community. Such a presentation of Punjabi history entirely begs the question of the historical construction of Sikh identity *as opposed to* a Hindu identity. In the case of Sikhism, which grew out of the Nanak *panth*, we are much more prepared to deconstruct the "ism" historically than in the case of Hinduism or Islam, but I would insist that also in the latter cases religious and social practices and ideologies have to be understood in their historical context.

Dumont is explicitly sceptical about a historical approach to his object of inquiry; he argues that India's system of values is indifferent to real history in the western sense of a significant and positively valued pattern of change. The Hindu notion of four cycles (*yugas*) devalues individual life and history. Again, this assertion is based on the privileging of certain Brahmanical discourses that do attempt to obscure history by their reference to Eternal Truth. By now we can perhaps see that the traditional India Dumont is writing about is an orientalist construction in which certain Brahmanical ideologies about kingship and time are sociologically interpreted as what Dumont calls a "global ideology," which is a set of ideas and values shared by all members of society (Dumont 1980: 343).

Dumont's argument can only be made by ignoring discourses that, for example, stress the sacredness of the king or the ascetic (Burghart 1978). In fact, apart from Brahmanical sources there is no evidence of desacralized kingship that depends on Brahmanical authority at any point in Indian history. Instead there is good evidence of a conception of the divinity and ritual centrality of the king and the dominant caste (Hocart 1970; Raheja 1988).

The argument that economic transactions in "traditional India" are embedded in a hierarchical orientation toward the whole of society that prevents the emergence of individual property rests on the anthropological myth of *jajmani* transactions as an encompassing system of exchange characteristic of the static and autarkic premarket economy of village India (cf. Fuller 1989). Similarly, Dumont's portrait of the modern West is also a construction that ignores the relation between religious and ethnic ideologies on the one hand and nationalist ideology on the other.

What are the consequences of Dumont's orientalist acceptance of Brahmanical ideology as an account of the values and ideas of Indian peoples of all times and places? Despite the overwhelming mass of historical sources, India becomes a society without history from 1200 until the arrival of the colonial powers. It is a frozen society that is only introduced into real history by its confrontation with the modern colonial world. Moreover, in India there are no individuals, each possessing a discrete subjectivity, until they are invented at the arrival of the British—there are only human species. You may say that this inert society had to be awakened from its oriental dream to find history and individuality. When it was awakened it could only infuse reality with its religious fantasies, which resulted in violent communalism. To deny human beings individuality and some degree of autonomous action within certain social constraints is to create the oriental other as a disposable entity. This other's violence is unpredictable and not related to rational ends, but only to the religious dreamworld of the other.

The Muslim Other

Dumont's refusal to deal in any direct way with the Muslim presence in Indian society and history is remarkable, but not exceptional among anthropologists. This neglect derives from the orientalist emphasis on the higher, Sanskritic civilization in understanding Indian society. As we have seen above, Dumont relates Partition to the existence of the mutually exclusive value systems of Hindus and Muslims. We have also seen that his analysis privileges value systems in the understanding of society. While this seems quite straightforward, it is only the Hindu value system that receives a full treatment, with the tacit assumption that the Muslim presence does not matter for its analysis. Indian Muslim society is discussed as a marginal case in Chapter X of *Homo Hierarchicus*, which is entitled "Comparison: Are there castes among Non-Hindus and Outside India?" Moreover, most attention is given here to the Swat Pathan of the High Indus, a Muslim society without Hindu presence that Dumont sees as a limiting case, and not to the Muslims of, say, Uttar Pradesh, who have always been in intimate interaction with Hindus.

There are two, seemingly opposed, arguments in Dumont's work that lead to the attribution of marginality to Indian Muslim society. The first is that the "foreignness" of Muslim culture makes Muslims marginal. The idea is that Islam comes from outside of India and is thus not "Indic." Moreover, Muslims form a minority in Indian society, which adds to their marginality in the Indic civilization as a whole. The second is that Indian Muslims are "just like" Hindus and therefore marginal. They are "natives of India" who have been nominally converted to Islam but continue their Indic social customs, such as those of caste.

To start with the first argument, it is clear to me that Indian Muslims have an Islamic culture that has to be understood in local contexts (cf. Eickelman 1982). What we have in India is one of the largest communities of Muslims in the world and an Islamic history of many centuries, so that the suggestion of the non-Indic nature of the Indian Muslim community and its culture is simply untenable. Indian Muslims do refer to traditions and religious centers outside of India, but that reference is historically variable and has to be contextualized in order to be understood. The reference to a universal community of believers centering on Mecca is crucial for Muslims today and it has been in the past. Certainly that reference has also always been important in Sufism, which before the nineteenth century was virtually coextensive with Islam (Fusfeld 1988: 20). Sufi orders define themselves in terms of lineages that stretch back to the very origins of Islam. Nevertheless, the central place of worship in a Sufi order is the tomb of a saint that draws attendance from a local (regional) community. Although this is also true for the mosque, the Sufi shrine tends to draw the entire local community. Not only Muslims visit the tomb but Hindus do also. Saint worship is thus a critical practice not only for the relation between Muslims and locality, but also for the relation between Hindus and Muslims. This implies that Muslim reformists in India have often related their condemnation of the worship of the local saint to the issue of the relation between Hindus and Muslims. Here again we see the extent to which Muslims have to understand and defend their practices within an arena in which the presence of Hindus and Hinduism looms large. So, even a purist argument about Islamic orthodoxy in India will often take a particular form by positioning itself in relation to "the influence of Hinduism" and the presence of Hindus. While this is true for both the precolonial and the colonial period, Islamic debate about orthodoxy goes through an important transformation when colonialism impinges on it with its orientalist discourse on the essential differences between Hindus and Muslims. This is too large a subject to deal with in this essay (see van der Veer 1992), but I would like to suggest that orientalism understands Indian Muslims within a framework of "foreignness" that ultimately derives from the long history of western (Christian)—Arab (Muslim) rivalry. The Muslim is the quintessential other in orientalist discourse, and this relates perfectly to precolonial Hindu discourses on Muslim "otherness" (*yavana, mleccha*) and also, ultimately, to Muslim discourses on their own distinctiveness.

A seemingly quite opposite line of thinking is expressed in the argument that Muslims are just like Hindus in important respects. This argument pertains to two levels of society, that of the Muslim state and that of village society. It is striking that Dumont can discuss the Hindu notions of kingship and dominance in his analysis of the caste system without taking into account the crucial historical fact that large parts of India over long periods of time have been ruled by Muslim rulers. The assumption seems to be either that there is not much difference between Hindu and Muslim conceptions of kingship or that differences did exist but did not have great consequences for society. This entirely begs the question on what the legitimacy and authority of Muslim kings rested. Clearly the Hindu conception of the king as the protector of Brahmans, cows, and temples cannot account for the authority and legitimacy of Muslim kings. Muslim rulers always had to be careful to prove their legitimacy in Islamic terms, which sometimes obliged them to levy capitation tax on the infidels or to destroy Hindu temples but which sometimes also allowed them to support Hindu institutions or contract marriage alliances with Rajput nobles. At least one element of their authority ultimately relates to safeguarding the Islamic Law and the Revelation. What this meant for their relation with Hindu subjects depends on historical context. Muslim kings were important patrons of Hindu temples and festivals. Conversely, Maratha war leaders in the eighteenth century may commonly be portrayed as anti-Muslim supporters of Hinduism who built many of the *ghat*s in Benares, but historical evidence shows that they also supported the Chishti Sufi shrine at Ajmer. Here, again, it is orientalism that essentializes these complex relations as Muslim despotic rule over Hindu subjects and as Hindu resistance to it in order to legitimate the colonial replacement of that rule.

The level of the village society poses again other problems. Dumont argues, basically, that Muslims replicate the Hindu caste system. He sees the Muslim case as parallel to that of the Hindu group of Lingayats of Karnataka in the sense that a sectarian identity is superimposed on the primary social fact of caste. This argument is quite hard to refute, since a refutation depends inevitably on a better understanding of the historical flexibility of the ideological notion of caste than we are able to provide now. It is clear that we cannot turn to ethnosociology for a solution, since it is an approach that is at least as orientalist as that of Dumont. The ethnosociological account of the Hindu cognitive system refers back to the Vedas and to Hindu modes of worship, but is nevertheless seen as broad enough to also account for Muslim communities in India (Marriott and Inden 1977; Marriott 1976).

On the other hand, it would clearly not further our understanding of Muslim village societies to oppose the so-called egalitarian values of the *'umma* to the so-called hierarchical values of Hindu caste society and to explain the fact that Muslims make hierarchical distinctions in terms of purity among themselves as well as in their relation with Hindus from a mixture of these value systems. It is quite clear from studies of Muslim societies outside of India that these also have endogamous, occupationally specialized groups that are hierarchically ranked (cf. Lindholm 1985). The notions of purity and pollution can also be found in these societies and, as in the case of India, they have to be understood in relation to other ideological notions. I would like to suggest that when we are interested in commonality of ideas and values we find it in the great emphasis on notions of honor (*izzat*) and shame (*sharam*) among Hindus and Muslims alike. These notions seem to structure a great number of intergroup and intragroup relations, notably those of gender and kinship (see, e.g., Jeffery, Jeffery and Lyon 1989). It is in the configuration that notions of honor and shame form with notions of purity and auspiciousness—and in its transformation through the influence of religious institutions and movements—that we may look for the similarities and differences between the values of Hindus and Muslims living in the same village.

Notions of purity and auspiciousness are probably less important aspects of regimes of social inequality among Muslims than among Hindus, but to understand their relevance we have to relate them to other notions of dominance and centrality, honor and shame. Hindus may not accept water from the hands of both dominant Muslim landowners and of untouchable weavers, but that does not mean that they would accord them the same social status. Alternatively, Muslims will easily make a clear social difference between a Brahman landlord and a sweeper, although both are from his religious point of view idolatrous infidels.

Finally, when we want to understand modern Hindu and Muslim communalism, we will have to deal with the subject of syncretism. What Dumont fails to take up in his discussion of the heterogeneity of Hindu and Muslim value systems are the religious configurations in which both Hindus and Muslims participate. Hindus often participate in Muslim cults of saints, and in at least some cases Hindus and Muslims seem to share a frame of understanding in respect to these cults (cf. S. Bayly 1989). There are obvious religious differences between Hindus and Muslims, but what these differences mean depends on historical and regional context. "Muslim" Bohras and Khojas in Gujarat may not have been very distinguishable from their so-called Hindu neighbors in the past, but they are now; Brahman Chaturvedis may have participated in the *t'aziya* processions of Lucknow in the nineteenth century, but they do not now. Moreover, religious differences are obviously sharper between Muslim *'ulama* and Brahman *pandits* than between Muslim and Hindu peasants who both go to visit Sufi shrines.

This is not to say that there has been a syncretistic, peaceful culture shared by Hindus and Muslims before the colonial period. On the contrary, while there have always been points of contact and commonality in religious and social practice between Hindus and Muslims and these exist to the present day, these commonalities have also always been subject to religious debate about orthodoxy. Moreover, the evidence of Hindu participation in Muslim religious activities does not preclude the existence of violent conflict between Hindus and Muslims in the same region and in the same period. In a recent paper, Chris Bayly (1985) has given a great number of examples of such conflicts before the nineteenth century. Some of them were related to public worship and were concerned with control over religious shrines or religious processions. We have to realize, however, that such conflicts existed also between Ramanandis and Dashanami Sannyasins, groups which were later to be lumped in a seemingly unambiguous category of "Hindu"; or, for that matter, between Shias and Sunnis, representatives of the "Muslim" community. Other conflicts were then as now directly related to deep economic antagonisms in the countryside as well as in the towns and should, according to Bayly (1985: 202–3), not be understood in terms of decontextualized communal consciousness, but as contingent on social and economic circumstances. In that sense, from Bayly's point of view, many so-called communal riots in the twentieth century can be understood in the same way as such conflicts in the eighteenth century.

Nevertheless, despite these continuities of debate and conflict the colonial period does bring some major transformations. Reformist movements in the late nineteenth and early twentieth centuries produced communal Hinduism and Islam as sets of unifying practices and ideas and created new understandings of religious as well as political and economic competition. Thus, conflicts that are contingent on social and economic circumstances are understood in terms of a communal discourse, fed by orientalism, that did not exist in that way before the nineteenth century. The question of the nature of Hindu-Muslim relations before the colonial period is often prejudiced by the easy assumptions made in orientalist discourse.

Comparison and Contextualization

One could object from the Dumontian perspective that attention to historical discontinuities and agency would lead to an endless fragmentation of the ethnographic and historical unity of India and that the major aim of Dumont's enterprise to formulate a comparative critique of the modern western ideology of individualism and equality would become impossible. I would be quite happy to accept that objection, because to my mind Dumont's opposition of the modern and the traditional leads to the unbridgeable and objectionable gap between Us and the Other rather than to an illuminative comparison of "lived experience." *Homo Hierarchicus* is largely constructed as the opposite of an equally constructed *homo equalis*. As Beteille (1986) has recently argued, it is dangerous to say that the individual counts for nothing in some societies and for everything in others, because it is evident that even in the same society people hold divergent beliefs and act in different ways. Moreover, it is obvious that the commitment to equality varies greatly within the same society between classes, between ethnic groups, and between men and women. Finally, the assumption of a relationship between individualism and equality is itself problematic. The individual who sees himself as an autonomous moral agent does not have to emphasize equality among individuals, but can also wish to distinguish himself from others. Individualists may believe in equality of opportunity, but also in competition and inequality of reward. Interestingly, in modern neoconservative writings the central idea seems to be that equality as a policy is bad, since it violates individual liberty as well as efficiency.

This discussion of the Enlightenment discourse of individual equality and of the essential differences between an individualistic West and a communal East is not merely academic. It leads us to one of the main issues in politics today, namely the relation between communal representation in politics and the policy of affirmative action. The British are often accused of having divided Hindus and Muslims by creating separate electorates and special communal representation. While this is not continued in independent India, there is a policy of affirmative action and compensatory privileges for certain caste groupings, primarily untouchables. We see here one of the basic contradictions of the democratic process in India as well as elsewhere. The difficulty is that there is a political will to reduce long-standing social discrimination of certain groups, but that by giving special privileges to such groups to redress these disadvantages one comes into conflict with the very principle of equality of opportunity. Clearly, this conflict is a major aspect of the allocation of resources in the political process and thereby one of the direct causes of violence all over India.

The implementation of positive discrimination takes very different shapes in different Indian states (see Frankel 1988). In Tamil Nadu, the total quantum of reservation of seats in educational institutions and jobs in the public sector is 68 percent, while the state estimates the percentage of the backward living in Tamil Nadu at 67.15 percent. The politics of positive discrimination relates more to the value of getting enough seats in the state assembly than to the value of equality. The most striking example of this is to be found in Gujarat. On the eve of the elections of 1984, the quantum of reservation was raised from 31 percent to 49 percent, and riots broke out all over the place.

The important thing in the context of this essay is that the discourse of positive discrimination in the context of a struggle for power between classes and regional castes becomes rapidly translated in terms of Hindu-Muslim antagonism. The Hindu communalist argument is that the state discriminates against its Hindu majority population and favors the Muslim minority, because the Congress party, the party in power, covets "the Muslim vote." This argument, which derives from what Tambiah (1986) has called "the minority-complex of the majority," is very forceful and is used to unite people on a Hindu platform. In the dynamics of rioting, it is remarkable how easily violence related to positive discrimination of Backward Castes can be deflected into communal violence against Muslims. The continuous violence in Ahmedabad, Gujarat, is a good example of this process. It is also remarkable that Hindu nationalism with its emphasis on the Muslim Other is often countered with a discourse that focuses on caste and class differences among Hindus. This was, for example, the case in 1990 when the Union Government, led by V. P. Singh, decided to implement a positive discrimination policy, from which Hindu Backward Castes could benefit, to take the wind from the sails of a Hindu nationalist movement led by the Vishva Hindu Parishad. It is our task to understand the discourses that lead to the linkage of positive discrimination and communalism. What we seem to witness here is the gradual transformation of the social life of large groups in Indian society that engenders many types of political mobilization in which public symbols and communal identities are infused with new meanings. The ideological emphasis on the existence of value systems and their incompatibility is part of the problem to be studied rather than part of the explanation.

All this means indeed that the study of Indian society becomes more fragmented and that the object of this study should be directed to the relations between social configurations in regions and countries in the subcontinent, as well as to their incorporation in a world economy, rather than to the comparison of Indian and Western civilizations.

Orientalism and Communalism

Communalist discourse in India feeds on the same orientalist assumptions that inform postcolonial sociological understandings of India. However, I need to give two caveats here. The first is that in highlighting the commonalities between communalist and sociological discourse I do not impute bad intentions to writers like Dumont. There is no doubt that such writers are engaged in the very activity in which I myself am engaged, namely the endeavor to attain a better understanding of Indian society. My argument is thus not related to personal intentions, but to theory and its relation to power. The second is that I do not think that orientalism is the cause of communalism. Rather I would argue that orientalism and Indian nationalism both belong to the discourse of modernity. Indian nationalism undoubtedly is an anticolonial force, but in its very anticolonialism it shares basic discursive premises with orientalism and with the nationalism of the colonizing British.

Indian nationalism is certainly not a monolithic entity. One way of seeing its complexity is to look at the common distinction between communalism and nationalism that informs Dumont's essay and much of political discourse in India. The striking thing is, of course, that the great leader of the Independence movement, M. K. Gandhi, rejected the basis of that distinction, secularism, as a western construct. The independent state of India that he helped form, however, has claimed to be secular from the start. A stark distinction between secular nationalism, espoused by Gandhi's Congress Party, and communalism, espoused by the Muslim League and the Hindu Mahasabha, would certainly not help our understanding of the events leading to Independence and Partition. In fact, what we have to realize is that the very distinction between religious and secular is a product of the Enlightenment that was used in orientalism to draw a sharp opposition between irrational, religious behavior of the Oriental and rational secularism, which enabled the westerner to rule the Oriental. Religious discourse and practice are defined as belonging to the private sphere and thereby separated from political action. It is this discourse of modernity that is inherited by Jawaharlal Nehru in his insistence on secularist politics. It is clearly also the discourse that informs Dumont's essay on nationalism and communalism.

At the same time, Gandhi's rejection of secularism and other rejections, such as those of the Muslim League and the Hindu Mahasabha, form alternatives not outside but within the same discursive framework. I would argue that the discourses of Gandhi and the Hindu militants who murdered him after Independence present variants of Hindu nationalism rather than totally different ways of thinking. The orientalist construction of Hinduism is a crucial aspect of these discourses and, as we have seen, of Dumont's sociology. It is in this construction that we can find the commonalities between Hindu nationalism and the postcolonial sociological interpretation of Indian society.

What orientalism has done is two things. It gave crucial support to the Brahmanical contention that Indian civilization is a unified whole based on a *shastrik*, authoritative tradition of which Brahman priests and sectarian preceptors are the principal bearers. Reformist movements, such as the Arya Samaj, certainly were a response to the vilification of Hindu beliefs and practices by Christian missionaries. Their ideology, however, as well as the ideology of their "orthodox" counterpart, the *Sanatan Dharm*, very much resulted from the interaction between the orientalist production of unchanging "Ur"-essences and Brahmanical ideology. Orientalists brought modern philological methods and concepts to bear on India's past. In critical editions of Hindu scriptures they replaced a fragmented, largely oral set of traditions with an unchanging, homogenized written canon. The critical editions of the Mahabharata and Ramayana as well as the ongoing Purana-projects show this process of selection and unification very well. In that way a "history," established by modern science, came to replace a traditional "past" (see also Ludden, in this volume).

Orientalism also canonized certain scriptures, such as the *Bhagavad Gita*, which prepared the ground for Mahatma Gandhi to make this Sanskrit work into a fundamental scripture of Modern Hinduism. By looking for the roots of western (Aryan) civilization in Vedic and early Hindu scriptures, it created an image of the decline of "Hindu society" after the "Muslim invasion." All this led to the Hindu nationalist construction of the glorious Hindu past and of the "foreignness" of Muslims. At the same time, the orientalist facts could also be used for a secularist alternative to Hindu nationalism in Nehru's *Discovery of India*.

One of the most fascinating convergences between orientalism, Hindu nationalism, and Dumont's sociology is in the discourse about "spirituality" and "renunciation." In the Indological study of Indian religious traditions, there has always been a strong interest in philosophy, mysticism, asceticism, and spirituality. This interest in "the Wisdom of the East" was at some point related to certain developments in German idealism, but it has continued to the present day in other forms. Dumont explains religious change in Hinduism by pointing at the innovative role of the renouncer who in his terms is an individual outside the world of caste. The notion that renunciation is the highest value in Hinduism is taken up by a great number of writers. Finally, Hindu nationalism both in its Gandhian variant and in its radically militant variant capitalize on "spirituality" as a defining feature of Hinduism.

Hindu spirituality is commonly seen as based on a set of philosophical scriptures in the Brahmanical tradition, called Vedanta. It is important to see that the notion of "Hindu Spirituality" that was crucial in the orientalist study of India was taken up and developed by westernized Indian intellectuals in Bengal in their reinterpretation of the Vedanta tradition. One of the major thinkers here was the founder of the Ramakrishna Mission, Vivekananda (1863–1902). He was able to systematize a disparate set of traditions that had been made available by the orientalist project and to make it into "Hindu Spirituality" as the sign of a Hindu nation that was superior to the materialist West. What we see here is a combination of Hindu spirituality and nationalism, informed by orientalism. Vivekananda's work inspired Gandhi and the philosopher-president Sarvepalli Radharkrishnan. It could be used to defend nonviolence and tolerance as ultimate Hindu values, seen to be embedded in the spirituality of the Vedanta. Very telling is Radhakrishnan's formula: "The Vedanta is not a religion, but religion itself in its most universal and deepest significance" (quoted in Halbfass 1988: 409). The point is that Hinduism, Islam, and Christianity could all be encompassed by this national, multicultural spirituality.

However, Vivekananda's work has also inspired Hindu nationalists with a somewhat different gloss on Hindu spirituality. One of the most important of them is Swami Chinmayananda, a religious leader who is the founder of the Vishva Hindu Parishad (VHP), an organisation that attempts to "reclaim" India for the "Hindu majority" (see van der Veer, in press). The VHP is at the forefront of an anti-Muslim movement in Indian politics in the 1980s that assails the secularism of the Indian state and attempts to make India into a Hindu nation-state. The discourse of the

VHP remains very similar to that of Gandhi and Radhakrishnan, but Muslims and Christians are blamed for not accepting the tolerance of Hindu spirituality. This discursive move enables us to see the inclusivist rather than tolerant nature that the notion of Hindu spirituality has had from the start for those who do not accept the lineage of the Vedanta. Muslims and Christians have to shed their "foreignness" and accept the inclusion of their religious traditions within the encompassing Hindu spirituality. It is striking in this connection that neither in Dumont's analysis of Renunciation nor in communalist discourse on Hindu spirituality is there any attempt to understand current Indian religions in terms of the historical interaction of Hindu and Muslim discourses and practices.

What figures like Vivekananda and Chinmayananda also permit us to see is the extent to which orientalist discourse about "Hindu spirituality" that is adopted in postcolonial sociology and in Hindu nationalism takes transcendental values as its object rather than the social history of institutions. Renunciation becomes an entirely different phenomenon, when one looks at it as a social institution with a particular history rather than as the essence of Hinduism. The VHP is in the first place an organization of religious leaders and their followers. These leaders have never been individuals outside of the world of caste, but rather successful entrepreneurs, both in the cultural and economic sense, within a world that is partly defined by caste (see van der Veer 1988). Awareness of the militant history of Indian "renouncers" and their vital role in warfare and trading helps in being prepared for the political militancy of Hindu monks today, despite the Gandhian (Tolstoyan) emphasis on nonviolence.

Finally, important in both Vivekananda and his current Hindu nationalist heirs is the dialectic of nationalism and transnationalism. Vivekananda became important in India only after he had gained a world audience, following his performance at the World Parliament of Religions in Chicago in 1893. In a way he addressed both the middle class in the West and the westernized middle class in India. The current VHP does very much the same. The construction of a unified Hindu identity is of utmost importance for Hindus who live outside India. They need a Hinduism that can be explained to outsiders as a respectable religion, that can be taught to their children in religious education, and that can form the basis for collective action. The VHP provides such a religious ideology, and it is thus not surprising that it has already gained great support among Indians in Britain, the United States, The Caribbean, Fiji, Holland. In an ironic twist of history, orientalism is now brought by Indians to Indians living in the West. It is reinforced by the orientalism that I have tried to show in postcolonial understandings of Indian society in the academy. Scholars who are working on India and especially Indologists are often invoked as authoritative interpreters of Indian tradition by the Indian communities in these countries. It is the postcolonial predicament that orientalism is reinvented in the dialectic of nationalism and transnationalism.

I wish to thank Arjun Appadurai and David Ludden for their helpful comments on an earlier version of this essay.

References

Appadurai, Arjun. 1981. "The Past as a Scarce Resource." *Man (NS)* 16: 201–19.

Asad, Talal. 1983. "Anthropological Conceptions of Religion: Reflections on Geertz." *Man (NS)* 18: 201–19.

Bayly, Christopher A. 1985. "The Pre-History of 'Communalism'? Religious Conflict in India, 1700–1860." *Modern Asian Studies* 19, 2: 177–203.

Bayly, Susan. 1989. "Islam and State Power in Pre-Colonial South India." *Itinerario* 12: 143–63.

Beteille, Andre. 1986. "Individualism and Equality." *Current Anthropology* 27, 2: 121–28.

Burghart, Richard. 1978. "Hierarchical Models of the Hindu Social System." *Man (NS)* 13: 519–36.

Burghart, Richard and Audrie Cantlie, eds. 1985. *Indian Religion*. London: Curzon Press.

Cohn, Bernard S. 1968. "Notes on the History of the Study of Indian Society and Culture." In Milton Singer and Bernard S. Cohn, eds, *Structure and Change in Indian Society*. Chicago: Aldine, 3–28.

———. 1988. *An Anthropologist Among the Historians and Other Essays*. Delhi: Oxford University Press.

Dumont, Louis. 1970. *Religion, Politics and History in India: Collected Papers in Indian Sociology*. The Hague: Mouton.

———. 1980. *Homo Hierarchicus: The Caste System and Its Implications*. Trans. Mark Sainsbury, Louis Dumont, and Basia Gulati, Chicago: University of Chicago Press.

Eickelman, Dale F. 1982. "The Study of Islam in Local Contexts." *Contributions to Asian Studies* 17: 1–16.

Frankel, Francine. 1988. "Middle Classes and Castes in India's Politics: Prospects for Political Accommodation." In Atul Kohli, ed., *India's Democracy: An Analysis of Changing State-Society Relations*. Princeton, NJ: Princeton University Press.

Fuller, C. 1989. "Misconceiving the Grain Heap: A Critique of the Concept of the

Indian Jajmani System." In J. Parry and M. Bloch, eds., *Money and the Morality of Exchange*. Cambridge: Cambridge University Press, 33–64.

Fusfeld, Warren. 1988. "The Boundaries of Islam and Infidelity." In Katharine Ewing, ed., *Shari'at and Ambiguity in South Asian Islam*. Berkeley: University of California Press, 205–20.

Halbfass, Wilhelm. 1988. *India and Europe: An Essay in Understanding*. Albany: State University of New York Press.

Handler, Richard. 1988. *Nationalism and the Politics of Culture in Quebec*. Madison: University of Wisconsin Press.

Hocart, A. M. [1938] 1970. *Kings and Councillors*. Chicago: University of Chicago Press.

Jeffery, Patricia, Roger Jeffery, and Andrew Lyon. 1989. *Labour Pains and Labour Power: Women and Childbearing in India*. London: Zed Books.

Kapferer, Bruce. 1988. *Legends of People, Myths of State: Violence, Intolerance, and Political Culture in Sri Lanka and Australia*. Washington, DC: Smithsonian Institution Press.

Lindholm, Charles. 1985. "A Critique of Theories of Caste Among Indian Muslims." *Archives Européennes de Sociologie*. 26: 131–41.

Marriott, McKim. 1976. "Hindu Transactions: Diversity Without Dualism." In Bruce Kapferer, ed., *Transaction and Meaning: Questions in the Anthropology of Exchange and Symbolic Behavior*. Philadelphia: Institute for the Study of Human Issues, 109–42.

Marriott, McKim and Ronald Inden. 1977. "Toward an Ethnosociology of South Asian Caste Systems." In Kenneth David, ed., *The New Wind: Changing Identities in South Asia*. The Hague: Mouton, 227–38.

Parry, Jonathan. 1985. "The Brahmanical Tradition and the Technology of the Intellect." In Joanna Overing, ed., *Reason and Morality*. London: Tavistock Publications, 200–25.

Raheja, Gloria. 1988. *The Poison in the Gift: Ritual, Prestation, and the Dominant Caste in a North Indian Village*. Chicago: University of Chicago Press.

Said, Edward W. 1978. *Orientalism*. New York: Vintage.

Spencer, Jonathan. 1990. "Writing Within: Anthropology, Nationalism and Culture in Sri Lanka." *Current Anthropology*. 31, 3: 283–300.

Tambiah, Stanley. 1986. *Sri Lanka: Ethnic Fratricide and the Dismantling of Democracy*. Chicago: University of Chicago Press.

van der Veer, Peter. 1988. *Gods on Earth: The Management of Religious Experience and Identity in a North Indian Pilgrimage Center*. London: Athlone Press.

———. 1992. "Playing or Praying; A Sufi Saint's Day in Surat." *Journal of Asian Studies* 51, 3.

———. In press. "Hindu Nationalism and the Discourse of Modernity: The Vishva Hindu Parishad." In Martin Marty and Scott Appleby, eds., *Accounting for Fundamentalisms*. Chicago: University of Chicago Press. The Fundamentalism Project, vol. 2.

Jayant Lele

2. Orientalism and the Social Sciences

Introduction

Although Edward Said's strictures against the representation of the Orient are insightful and correct, there are a number of ways in which his analysis needs to be enriched. I hope to show that orientalism, while it serves the purpose of successful control and exploitation of the Orient, can only do so by insulating the common people of the Occident from the self-examination that can result from contact with the rest of the world. This claim is demonstrated through an examination of development theory in general and of studies of the politics of modernization in India in particular.

As a backdrop for his selectively constructed discourse paradigm of Islamic orientalism, Said constructs an Occidentalism in the garb of historicism. Said's (1978) critique of orientalism in the social sciences offers a number of insights on how and why systematic misconceptions and willful constructions of "the other" perpetuate themselves under the garb of "positive" knowledge. However, his nuanced and sensitive discourse seems to rest in part on a strategy that he himself criticizes. While specifically rejecting it as an alternative to orientalism (328) Said nonetheless constructs an all-inclusive "occidentalism" within which he locates the social sciences as manifestations of a metanarrative, another monolithic construct called historicism. The main consequence of this strategy is that the internal dynamics of the western intellectual tradition—anchored in the dramatic changes in the rational basis of social thought that occurred over the centuries when the social sciences came into existence and engaged in many self-critical exercises—is flattened out in a manner that is counterproductive to Said's own attempt to explain why the West continued to see the Orient as its other.

A detailed analysis of how the critical and hegemonic moments of western tradition unfold and enter the progression of social thought is beyond the scope of this chapter. However, some links can be tentatively sketched. The transformation of the bourgeoisie as the dominant class was associated with the rise of Henri Saint Simon and Augusté Comte along with their affirmative social science (Zeitlin 1981). Hobbes's social philosophy, his notions of social contract, and the objective conditions of the seventeenth century were similarly closely linked. The centralization and bureaucratization of power within the absolutist state apparatus and the expansion of mercantilist commodity trade went together with the justification of their governance under "the supreme authority which was just beginning to attain sovereignty" (Habermas 1973: 62). During the Enlightenment, celebration of reason, science, and progress was associated with the industrial bourgeoisie's aspirations to become the "universal class" (Avineri 1970: 48–52).

The subsequent changes experienced by capitalism in confronting its crises also find their reflection in the developments in the social sciences. It seems plausible, for example, to associate the predominance of structural-functionalism with the postwar stabilization of welfare state mass democracy under monopoly capitalism, and its decline and fall with the subsequent crisis and ongoing restructuring of the Fordist phase of industrial capitalism (Gouldner 1970; Lipietz 1987). The concurrent development of decentered perspectives and system theoretic metanarratives is similarly linked to late capitalism. Throughout the history of capitalism, these dominant epistemological discourses have faced and responded to critical challenges from within. Capitalism has had to consciously confront and not only silence but systematically and functionally appropriate the critical discourses of resistance from its own majorities while similarly dealing with "the non-synchronous experiences of Europe's Other" (Said 1986: 223).

Said adopts a structuralist conception of power, instead of seeing domination and critique as recurring moments in the history of a society. This decontextualized conception of power both renders the authors of the dominant discourse and those whose discourse capability has been silenced by it irrelevant for a critical analysis of power relations. It encompasses the entire history of the western enterprise of knowledge production into a fortuitously constructed monolith of power. It becomes a monument, a sculpture to which those silenced by it are linked not in an integral manner but as pieces of rock that have been chipped away. Such a conception merely reaffirms and thus perpetuates the marginal status of the silenced by giving them, at best, an important moral aura as victims of an unintended conspiracy. By default, it contributes to the entrenchment of the totalizing power of the ruling classes.

Today there are two main tendencies in the social sciences: the microperspectivism of the empirical-analytical, the hermeneutic-phenomenological, and the structuralist/poststructuralist disciplines; and the universalism of the comprehensively designed systems and communicative action theories. These tendencies together contribute to an affirmative celebration of the fragmented life of western modernity under late capitalism. Their justifications are value-neutrality (scientism), criticism of the part but approval of the whole (rationalism), or general functionality of social life for the reasons of the state and economy (functionalism). Together they accomplish the task of defusing the already remote possibility of a comprehensive critique of the oppressive social practice in the West. Entrenched instrumentalism as hegemonic ideology is continuously bolstered by a "consciousness industry" (Enzenbergber 1974). Affirmative social scientists empirically confirm the asocial socialization of citizens (Sixel 1988: 43–45) as a matter of fact and the lack of critical, collectively rebellious action as a proof of satisfaction and happiness (see, e.g., Almond and Verba 1965: 343–44). Differential socialization of hegemonic and working classes and genders through schools, child raising, and religious affiliations prepares a few for leadership roles and instills others with self-derogatory fatalism for failing in a world of "fair" competition (Habermas 1975: 74–84). Those who remain inadequately socialized along these lines are managed through marginalizing institutions and associated discourses.

Suppression of aesthetic authenticity of the utopian needs of the ordinary people was the theme of Nietzsche's and Foucault's critique of western modernity. However, both failed to address the central role played by the fragmentation of value spheres in silencing the spontaneity of those who try to cultivate it in everyday life, even though both were acutely aware of the human urge for authentic and unfiltered experience of joy and suffering. Differentiated value spheres under western modernity have made that urge invisible but not extinct. The material and nonmaterial dimensions of our existence still remain closely intertwined. Pacification and depoliticization of citizens and appropriation, falsification, and exploitation of their authentic "utopian needs" still requires a massive systematic effort. Because these suppressed desires for participation and undistorted aesthetic experience have physiological roots, they are the "harbinger of something else. Consumption as spectacle contains the promise that want will disappear" (Enzeberger 1974: 111–12, also Lefebvre

1971). Most other critical attempts to capture this hidden contradiction of western modernity—the denial of mass spontaneity (through theories of "mass culture" and "mass society"), its attempted assimilation (through the theses of pluralism, relativism, and liberal tolerance) or its quarantined celebration as deviance (with countercultural studies and practices)—have also failed to see the material anchoring of the disaffections of modern life.

Western social thought, in its prescientific and social scientific forms, was primarily obsessed with the dramatic transition in its own social formation, which it understood as modernization. Within that thought, the salience of critical and affirmative interpretations varied with changing perceptions of crisis and stability. In all these cogitations, the nonwestern world was kept as largely peripheral by the West except, at times, as a convenient mirror to assess or admire itself. There was neither the interest nor the cultural sophistication necessary for understanding the other on its own terms. Consequently, both its own self-understanding and its understanding of the Orient became systematically distorted.

Even anthropologists met the challenge of encountering other cultures by establishing anthropology "as an allochronic discourse" (Fabian 1983), a characteristic shared by all the paradigms (see Ortner 1984) that were still dominant at the end of the 1950s. Even later, the recognition of "coevalness" of the other, a sense for the fact that "we Europeans are what Africans see as 'other cultures,'" their 'primitives,' their 'ethnics'" (Goody 1982: 55), was limited to a few. It has failed to produce an adequate methodology (Sixel 1988: 55–56) and has most certainly not become part of the central agenda of anthropology.

Today when social sciences scholars claim to understand and interpret the Orient (and for us, more specifically, India), they do so without having resolved their internal dilemmas and without having understood the societal contradictions that produce them. Before the nineteenth century, while the fragile unity of theoretical and moral-practical knowledge was still kept together by theology and metaphysics, we notice attempts to use the Orient as a counterfoil of self-reflection by the West. The two pre-Napoleonic projects of Anquetil-Duperron and William Jones, for example, fall within what Said calls "simple comparatism" that may have "helped a European to know himself better" (1978: 117). Even after industrial capitalism had become hegemonic in the nineteenth century, there are traces of self-reflection in the dichotomies such as "community-society, authority-power, status-class, sacred-secular, alienation-progress' (Nisbet 1966: 7), which express concern about the direction taken by western modernity. This pathos of passage is at times expressed with nostalgic references to the Orient.

Orientalism in Development Theory

The post-World War II era presented the social sciences with new challenges at home and around the world. At home in the economic domain, the Fordist compromise, which "incorporated both productivity rises and the corresponding rise in popular consumption into the determination of wages and nominal profits, *a priori*" (Lipietz 1987; 35), produced an aura of affluence. It was matched, in the political domain, by high levels of civil privatism—"political abstinence combined with an orientation to career, leisure and consumption"—under a formal democracy of "passive citizens with only the right to withhold acclamation" (Habermas 1975: 37). Globally, the emergence of the United States as the dominant power of the world capitalist system, the consolidation of the Soviet Union as a countervailing power, the success of the Chinese Communist party, and, in much of Asia and Africa, the decolonization through political independence or the intensification of liberation struggles were the events that could not be ignored. The countries that could not or did not make a radical break from their past, by instituting basic structural changes within, called for projects of active intervention to promote "development." A reexamination of earlier assumptions about themes such as stability and change, and state intervention and individual liberty led to the emergence and dominance of a new social science paradigm in the form of structural-functionalism.

Consistent with the requirements of the new regimes in postwar political economy of the western industrial nations, Parsons and Smelser (1956: 22) claimed that the goal of the economy is "the maximization of production related to the whole complex of institutionalised value-systems and functions of society." Parsons had earlier argued that economic rationality is only one, functionally specific, form of rationality in general, of which ends, means, and conditions of action are all constitutive elements (1949: 698). In modern societies, Parsons argued, the relative salience of the various forms of means-ends rationality is determined through specific processes for which the polity is the functionally differentiated subsystem and the state its primary institution. Thus, Parsons's opus of conceptual and descriptive elaborations provided a sufficiently abstract characterization of the early postwar era along with a scientistic, affirmative justification of state intervention and global planning for an essentially private enterprise economy. For many social scientists, it provided a broadly plausible conceptual apparatus for the study of various aspects of industrialized welfare-state mass democracies.

For the social scientists interested in the new nations, structural-functionalism held a special appeal because of its evolutionism. Based on the recent experience of European reconstruction, economists were the first to dominate the disciplinary domain of development. For them, economic growth was a precondition for, if not the same as, development. Industrialization, capital accumulation, planning, and an interventionist state were stressed as the basic elements of theory and practice (Sen 1984). Even then the policies and models based on neoclassical principles proved to be inadequate, and an increasing number of disciplines brought their own specialized paradigms to bear on the puzzle. An at times invisible coherence was provided by the Parsonian synthesis of the western self-understanding of its own modernization. Despite their significant differences, the two eminent economic historians Rostow (1960) and Gerschenkron (1962) shared the basic premise of that self-understanding, namely, its linear evolutionism (Blomström and Hettne 1984: 19, 22). With the Parsonian systems theory, the inadequacy of the economic models could be explained as a consequence of inadequate structural differentiation. Since the four basic functions (Parsons 1951) were assumed to be universally operative at all levels and for all types of social interactions, a country's level of development could be evaluated and policy proposals for accelerating differentiation could be visualized. The practitioners of the modernization paradigm, psychologists, sociologists, anthropologists, economists, and political scientists, became convinced that in the new nations, personalities, roles, norms, values, and institutions will gradually differentiate into "rational" structures, patterns, processes, and communications media, through scientific state intervention and external aid. Like the Comtean "positive age," the Fordist "golden age" (see Lipietz 1987: 36–39) seemed globally realizable.

The cultural consequences of Fordism were revealed in crisis tendencies symbolized by civil rights and student movements. At first, this bourgeois revolt against the principles of bourgeois society, "almost successfully functioning according to its own standing," objected to the price being paid for affluence in the form "of a society dominated by competition for status and achievement and by the bureaucratization of all regions of life" (Habermas 1970: 28, 39). It attacked discrimination against late Capitalism's backwash: the youth, the unemployed, the aged, and the black, who could not be absorbed within the Fordist compromise. The premonitory signs of the economic crisis of Fordism had also become visible in the 1967 recession (Lipietz 1987: 41). The uncertainties at home were matched, globally, by the disintegration of the inherited neocolonial, formal state structures in most former colonies and by the continuing appeal of communism for the elites and masses of the new nations. The evolutionary optimism about stability and progress at home and the gradual diffusion of western rationality abroad suffered rapid erosion. Domestically, there was a shift away from optimistic expectations of theoretical convergence and political institutional stability and toward the avoidance of metanarratives in preference for micro studies. Subsequently, concern about the crises of ungovernability and the need for reliable strategies of communication and policy making came to dominate empirical research. Globally, the evolutionary optimism about the spread of democratic institutions, derived from metatheories, yielded to an emphasis on counterinsurgency research as well as concern about the capability of the new nation-states to withstand the escalation of internal "demand overloads" (see O'Brien 1972). More recently, the dramatic differences in the developmental performance of different nations have led to cultural relativism as an explanatory strategy.

Thus one notices a general shift away from overt adherence to larger paradigms about the functioning or transformation of societies. Specific issues in political economy, studies of policy alternatives, and rational choices are in vogue. Research is increasingly focused on specific problems, possible solutions, likely outcomes, and the capabilities of the state apparatus to meet these challenges. The result has been a dramatic increase in the flexibility of information generation and processing. It is consistent with and complements the "complexity-reductive" requirements of the more sophisticated forms of systems and related theories such as Luhmann's (see Luhmann 1982; Bell 1980). Both theorists and practitioners of the systems enterprise conceive of social evolution as a process of expanding problem-solving capabilities through structural change. They disavow normative commitments and seek to judge the outcomes of problem-solving processes only in terms of survival and stability of the designated systems. The success of differentiation (of personality, roles, norms, values, and institutions) is determined by the capacity for complexity reduction and crisis management. Advocacy for democracy (with attendant moralistic notions of freedom, equality, justice) has yielded to sheer instrumentalism as the only evaluative standard.

The Politics of Modernization

The recent self-evaluations by modernization theorists are also consistent with these instrumentalist demands of a post-Fordist world economy, as the following few examples will show. While acknowledging the surprises administered by the elites and the people of the new nations to the naive expectations of modernist theorists about the rapid spread of revolutions or formal democracy, Weiner (1987: 45, 47) offers as explanations a few specific local circumstances such as "security considerations," siege mentality, and "Confucian pattern of authority" (for South Korea and Taiwan). A long list of failures of popular movements, ending in the establishment of military, authoritarian, autocratic, and brutal regimes, is offered (Pakistan, Iran, Kampuchea, Vietnam), followed by a reference to the Philippines as the single success story of democratization! Presumably similar, specific, and contingent explanations can be offered for each one of these cases. Only a few generalizations are attempted, and they are characteristic of what now minimally unites the modernization paradigm: a drive to disprove the significance of class analysis. In its support, two generalizations are offered about "the most popular widespread political movements": (a) they were not organized around class or economic issues but centered around religion or ethnicity and (b) they attracted the most modern, the most educated, and most developed sectors of society, not the most deprived, lowest income groups. Although not entirely incorrect, it is the intention behind these claims that is worth noting. They reappear in different forms in most of the recent modernization analyses to offer a feeble counterattack on the massive edifice of critical scholarship on development.

As a specialist, Weiner (1989: 21–37, 77–95) also tries to explain the persistence of formal democracy in India, despite many dire predictions about its imminent demise, made primarily by modernization theorists themselves. He offers us one generalization, namely, that the United Kingdom has an impressive record of leaving behind its distinctive political institutions. This contention is accompanied by a list of exceptions that includes a large number of African and two South Asian countries for which this is not true and several others in which it may soon not be true

(77–78). From this point on, there is a steady retreat into increasingly more contingent explanations such as "the conflict managing role of the Congress Party"(33)—a party which, it is immediately admitted, is now in a state of decay. Other felicitous conjunctures such as the combination of social structures and constitutional forms that "quarantine violent social conflict and political instability at the state level" are then listed (36). Such conjunctures, since they are not traced to their structural roots, can change without reason, at any time. The scientific enterprise is thus reduced to "if-then" types of alternate scenarios (74–75), in which both terms are seen as flexible and alterable as basically independent and only "mutually dependent" variables. See, for example, the profound proposition that "the major concerns of any Indian government—the maintenance of order and the management of economy—depend on the character of governmental administration" (95).

Rudolph and Rudolph (1987) candidly admit that typically "events have pulled the rug from under our scholarly feet" (xv). Their solution to the problem is innovative: continue, as usual, to interpret India in terms of structures and models of rational choice (and call it political economy), since these terms and devices have become the main crutches of contemporary political science, but then claim no responsibility for predicting final outcomes of policies. Leave it instead to Lakshmi, the fickle goddess of fortune (393). Because, even after rising "above the flotsam and jetsam on the surface of political and economic events" and after confidently reaching "for the more durable elements beneath," they say "we are aware that we are still at the mercy of conjunctures" (xvi). This show of humility is not the result of a recognition of the enormous complexity of a civilization that is five thousand years old and of the adolescent quality of the framework into which modernization theory has tried to force it. However, equivocal, generalizations are still produced, as can be seen from this example: "Politics seems not to matter as much for economic performance as politicians and political scientists would like to think" (224). This is seen neither as a result of nor as a hypothesis about structural constraints on political regimes, both internal and international. In fact, there is little sense for these structures as producers of performance outcomes that are stable despite changes in regime types and also as forces that are often responsible for such changes. Kamat (1979) in the early years of the old Janata regime and Dutt (1984), Kaviraj (1988), and Kurien (1989) more recently have offered insightful analysis of the regime-structure-policy performance relationship. Neither Kamat nor Dutt are included Rudolph and

Rudolph's author index, with its more than four hundred entries. Instead, we are offered some new paradoxical juxtapositions (similar to the old one of 1967, about "the modernity of tradition"). The Indian state is characterized as weak-strong and the economy as rich-poor. New taxonomic concepts are supposed to explain these paradoxes. The notions of "demand politics" (an idealized notion of electoral democracy and interest group activity), "command politics" (an idealized version of benevolent despotism), bullock capitalists (for rich and middle farmers), and involuted pluralism (as a negative judgment on the presence of too many and relatively short-lived interest groups and movements) are offered to give an appearance of novel and profound analytical breakthroughs.

The general strategy of the new modernization theory of India, after its rejection of metanarratives (referred to as liberal and Marxist models), is not, however, that of producing strictly factual ethnographic narratives of events. Instead, the modernization theory offers plausible, often indiscriminate, generalizations, with appropriate caveats where necessary to avoid later embarrassment, since both people and events in the new nations often refuse to conform to its expectations. Such caution is seen as unnecessary when offering sweeping cultural explanations: "For Indians politics means acquiring power over others, maintaining or elevating one's status, and using power to provide patronage to one's supporters" (Weiner 1989: 64). It would seem appropriate for a practitioner of comparative politics to follow this assertion by a reference to assessments of what politics means to Americans or to politicians and citizens in other western mass democracies. Critical literature is full of such insightful observations (Offe 1984; Held and Pollitt 1986; Habermas 1975). Why not refer to Habermas (1975: 75) and his characterization of formal democracies as places where citizens support a regime as long as interests in consumption, leisure, career, and status are being met by policy outcomes produced through administrative mechanisms? Most citizens care or know little about policies and issues. In other words, as long as the privatistic demands are met, the citizens of industrialized mass democracies are happy to treat politics as a spectator sport. Why are such comparative self-reflections so alien to Weiner's social science? Instead we are treated to an "American liberal view" of Arthur Schlesinger that "politics is in the art of problem solving" and hence has to do with policies and issues, with the implication that that is the substantive reality of American politics.

That the propensity for unabashed and sweeping generalization has not diminished in the reformed modernization theory becomes clear when we encounter an easy to digest summary (Pye 1985) of the "complex culture of the Indian subcontinent" and its philosophy as those which "abound in contradictions, ignore the canons of the logic and the rules of cause and effect and label and categorize things without going on to seek analytical explanation" (133). These irrationalities are resolved for us completely in the next twenty-three pages with choice distillations such as "the amoral and violence legitimating propensity of Indian political culture" (139) and "Hindu propensity to defer automatically to rulers of rank and status." The Hindu concept of power is said to derive from the concept of *danda*, which "stressed punishment and the ruler's power to coerce" (138). The presumed "extreme separation of status and power of religion and politics" is explained by one-liner appeals to *karma* and *danda* and selective references to a few of the "nineteen great thinkers" of statecraft, with a specially detailed (two paragraphs) attention to Kautilya's *Arthaśāstra*. Having disembodied and fossilized centuries of reflection, rooted in specific, dramatically different sociohistorical contexts, as "Hindu thought," Pye has no difficulty in drawing plausible, pithy conclusions about today's Indian society that are easily palatable to his eager audience.[1]

Nuanced and sensitive analyses of the evolution of the state and ideology, of popular challenges and critical reflections that arose in response to the excesses of state power in ancient, medieval, and colonial India, and of the dynamics of India's tradition are, of course, available (in English) for anyone with a bit of time to explore them (Kosambi 1975; Sharma 1980; Thapar 1978, 1984; Chanana 1960; and Patil 1982, to name a few). Thapar (1984) speaks of *Arthaśāstra* as the first treatise to offer a full definition of the (newly evolved) state in terms of its seven elements (*prakrtis*) and points out that *danda* does not refer only to army, access to legitimate physical force, or broader coercion alone, but "even to power of law and authority" (122). In tracing the emergence of the state system in India to the mid-first millennium B.C. and in unraveling the complex social formations that preceded and followed this emergence, Thapar warns us that many terms in the ancient texts were carried over from one society to the other but that their connotations changed and hence must be viewed in the context of that change (155).

There are other western scholars of the politics of modernization in India who are aware of its enormous complexity and offer interesting insights, that may not occur to scholars from within, about regions to which they have devoted their sustained attention. Brass on U.P. (1965), Frankel on Bihar (1989a) and Manor on Karnataka (1980) are the obvious examples. But even they, when forced by professional requirements to expound on "India in general" or "development theory in general," display the severe limits to comparative self-reflection imposed on them by their training. Take Frankel (1989b) for example. She justly criticizes the old modernization theorists who "so easily jettisoned" democracy as an ideal while retaining economic growth as a goal attainable "with the existing set of institutions" (98). There is no reflection here on the political-economic context in which political scientists, both at home and in their study of the third world, abandoned optimism and turned to considerations of order and to the micropolitics of policy studies and to detailed descriptions of "political economy." Frankel cites Geertz and his gloomy conclusion that the watchword in new regimes everywhere had become "not mobilization of the populace but its depoliticization" (95). You will look in vain, however, for a comparison with or reference to the postwar depoliticization of the populace of her own country or of the continent whose tradition it claims to uphold.

Thus a double strategy of isolation, subtle and invisible only to its practitioners, characterizes the new modernization paradigm:

(a) It isolates the third world experience, with its discrepancies and contradictions (as traditional), from being a source of reflection and enlightenment about the pathologies of the western (modern) social formation.

(b) It ignores the work of sensitive scholars who operate within a broadly critical framework and offer rich empirical studies of interaction between classes and other identities (gender, race, caste, tribe). In a fake display of evenhandedness,[2] it conflates and criticizes the so-called liberal and neo-Marxist theories as advancing "a global model of development" and for seeing the process as "historically determined or universally pursued" (Frankel 1989a: 17). Both theories are then condemned as having been empirically falsified. In their place an "agnostic," "empirical," and presumably "value free" theory and "investigations to gain practical knowledge about specific conditions" (Frankel 1989b: 108) are advocated.

In the actual practice of this empiricist agnosticism, the biggest victim is the analysis of enduring structural forces that have produced major noticeable changes in the Indian polity over the last forty-five years. The new modernization theorists of Indian politics do note some of these changes but only in terms of "deinstitutionalization" or "decay" of the Congress party and/or the increasing tendency toward "centrism" in its leadership. By focusing on these events as outcomes, these theorists can point to some symptomatic events as contingent explanations of others, or just reverse the process. Generational change (disappearance of committed nationalist leaders), the rise of state level bosses (which is compared to the old "machine politics" in the United States), the character, cunning, and/or disingenuous behavior of the Gandhis (Indira, Sanjay, and Rajiv), and a shift from coalitional to populist ("plebiscitary") politics are offered as explanations, as if they are in themselves adequate. The structural basis of the emergence of coalitional politics was succinctly identified by Kamat (1979). The dominant and vocal classes and interests had coalesced under the Congress umbrella within the international context of the declining relevance of British imperialism for all dominant classes in India (Lele 1990a). That coalition had endured for almost two decades after independence because of its anchoring in the cultural-economic hegemony of the dominant caste-class nexus of the rich peasantry (Lele 1990b). The uneasy but mutually rewarding alliance between the internally differentiated capital and peasantry was sustained by a formally democratic state. The price paid in terms of slow surplus transfer and slow growth rates (reviled as the "Hindu rate of growth") was richly rewarded by temporary political stability and surface consensus of the Nehru era. The aura of prosperity of that period eroded just as the signs of the crisis of Fordism began to surface in the West around 1967. The internal and external structural pressures for a change in the course of policy, beginning with the Ford Foundation report on food policy, have taken a variety of forms. The anticipated conflict between the capitalists and the rich peasants (Byers 1974) has been intensified and was reflected in regime changes such as the Emergency and the two Janata interludes. Whereas Rudolph and Rudolph were able, through their aggregate data analysis, to notice the fact that economic performance has tended to be "regime neutral" (1987: 225:44), their agnostic empiricism has prohibited them from noticing, let alone engaging, the structural analyses that show how the regimes themselves have been all along vulnerable to the broader structural forces (Patnaik 1986; Prasad 1990).

Shanin (1982: xi) reminds us that coming "to grips with a social reality that is systematically different from one's own, and to explain its specific logic and momentum are most difficult conceptual and pedagogical tasks." I have argued in these pages that the intellectual opportunism preached and practiced by the new politics of modernization, its refusal to confront and engage structural analyses, and its incapacity for critical self-reflection have effectively sealed it from being able to fulfill this task. This is true of the affirmative social science in general, both at home and on the periphery. Furthermore, this has been the pattern of almost all the western encounters with the Orient, since Napoleon. Despite the absence of self-reflexivity, through singular affirmation of one's own condition as positive and worthy of emulation, these encounters did produce "correct" knowledge (or what Said [1974: 54] calls "positive" knowledge) that allows conquerors to subjugate and control people politically and to exploit them economically. The incorporation of this correct knowledge into a broader self-affirmative framework of interpretation (what Said refers to as "imaginative" knowledge) has had a different task: to insulate one's own worldview from a possible critique through an open exposure to other ways of making sense.

Simple means-ends rationality of the early capitalist era accompanied the entrenchment of British rule in India. In the generation of correct knowledge, the British administrators were assisted by Indian accomplices of what the British described as "the advanced castes." Knowledge thus generated was used and transmitted to the core through documents and reports that employed a larger framework that was at times Christian (defensive or against the faith), broadly liberal, or narrowly utilitarian in character. The presence of an ancient and highly sophisticated civilization could not be ignored, although admitting its presence in the simple folk wisdom and everyday life practice of a peasant would have been contrary to the project of control and exploitation. It would have also been inconsistent with the administrator's self-understanding, with his relationship to his own past. With the assistance of the local cultural compradors, mostly Brahmans, who had their own hegemonic agenda dating back to Manu (see Lele 1990c), a new explanatory narrative was constructed. Orientalists (and administrators) "invariably made a distinction between popular Hinduism, which they did not deem worthy of study, and 'philosophical' Hinduism, which they tried to define as a set of hard and fast doctrinal propositions and place in current theories about the nature and history of religion" (Marshall 1970: 43).

This "disembodiment" of Indian thought was consistent with the emerging disenchantment in Europe with its own past. It was employed in the debates about the virtues and vices of Christianity, debates that were an important part of European self-assessment. In India, the Brahmanic assessment of the contemporary era, as *kaliyuga*, coincided with the European view of India's intellectual stagnation to offer a justification for the collaboration between the new rulers and the "new Brahmans" as agents of reform and progress. The early modernization theory had also retained this liberal reformist zeal for progress through economic growth and political democracy during the era of postwar prosperity at home. The new modernization theory, in criticizing its "liberal" predecessors, reveals the triumph of instrumentalist logic as it tries to affirm the virtues of late capitalism, under conditions of a Fordist crisis. It calls for a renewal of value neutrality in social sciences. It aspires to greater honesty (?) and detachment. It is forced to grant some credence to the Marxist analyses but only as they pertain to the West. Thus, we find occasional references to the domestic scene in claims such as "the intellectual tradition of Europe and American area studies is older and better established. The professional core is larger" (Almond 1987: 476). Or, we are told that "the belief that an excess of democracy constrains economic growth and jeopardizes governability had a certain currency" in the 1970s in India and "in developed countries too" (Rudolphs 1987: 222). The neo-Marxist scholarship on the West is praised for being more mature, in the first case, and Offe (1984) is cited for having talked about "ungovernability," in the second. No further comparative reflection on the structural sources of the rise of neoconservatism in the West and its repercussions on the regime in India is deemed necessary. Such a disciplinary dualism is nothing but covert adherence to the Gibbian principle, as cited by Said (1974: 107): "to apply the psychology and mechanics of Western political institutions to Asian or Arab states is pure Walt Disney." I am arguing, however, that the purpose of this dualism is to ensure that an honest comparative analysis does not lead to critical analyses of the society at home and a desire to explore and challenge the sources of hypocrisy and oppression on which that social order rests. The fear of a self-critical public attitude and the need for successful (i.e. correct) knowledge, so as to control and exploit the other, are the two elements behind what Said describes as the "textual attitude" (92–94). They drive the social sciences toward misunderstanding and misrepresentation. The burgeoning "consciousness industry" (Enzenberger 1974) distorts and misrepresents to the western people their own authentic dreams and aspirations. It also distorts, often by employing social scientific knowledge, the nonwestern people, their civilizations, their resistance, and their own distinct and imaginative responses to alien invasions and conquests. The two are part of the same project of control and exploitation through a culturally imposed stupefaction of its own people.

Paradoxically, critical and humane self-reflection, open to intersubjective enlightenment and not as the instrumental reflexivity of modern science, was to be the cornerstone of western modernity, according to its own theorists. The notions of "partiality for reason" and "European human dignity" (Habermas 1975: 142–43), which were central to that project, now have a hollow ring. The ongoing subversion of that capability originated in the fragmentation of the lifeworld in the seventeenth century, if not earlier (Gadamer 1981), and was accelerated by the triumphant march of capitalism at home and around the world. It now sustains the cultural reproduction of late Capitalism through the omnipotent consciousness industry. At the same time, perspectivism at home and cultural relativism (see Huntington 1987: 22) about the rest of the world, as a strategy for explaining a social reality that is so substantially different, allows production of discrete pieces of information. The rejection of metanarratives on the grounds of their value-ladenness and ethnocentrism (or as "liberal" or "Marxist" or "structural-functionalist"), by social researchers and area specialists, does not prohibit policymakers and other manipulators of people's memories and dreams from using them to reduce the complexity of amassed information and to flexibly employ them to ensure control and exploitation.

There is every reason to fear the rapid spread of that subversion of reflexivity to the new nations. Said (1978: 322) speaks of "accommodation between the intellectual class" in the Orient and "the new imperialism." One must not forget that such an accommodation did not occur without resistance and was never complete. As I have shown elsewhere (Lele 1989), some of the early encounters between the colonial masters and the Indian intellectuals who took their "purportedly Liberal culture" (see, Said 1978: 254) seriously led to critical self-reflections that exposed the hypocrisy of European as well as Indian dominant discourses. Thus emerged a universalistic humanism of men like Ranade and Phule. The subsequent dissipation of their insights, for want of a material-social base and as a result of instrumentalist colonial policies of promotion of interest group competition, did not necessarily eliminate the critical potential available in them. Immanent subaltern challenges have kept surfacing within that tradition, as was shown by Ambedkar (see Lele 1991). It seems reasonable to expect that similar explorations of the responses of the colonized peoples elsewhere, with their enormous variations and cultural specificity, may still point to the fundamental unity of their resistance, to the basic elements of a universal discourse of the unprivileged (see Lele and Singh 1989: 96–109). We should heed the plea in Fabian (1983: 161) and make embodied "consciousness, individual and collective, the starting point"—and thus authentically unravel the modernity of each tradition (see Lele 1981). It may thus become possible to demonstrate, more fully, the inadequacies and ethnocentrism of perspectivist and relativist methodologies.

Dependency Theory as Culture Critique

Shanin (1982: xi), while pointing to the specific logic and momentum of third world societies, also stresses the unity of their experience "of relationships past and present with the countries of advanced capitalism and industrialisation." The dependency perspective tried to capture this common experience, as the "development of underdevelopment," and to make it the central theme of development theory. For Latin America, the home of dependency school, the most important element of that experience has been the overwhelming presence of an imperial power. Its paternalism and coercive might were matched by the subservience of the ruling classes in the Latin countries, regardless of the authoritarian or democratic veneer of their regimes. Since that paternalism permeated the thinking behind the modernization paradigm, it also came under a severe critical scrutiny. Andre Gunder Frank (1969) was one of the first to offer a Marxist analysis of modernization theory. With his intimate knowledge of American social science and its cultural ideological underpinnings, Frank was able to mount a devastating critique of the theoretical, empirical, and practical inadequacies of the dominant paradigms. It is refreshing to find, in an essay written in 1965 (1969: 21–94), a critique of all the major themes in the new modernization theory: instrumentalism, cultural relativism, self-imposed asceticism toward structural analysis, and the inability for self-reflection. Through a telling reference to a cover of the *New Yorker* depicting Santa Claus and Freud together, Frank captures the two main legitimating devices of the American myth of progress through capitalist growth: the promise of automatic success through adherence to the naturalistic rule of the market forces (as "being good" for Santa Claus) and the corresponding blaming of the victim's inadequate motivation (low "'n' achievement" and hence need for "analysis") in an unequal race for success. He shows how these myths are now being diffused to the third world by the practitioners of modernization theory. His reference to the "Freudianization" of Weber (68) is a critique that applies to all scientism, which thrives on the pacification of the human subject both in the West and in the new nations. An awareness of the absence of self-reflection and the need for it is reflected in Frank's advice to the anthropologists to work in and for their own cultural context. Frank also shows how futile comparative studies can be without a prior commitment to and openness for self-criticism (137–45).

These contributions of Frank, a culture-critique of the roots of modernization theory and of its role as the ideological-epistemological arm of imperialism (138), have been overshadowed by the debates generated through his economic generalizations about the possibility of autonomous capitalist development on the periphery. Frank, the other contributors to the dependency perspective, and their critics, on the Left and the Right, have reduced the broader, all-encompassing view of the relationship between industrial capitalist countries and the new nations to a sterile debate about the "progressive" role of capitalism and the national bourgeoisie. Excessive claims about the inevitability of underdevelopment, interpreted narrowly as lack or slow growth of industrialism, have been made the object of criticism. Attention is thus deflected from the fact of uneven international development and its cultural hegemonic as well as political-coercive antecedents and consequences. Dependency theory had effectively focused its attention on the distortions that imperialism, as a moment of the *political* economy of capitalism, implants into colonies, possessions, and "the spheres of influence." It also identified the local agents charged with the legitimation of the ruthless methods of surplus extraction. When critics of dependency theory advance the claims of the progressive role of capitalism, assert the necessity or inevitability of capitalist development at any cost, and believe that, in reality, capitalism follows the same lawlike processes of emergence and expansion everywhere, they become, naively or purposely, the advocates and legitimizers of ignorance, distress, poverty, dirt, abandonment, and downtroddenness. Like the new modernization theory's cultural relativists, those who stress only the internal specificity of each separate social formation, while celebrating as necessary the universally dehumanizing cultural consequences of capitalism, seem to believe that salvation can come only through (although, perhaps, not in) capitalism.

In Africa as in Latin America, the dependency thesis was used, abused, and resurrected to assert the lack or necessity of encouragement to entrepreneurship, domestic or international, and to denounce the inferior commitment of the ruling African elite to capitalist expansion. The cultural consequences of colonialism, in enhancing a truncated form of growth and capitalist expansion and in nurturing an irresponsible elite, did not form part of this debate. Neither the economistic abridgment of dependency theory, nor its dismissal as a poor predictor of peripheral capitalist expansion, have found much favor in India. There, from the beginning, many of the intellectuals, even as they collaborated with the alien regime, became sensitive to its pathogenic quality and its zeal for a dependent transformation of the national economy. Its hypocrisy and double standards, its instrumentalism, its encouragement of egofocality, and its amoral pursuit of individual gain led many to a critical evaluation of their own role and often to an advocacy of the masses, against the injustices, oppression, and drain inflicted on them by the "Un-British rule in India" (Naoroji 1962; also Ranade 1915). Self-reliance as a strategy of resistance to the pathogens that seem to inevitably accompany the advance of capitalism thus dates back in India to the 1870s. That theme of a critique of colonial capitalism also led to M. N. Roy's confrontation with Lenin at the Second Congress of the Third International in 1920 (see Roy 1964). Today also it remains the central concern of critical social science in India. As the inheritors of that legacy of colonial experience and as the descendants of the colonized and not the colonizers, even the advocates of capitalism as a necessary stage seem more subdued in their defense than the "Warrenites" (see Warren 1980; Sender and Smith 1986).

Despite some of its sophistry, the "modes of production" debate in India nowhere approaches the sterility of its counterpart in the West (for a summary, see Thorner 1982). One of the debate's salient contributions was to identify the political, cultural, and economic mechanisms used by the local and imperial agents for extraction and appropriation of socially unnecessary surplus. It showed how the lack of differentiation of the roles of the producers and extractors of surplus produced radical or reactionary alliances or how caste played the ideological role of masking class relations. In most of its empirical explorations and interpretive controversies, it still kept alive the moral-practical question that was central to the appeal of dependency theory: how to resist and overcome the ravages of capitalist transformation in the age of imperialism. The comment by Sau (1975: 1003) on Latin America may apply equally as an explicit or implicit judgment in the Indian debate on the nature and prospects of capitalist development: "That is to say, bourgeois-democratic revolution (Debray) or no bourgeois-democratic revolution (Frank), the 'national bourgeoisie' in Latin America is neither effectively national, nor truly a bourgeoisie in its full classical revolutionary glory." Despite their disagreements on the relative significance of class or caste or region, for analysis or for political mobilization, the central question for the critical social scientists in India has been the same: when and how to lift the various specific struggles to the level of people's war or when must an anti-feudal and anti-imperialist revolution transform itself into an anti-capitalist-socialist revolution (Sen 1984).

However, its vibrancy notwithstanding, the colonial ancestry of the critical social analysis in India still extracts a heavy price. Indian scholars are remarkably sensitive to the dialectical nonmechanistic, universalistic,

and humane dimensions in Marx and to the insights of those who followed in his footsteps, including Lenin, Luxemburg, Gramsci, and Mao
(see, for example, Bagchi 1983; Patnaik, A. 1988; Chatterjee 1988; Sen 1984,
1988). With a clear understanding of the inevitability of their situation, the
very condition of their intellectual discourse that forces them to "speak the
language of European philosophy" (Chatterjee 1990: 120; also see Sen
1984), these Indian scholars expose the provincialism of the European concepts that parade as universal (such as "civil society") while unlocking
those that have been systematically suppressed as "traditional" and "parochial" (such as "community") by the narrative of capitalism. Only by ignoring the contributions of Indians as peripheral outsiders do the western
social scientists retain their insularity from self-criticism.

The critical sensitivity shown toward the western philosophical tradition does not seem to have the same cutting edge, if and when these
Indian intellectuals address their own tradition. In a way this is not surprising. As in the West, the quarantined discursive freedom "framed
through disciplinary practices in the universities and in the international
academic community" (Chatterjee 1990: 120) encourages sterility by restricting access to everyday life, through its scientization or philosophi-
zation (Lefebvre 1971: 1–67). In India, the distance is accentuated by a
definitional gulf that separates everyday life of the common people as the
Little Tradition from the disembodied philosophical discourses that are
taught in the universities as the Great Tradition. For most professionals,
who "coexist peacefully" in "traditional" and "modern" cultures, or uphold a universal "composite" culture, the problem is resolved through a
dualistic adoption of conflicting epistemological postures (Lele and Singh
1989: 44–50). An easy temptation is to suspect all commonly held beliefs
as an opiate, an ideology that clouds realistic consciousness and thus to
offer a critique from the outside, ignoring the possibility of and thus rejecting any access to their inner, immanent dynamics. As a corollary, the
professionally privileged, functionally critical intellectual may construct or
search for counterdiscourses that challenge common beliefs as products of
a dominant discourse. One may then concentrate only on those subalterns
who become visible through overt resistance in the form of "jacquerie,
revolt, uprising, etc., or to use their Indian designations—*alhing*, *bidroha*,
ulgulan, *fituri*, and so on" (Guha 1983: 4).

Marx himself and some recent Marxists, informed by the insights of
phenomenology and hermeneutics, "bestowed an epistemological status
upon the categories of everyday action, speech and common life." Today's

postmodern intellectuals—Indian and Western—while trying to establish links with the unprivileged often tend to so direct "their gaze to the phenomena of the extraordinary that they contemptuously glide over the practice of everyday life as something derivative or inauthentic" (Habermas 1987: 339). Such degradation of everyday life is easier in India because of the westward orientation and training of its intellectuals. The preferred option of many critical social scientists seems to be to treat the dominant discourses as monoliths, in an essentialist manner; to suspect them because of their universalistic, inclusive claims; and to treat those who believe in them and live by them as silent, uncomprehending victims. In proposing discrete critical activities out of "decentered consciousness," social scientists are also likely to suspect such simple notions as our essential materiality, unique but universal, as human beings. An awareness that we are capable of experiencing and sharing our joy and suffering through social labor, including linguistic labor, and across cultural barriers is likely to be labeled "recycled Marxism" (see Said 1986: 223).

Due to their disaffection with the abuse of Enlightenment values of reason, progress, truth, or freedom, Foucault and the other successors of Nietzsche want to suspect and dismantle the entire European critical tradition. This is possible only by conflating it with its distortions and suppressions entrenched under late Capitalism and serviced by the affirmative social sciences. Precisely those insights that throw light on the processes by which suppression of critical sensitivity occurs are now being suspected or ignored. One can enter the postmodernist discourse either from the left or from the right. The two paths are distinguished only by the personal preferences of the entrants. One can celebrate spontaneity, uniqueness, and dissidence and oppose bureaucratic control, economic growth, and the existing political institutions either with and on behalf of the unprivileged or against them. Having unraveled the sources of perspectivism and relativism in the post-Fordist western social formations, it is difficult not to see all of these, often contradictory and chaotic, initiatives as being consistent with, if not the consequences of, instrumentalism. Said (1986: 228–29), fully aware of the dangers of "parochial dominations and fussy defensiveness" that accompany the new decentered discourses, is still unable to find the possible basis on which the collectively maintained dominations could be collectively fought. Precisely what that basis can be has been the source of major debates in the western critical tradition. If we wish to uncover the insights generated by it and interpret them, in ways appropriate to our times, we must first engage that tradition on its own terms. Instead, Said has chosen to "stand outside the family-quarrel of the Western philosophical tradition" (Bhatnagar 1986: 15). He merely suspects it, in its entirety, through Foucauldian eyes. He misses the crucial elements in the Vico-Marx-Gramsci tradition, elements that are central to his project. Consequently, his insightful analysis of orientalism still remains one-sided and incomplete.

The responses to Said's book have been, therefore, predictable. The practitioners of the new modernization theory have ignored him as they have ignored most other critical scholarship. His "unscientific method," his "passionate rage," and his moral anger would no doubt discourage them, as an unscholarly display of "bitterness, repetitiveness and tendentiousness" (see Kopf 1980). Others seem to have taken a "shrug of the shoulder" approach and decided to "get on with the scholarly work at hand, since the alternative is to "depart from the scene of the struggle—into silence or into some other walk of life" (Kapp 1980: 483–84). It is a mistake to dismiss without explanation this sense of helplessness as paralysis specific to first world scholars (Bhatnagar 1986: 14). It points as much to Said's failure to locate that paralysis within the broader context of the western social formation and to his inability to offer anything more than a naive hope of establishing cross-cultural understanding and a new, benign intra-cultural subjectivity through self-cleansing genealogical exercises. Kapp himself offers a clue that reveals the all pervasive instrumentalism as the source of the paralysis in his admission that dispassionate confessions about the manipulative aspects of scholarship left a class of undergraduates nearly asleep within minutes. They were neither surprised nor shocked nor did they expect it to be a question on their final examination. At the same time, Indian scholars can ill afford to laugh at Kapp's predicament. If they believe that their life is or can remain immune to the same malaise, they are wrong.

Beyond Orientalism?

In the end we are still left with Said's most pertinent but unanswered question (1978: 45):

Can one divide human reality, as indeed human reality seems to be genuinely divided, into clearly different cultures, histories, traditions, societies, even races, and survive the consequences humanly? By surviving the consequences humanly, I mean to ask whether there is any way of avoiding the hostility expressed by the division, say of men into "us" (Westerners) and "they" (Orientals).

Despite its major methodological achievements, critical hermeneutics, like phenomenological and critical Marxism, leads a quarantined existence as yet another "theoretical framework" for doctoral dissertations. All of the approaches that seek to answer Said's question by privileging the other, by taking only the local perspective, and by choosing to speak only for or to specific, decentered, marginalized constituencies, remain amenable to functional absorption into metatheories. Specific, practical activities that challenge specific oppressive practices are also routinely ignored or given salience and ameliorated on terms set by the dominant interests. Thus, those who merely suspect the entire western tradition, including its earlier critical-revolutionary moments, as a conspiracy, seem to join those whom they oppose as oppressors. Together, they celebrate the western fragmentation of life and thought as the achievement of modernity or postmodernity.

I have argued in these pages that the western tradition labeled "historicism" by Said and dismissed for its lack of sensitivity to the Orient had in fact developed insights about reliable knowledge that are still relevant once appropriately interpreted for the contemporary context. They emerged at a major moment of crisis in western history, and their suppression and distortion was associated with the changing social context of the rise, survival, and entrenchment of capitalism in Europe and its spread around the world. That spread was ensured and accelerated by the cultural, political, coercive, and economic arms of imperialism. Those who became the victims of that onslaught responded in highly innovative and subtle ways, often through critical self-reflection. Consequently, imperialism also had to respond and change, causing in its wake changes in the structure of capitalism.

However, even the critical impulses produced by the crises of capitalism have ignored or systematically misunderstood the ways of the people of the non-Western world. Western critics of western society remain narcissistically immune to the lessons of innovative self-reflection that occurred on the periphery. This narcissism was integral to the project of imperialism. Its power was and is predicated on a systematically cultivated cognitive poverty (Sixel 1979). Marx, writing during the early stages of the crisis of capitalism, had grasped, however opaquely, the basic elements of our universality as those who are materially united and hence capable of symbolically communicating that universality across cultures. Hence he remains central to the critical enterprise, globally. Today the philosophical terrain in the West is dominated by metanarratives on the one hand and microperspectives as well as decentered discourses on the other. In the process, the central critical insights of Marx and his predecessors and successors are being dissipated into a super market of ungrounded perspectivism, and economistic or evolutionary orthodoxies. These tendencies correspond to the requirements of late Capitalism and should, therefore, be treated as suspect. A strategy of imitation is fraught with particular danger for third world scholars because of the tendency in these discourses toward a linear devaluation of tradition. Marx was aware of the temptation of linear devaluation of tradition when he spoke of the latest form that regards the previous ones as steps leading toward itself. He also noted that societies do produce movements of critical self-reflection, where they are able to overcome one-sidedness. This happens under conditions of crisis. He was also aware of the human incapability to not learn, except under conditions of ideological stupefaction. Thus, in everyday life also, moments of critical self-reflection occur through social labor of work and speech. In this sense, if reflexivity is the crucial element of modernity, it is also the singular attribute of the human species. Thus for humans, to use Habermas (1975: 15) against his own evolutionism, "Not *learning* but *not-learning* is the phenomenon that calls for explanation." As my analysis of development theory has shown, the all pervasive instrumentalism, in everyday life and in academic discourses, acts as a nurtured antidote to the potential for self-reflection.

Out of an understanding of Marx's anti-orientalism has come the plea by Fabian (1983) for making "consciousness with a body" the starting point in anthropology. It is also a source of my proposal for the recognition of an ongoing modernity of tradition. Traditions are capable of generating, from within, a critique of oppressive social practices and of their legitimating ideologies. Such a critique is grounded in a rational recognition of a forcibly denied potential social order. In situations where an adequate material basis for an epochal transformation has emerged, the critique may point to a future where all of the existing oppressions are seen as coming to an end. Where such preconditions have yet to emerge, it appeals to the anchoring principles of tradition and demands that "unnecessary oppression," socioculturally determined within the parameters of a given tradition, be abolished. Discrepancies between the principles affirmed and promises made by the appropriators of social surplus, and the actual life experience of active producers have been the source of social movements in all traditions.

The experience of these past struggles is incorporated and kept alive in the symbols, rituals, and texts. It remains accessible as a source of inspiration for collective social action under appropriate conditions and through contextualized reinterpretations. These past points of departure, while they remain mystified and mythologized, serve as sources of legitimation. They are used to support the claim that the existing social order, as the product of previous struggles, is a socially cherished end in itself or at least a socially sanctioned way to fulfill those as yet denied dreams and aspirations at some future date. However, mystifications of this kind are not automatic outcomes or inert end points of social struggles. They have to be and are systematically constructed (Lele in press).

The paralysis of today's western intellectuals is matched by the estrangement of the Indian intellectuals from their own tradition. That tradition is still constitutive of a meaningful lifeworld of the Indian people. Chatterjee (1990: 120) correctly argues that the "modern" intellectuals from the third world "cannot pretend to occupy an alternative subject-position merely by privileging the concepts" of their own philosophies. "Alternative subject positions, if they are to emerge, must be fought for through contestations within the site of European philosophy by pushing its terms beyond its own discursive boundaries." Such a project cannot help western thought overcome its narcissism, unless the terrain beyond the boundaries is marked by a critical reappropriation of one's own tradition. The Indian intellectuals must be willing to return to their own past, concurrently, and be able to appreciate the rationality of the discourses of the unprivileged embedded in their own tradition and encrusted in the sedimentations of centuries of hegemonic and ideological distortions.

Informed by a critique of orientalism, the new social science enterprise in India must begin with the recognition that researchers always departed from the vantage point of a dominant discourse. The only bond that unites them with those they seek to know is the *possibility* of a new understanding, based on a bodily-felt urge to make sense together. The memories of past struggles and dreams of a denied future give meaning to the events of daily life of the people, and hence to know them is to first understand what they mean locally. This does not call for a prior renunciation of one's own ways of making sense. That is impossible, in any case.

When the two ways do come in conflict, the willingness to suspect one's own ways, to engage in self-reflection, and to be capable of being truly modern constitute the only preconditions for a new understanding that encompasses the truth of both by going beyond them.

In concrete terms relevant for our own times, I see the need to find a mode of analysis that can take into account small, localized accretions to a tradition of critique, the virtualization of historical experience, and the moments, however fleeting, of its critical rejuvenation. Man cannot become a child again, said Marx, or he becomes childish. But he must strive to reproduce the truth of his childhood, its naivete, at a higher stage (1973: III). To the extent that tradition carries within it the naive dreams and aspirations of humanity anchored in its historic childhood, it reconstitutes its modernity in trying to reproduce the truth of that naivete at moments of crisis brought on by excessive or unnecessary suppression of the bodily felt spontaneity and naivete. Access to that naivete, in one's own tradition or that of the other, remains closed because of our unwillingness or inability to enter the worldview of the other with the two qualities that Jnanesvar begged from his thirteenth-century audience: gentle humility (*haluvarpana*) and alertness (*avadhana*). The art of listening to those who believe, while unmasking the hypocrisy and falsehood of the beliefs themselves by suspecting them (Ricoeur 1978), requires that we move not with Nietzsche or Foucault alone but with Marx and Gramsci as well.

Notes

1. One wonders whether Harvard University Press would publish a book on the cultural dimension of American power and politics that described it as being based on "disregard for the organization of the society" and the recognition of "a state of war as universal and in principle irremovable." This may not seem any less plausible in view of the Gulf War of 1991. After all, Machiavelli is as much a theorist of western politics as Manu or Chanakya is of Indian, and Habermas (1973: 50) is at least as respectable an authority on the Occident as Ashis Nandy is on India.

2. Why, otherwise, would Weiner (1989: 24–25) derive his understanding of Marxism from a "distinguished Indian sociologist" known neither for his deep study nor for a sympathetic understanding of Marx's enormously large and varied opus. It is also difficult to explain why, in a listing of those in the "Marxist circles" who are dissatisfied with the simplistic character of Marx's class analysis, the entire corpus of critical theory is excluded and only the neoclassical reductionists are given the place of honor. Frankel (1989b: 18) also conveniently ignores the contributions of Omvedt, Patil, and other critical scholars to a sensitive analysis of caste-

class mediations and concludes that Marxist theory presumes that "caste will be suppressed by the formation of economic classes associated with the capitalist mode of production." Much of the nuanced analysis of how capitalism thrives on caste-race-gender segmentation of the labor market does not seem to make much sense to her.

References

Almond, Gabriel A. 1987. "The Development of Political Development." In Myron Weiner and Samuel P. Huntington, eds., *Understanding Political Development: An Analytical Study*. Boston: Little, Brown.

Almond, Gabriel A. and Sidney Verba. 1965. *The Civic Culture: Political Attitudes and Democracy in Five Nations*. Boston: Little, Brown.

Anderson, Perry. 1974. *Lineages of the Absolutist State*. London: NLB/Verso.

Aron, Raymond. 1965. *Main Currents in Sociological Thought*, vol. I. Trans. Richard Howard and Helen Weaver. New York: Basic Books.

Avineri, Shlomo. 1970. *The Social and Political Thought of Karl Marx*. Cambridge: Cambridge University Press.

Bagchi, A. K. 1983. "Toward a Correct Reading of Lenin's Theory of Imperialism." *Economic and Political Weekly* 18, 31.

Bell, Daniel. 1980. "The Social Framework of the Information Society." In Tom Forester, ed., *The Microelectronics Revolution: The Complete Guide to New Technology and Its Impact on Society*. Cambridge, MA: MIT Press.

Bhatnagar, Rashmi. 1986. "Uses and Limits of Foucault: A Study of the Theme of Origins in Edward Said's 'Orientalism.'" *Social Scientist*, 16, 7: 3–22.

Blomström, Magnus and Björn Hettne. 1984. *Development Theory in Transition: The Dependency Debate and Beyond*. London: Zed Books.

Brass, Paul R. 1965. *Factional Politics in an Indian State: The Congress Party in Uttar Pradesh*. Berkeley: University of California Press.

Byers, T. J. 1974. "Land Reforms, Industrialization and the Marketed Surplus in India: An Essay on the Power of Rural Bias." In David Lehmann, ed., *Agrarian Reforms and Agrarian Reformism: Studies of Peru, Chile, China, and India*. London: Faber and Faber.

Chanana, D. R. 1960. *Slavery in Ancient India*. New Delhi: People's Publishing House.

Chatterjee, Partha. 1988. "On Gramsci's 'Fundamental Mistake.'" *Economic and Political Weekly* 23, 5.

———. 1990. "A Response to Taylor's 'Modes of Civil Society.'" *Public Culture* 3, 1.

Dutt, Srikant. 1984. *India and the Third World: Altruism or Hegemony?* London: Zed Books.

Enzenberger, Hans Magnus. 1974. *The Consciousness Industry: On Literature, Politics and the Media*. New York: Seabury Press.

Fabian, Johannes. 1983. *Time and the Other: How Anthropology Makes Its Object*. New York: Columbia University Press.

Foucault, Michel. 1977. *Language, Counter-Memory, Practice: Selected Essays and Interviews*. Ed. Donald Bouchard, trans. Donald Bouchard and Sherry Simon. Ithaca, NY: Cornell University Press.

———. 1980. *Power/Knowledge: Selected Interviews and Other Writings, 1972–1977*. Ed. and trans. Colin Gordon. New York: Pantheon Books.

Frank, Andre Gunder. 1969. *Latin America: Underdevelopment or Revolution: Essays on Underdevelopment and the Immediate Enemy*. New York: Monthly Review Press.

Frankel, Francine. 1989a. "Caste, Land and Dominance in Bihar: Breakdown of the Brahmanical Social Order." In Francine Frankel and M. S. A. Rao, eds., *Dominance and State Power in Modern India: Decline of a Social Order*, vol. I. Delhi: Oxford University Press.

———. 1989b. "Modernization and Dependency Theories: Is a Social Science of Development Possible?" In Iqbal Narain, ed., *Development, Politics, and Social Theory*. New Delhi: Sterling.

Gadamer, Hans-Georg. 1981. *Reason in the Age of Science*. Trans. Frederick Lawrence. Cambridge, MA: MIT Press.

Gershenkron, A. 1962. *Economic Backwardness in Historical Perspective*. Cambridge, MA: Harvard University Press.

Goody, Jack. 1982. *Cooking, Cuisine and Class: A Study in Comparative Sociology*. Cambridge: Cambridge University Press.

Gouldner, Alvin W. 1970. *The Coming Crisis of Western Sociology*. New York: Basic Books.

Gramsci, Antonio. 1971. *Selections from the Prison Notebooks*. Ed. and trans. Quintin Hoare and Geoffrey Smith. London: Lawrence and Wishart; New York: International Publishers.

Guha, Ranajit. 1983. *Elementary Aspects of Peasant Insurgency in Colonial India*. Delhi: Oxford University Press.

Habermas, Jürgen. 1970. *Toward A Rational Society: Student Protest, Science, and Politics*. Trans. Jeremy Shapiro. Boston: Beacon Press.

———. 1973. *Theory and Practice*. Trans. John Viertel. Boston: Beacon Press.

———. 1975. *Legitimation Crisis*. Trans. Thomas McCarthy. Boston: Beacon Press.

———. 1984. *The Theory of Communicative Action. Volume One: Reason and the Rationalization of Society*. Trans. Thomas McCarthy. Boston: Beacon Press.

———. 1987. *The Philosophical Discourse of Modernity: Twelve Lectures*. Trans. Frederick Lawrence. Cambridge, MA: MIT Press.

———. 1989. *The Structural Transformation of the Public Sphere: An Inquiry into a Category of Bourgeois Society*. Trans. Thomas Burger. Cambridge, MA: MIT Press.

Held, David and Christopher Pollitt, eds. 1986. *New Forms of Democracy*. London: Sage.

Huntington, Samuel P. 1987. "The Goals of Development." In Myron Weiner and Samuel P. Huntington, eds., *Understanding Political Development: An Analytic Study*. Boston: Little, Brown.

Ingram, David. 1987. *Habermas and the Dialectic of Reason*. New Haven, CT: Yale University Press.

Kamat, A. R. 1979. "The Emerging Situation: A Socio-Structural Analysis." *Economic and Political Weekly* 14, 7–8: 349–54.

Kapp, Robert A. 1980. "Introduction: Review Symposium: Edward Said's Orientalism" *Journal of Asian Studies* 39, 3.

Kaviraj, Sudipta. 1988. "A Critique of the Passive Revolution." *Economic and Political Weekly* 23, 45–47: 2429–44.

Kopf, David. 1980. "Hermeneutics Versus History." *Journal of Asian Studies* 39, 3.

Kosambi, Damodar Dharmananda. 1975. *An Introduction to the Study of Indian History*. Bombay: Popular Prakashan.

Kurien, C. T. 1989. "Indian Economy in the 1980s and on to the 1990s." *Economic and Political Weekly* 24, 15: 787–98.

Lefebvre, Henri. 1971. *Everyday Life in the Modern World*. New York: Harper Torchbooks.

Lele, Jayant K., ed. 1981. *Tradition and Modernity in Bhakti Movements*. Leiden: E. J. Brill.

———. 1989. "Tradition and Intellectuals in a Third World Society." In Jayant K. Lele and R. Singh, *Language and Society: Steps Towards an Integrated Theory*. Leiden: E. J. Brill.

———. 1990a. "Caste, Class and Dominance: Political Mobilization in Maharashtra." In Francine Frankel and M. S. A. Rao, eds., *Dominance and State Power in Modern India: Decline of a Social Order*, Vol. 2. Delhi: Oxford University Press.

———. 1990b. "The Legitimacy Question." *Seminar 367: The Politics of the State* (March).

———. 1990c. "On Regaining the Meaning of the Bhagavad Gita." *Journal of South Asian Literature* 23, 2: 150–67.

———. 1991. "The Implications of Dr. B. R. Ambedkar's Conversion to Buddhism." In John McRae, ed., *Proceedings of the Fo Kuang Shan International Conference on Buddhism in the Modern World*. Kaosiung: Fo Kuang Shan.

———. In press. "The Political Appropriation of Bhakti: Hegemony and Dominance in Medieval Maharashtra." In Majid Siddiqui, Daniel Little, and Anton Blok, eds., *Peasant Culture and Consciousness: Essays in Peasant Studies*.

Lele, Jayant K. and R. Singh. 1989. *Language and Society: Steps Towards an Integrated Theory*. Leiden: E. J. Brill.

Lipietz, Alain. 1987. *Mirages and Miracles: The Crises of Global Fordism*. London: NLB-Verso.

Luhmann, Niklas. 1982. *The Differentiation of Society*. Trans. Stephen Holmes and Charles Larmore. New York: Columbia University Press.

Manor, James. 1980. "Pragmatic Progressives in Regional Politics: The Case of Devaraj Urs." *Economic and Political Weekly* 15, 5–7: 201–13.

Marcuse, Herbert. 1960. *Reason and Revolution: Hegel and the Rise of Social Theory*. Boston: Beacon Press.

Marshall, P. J., ed. 1970. *The British Discovery of Hinduism in the Eighteenth Century*. Cambridge: Cambridge University Press.

Marx, Karl. 1973. *Grundrisse: Introduction to the Critique of Political Economy*. Trans. Martin Nicolaus. Harmondsworth: Penguin; New York: Random House.

McCarthy, Thomas. 1982. "Rationality and Relativism: Habermas's 'Overcoming' of Hermeneutics." In John B. Thompson and David Held, eds., *Habermas: Critical Debates*. Cambridge, MA: MIT Press.

Naoroji, D. 1962. *Poverty and Un-British Rule in India*. Delhi: Publications Division.

Nisbet, Robert A. 1966. *The Sociological Tradition*. New York: Basic Books.

O'Brien, Donald Cruise. 1972. "Modernization, Order, and the Erosion of a Democratic Ideal: American Political Science 1960–70." *Journal of Development Studies* 8, 4: 351–78.

Offe, Claus. 1984. *Contradictions of the Welfare State*. Cambridge, MA: MIT Press.

Ortner, Sherry B. 1984. "Theory in Anthropology Since the Sixties." *Comparative Studies in Society and History* 26, 4: 126–66.

Parsons, Talcott, 1949. *The Structure of Social Action*. Glencoe, IL: Free Press.

———. 1951. *The Social System*. New York: Free Press.

Parsons, Talcott and Neil J. Smelser. 1956. *Economy and Society: A Study in the Integration of Economic and Social Theory*. Glencoe, IL: Free Press.

Patil, Sharad. 1982. *Dasa-Sudra Slavery*. New Delhi: Allied Publishers.

Patnaik, Arun K. 1988. "Gramsci's Concept of Common Sense: Towards a Theory of Subaltern Consciousness in Hegemony Processes." *Economic and Political Weekly* 23, 5.

Patnaik, Prabhas. 1986. "New Turn in Economic Policy." *Economic and Political Weekly* 21, 23.

Prasad, Pradhan H. 1990. "Political Economy of India's Retarded Development." *Economic and Political Weekly* 25, 4: PE 29–46.

Pye, Lucien W. 1985. *Asian Power and Politics: The Cultural Dimensions of Authority*. Cambridge, MA: Harvard University Press.

Ranade, M. G. 1915. *Miscellaneous Writings of the Late Hon'ble Mr. Justice M. G. Ranade*. Bombay: Manoranjan Press.

Ricoeur, Paul. 1978. *The Philosophy of Paul Ricoeur*. Boston: Beacon Press.

Roy, M. N. 1964. *M. N. Roy's Memoirs*. Bombay: Allied Publishers.

Rostow, Walt W. 1960. *The Stages of Economic Growth: A Non-Communist Manifesto*. Cambridge: Cambridge University Press.

Rudolph, Lloyd I. and Susanne H. Rudolph. 1967. *The Modernity of Tradition: Political Development in India*. Chicago: University of Chicago Press.

Rudolph, Lloyd I. and Susanne H. Rudolph. 1987. *In Pursuit of Lakshmi: The Political Economy of the Indian State*. Chicago: University of Chicago Press.

Said, Edward W. 1978. *Orientalism*. New York: Vintage Books.

———. 1986. "Orientalism Reconsidered." In Francis Barker, P. Hulme, M. Iversen, and D. Loxley, eds., *Literature, Politics and Theory: Papers from the Essex Conference, 1976–84*. London: Methuen.

Sau, Ranjit. 1975. "The Dialectics of Development." *Economic and Political Weekly* 10, 27.

Sen, Amartya K. 1984. "Development: Which Way Now?" In Sen, ed., *Resources, Values and Development*. Oxford: Blackwell; Cambridge, MA: Harvard University Press.

Sen, Asok. 1984. "The Transition from Feudalism to Capitalism." *Economic and Political Weekly* 19, 3.

————. 1988. "The Frontiers of the 'Prison Notebooks.'" *Economic and Political Weekly* 23, 5.

Sender, John and Sheila Smith. 1986. *The Development of Capitalism in Africa*. New York: Methuen.

Shanin, Teodor. 1982. "Preface." In Hamza Alavi and Teodor Shanin, eds., *Introduction to the Sociology of "Developing Societies."* New York: Monthly Review Press.

Sharma, R. S. 1980. *Sudras in Ancient India*. Delhi: Motilal Banarasidas.

Sixel, Friedrich W. 1979. "Images of Indians: A few Ideas for a Study of the Cognitive Poverty of Power." In R. Hartmann and V. Oberem, eds., *Estudios Americanistas II: Homenaje a H. Trimborn*. St. Augustine, Coll. Inst. Anthr. 21.

————. 1988. *Crisis and Critique: On the "Logic" of Late Capitalism*. Leiden: E. J. Brill.

Thapar, Romila. 1978. *Ancient Indian Social History*. Bombay: Orient Longmans.

————. 1984. *From Lineage to State*. Bombay: Oxford University Press.

Thorner, Alice. 1982. "Semi-Feudalism or Capitalism? Contemporary Debate on Classes and Modes of Production in India." *Economic and Political Weekly* 17, 47–51.

Warren, Bill. 1980. *Imperialism: Pioneer of Capitalism*. London: New Left Books.

Weiner, Myron. 1987. "Political Change: Asia, Africa and the Middle East." In Myron Weiner and Samuel Huntington, eds., *Understanding Political Development*. Boston: Little, Brown.

————. 1989. *The Indian Paradox: Essays in Indian Politics*. New Delhi: Sage.

Zeitlin, Irving M. 1981. *Ideology and the Development of Sociological Theory*. Englewood Cliffs, NJ: Prentice-Hall.

Sheldon Pollock

3. Deep Orientalism?
Notes on Sanskrit and Power Beyond the Raj

smṛtibhraṃśād buddhināśaḥ
(*Bhagavadgītā* 2.63)

Orientalism and Indology

This paper brings together two projects, both still in progress, and frames them within the general problematic of orientalism, which, as it is usually conceived, may seem peripheral to both. Thinking about German Indology during the years 1933–45 and about forms of precolonial domination in South Asia in this framework, however, suggests that the question orientalism, at least in its common contemporary sense, is usually thought to pose—to what degree were European scholarship of Asia and the colonial domination of Asia mutually constitutive?—may be too narrow. The case of German Indology, a dominant form of European orientalism, leads us to ask whether orientalism cannot be as powerfully understood with reference to the national political culture within which it is practiced as to the colony toward which it is directed; whereas examining forms of social power in India before the Raj leads me to believe that "orientalist constructions" in the service of colonial domination may be only a specific historical instance of a larger, transhistorical, albeit locally inflected, interaction of knowledge and power. I will enlarge on these questions a little more broadly before turning to them individually.

The history of classical Indology in the West, more particularly of Sanskrit studies, discloses a process of knowledge production fundamentally informed by, and serving to enhance, European power in Asia.[1] This is all well known—although in isolating three specific forms of such power my assessment may be idiosyncratic—and I will be brief about it here. What this orientalist commonplace cannot readily accommodate, however, is German Indology. One way to theorize this case is to consider the possibility that the movement of orientalist knowledge may be multidirectional. We usually imagine its vector as directed outward—toward the colonization and domination of Asia; in the case of German Indology we might conceive of it as potentially directed inward—toward the colonization and domination of Europe itself. Orientalism may be said to create an opposite when this "othering" fits both with historical paradigms and with political needs, as in the Middle Eastern matrix of semite, infidel, colonized, and so on charted in the studies of Edward Said. In the case of the Germans who continued, however subliminally, to hold the nineteenth-century conviction that the origin of European civilization was to be found in India (or at least that India constituted a genetically related sibling), and who at the same time had none of the requisite political needs, orientalism as an ideological formation on the model of Said simply could not arise. On the contrary, their "othering" and orientalization were played out at home. At least this seems to me one way to understand Indology in the National Socialist (NS) state, for which I give a brief institutional and intellectual-historical sketch below.

A fundamental thing about orientalism is that it offers an extreme and often transparent instance of knowledge generating and sustaining power and the domination that defines it. How might we apply this insight of the orientalist critique to precolonial forms of domination? Pared to the bone, orientalism is disclosed as a species of a larger discourse of power that divides the world into "betters and lessers" and thus facilitates the domination (or "orientalization" or "colonization") of any group.[2] From this perspective, indigenous discourses of power—the various systematized and totalized constructions of inequality in traditional India—might be viewed as a preform of orientalism. Raising such a possibility, at all events, might encourage extending to premodern Indian cultures the problematics of power and domination necessary to help us interpret their products.

The status of these indigenous discourses of power in everyday relations of domination has been a principal target of the critique of orientalism in India, a critique conducted, however, largely in the absence of adequate analysis of the discourses themselves. Sanskrit knowledge presents itself to us as a major vehicle of the ideological form of social power in traditional India, and I want to look at this self-presentation and some of the questions that have been raised about its status as an "orientalist construction." At the same time, I will examine briefly one feature of this ideological form of Sanskrit knowledge, namely, its monopolization, and thematize the restriction of access to Sanskrit "literacy" as a principal mode of domination. Admittedly, these are "mandarin materials" I am working with, but much ideological discourse, almost by definition, consists of mandarin materials. I also acknowledge that I do not attain (or seek) at present much institutional, regional, or historical specificity. But the lack of a social-historical framework of analysis for domination doesn't entail the lack of its historical social reality.

Widening the scope of orientalism to include discursively similar phenomena is not meant as an attempt to relativize and thereby detoxify European colonialism. Nor, of course, does focusing on the contributions of German Indology to the discourse of National Socialism, or of high Brahmanism to the ideological formations of precolonial India, mean to suggest that other discourses of power—directed at Palestinians on the West Bank, Brahman communities in contemporary Tamil Nad, or whomever—do not exist. On the contrary, it is precisely by expanding our analysis that we may be able to isolate a certain morphology of domination that many such discourses share—in their invoking higher knowledge naturalizing cultural inequality ("revelation," "science," "intuition of the blood"), creating the idea of race and concurrently legislating racial exclusivity, asserting linguistic hierarchy and claiming superiority for the language of the masters, and securing an order of domination by monopolizing "life chances" such as forms of literacy.

It might be argued that expanding the term "orientalism" to cover phenomena beyond, and before, colonialism jeopardizes the heuristic historical specificity of the very concept. To a degree this criticism is valid, yet I think we may lose something still greater if not doing so constrains our understanding of the two other historical phenomena.

Both sets of problems, German Indology in the period of National Socialism and social power in precolonial India and the interpretation of Sanskrit cultural products, are complicated issues that I do not pretend in either instance to be fully competent to adjudicate. German Indology presents so many problems that I see I have often been driven in what follows from the more central—a consideration of academic-political discursive formations—to the more peripheral—a narrative of "personal politics." (The tendency for histories of academic disciplines for the NS period to veer toward *Personalpolitik* suggests others share my conceptual difficulties.) The question is whether the motivating impulse, the very epistemological foundation of so much German Indology up to the end of the Second World War (which I think is the German search for national self-understanding) is in its very nature a reactionary impulse. If not, how did such scholarship find itself, so easily and so vastly, contributing to reactionary politics? How did even those whose overt politics seem to have had little to do with National Socialism come so readily to contribute to precisely the same discourse as officers in the SS? Finally and more broadly, how far do regnant discourses—and these are, ultimately, the discourses that are politically regnant—constrain what we can know and why we want to know it?

As for the work currently being done to "de-orientalize" the study of South Asia, I have come to regard it as an essential precondition for classical Indology, and as the most exciting development in the field in this generation. Yet at the same time, I have begun to sense that some arguments and perspectives currently dominant could benefit from a more capacious historical view and a more nuanced methodological reflection on what ideological power—projected, imagined, hoped-for power—in addition to "real" power might mean for our interpretation of Indian cultures. It is crucial to ask to what degree we must take into consideration asymmetries of power, interpreted though all the accounts of them must be, in the context of "Sanskrit culture" when trying to understand its products. Can we not argue that redirecting our work to this problematic is required not only by a morally sensitive scholarship, but even more compellingly, perhaps, by an epistemological necessity, given that social contextuality—however infinitely expandable it may be—and, correlatively, relations of social power, form the condition of possibility for any cultural meaning?

I have no illusions that I have successfully negotiated all the strong whirlpools, epistemological, political, and moral whirlpools, that confront anyone approaching the history of German Indology, still less so the problem of writing a history of cultural power in a precolonial world from within a postcolonial one (particularly the problem that such cultural critique sometimes might seem to recapitulate the very colonial discourse it seeks to transcend). The "Notes" in the subtitle is meant at least to circumscribe the ambitions I have and the claims I am prepared to make. But I want to share these notes because I think the issues in each of the two cases are too central to what, ultimately, Indologists do to permit the luxury of silence on the plea of specialization.

Finally, placing my two projects within the framework of "orientalism" reinforces the necessity to think about the critical dimension of this scholarship. A history of Indology, extracolonial no less than colonial, that finds it to be enmeshed in power from its very beginnings, and an analysis of the object of Indology, or at least of Sanskrit studies, as an indigenous form of knowledge production equally saturated with domination, have important implications. We are forced to ask ourselves whether the Indology we ourselves practice continues its past role. Which of those forms of traditional domination that have existed in India remain sedimented in contemporary society? What can we learn about our own history as well as Indian history from all this, and what might be some components of a critical Indology that confronts domination in both the scholarly process and the scholarly object?

Indology, Power, and the Case of Germany

The early history of Indology is constituted out of a network of factors, economic, social, political, and cultural, that make any generalization about it at the same time simplification. With that caution understood, I think we can broadly identify three constituents in early Indian studies as especially important for their historical effectiveness and continuing vitality. These are British colonialism, Christian evangelism (and its flip side, theosophy and related irrationalisms), and German romanticism-Wissenschaft.

In the West, Sanskrit studies from the beginning developed from the impetus provided by one or another of these constituents. The earliest grammars of the language, for example, are the work of German and Austrian missionaries of the seventeenth and eighteen centuries (Hanxleden, Paulinus; Roth 1988); many of the first Sanskrit manuscripts in Europe were collected by French missionaries, some of the first attempts at Sanskrit editing and publishing are those of the British Baptists at Serampore in Bengal (e.g., Carey and Marshman 1806–10). One of the first Europeans to learn Sanskrit well enough to make use of it was—obligatory reference—William Jones, supreme court judge under the East India Company (1785; Cannon 1970: 646, 666, 682ff.), whose principal motive, like that of another important early Sanskritist, Colebrook, was the administration of law in British India. One of the critical moments in the academicization of Sanskrit studies was the encounter in Paris (1803–04) of the dominant character in German romanticism, Friedrich von Schlegel, with Alexander Hamilton of the East India Company (Rocher 1968). From Hamilton, Schlegel learned enough Sanskrit (*Über die Sprache und Weisheit der Indier*, 1808; Oppenberg 1965) to encourage his brother, August Wilhelm, to learn more, and it was A. W. von Schlegel who went on to hold the first chair for Sanskrit in Germany, at the University in Bonn (1818).

All of this history is certainly well known. I review it here to disentangle the three principal components so that, by arranging them side by side in their bare outline, we can appreciate more fully the fact that it was particular institutions of European power, the church, the corporation, the university, that created and later sponsored Indology; that, however we may wish to characterize the ends of these various institutions, it was their ends that Indology was invented to serve.

The principal target of the orientalist critique in South Asia has been the intimate and often complicated tie, sometimes the crudely heavy link, between Indology and British colonialism, and we now possess sharp analyses of some of its most subtle forms (for instance, Cohn 1987).[3] Some of the postulates in this critique about precolonial power, and the more complex and challenging issue of a postcolonial "European epistemological hegemony," I will discuss below. But the creation of Indological knowledge and its function in colonial domination need no elaboration here.

The various forms of cultural and spiritual domination represented by missionary Indology do not require special comment here either, although its cognate phenomenon, nineteenth-century theosophy and its wide range of modern-day incarnations, merit discussion within an orientalist analysis. It would be worth examining how these representations, especially in their highly commodified, scientistically packaged, and aggressively marketed contemporary forms, continue to nourish one of the most venerable orientalist constructions, the fantasy of a uniquely religion-obsessed India (and a uniquely transcendent Indian wisdom), and how this fantasy in turn continuously reproduces itself in contemporary scholarship, given the institutional monopolization of Indian studies by the "history of religions," and presents one of the most serious obstacles to the creation of a critical Indology.

The third major component of Indology, my oddly hyphenated German romanticism-Wissenschaft, is less easily accommodated within an explanatory framework of colonial instrumentality and thus not accidentally was the one major form that Said left unaccounted for in his analysis.[4] Trying to conceptualize in larger terms the meanings and functions of German orientalism invites us to think differently, or at least more expansively, about orientalism in general. It directs our attention momentarily away from the periphery to the national political culture and the relationship of knowledge and power at the core—directs us, potentially, toward forms of internal colonialism, and certainly toward the domestic politics of scholarship.

No serious encounter with orientalism as it relates to traditional India can avoid the case of Germany. There are two reasons that are immediately obvious, because of their very materiality: the size of the investment on the part of the German state in Indological studies throughout the nineteenth and the first half of the twentieth centuries (without this involving, it bears repeating, any direct colonial instrumentality) and the volume of the production of German orientalist knowledge. On both counts Germany almost certainly surpassed all the rest of Europe and America combined.[5]

In dissecting what accordingly has to be seen as the dominant form of Indianist orientalism, both in sheer quantity and in intellectual influence, two components seems worth isolating: the German romantic quest for identity and what was eventually to become one of its vehicles, the emerging vision of *Wissenschaft*.

The romantic search for self-definition (beginning in the early nineteenth century but with impulses continuing halfway into the twentieth, and perhaps beyond) comprised initially a complex confrontation with, on the one hand, Latin-Christian Europe, and on the other, the universalizing Enlightenment project of humanism. The discovery of Sanskrit was one of the crucial components in this search. As a British historian put it in 1879: "Not in a merely scientific or literary point of view, but in one strictly practical, the world is not the same world as it was when men had not yet dreamed of the kindred between Sanscrit, Greek, and English"—and, he should have added, German.[6] As is manifest in the responses of the first Germans to learn the language (Friedrich von Schlegel and Othmar Frank, among others), Sanskrit was thought to give evidence of a historical culture, and spiritual and ultimately racial consanguinity, for Germans independent of, and far more ancient than, Latin or Christian culture.

This romantic dream seems to have sharpened into the vision of an Indo-Germanic *Geisteswelt* only gradually. The principal German cultural dichotomy in the early nineteenth century had juxtaposed Germania and Rome. This came to be replaced by the antithesis and finally essentialized dichotomy between "Indo-German" and "Semite." Indo-German, according to one of the best short accounts, was largely a *Kontrastbegriff*, called into being by the social and economic emancipation of Jews in the course of the century (von See 1970). But what made it possible to construct and consolidate this dichotomy, in addition to an "orientilizing" epistemology, was "orientalist" knowledge itself.

The discourse on Aryanism that this orientalist knowledge generated was, to a degree not often realized, available to the Germans already largely formulated for them at the hands of British scholarship by the middle of the nineteenth century. This discourse included a generous selection of what were to become the topoi of 1930s Germany: the celebration of Aryan superiority; the willingness to recognize racial kinship between European and Indian coupled with a readiness to establish (where this was politically useful) and explain (with the commonplaces that recur in 1933) the degeneracy of the South Asian Aryans; the politically driven disputes on the original homeland; even proposals for a eugenics program in India (calling for a revivification through racial planning of the debilitated South Asian Aryan stock). It might even be said that Aryanism was one conceptual building block in the totalizing projects of a good deal of nineteenth-century British work on India (H. S. Maine, J. W. Jackson, F. Max Mueller—a list easily extended).[7]

In the German instance, however, orientalism as a complex of knowledge-power has to be seen as vectored not outward to the Orient but inward to Europe itself, to constructing the conception of a historical German essence and to defining Germany's place in Europe's destiny. If the "German problem" is a problem of identity, and "the German figure of totalitarianism" racism (Lacoue-Labarthe and Nancy 1990: 296), the discourse of Aryanism and, consequently, the orientalism on which it rested was empowered to play a role in Germany it never could play in England.

There is no need to trace further here the beginnings in the nineteenth century of the orientalist creation of Indo-German as counteridentity to Semite, still less the general place of India in the rise of German romanticism, for a good deal of work has already been done on those topics (e.g., Schwab 1950: 74ff.; Willson 1964; Stern 1961: 3–94; Römer 1985: 62ff.). What I want to focus on instead is the end point of the process, by which I mean not so much its chronological end but its consummation, in the period of National Socialism. In this culminating instance, I think two things happen: First, there come to be merged what hitherto seemed by and large discrete components of German orientalism, romanticism and Wissenschaft. Second, "orientalist" knowledge becomes part of the official worldview of a newly imagined empire, and in this German allomorph of British imperialism—the attempt to colonize Europe, and Germany itself, from within—orientalism has its special function to discharge.[8]

With some exceptions (the Göttingen orientalist, though not Indologist, Paul de Lagarde in the last third of the nineteenth century, for instance), the emerging vision of science/scholarship, *Wissenschaft*, seemed to be a current running parallel to and rarely intersecting with the quasi-mystical nativism of romanticism; indeed, this disjunction seems somehow prefigured already in the characters and careers of those fellow Sanskrit students in Paris in 1815, the romantic A. W. von Schlegel and the scientist Franz Bopp (the latter of whom in 1816 was the first systematically to demonstrate the cognate relationship between Indic and European languages).[9] And I suggest it was precisely a new interpenetration of "science" and nativism that in the 1930s endowed German Indology with its specific power and significance. Indeed, the conjunction in NS Indology of cultural-nationalist primitivism and high intellectual technology presents an instance at the level of the academy of a much broader phenomenon fundamental to National Socialist culture, which a recent scholar has appositely characterized as "reactionary modernism."[10]

The characteristics of this "science" merit historical analysis no less than the constructions of romanticism. An inventory of the epistemological instruments of *Indologie* would include, besides Bopp's comparative linguistics, other nineteenth-century intellectual technologies developed for the human sciences, such as the text-criticism of Wolf and Lachmann, the philology of Böckh, and the historiography of Ranke. What above all interests me here, however, is the general conceptual framework within which these components combine to operate. Part of this framework consists in the claim of objectivity, of "value-free scholarship," which seems to have been more vigorously asserted the deeper the crisis of European culture grew.

I want to look very briefly at one of the more forceful and historically significant apologies for such scholarship, the programmatic lecture "Wissenschaft als Beruf" (Science/Scholarship as Vocation/Profession) that Max Weber delivered before students of the University of Munich only months before his death. There is nothing in itself "orientalist" about this defense, which was made by a political economist and meant to apply broadly to the human sciences. But it is worth singling out by way of preface to a discussion of National Socialist Indological scholarship partly because of its historical location—it was presented in late 1918 or the beginning of 1919, the liminal moment in modern German history;[11] partly because it gives lucid expression to a set of beliefs about scholarship and to a justification of method that seem to infuse the scholarship of the period, including academic Indology; and partly because of what may be a deep and enduring self-deception. I think it is all-important to try to understand the set of presuppositions that sustained belief in the possibility of producing "serious scholarly work," which viewed itself as utterly distinct from other modes of state discourse such as propaganda, directly under the aegis of the swastika. In a way, Weber's lecture, intended as an attack on the politicization of scholarship, and indeed, viewed with suspicion and hostility especially by conservatives,[12] may help us grasp one basic ideological precondition for the intersection of scholarship and state power, at the very moment when that intersection was about to become interpenetration.

What for Weber were the "least problematic" issues of scholarship need no problematizing here. It is irrelevant for understanding much NS-era Indology to question the formal and positivistic ideals of scholarship (consistency, noncontradiction, evidence, argument, philological and historical precision), for they were also accepted as ideals generally by NS scholars. Nor is there anything very troubling about Weber's claim that, given the fundamental undecidability of competing value systems, scholarship should attempt to remain value-neutral. What is surprising is his reluctance to extend this relativism to "science" itself, to its descriptions, representations, constructions. We are presented at once with a conception of the "political," as open advocacy of partisanship, that seems wilfully shallow, and with an unquestioned assumption that, despite the fundamentally political nature of social and cultural existence, including scholarly existence, the transcendence of political values really is possible. Weber demands, for example, of the students listening that they should just "establish the facts." He offers to prove "in the works of our historians that, wherever the man of scholarship comes forth with his own value judgments, the full understanding of the facts ceases" (Weber 1984: 26). In all of this there is little acknowledgment that historical or cultural facts (Weber takes "democracy," that most ideologically protean entity, as his example) may not actually be lying about like so many brute existents waiting merely to be assembled, but are actually constituted as "facts" by the prejudgments—by the values—of the historians and "men of scholarship" themselves. Relentless in driving politics from the lecture room, Weber seems to have left it to rule untroubled in the study.

The objectivism Weber enshrines was no more questioned in Indology than it was in any other institutional scholarship in the Germany of the period. And what I am wondering is whether it is the putative separability of "fact" from "value," to which Weber gives expression in his lecture, and consequently the decontextualization and dehistoricization of the scholarly act itself, the objectification of scholarship—and all in the

interests of a depoliticization of scholarship in the face of war and revolution—that enabled some of the most politically deformed scholarship in
history, including Indological history, to come into existence. I want at
least to entertain this hypothesis when examining institutional Indology
in Germany during the period of NS power, 1933–45, although the paradox of NS scholarship is more complicated: While denouncing a Weberian
objectivism as alien to the spirit of scholarship meant to serve the new
Germany,[13] the Indologists in fact believed that the scholarship they were
producing to that end was scientific and objective. The NS Indologists, it
seems, were Weberians in reverse: relentless in driving "objectivism" from
the classroom, they yet felt it had to rule, and could indeed rule, in the
study.

Ex Oriente Nox: Indology in the Total State

Before the logical aporia of legitimacy, political systems have only a relatively limited repertory of methods of legitimation. Some political systems
(certain once-existing "socialist" systems, for example) employ myths of
utopia, while fascist systems employ myths of origins (Lyotard 1987). The
NS state sought legitimation in part by the myth of "Aryan" origins. This,
as we have seen, had been provided early in nineteenth-century Indian
orientalism—a benchmark is Friedrich von Schlegel's identification (1819)
of the "Arier" as "our Germanic ancestors, while they were still in Asia"
(Sieferle 1987: 460). In the later NS search for authenticity, Sanskritists,
like other intellectuals—"experts in legitimation," as Gramsci put it—
did their part in extrapolating and deepening this discourse. They finally
would heed the words of the nineteenth-century proto-fascist (and "Wahl-
deutscher") Houston Stuart Chamberlain: "Indology must help us to fix
our sights more clearly on the goals of our culture. A great humanistic task
has fallen to our lot to accomplish; and thereto is aryan India summoned."

   The myth of Aryan origins burst from the world of dream into that
of reality when the process of what I suggest we think of as an internal
colonization of Europe began to be, so to speak, shastrically codified,
within two months of the National Socialists' capturing power (April
1933). The "Law on the Reconstitution of the German Civil Service," the
"Law on the Overcrowding of German Schools," and a host of supplementary laws and codicils of that same month were the first in a decade
dense with legal measures designed to exclude Jews and other minority

communities from the apparatuses of power (including "authoritative" power, the schools and universities), and to regulate a wide range of social, economic, and biological activities.

For some, linguistic activity should have been included. The Kiel (later Munich) Sanskrit and Iranist Hermann Güntert had already in 1932 expressed a view on the relationship of race and language consonant with such control, which he elaborated in a manifesto in 1938, "New Times, New Goals," when he became editor of the journal *Wörter und Sachen*.

> A man alien to a given ethnic and racial group does not become, simply because he speaks their language—one originally alien to him—and "beholds the world" via the constructions of that language, a comrade of the folk [*Volks-genosse*], even if the language—which was originally alien—had been used already by his forebears. For far more potently, deterministically, uncon-sciously do primal dispositions and peculiarities of his inherited substance issue forth, whereas language is far more easily changed and transformed than those deep spiritual dispositions such as customs, notions of justice, Weltan-schauung, and the general emotional life. Should those who are alien to the race have long-term influence, they would transform the language according to their own nature and try to adapt it as far as possible to their spiritual natures—that is to say, they would become pests upon, corrupters of this language. It is therefore perfectly clear: A people creates itself a language appropriate to it, and not vice versa! A people is the power that commands all the life of a language.[14]

The whole weight of these early laws rested on the concept "Aryan" (or rather, somehow significantly, at first on its negation[15]): "Beamte, die *nicht arischer* Abstammung sind, sind in den Ruhestand zu versetzen" ("Civil servants *not of aryan* descent are to be pensioned off"); " . . . die Zahl der *Nichtarier* [soll] ihren Anteil an der Gesamtbevölkerung des Reichs nicht übersteigen" ("The number of *non-aryans* [allowed into schools] [shall] not exceed their percentage among the general population of the empire") (Walk 1981: 12ff.).[16] It is not necessary to review here the long and rather complex prehistory of the term *Arier*—the essence is caught in the remark of Victor Klemperer, that "'aryan man' is rooted in philology, not natural science" (Klemperer [1947] 1987: 148)[17]—nor to analyze the justification of the category constructed by "race-science," which was the master conceptual scheme in operation here and which itself had signficant orientalist dimensions.[18] The point I want to make has nothing whatever to do with historical truth or scientificity of termi-nology; it has to do with the mobilization of meaning for the purpose of domination as it is contextaully bound to Germany in the years 1933–45.

In this connection, two points are worth stressing. First, the concept of *Arier*, which was ambiguous to the scholarly mind and opaque to the popular, absurdly so for a juridical term, required substantial exegesis, as the initial supplementary decrees for the execution of the *Arierparagraph* make clear.[19] Second, to contribute uncritically to this exegesis was to justify what Löwith aptly terms "political zoology" and to contribute to the marginalization, exclusion, dehumanization, and ultimately extermination of "lesser" peoples in a manner congruent with, if exceeding, standard-issue colonialism. In this project, German Indology participated in some crucial ways. I want to explore a few of these, adopting Haug's formulation and asking how German Indologists *qua Indologists*, by means of their specific epistemological tools and sense of scholarly purpose as Indologists, helped to effect the "fascisization" of Germany Indologically (cf. Haug 1989: 5).

Regarding the role of "ideology" in the consolidation and execution of NS power, I will only allude here briefly to the ongoing debates on functionalist and "idealist" explanations that have long been contending in the analysis of National Socialism (as indeed of other political formations). The importance and effectivity of the notional, of the intellectual and ideological and "weltanschaulich," in addition to or even independent of the material, seem to have gained at least parity in current re-thinking in the historiography of the movement. This seems in part attributable to the fuller history of the Holocaust now available, since the extermination of the Jews would seem to pose a serious challenge to any purely functionalist explanation of National Socialism.[20] Yet, whatever the actual effectivty of the ideational dimension of National Socialism may have been, there is no doubt that the builders of the movement believed in the necessity of providing it with an intellectually convincing doctrine. And this was to become one that in the end relied, more than any other state doctrine in European history, on the putative results of scholarly—archaeological, philological, anthropological, Indological—research.

I can examine here in some detail only a few examples of Indology as practiced in NS Germany; an exhaustive typology and analysis are premature. The range of contribution is wide and multifaceted (and bibliographically altogether unsystematized); the degree of candor and self-consciousness about congruence with state discourse differs markedly in these contributions; and the interpretation of most of them necessitates a confrontation with serious problems of scholarly method and purpose. Yet one thing that is uniform and clear about these texts is the set of basic "orientalist" ideologemes they adopt—about an Aryan culture of the past, its survival into and meaning for the German present, the role and ability of Indology in capturing its nature, its superiority and the concomitant debasement of others—and the scholarly foundations with which these components are supplied.

The earliest Indological intervention after the National Socialists took power, within months of the law on the "Reconstitution" of the civil service mentioned above, and a model for what was to come, is the programmatic article "German Antiquity and the History of Aryan Thought" by Walther Wüst, Vedic specialist at the University of Munich, student of Wilhelm Geiger, successor to Hans Oertel, later rector of the university (Wüst 1934).[21] What the first adjective in the title means, says Wüst, everyone knows; the second one, however, is far less clear, although "by reason of the laws of racial protection it has become more familiar than any other word in the German language." To explicate it, Wüst brings to bear the full and ponderous apparatus of philological and historical Indology. Etymology, literary history, comparative religion, folklore, and archaeology are all summoned to testify that the ancient *āryas* of India were those who felt themselves to be the "privileged, the legitimate" (Wüst's interpretation of *ārya*) because they established the superiority of their race, their culture, their religion, and their worldview in the course of struggle with host populations. The "deep significance" and "indestructible grandeur" attaching to the terms *Arier, arisch* have been preserved into the present thanks to tradition and racial memory (*Erberinnerung*). The *RgVeda* as an Aryan text "free of any taint of Semitic contact"; the "almost Nordic zeal" that lies in the Buddhist conception of the *mārga*; the "Indo-Germanic religion-force" of yoga; the sense of race and the "conscious desire for racial protection"; the "*volksnahe* kingship"—such is the meaning of the Indo-Aryan past for the National Socialist present, a present that, for Wüst, could not be understood without this past.

The search for German identity and NS self-legitimation in the Aryan past found in Wüst's early essay is characteristic of a great deal of Indological work of the period; his article in fact is a catalog of commonplaces. But equally characteristic, and crucial for us to note, is the "scholarly" dimension. Wüst repeatedly distances himself from amateurs, charlatans, and ignorant nonspecialists (*Sachunkundigen*) and invokes and exploits to a fault the standards of philological and historical scholarship. More than anything, it is this commitment to "science" to substantiate the order of the state, and the vision that scholarship could gain access to a realm of objective truth independent of historical interests and values, that makes this orientalist scholarship so typical of the period and so disquieting.

Lest we isolate this scholarly activity from the world of concrete power, it is worth recounting a speech given by Wüst (in his capacity as [then] SS-Hauptsturmführer) on March 10, 1937, in the Hacker-Keller, Munich, before the commanders of the SS officer corps South and the SS subordinate commanders and regulars of the Munich garrison. In "The Führer's Book 'Mein Kampf' as a Mirror of the Aryan World-View" (1937), Wüst seeks to establish a general set of continuities between ancient Indian and contemporary German thought (or rather *Weltanschauung*, for which he offers a long etymological excursus).[22] After providing a catalog of what he takes to be basic "Indo-Aryan" representations (the world as ordered and "bright," existence as growth, the eye as a microcosmic sun, god as the father, the law of fate, and the like), he argues that all of it is to be found in Hitler's *Mein Kampf*, a text that thus evinces a spiritual continuum stretching from the second millennium B.C. to the present. "But we see these connections in their maturest state," he adds, "perhaps in personality. In this context, I would like to make reference to a particularly significant connection." He proceeds to recount the Buddha's sermon on the Middle Way, the realization that fulfillment lay between self-indulgence and self-denial, and then proceeds to argue that

> this very closely correlates with an experience the Führer had during his Vienna period, when as part-time worker he came face to face with suffering, and went through the wretched dwellings of the workers and saw their want. There the Führer spoke the profound words: "At that time I was warned not to choke on Theory nor to become shallow on Reality" ["Damals wurde ich gewarnt, entweder in der Theorie zu ersticken oder in der Wirklichkeit zu verflachen"]. I know of no more striking example of this hereditary, long-term tradition than the ingenious synopsis contained in the brief words of the Führer and the longer confession of the great aryan personality of antiquity, the Buddha. There is only one explanation for this, and that is the basic explanation for components of the National-Socialist world-view—the circumstance, the basic fact of racial constitution. And thanks to fate, this was preserved through the millennia . . . [through] the holy concept of ancestral heritage [*Ahnenerbe*]. (Wüst 1937: 17–18)[23]

Neither Wüst's improbable thesis, nor the spectacle of a professor of Sanskrit lecturing before members of the central apparatus of Nazi terror on Indo-European etymologies and Buddhist *sūtras* to prove the "absolute fact" of the superiority of Aryan cosmology and its afterlife, should blind us to what is significant here: the propriety and need Wüst felt of legitimating the NS *Weltanschauung* by anchoring it in an ancient Indian *darśana*.

As an example of pedantic *wissenschaftliche* antiquarianism coupled with a primitivism and irrational cultural nostalgia that finds itself suddenly, incredibly, and perilously invited into the inner sanctum of political power, the work and career of Wüst may be extreme.[24] What is typical, however, is again the "orientalist" character of his scholarship, in every essential dimension of the term, both as representing an ontological and epistemological division between an "us" and some "them," and as serving to sustain a structure of manifest domination.

A fuller account of the more notable expressions of NS Indology would include the work of Ludwig Alsdorf, Professor of Sanskrit and Jainology at Münster and Berlin (Alsdorf 1942 is a *Fachgeschichte* of Indology that gives unusually clear voice to its ethnic and national purposes);[25] Jakob Wilhelm Hauer, Professor of the History of Religions at Tübingen (Hauer 1934 argues that the *Bhagavad Gītā* is an "Aryan" text; Hauer 1937 offers an assemblage of the principle NS themes on Indo-Aryan antiquity);[26] and Hermann Lommel, Professor of Sanskrit and Iranian at Frankfurt (Lommel 1935 makes the attempt to distill the "authentic Aryan spirit" of the oldest cultural monuments to achieve an awareness of "our own historically evolved and genetically [*blutmässig*] inherited way of being"; Lommel 1939 [!] is a disquisition on the Aryan god of war). Requiring more complex theorization are those texts—issuing in a flood after 1933— that, without any overt commitment to National Socialism, fully embrace the terms of its discourse by their unchallenged participation in and acceptance of the *Fragestellungen*, the thematics, of NS Indology. An example of this more sophisticated orientalism is the work of Paul Thieme (1938), an analysis of the Sanskrit word *arya*, where at the end he adverts to the main point of his research: to go beyond India in order to catch the "distant echo of Indo-germanic customs" (p. 168). Apparently arcane articles on such topics as "Alt-indoarisch *matya*-, n. 'Knüppel als bauerliches Werkzeug'" (Ernst Schneider, *WZKM* 47 [1940]: 267ff.) feed into, and were intended to feed into, a complex state doctrine of *Blut und Boden*, Indo-Germanic farmers versus nomadic Orientals, Nordic heroes versus Semitic traders, and so forth.

One focal point of Indological work during the NS period that merits more than the brief observations possible here was the question of the *Urheimat* (the original home of the Aryans). To a degree the Urheimat issue had always been a scholarly question prompted and driven by the ideological demands of the European polities in which this discourse originated. Yet no matter how squarely situated at the intersection of scholarship and politics the question shows itself to be, as in Germany in the 1930s, it has almost universally been debated with a breathtaking pretense of political detachment. The first major scholarly salvo of the 1930s was fired with the publication of *Germanen und Indogermanen . . . Festschrift für Herman Hirt* (1936).[27] In his introduction, Helmuth Arntz, the editor, asserts the purely scholarly nature of their investigations: "Much poison has been poured out, even upon our scholarship; much hate and bitterness does the world fling at the Third Reich, the new state we have finally built for ourselves. That our scholarship is no longer free, but muzzled and misused for propaganda purposes—that is the worst reproach. This Festschrift refutes that. Each of the participating scholars was free to say what he wishes; and the fact that high scholarship is a cultural factor of propagandistic value holds for other nations as well as ours" (p. viii).[28] The volume edited later that same year by the ethnologist of tribal South Asia, the Austrian W. Koppers, *Die Indogermanen- und Germanenfrage*, was meant to provide a counterweight to the *Hirt Festschrift*.[29] Also in 1936 (in what hardly seems an accidental *Stellungnahme*), the whole debate is deflated by the great Russian phonologist Trubetskoy. Speaking before the Cercle linguistique de Prague in December, he argued that there may never have taken place a "Proto-Indo-Germanic language" diffusion carried by Indo-German groupings—in fact, there never may have existed a Proto-Indo-Germanic language—but only "a gradual approximation of languages, the one to the other, through mutual borrowing over time."[30] From among the complexities of NS analysis of the Urheimat question it is worth calling attention to the way the nineteenth-century view expressed by Schlegel was reversed: the original Indo-Europeans were now variously relocated in regions of the Greater German Reich; German thereby became the language of the core (*Binnensprache*), whereas Sanskrit was transformed into one of its peripheral, "colonial" forms.[31]

Of course, more "traditional" Indological work, of a text-critical, lexical, epigraphic, numismatic variety, was taking place during the period—the same sort of work produced, say, under the sign of nineteenth-century French orientalism for Arabic (of the genre wherein, given the context of NS deformities, some postwar historians like Rothfels were prepared to see an "inner emigration" and a "sort of opposition"). But such philological work, despite illusions as to its rocklike imperviousness to political-social life that are still widespread in the field, is an instrument of meaning—social, historical, ideological—and presupposes questions of such meaning whether these are articulated or not. And when such questions of meaning did find articulation in Germany in the years 1933–45, they seem to have been in the main purely "orientalist" questions.[32]

I want to illustrate the typicality noted above in regard to Wüst's scholarship by a brief account of the final phase of orientalism in the NS period, the wartime program funded by the Imperial Ministry of Education called the "War Effort of the Humanities" (*Kriegseinsatz der Geisteswissenschaften*, 1941–42).

The task of the "War Effort" (or "Aktion Ritterbusch" as it was sometimes called after the Kiel legal scholar who initiated the *Einsatz*), was to encourage scholars of the humanities "to place in the foreground of their work the idea of a new European order."[33] As part of this effort, and at the suggestion of the executive committee of the German Oriental Society,[34] a "Working Session of German Orientalists and German Orientalist Archaeologists" was convened in Berlin in 1942. Ritterbusch's opening statement adequately conveys the self-understanding of much German scholarship of the period with respect to its relationship with state power:

> I do not have to emphasize again here how acutely aware the German humanities are of their political-historical responsibility, and how very much they wish to prove, through their own learning and initiative, that they are not only a great, indeed, critical power of our popular [*völkisch*] life, but that they wish to contribute to the formation of world-historical decisions and dispositions that are coming to maturity and being decided upon in this war—to contribute and to participate for the benefit of the people and the Führer and the historical mission of the Empire. (Schaeder 1944: 5)

What interests me particularly in this scholarly convention of orientalists contributing to the mission of empire is the contribution of Erich Frauwallner, Professor of Sanskrit at the University of Vienna, who is widely regarded as the preeminent authority on Indian philosophy of his generation (and member of the National Socialist German Workers Party [NSDAP] since 1932, when the party was still illegal in Austria). In his presentation, Frauwallner argued that the special meaning of Indian philosophy lay in its being "a typical creation of an aryan people," that its similarities with western philosophy derived from "the same racially determined talent," and that it was a principal scholarly task of Indology to demonstrate this fact. Reiterating an axiom of NS doctrine, that "Wissenschaft in the strict sense of the word is something that could be created only by nordic Indo-Germans," Frauwallner adds, "From the agreement in scientific character of Indian and European philosophy, we can draw the further conclusion that philosophy as an attempt to explain the world according to scientific method is likewise a typical creation of the Aryan mind" (Frauwallner 1944; cf. 1939).

Indian knowledge, again, is meaningful to the degree that it assists in the self-revelation of "Aryan" identity. The very raison d'être of Indology for Frauwallner, as it seems to have been for so many scholars of the period, is fundamentally conditioned by this racialism. The ideology of objective "science," moreover, not only governs Frauwallner's presentation; his whole purpose is to demonstrate that this science exists in a realm beyond ideology—that it is a fact of biology. What alone enables him to do this, I think, is "orientalist" knowledge production.

I have observed often enough that all the Indologists cited above are "serious" scholars; their work was argued out on sophisticated historical and philological grounds, not on the "intuitive" principles of crude propagandists like the chief party idealogue Rosenberg (although no German Indologist ever felt the call to criticize Rosenberg, and some, like Alsdorf [1942: 86] cite him as authoritative). They are for the most part unimpeachable with respect to scholarly "standards." What is of the essence to see is that it is within the realm of Wissenschaft that this knowledge production is taking place, Wissenschaft that provided the warrent of objective truth that constituted it as scholarship.

To what degree this work was motivated by opportunism or cynicism it is not easy to discover. It may be pointed out, however, that German Indology shows a support for National Socialism noteworthy among the humanities for its breadth.[35] In the early and important *Declaration of Allegiance . . . to Adolph Hitler* (*Bekenntnis . . . zu Adolph Hitler* [Dresden n.d. (November 11, 1933)]), the names of a good number of the most distinguished Indologists of the period are prominent (including Schubring, Sieg, Nobel, Hertel, F. Weller). Of the twenty-five or so Indology professors of the NS period (leaving aside Dozenten, etc.), perhaps a third were active participants in the party or the SS, according to documents preserved in the Berlin Document Center. (Some examples, from a first, incomplete census: Ludwig Alsdorf, NSDAP No. 2697931 [entry into party 1 August 1933]; Bernhard Breloer, NSDAP No. 5846531 [1 May 1937], SS-Unterscharführer, SS No. 230317 [26 June 1933]; Erich Frauwallner, NSDAP No. 1387121 [29 November 1932]; Jakob Wilhelm Hauer, SS-Untersturmführer, SS No. 107179, NSDAP No. 50574 [1 May 1937]; Richard Schmidt, NSDAP No. 2492244 [1 June 1933], SS-Obersturmführer.[36]) No

German Indologist made any public statement on the state appropriation of Indological learning—perhaps none could have made such a statement, since there was little discernible appreciation of the politics of interpretation. Apart from the Indologists victimized by the "Aryan paragraphs" whether as Jews themselves or because they were married to Jews (including Bette Heimann [emigrated], Walter Neisser [suicide, 1941], Walter Ruben [emigrated], Isidore Scheftelowitz [emigrated], Richard Simon [died 1934], Moritz Spitzer [fate unknown], Otto Stein [died in Łódź Ghetto, 1942], Otto Strauss [died in flight in Holland, 1940], Heinrich Zimmer [emigrated]), none publicly opposed the regime, or left the country. As far as I can tell, only one, Heinrich Lüders, ran afoul of the NS state, being forced to take early retirement from his position at the University of Berlin in 1935.[37] Quite as important, to my knowledge no German—or indeed, any other—Indologist has undertaken an analysis of the field and the relationship of the questions of scholarship and the questions of state since the war. In the flood of work since the late 1960s on every conceivable dimension of scholarship in the National Socialist period, it is noteworthy that there has been no publication on the topic from within the Indological community (even on an autobiographical occasion; typical is the silence of von Glasenapp in *Meine Lebensreise* [1964]). I would also like to call attention to the substantial increase in the investment on the part of the NS state in Indology and "Indo-Germanistik." Both Himmler and Rosenberg sponsored institutes centrally concerned with "Indo-Germanische Geistesgeschichte."[38] There is preserved a planning memo on the postwar Institut für arische Geistesgeschichte approved by Hitler in 1940, in which Rosenberg wrote:

> The nineteenth century left behind extensive research on the history of the Indians, Iranians, and Greeks, and their intellectual/cultural creations. With the exception of Greek literature, Indian and Iranian thought has not penetrated European consciousness very deeply. To strengthen this consciousness, [and]—given the collapse of the entire Palestinian [i.e., Jewish] tradition—to free a more ancient and far more venerable one from its concealment, is the critical *weltanschauliche* task of the Munich institute. Therefore it will also be its task, in addition to working up the important sources and presenting syntheses of them, to re-issue those works that are essential for National Socialist *Weltanschauunng*, and for the development of an intellectual tradition, e.g., L. v. Schroeder, *Indians Literatur und Kultur;*[39] Böthlink [sic], *Indische Sprüche*. (Document reproduced in Poliakov and Wulf 1983: 133ff.)

Motives are not always easy to discern, no doubt. All we can know is that between this scholarship and basic ideologemes of the NS state there is distinct congruence; what we need to know is what made this congruence possible and how it worked. In German Indology of the NS era, a largely nonscholarly mystical nativism deriving ultimately from a mixture of romanticism and protonationalism merged with that objectivism of Wissenschaft earlier described, and together they fostered the ultimate "orientalist" project, the legitimation of genocide. Whatever other enduring lessons this may teach us, it offers a superb illustration of the empirical fact that disinterested scholarship in the human sciences, like any other social act, takes place within the realm of interests; that its objectivity is bounded by subjectivity; and that the only form of it that can appear value-free is the one that conforms fully to the dominant ideology, which alone remains, in the absence of critique, invisible as ideology.

As one of its dominant forms, German Indology has to be accommodated in any adequate theorization of orientalism. But the German case also suggests that orientalism, thought of as knowledge serving to create and marginalize degraded communities—even members of one's own community—and thus to sustain relations of domination over them, reveals itself as a subset of ideological discourse as such.[40] If consideration of the British use of forms of orientalist knowledge for domination within India might help us theorize the German use of comparable forms for domination within Germany, the latter may help us theorize how Indian forms of knowledge serve in the exercise of domination in India—may suggest a sort of eastern orientalism, in the service of a precolonial colonialism. The self-representation of Indians no more escapes the realm of interests than the representations of their oppressors; and just as there have been other imperialisms than that forming the last stage of capitalism, so there may have been other "orientalisms" to sustain them.

Pre-Orientalist "Orientalism"

It has in part been the critique of orientalism in Indian studies over the past decade that has led to a notable reformulation of the history of social power in India. One way this is expressed, to touch on a central tenet of what we might call a new archaeology of colonialism, is to claim that colonialism "elevated Brahmanic formulations to the level of hegemonic text" (Raheja 1988: 498), or, in other words, that it "created . . . an autonomous caste structure with the Brahman clearly at the head" (Dirks 1987: 8; cf. 1989: 45). From the very specific—"the colonial domination of

India, meaning the late nineteenth-century Orientalism . . . infect[ed] concepts of caste," "overpowered Indian beliefs," and introduced "the notion of . . . inherited [physical] properties" (Fox: 1985: 154)—to the very general—orientalism invented "much of India's ancient past . . . and, not least, the past of Asiatic Despotism" (Washbrook 1988: 83)—the implication seems generally to be the same: that to a substantial degree it was British colonialism that, in cooperation with orientalism, "traditionalized" society in such a way that it took on a form, a hegemonic Sanskritized form, that it may never really have had.

I hope this summary does not caricature the analysis of the post-orientalist anthropologists and historians, and I certainly do not mean to dismiss their deep insights out of hand, for much of the argument—for example, concerning the objectification, by the very categories of the British census, of caste hierarchies that previously had been far more flexible and mobile—is compelling. What troubles me is, first, the stronger formulation of this interpretation, whose logical extension is that colonialism in South Asia produced certain forms of domination *tout court*; and second, the thinness of the history of precolonial domination on which, ironically, this new historicism is based, and, moreover, its potential for precluding such an analysis.[41]

As for the stronger formulation, it may be that, out of repugnanace toward India's colonial past and orientalism's complicity in it, post-orientalist Euro-American Indology, like Indian nationalist Indology before it, has become prone to idealized India's precolonial past. Even if this idealization has not always found actual expression, the now widespread thesis seems unavoidably to entail a far more positive valorization of what preceded colonialism's "'Brahmanization' of society . . . [which made] the values of one section of present society [Brahmans] artificially dominant over those of others" (Washbrook 1988: 82). This is a valorization that can also be found in much contemporary South Asian scholarship.[42] When we combine this with the fallout from books like *Homo Hierarchicus*—leading the general reader to such New Age characterizations of caste as "an expression of holistic unity of opposites that is as much a part of the structure of human thought as . . . binary oppositions" (Jay 1988: 47)—we soon find ourselves launched into some Oriental Paradise Lost.

To make my objection a little clearer, I will examine this post-orientalist theme in two specific cases and then try to think a little more epistemologically, if you will, about problems we face interpreting pre-modern Indian, or indeed any, cultural products.

The first case is an argument recently made by Burton Stein.

What I am calling "indologism" is different in crucial ways [from "Indology"]. The ideology of divine hierarchy, *varnāshramadharma*, is an important part of the ancient knowledge of India, beginning with the post-Vedic *Brahmana* texts, with their neat order of social differences within a moral unity, and continuing through medieval *dharmaśastra* texts, with their more messy, contingent and regionally varied codes. These texts—particularly the former—received a new life lease and legitimacy at the hands of European orientalists who constructed the knowledge we call "indology" and which I, polemically, call "indologism." By the latter I mean the conversion of the findings of a valid knowledge and discourse, based upon ancient texts, into a social theory allegedly pertinent . . . to pre-modern socieites of South Asia, where it can have at best a partial validity (and that to be demonstrated). (1985: 36–37)

We might want for a moment to consider, as one illustrative instance, the new life lease and legitimacy that these texts, particularly the former,[43] received at the hands of Indian "orientalists" in the eleventh and twelfth centuries. It is then that we find, especially in North and central India, a sudden (or so it appears to me) and certainly luxurious efflorescence of scholarly production relating to such texts. This production brings us for the first time identifiably authored and securely datable *dharmaśāstra* works. All of these emerge from the court circles of the ruling elites of the period. Within a century and a half we witness extraordinary activity: the (now lost) codes of Bhoja, king of Dhārā (ca. 1030); the great commentary on the *Yājñavalkyasmṛti* by Vijñaneśvara, patronized by Vikramāditya VI of the Kalyāṇa Cāḷukyas (ca. 1100); the commentary on the same text by Aparārka, of the Śilāhāra dynasty of the Konkan (ca. 1130); the vast digest (the earliest one extant) by Lakṣmīdhara, chief minister of King Govindacandra of the Gāhaḍavālas of Kanauj (ca. 1130), on whom more below; the five huge works on *dharma* composed at the court of (or perhaps even by) King Ballālasena of Bengal (ca. 1175); the capacious code of Hemādri, minister of Mahādeva, the Yādava king of Devagiri (ca. 1265), and, at the end of this period, the monumental work on *Parāśara* by Mādhava, hereditary teacher and minister to the first kings of Vijayanagar (early fourteenth century).

Such vast intellectual output surely needs to be theorized in some way. No one is insisting that such texts be read as reflections of reality: texts cannot simply "reflect" what in some measure they help to constitute. But at the very least, it is conceivable that demonstrating commitment to a certain—perhaps even antiquarian or nostalgic—ideal of social order, a kind of pre-modern "traditionalization" of it, was a major concern of the ruling strata in this two or three hundred year period, when, significantly, the Sultanate was in process of consolidating itself (see below). I do not see how we can understand this concern and thus approach an adequate understanding of the nature of social power during this period if we dismiss as not pertinent such massively subsidized intellectual work emanating from within the very center of the political culture of the time. It is possible to argue, in fact, just the opposite of Stein's position: that it is precisely the fact that this textual material "has served (and still does) as a justification for class oppression" that supplies a "powerful reason" for *not* "questioning its standing as relevant social theory for the reconstruction of medieval societies" (1985: 37). These texts may well in part be "models for" rather than "models of," but whereas this distinction nuances our sense of their material reality, it does not empty them of ideological reality.

My second example is a recent essay on the nineteenth-century debate on *satī*, which illustrates many of the strengths and some of the weaknesses of the current postcolonial archaeology of power in South Asia (Mani 1987). In important and useful ways, the author draws attention to the way the discursive strategies of the entire debate on the burning of widows worked to silence the voice of the victim and foreclose the question of female agency. But the more central concerns of the essay are stated to be textual authority, "law," and "tradition," and here the argument is on shakier ground. "Tradition," for instance, is said to be "reconstituted under colonial rule"; "brahmanic scriptures" are falsely postulated as "locus"—and prescriptive locus—of "what constitutes authentic cultural tradition" (pp. 121–22). "[T]his privileging of brahmanic scripture and the equation of tradition with scripture is . . . an effect of a colonial discourse on India" (p. 122). Though the main intention throughout the essay is to raise "questions regarding the place of brahmanic scripture in precolonial India, the nature and functioning of precolonial legal systems and pre-British indigenous discourses on tradition and social reform" (p. 123), we never leave the colonial arena in pursuit of these goals. To discover whether "a legal discourse on scripture is a colonial phenomenon" (p. 149), we don't proceed to the logically prior question, "whether brahmanic texts [have] always been prioritized as the source of law" (a good, though conceptually and historically complex, question), but to "a careful reading of the Parliamentary Papers" (p. 133). If we want to argue that colonialism reconstituted tradition, should we not do a careful reading of the earlier tradition (or rather, traditions) that was the object of transformation? Would we not want to look, for example, at real texts with real dates and authors we can place in a social world, in addition to the interpretative practices of the Company pandits (themselves not so easy to interpret)?

Were we to do this we would find a process of hierarchizing textualization, a regime of truth, in precolonial India comparable to what we find in the early Raj. To argue that "the equation between scripture and law" (terminology never theorized in the essay, and far more dichotomous than that in use in precolonial India) is a process that takes place under the sign of colonialism or that the debate on *satī* is "a modern discourse on tradition" in which "tradition" as such is "produced" (pp. 150–51), is to ignore perhaps a millennium of debate in India over what constitutes "traditional" textuality and how local practices interact with that textuality. Critique, rejection, and reform do not begin in 1800 in India, and their epistemological building blocks, "authentic tradition" and the like, are not ideas that spring forth for the first time from the fevered brains of Colebrook, Bentinck, and Rammohun Roy.

In fact, much of the discourse as we find it in the nineteenth-century Raj could easily have derived, and may have actually derived, from a text like the twelfth-century digest I examine further below, the *Kṛtyakalpataru* of Lakṣmīdhara. Here the discussion of *sahamaraṇa* (*satī*) takes place in the context of *vyavahāra,* which is precisely what we would call juridical procedure and substantive law, rather than in the discourses on "domestic" duties, "religious" vows, or "ritual" purity. The treatment follows a section on criminal law and is directly preceded by points of law relating to sexual behavior outside marriage—rape, adultery, fornication, heterosexual and homosexual child molestation, bestiality; it is placed within the framework of sexual law within marriage and is itself followed by discussion of levirate, remarriage, and inheritance laws.[44] *Sahamaraṇa* is thus regarded by the author simply as a further dimension of legal obligation within the sexual sphere. Lakṣmīdhara cites the same "scriptural" passages as those adduced by the pandit of the Nizamat Adalat in 1821 (Mani 1987: 131), and other texts, for example, the *Brahmapurāṇa,* that appeal for authority to the *Rgveda* verse (7.6.27) whose interpretation was so much to vex Rammohun (p. 136; *Kṛtyakalpataru* p. 634).[45] Lakṣmīdhara concludes, "After examining all these textes, one may affirm that all women, Brahman and others—except those who are pregnant, or have small children, and so on—who seek particular rewards for the husbands in heaven are entitled (or obligated) to die with him [if he dies at home] or subsequent to him [if he dies abroad]."⁴⁶ He then proceeds to cite additional authorities (Bṛhaspati, Viṣṇu, Hārīta, Yama, and of course the ubiquitous Manu) who allow the alternative of asceticism, without himself commenting on the option.

In brief, this whole discussion—and others of the same sort in other digests and commentaries (like Medhātithi on *Manusmṛti* 5.117ff., who denies the very possibility of the legality of *sahamaraṇa,* calling it suicide)—illustrates not only the premodern interpenetration of "law" and "scripture," but the "contentiousness" of "pre-traditionalized" tradition itself. Indeed, the very existence of the sophisticated hermeneutic science, Pūrvamīmāṃsā, that I discuss below is predicated on antinomies internal to the Sanskrit tradition, respecting everything from the performance of basic rituals to the very conceptualization of "tradition" itself.

If there was a British "Brahmanizing tendency," then, it may largely have recapitulated a precolonial Brahmanizing tendency on the part of medieval ruling elites. This is to make no claim that other regulating structures of social life—"lineage, sect, and little king," for instance⁴⁷—may not, in fact, have been more relevant in everyday reality (whatever "everyday reality" might mean). It is only to recall that elite Sanskrit textuality laid claim to omnipotence and to suggest that the social origins and epistemological modalities of such claims require that we take them seriously. It bears repeating that the fact that the colonial debate on *sati* "turned on the issue of its scriptural grounding" (p. 140) makes a crucial point about the displacement of real violence against women onto textuality, but this is a displacement that occurred earlier, for "tradition" itself in India invariably scripturalizes deliberation of what should and should not be done in social life. The textualization of *sati,* thus, seems yet another instance where indigenous discourses of power intersected with the colonial variety (as is justly acknowledged with respect to the denial of female subjectivity, p. 152). What might in fact be worth assembling is just such an inventory of ideologemes, for the preexistence of a shared ideological base among indigenous and colonial elites may have been one contributing factor to the effectiveness with which England consolidated and maintained its rule in India.

The epistemological problems—concerning the interpretation of texts, ideology, social action—implicit in so much of the discussion of "Indologism" certainly merit more sustained reflection than they have received.

To take a commonplace example, consider the following verse from the beginning of the *Vālmīki Rāmāyaṇa*, describing the social world of the kingdom of Kosala:

kṣatraṃ brahmamukhaṃ cāsīd vaiśyāḥ kṣatram anuvratāḥ/
śūdrāḥ svakarmaniratās trīn varṇān upacāriṇaḥ//
("The kṣatriya order followed the lead of the brahman order, the vaiśya that of the kṣatriya, whereas the śūdras, devoted to their proper duties, served the other three *varṇas*.") (*Rām.* 1.6.17 ed. crit.)

What are we to do with such a statement in light of the above-mentioned claims about the transformative impact of colonialism and in our attempt to reconstruct a "poetics of power" for precolonial India? (I am not interested here in the specific problem of brahman versus kṣatriya dominance—a dichotomy wildly overdrawn given what we actually know of Indian social and political history—but only in the general question of how we evelute representations of power.) It will not do to object that the *Rāmāyaṇa* gives us mere fiction (*kāvya*), or just a dream of power. It is not just that the "tradition" itself regards the epic as absolutely true, or that nonfictional normative texts (*śāstra*) promulgate precisely the same sort of stratification, for similar objections of historicity could be raised.[48] What is more to the point is to examine the foundations of this historicity itself. What are the historical controls by which fictionality can be identified and excluded? Where a historical context can be constructed only via texts, and since the line between the documentary/constative text on the one hand and the "worklike"/performative text on the other is thoroughly permeable,[49] how can we tell the fiction from the fact? We have always known that people make their stories from their histories, and recently we have come to appreciate the degree to which people make their histories from their stories. Furthermore, even if we could somehow ascertain that this is only a dream of power, dreams, *l'imaginaire*, are no less historical, no less real—by the very fact of their being dreamed—and potentially no less effective than any other fact or event. A widely shared illusion can be more real than a "fact" that is disbelieved; the broad inculcation of belief in the existence of authoritative texts and their discourses of false necessity can reify practice in a very general but still crucial way (a question in essence no less relevant to the discussion of any normative discourse, legal discourse in particular, anywhere).

These are matters historians elsewhere have of course reflected on, though such reflections are rarely if ever brought to bear on the Indological problem. It may be instructive, therefore, to cite the following extended thoughts of the historian of medieval France, Georges Duby.

> In effect, in order to understand the ordering of human societies and to discern their evolutionary forces, we have to direct our attention equally to mental phenomena [in addition to material structures], whose intervention is unquestionably just as determinative as that of economic and demographic phenomena. For it is not as a consequence of their actual condition, but rather of the image they have of it—which is never a faithful reflection—that people regulate their conduct. . . . Reconstructing ideological systems of the past via their disparate fragments, or following the tracks of the transformations they have undergone, is in truth nothing but preparation for a much more difficult task, which consists in defining the relationships that ideologies in the course of their history have had with lived social reality. Here we would suggest conducting research in two stages: A) Ideologies present themselves as the interpretation of concrete situations. They are prone, consequently, to reflect any changes in these situations. They are slow in doing this, however, since they are by nature conservative. The adjustments finally produced in them often come only after a very long delay, and remain only partial. Measuring the deviations between the history of ideologies and the history of lived social relations is all the more difficult in that, by the play of a subtle dialectic, the weight of systems of representations can slow down, or at times even arrest, the movement of economic and political structures themselves. It is, nevertheless, the task of historians to establish as carefully as possible the chronologies of these discrepancies. And on these chronologies all subsequent investigation and interpretation should be based. B) Such an analysis of temporal deviations should naturally lead the social historian in due course to critique the coherent systems that ideologies of the past represent, to demystify them a posteriori by showing how, at every moment in the historical evolution, the discernible features of the material conditions of social life are more or less travestied within the mental images of them. That is, the historian should measure, as exactly as possible—and given the fact that in the majority of documents the expressions of lived reality and of dreamed reality are found to be confusinglfy mixed up, this enterprise is rendered exceedingly arduous—the concordances and discordances that are located, in every point of the diachrony, in three variables: on the one hand, between the objective situation of groups/individuals and the illusory image wherein they take comfort and find justification; and on the other, between this image and individual/collective behavior. (1974: 203–4, 217–18)

The problem remains, of course, how we can possibly determine the "objective situation." But the fact that India's past confronts us with real dreams of power as well as with real power, and that a critical historiography should aim at, among other things, measuring the fit or lack of fit between them, is something that I think we have yet to confront in classical Indology.

How it is possible, then, to survey the constructions of colonial domination without a detailed topography of precolonial domination, I cannot see.[50] And this topography, charted throughout the expanse of Sanskrit cultural production, does not really yet exist, a lacuna for which classical Indology itself is partly responsible. The failure to trace with any adequacy a historical map of social power in traditional India, which alone can anchor our estimations of the impact of colonialism, is all the more surprising considering what appear to be the extraordinary density, longevity, and effectivity of authoritative power—or at least of its normative claims, though the two are not easily distinguishable—in the high culture of early India.[51] One reason classicists have failed to write this history might emerge if we contextualize our own profession: The privileged elite from which Indology has historically drawn its members could hardly be expected to pose to an alien culture questions of domination it was unable, or unwilling, to pose to its own.

Such subjective impediments to tracing this map are, however, matched by the objective impediments of an inadequate, or rather stunted, historical record; inadequate given the typical hazards of studying an ancient society; stunted in the case of South Asia by a pervasive dehistorizing component in the dominant ideology itself. For a large part of its textual production, the model of truth available for most discourse in Sanskrit— the Veda, broadly conceived—and the conditions of truth that model entailed—historical transcendence—has produced a body of texts that actively aspired to, and largely secured, a condition of timelessness, one correlating with the naturalization of the social toward which this ideology aimed.[52]

An adequate historical analysis of ideology as accessible to us in one important and paradigmatic sector of traditional India, the culture of orthodox Sanskrit texts, is no small order, to be sure; I could not even begin to detail what such a project might encompass (not even what precisely "orthodox" might mean over time), though I will try to sketch out a few preliminary ideas. One suggestion is that what we may find to be central in this morphology is something close to the problem we encounter in the analysis of orientalism, above all the problem of knowledge and domination: Here it is not just the instrumental use of knowledge (indeed, of *veda*) in the essentialization and dichotomization of the social order, but the very control of knowledge that constitutes one of its elementary forms. The monopolization of "access to authoritative resources"—the most authoritative of all resources, Sanskrit (*vaidika*) learning—becomes itself a basic component in the construction and reproduction of the idea of inequality and thus in what, again, can be viewed as a process analogous to colonization in precolonial India.

Rather than any singular "idea of inequality," it is truer to speak of plural "ideas of inequalities," for there are many forms of difference— gender, ethnos, race—constructed in many diverse ways as inequalities. A fertile source for understanding the variety of inequality constructions, and in their very structure a potential template for a morphology of social power, are the *nibandhas* of medieval India I mention above. These digests of social/religious codes of conduct, which define what may be viewed as the total society (*varṇāśramadharma*), are compendia of rules and exegeses based on earlier material from *dharmaśāstra* and its "metalegal" framework, Pūrvamīmāṃsā, both of which have long and highly sophisticated traditions of their own. I want to look, very briefly, at a few themes of unequal power, "allocative" and "authoritative" power, before following up on one of them in a little more detail, as these themes are presented in one of the earliest of the great *nibandhas*, the *Kṛtyakalpataru*. This massive work, in fourteen volumes (twelve so far published) was composed, as I noted above, for King Govindacandra of the Gāhaḍavāla dynasty of Kanauj, the ruler of much of North India in the middle of the twelfth century, by Bhaṭṭa Lakṣmīdhara. Not only was Lakṣmīdhara "foreign minister" (*mahāsāndhivigrahika*) of the king, but he also appears to have been a judge who rendered decisions in a wide variety of cases.[53]

Why is the first great *nibandha* composed—why should an encyclopedic synthesis of an entire way of life be undertaken—precisely in that time and place? Evidently it has to do with some acknowledgment on the part of the Gāhaḍavāla king of a need for special reaffirmation of *dharma*, but why just then? Was it because, for the first time since the development of the *dharmaśāstras*, that way of life confronted, in the Central Asian Turks, something radically different, a resolutely unassimilating social and religious formation (far more confirmed in its difference than, say, the assimilationist Śakas a millennium earlier, or the Hūṇas of a half a millennium earlier)? The fact that the production of *dharmanibandha* discourse, as noted above, almost perfectly follows the path of advance of the Sultanate from the Doab to Devagiri to the Deccan (Lakṣmīdhara, Hemādri, Mādhava) suggests, on the one hand, that totalizing conceptualizations of society became possible only by juxtaposition with alternative lifeworlds, and on the other, that they became necessary only at the moment when the total form of the society was for the first time believed, by the privileged theorists of society, to be threatened. These political developments certainly mark the dynasty in other ways. The first invasions of Mahmud of Ghazni had started one hundred years before Lakṣmīdhara began his work (when, in fact, the efflorescence in shastric production noted above was initiated). We know that the king's grandfather, Candradeva, was involved in major campaigns against the Turks and had established the supplemental tax called the *turuṣkadaṇḍa* to raise money to that end.[54] One of his records represents him as "Svayambhū himself born upon the earth to restore *dharma* and the Veda, whose sounds had almost been silenced" (*IA* 18: 14–19, vs. 3). In one of Govinda's inscriptions he is said to be "Hari [Viṣṇu] himself born into this world at the request of Hara [Śiva], since he is the only one capable of protecting Vārāṇasi from the wicked Turk warrior."[55] Within little more than a generation, the dynasty would come to an end when Govinda's grandson, Jayacandra, died in battle with the Turks, and Banaras was sacked (A.D. 1193).[56]

To situate the arguments of Lakṣmīdhara, it is necessary to bear in mind certain basic postulates of *dharmaśāstra* discourse. One of these is that, since *dharmaśāstra* informs us of types of action that have nonutilitarian, transcendent ends (*adṛṣṭārtha*)—informs us, that is, of things we would not normally do for ends we would not otherwise know about[57]—its authority must likewise derive from some transcendent source. Only the Veda, consequently, qualifies to function as source of our knowledge of *dharma*. Thus, according to our earliest systematic analysis of the topic, in the *Pūrvamīmāṃsāsūtra, dharma* is rule-governed sacrificial ritual (*yā-gādi*) deriving its authority from texts that are transcendent, existing out of historical time, composed neither by man nor god (*apauruṣeya*). All of this constitutes a central representation, an episteme, of the *vaidika* worldview, with large consequences for social existence within and at the margins of the "orthodox" culture this worldview defines.[58]

In the course of Indian social-intellectual history, however, more came to count as *dharma* than could be accounted for in Vedic texts. (What is therefore paradoxical, if that is the right word, is not that the Veda has so little to do with *dharma*, as Jan Heesterman has so often argued [e.g., Heesterman 1978, 1981], but that *dharma* had, originally, little to do with anything but Vedic ritual.) This massive expansion of the realm of transcendentally enjoined practices represents historically, I would argue, a response to the Buddhist critique of *vaidika* culture and the ensuing disenchantment of the social world. In this process of expansion, "memories" of the Veda (the primary connotation of *smṛti* in this context) and the actions of those who participate in Vedic culture became essential authorities supplemental to existing Vedic texts, so long as these did not contradict the explicit word of the Veda or evince clear evidence of self-interest. But the difficulty of establishing contradiction between "memories" or "practices" and Holy Word is something the eighth-century Mīmāṃsaka Kumārila demonstrates with overpowering logic. At the same time, self-interest is never clearly thematized or seriously defined.[59] The way is thus opened for a vast textualization and ritualization of social-cultural life. It is in this context that Lakṣmīdhara adduces a foundational principle of the traditional Indian discourse of power: "Whatever act the *āryas* who know the Vedas claim to be *dharma, is dharma*; whatever they reject is said to be *adharma*."[60]

The term *ārya* itself merits intellectual-historical study (and I mean diachronic analysis, not static etymology) for premodern India at least of the sort *Arier* has received for modern Europe.[61] The binary pair *ārya/anārya* is one of several discursive definitions by which the Sanskrit cultural order constitutes itself. It overarches the world of traditional Indian inequality—"A non-*ārya* may act like an *ārya*, and *ārya* like a non-*ārya* . . . and though they may be equal [*samau*] in this [i.e., in transgressing caste duty] they never are [otherwise] equal" (*Manusmṛti* 10.73). Another antithesis, *ārya/mleccha*, seems to add little new, though again, the second valence here also awaits detailed analysis;[62] Lakṣmīdhara (for whom the word almost certainly already had reference to the Central Asian Turks, as it usually does later) cites a verse symptomatic of the xenophobic energy it channelized: "One should never perform a *śrāddha* in the land of the *mlecchas*; one should never go to the land of the *mlecchas*. If one drinks water from the wells of the Others, one becomes like them."[63] Added to these fundamental dichotomies is a biogenetic paradigm with which Lakṣmīdhara feels it necessary to supplement the social inequality already warranted as *dharma* by promulgation in the Veda.[64] Social action (*karma*) on the part of the various orders of the social world is differentiated by reason of the heterogeneous psychophysical constituents, peculiar to their specific natures, that make up the members of these orders.[65]

From such factors as the semantic realm of the distinction *ārya/anārya* and the biogenetic map of inequality (along with less theorized material, from Vedic and epic literature, for instance), it may seem warranted to speak about a "pre-form of racism" in early India (Geissen 1988: 48ff.), especially in a discussion of indigenous "orientalism," since in both its classic colonial and its National Socialist form orientalism is inseparable from racism. This question like many others raised here deserves reexamination, for work done to date strikes me as inadequate for the precolonial period.[66] At present, however, I want to stay with the indigenous rationale of inequality by isolating a principle internal to the *dharmaśāstra* tradition, which contributes as much to the construction of illegitimate hierarchy as any other, though not usually treated as such. This is the prohibition of knowledge, the denial of (*vaidika*) literacy, and the radical censorship this entails for "śūdras" and all communities outside the "twice-born."

Lakṣmīdhara introduces this prohibition via a detailed analysis of the "livelihood, action, and *dharma*" of śūdras, which I summarize for reference though much of this material will be familiar.[67] Numerous authorities of *dharmaśāstra* are adduced to confirm that "The one and only *dharma* of a śūdra is obedience to the twice-born; anything he does other than that will be fruitless" (p. 266). The śūdra is to work for an *ārya* (I omit the exfoliation of occupational detail), who is to provide the śūdra with leftover food, old clothing and furnishings, and the like (the qualitative inferiority that is a necessary complement of the quantitative inferiority of resources permitted the despised). The śūdra is to be supported by the *ārya* even if he is too old to work and must in turn support an *ārya* with whatever wealth he might have (p. 267); in general, however, "a śūdra even if capable must never have a surplus of wealth, for a śūdra with wealth will injure brahmans" (p. 271). These specific socioeconomic relations of domination are enjoined on the śūdra with full transcendent legitimacy— they are *śūdradharma*;[68] at the same time, the śūdra is obliged to conform with the general social ethic (*sādhāraṇa dharma*), purity/honesty, humility, and the like (p. 265; Vol. 1, p. 10)—that is, he has the obligations of humanity without its privileges. Add to these antinomies the most important: the śūdra's *dharma* paradoxically excludes him from the realm of *dharma*: " . . . The śūdra merits no ritual [initiation], enjoys no *dharma* as derived from Holy Word, nor [is subject to] prohibitions deriving from *dharma* as expressed in Holy Word" (p. 271).

The prohibition of knowledge is the subject taken up in detail by Lakṣmīdhara in chapter 29 of Book 2, "What Must Not Be Given a Śūdra." "One must never bestow learning[69] upon a śūdra . . . never teach him *dharma*, never instruct him in other vows. Whoever tells him about *dharma*, or instructs him in vows, will go to the hell called Vast Darkness, along with the śūdra himself."[70] Lakṣmīdhara's construal of this passage is indicated by his next citation, from Yama: "Whoever becomes the teacher of a *vṛṣala* [śūdra], and whatever *vṛṣala* becomes a student—both sink down to hell and dwell there a hundred years." Such injunctions restricting participation in Sanskrit high culture and access to Vedic "literacy"—something fundamental to the world conception of elite Sanskrit culture, and one of the elementary forms and formulations of inequality in traditional India—are not argued out in detail in the digests of *dharmaśāstra*. The principal theorization is found in Pūrvamīmāṃsā, where a separate "topic" is devoted to it entitled "Exclusion of the Śūdra."[71] The arguments here are rather technical and complex, but it is possible to summarize the basic issues and draw some provisional conclusions without too much misrepresentation.

The Mīmāṃsā discussion centers on a conception that might almost be called a fulcrum of inequality in *vaidika* India: *adhikāra*, "qualification" or even "right" of a person to possess the results of an act of *dharma*.[72] There are certain logical prerequisites (not necessarily directly enunciated by Vedic rules) of this "qualification": The person must have the knowledge to perform the rite, must be in possession of the ritual means (in particular the sacrificial fires), and must be physically and economically capable of executing the rite.

According to the Mīmāṃsā discussion, the simple "desire for heaven" is insufficient to qualify one for participation in the Vedic sacrifice. Even though the Vedas command, "He who desires heaven should sacrifice," sacrificing presupposes being in possession of the sacrifical fires, and in the Vedic injunction for building these fires[73] only the first three *varṇas* are mentioned (6.1. 25–26). According to some earlier authorities indeed (Bādari is cited as one), the injunction to build the fires ("a brahman should build the fires in the spring, a kṣatriya in the summer, a vaiśya in the autumn") was only intended to specify conditions for doing the building, not to ordain who could do it,[74] for "the śūdra desires heaven, too . . . and what is it in a sacrifice that any man can do but that the śūdra is unable to do?"[75] The insistence that only those actually mentioned have the "qualification" is, however, confirmed via the additional condition of knowledge: a Vedic injunction requires the initiation (*upanayana*) of a Brahman in the spring, a kṣatriya in the summer, a vaiśya in the autumn, whereas the śūdra and all the others below him again are not mentioned. The claim that these others might study the Veda alone is denied: the Veda explicitly prohibits this.[76]

Arcane and convoluted as this discussion may seem, it suggests several important things about inequality and its representation in the elite culture of traditional India; I want briefly to address three of them. First, the restriction on Vedic "literacy" discussed above is not peripheral to the Mīmāṃsā system but foundational to it and implicit from the very first *sūtra* (Verpoorten 1987). Second, it is by means of precisely such an exclusion that communities of the despised are ideationally created as such in early India. While a biogenetic disqualification is sometimes adduced elsewhere, śūdras and other despised communities are here not excluded from Vedic literacy on the grounds of physical or intellectual inferiority. On the contrary, "Śūdras are as capable of learning as the twice-born are"; "in the matters of this world *āryas* and *mlecchas* have equal capabilities."[77] The trouble is that, with the vast expansion of the realm of *dharma* alluded to above—the ritualization and shastra-ization that ultimately encompasses the whole of life, including the life of the śūdra—the "other world," of Vedic authority and the resources of power it controlled, had virtually subsumed this one. *Dharma* was total, and in *dharma* transcendent rules operated. In the world of Mīmāṃsā, therefore—the master science of the Veda, the foundation of *dharmaśāstra*, and so the heart of that orthodoxy that defines the high culture of traditional India—inequality in the final analysis becomes more than natural. Resulting from Vedic injunction, or rather a chain of Vedic injunctions, it is not simply beyond instrumental reason, but a matter of truth-transcending-reason (*adṛṣṭārtha*); like sacrificial violence, for example, it becomes understandable precisely because it is incomprehensible. Nowhere I think is Bourdieu's notion of "theodicy of privilege" better exemplified.

Third, the very fact that the Mīmāṃsā discussion should take place— a rationalization of the irrationalism of domination—betrays to my mind the consciousness in the tradition itself of the asymmetry of power that characterized it and the awareness of a need for its legitimation. This is the implication, too, of the many responses to it from within the tradition, from Bādāri in the Mīmāṃsā school itself to the *ViṣṇuPurāṇa* (6.2.22ff.), which celebrates the "freedom" from Vedic obligations thus provided the śūdra, who need only serve the twice-born in order to win the "higher words"; to (initially) countermovements like Buddhism, which sought to valorize other forms of literacy (Thapar 1975: 130);[78] and to sectarian movements like Pāñcarātra, which provided the missing "Vedic" injunctions authorizing initiation of the śūdra.[79] But none of this palliation makes itself felt in the totalizing constructions of the social order, like Lakṣīmīdhara's *Kṛtyakalpataru*, that were produced in North and central India in the two centuries leading up to the Turkic conquest. (Quite the contrary, the very form of the *nibandha* conspires to produce the impression of the massive and monolithic weight of tradition, at least on the questions I treat here.) Restrictions on access to high-culture literacy, along with other juridical structures of inequality in the orthodix Sanskrit tradition—particularly differentiation in (judicial) punishment and in (religious) penance, which seems to constitute almost an indigenous economy of human worth—are among the components of a program of domination whose true spirit we might begin to conjure with other comparable programs, such as the *Arierparagraphen* of the NS state.[80]

For a Critical Indology

Reviewing Indology in the way we have just done, we encounter a field of knowledge whose history and object both have been permeated with power. From its colonial origins in Justice Sir William to its consummation in SS Obersturmführer Wüst, Sanskrit and Indian studies have contributed directly to consolidating and sustaining programs of domination. In this (noteworthy orthogenesis) these studies have recapitulated the character of their subject, that indigenous discourse of power for which Sanskrit has been one major vehicle and which has shown a notable longevity and resilience.

In a postcolonial and post-Holocaust world, however, these traditional foundations and uses of Indology have disappeared, and the current self-interrogations within our field may, with typical scholarly tardiness, somehow be responding to this new impotence and the loss of purpose in scholarly activity that it implies. In other words, if Indological knowledge has historically been coexistent with vanished institutions of coercive power, then the production of such knowledge no longer serves its primary and defining purpose. Our obsession with orientalism over the past decade might suggest that Indologists, who have begun to realize their historical implication in domination only now that it has ended, no longer know why they are doing what they do.

The rise of a new empire and its continued production and utilization of orientalist knowledge may preemptively suggest that this assessment is not altogether correct. The colonial foundations of Indology may have given way, but neocolonial foundations have been built in their place. These await careful analysis, and our ignorance of our own role in the reproduction of power may account in part for the acute sense of confusion about our work some of us feel. But I can see at least three other sources for our turmoil.

German Indology, construed as part of a whole, leads us to confront a very large set of worries, the crisis of the culture of humanistic scholarship as such. As a component of domination, German Indology was hardly different from the rest of German scholarship of the period. Numerous studies over the past fifteen to twenty years have demonstrated clearly the painful truth Steiner has caught in a memorable phrase: The humanities in Germany failed to humanize.

> Not very many have asked, or pressed home the question, as to the internal relations between the structures of the inhuman and the surrounding, contemporary matrix of high civilization.[81] Yet the barbarism which we have undergone reflects, at numerous and precise points, the culture which it sprang from and set out to desecrate. . . . Why did humanistic traditions and models of conduct prove so fragile a barrier against political bestiality? In fact, were they a barrier, or is it more realistic to perceive in humanistic culture express solicitations of authoritarian rule and cruelty? (Steiner 1971: 30)

Like the predicament of Indology, that of humanistic studies in general has belatedly seized the attention of scholars, as "Der Fall Heidegger" demonstrates. This case is important not only because it posits in such stark terms the potential copresence of philosophy and barbarism, but because it is depressingly commonplace, as we are beginning to learn.[82] Can we continue to believe innocently in the value of such scholarship to life when this scholarship, often foundational each to its particular field, so readily served forms of repressive power through active contribution to the discourses that sustained these forms, or through "active indifference," "collaborative unknowing"?

Two other factors that I think contribute to the malaise I mention above are the management of critique perfected by contemporary capitalism and the theoretical challenge (yet again) to the scholarly dogma of objectivity.

A self-consciously responsible scholarship in late twentieth-century America may recognize and attempt to escape its implication in new forms of coercive power by fostering a critique of the imperial conditions of our scholarly production. A good example of this scholarship, and a sort of programmatic statement, is Edward Said's 1989 address to the American Association of Anthropologists, "Representing the Colonized: Anthropology's Interlocutors." Here he argues in favor of some (still largely unspecified) "alternative and emergent counterdominant" scholarly practices to break the link between area studies and neocolonial policy. "These are matters not just of theoretical but of quotidian importance. Imperialism, the control of overseas territories and peoples, develops in a continuum with variously envisaged histories, current practices and policies, and with differently plotted cultural trajectories."

Now what, as Weber might have asked, are the "external relation-ships," the "material conditions" of such scholarly pronouncements as this? What does it mean to warn against "the formidable difficulties of empire" before a professional organization of anthropologists, and in a scholarly journal published by the University of Chicago, and with all expenses paid by Columbia University? Why, in other words, should central ideological apparatuses of the empire so hospitably embrace those who seek to contest it, and why is it that the empire all the while should be so thoroughly unconcerned? It may be a tired and tiresome issue (a reprise of the 1960s hit "Repressive Desublimation"), but late capital-ism's blithe insouciance toward its unmaskers, its apparently successful do-mestication of anti-imperialist scholarship, and its commodification of oppositional theory are hard to ignore and certainly give pause to those who seriously envision some role for critique in the project of progressive change.

Said's essay may also serve as entry point for the second factor men-tioned, the problem of objectivity, something already raised above in the context of Weber's *Wissenschaft als Beruf*. There, a vision of science as value-free seems to have enabled, or certainly was spectacularly unable to prevent, the easy coexistence of scholarship and state violence. Challeng-ing this vision at the most fundamental level has been among the main themes of theoretical work in the humanities during the past two decades. Central here are hermeneutical criticism, ideology critique, and the rhe-toricization of historiography (as argued by Hayden White, Hans Kellner, and others). The prejudgments, theory-ladenness, and perspectival par-tiality out of and with which we perceive any object, especially a cultural object; the way discourses serve in class-divided societies to sustain forms of domination; the purely rhetorical (rather than ontological) status of the truth claims of historical description (LaCapra even wants to challenge the facticity of dates)—all of this conspires fundamentally to deny more forcefully than ever the very conditions of possibility of objective scholar-ship, including de-orientalizing scholarship.[83]

The problem of orientalism, therefore, thrusts itself on our attention not just because we now recognize that underwriting relations of power, in however modest a way, has been central to its existence; and probably not because of a perverse sense of impotence now that the traditional foun-dations of Indology have crumbled (for new foundations have replaced them). It's more than this; the whole project of humanistic scholarship, by reason of its capitulations and collusions, seems suspect. At the same time, the escalating critique of objectivism is nearing victory, but what a victory:

It ends in disarming the seekers of truth who advanced it—and who, even armed to the teeth, seem perfectly welcome in the new empire.

What, then, are the prospects of a scholarship that is "postmodern" with respect both to the subject and to the object of scholarship? How, concretely, does one do Indology beyond the Raj and Auschwitz in a world of pretty well tattered scholarly paradigms? I can only offer some very tentative thoughts, little more than notes to my "Notes."

1. The problem of "objectivism" is bedeviling more of us more profoundly than ever, and I cannot offer much that is original. One response may be programmatically to recognize and asseverate one's own interests and value-judgments, for does not the danger of "subjectivism" in part lie in suppressing it? Might the same self-consciousness not effectively confront if not neutralize the potential self-negation of the critique of ideology? Or perhaps we must finally acknowledge, as Joan Scott somewhere urges, that in the last analysis the fundamental question is not the "truth" of the human sciences but their relationship to power, whether as forms of knowledge that sustain illegitimate force or challenge it (a thesis for which NS Indology provides an important historical example). Another, more attractive response is one offered by the Critical Legal Studies (CLS) and Law and Society movements, where some of the more creative thinking about these problems is going on. Our focus should perhaps not be the dichotomy between objectivism and subjectivism, between accurate description and values, but rather the dominant paradigm of research itself, and its basic assumptions. We should construct new perspectives that, for classical Indology as for CLS, would include giving priority to what has hitherto been "marginal, invisible, and unheard."[84] Given the radical silencing and screening out of communities effected by "classical" culture, this is, admittedly, a very arduous task indeed; disembedding the discursive structures by which such censorship and occulation were effected, as I attempt to do in the discussion of pre-orientalist orientalism, has, I am fully aware, a barely provisional adequacy.[85]

As for method and the current fever of methodism, I am not sure that more is desireable than a minimalist position: Since cultural processes and social relations (constituted through hierarchies of class/caste, gender, etc.) are inseparable, and social relations are relations of power, cultural processes have to be seen as arenas where questions of power are constantly engaged (cf. Johnson 1986).

2. A postcolonial Indology should challenge the residual conceptual categories of colonialism, what was referred to above as "European episte-

mological hegemony." This may seem at times like some untranscendable hermeneutic horizen, but I don't think it is that serious; hermeneutical (or ideological or narratological) imprisonment is more terrifying in theory than in practice. An instance of the kind of challenge meant, from the side of economic history, is offered by Frank Perlin (e.g., 1983). He proceeds against the grain of the standard view, that the world system is modern and European, by demonstrating that a world system existed prior to the eighteenth century and that in this world system Europe was basically peripheral, while India may have possessed upward of one quarter of the manufacturing capacity in the world. Perlin's economic-historical project suggests something of a conceptual paradigm for thinking anew South Asian societies and cultures. Washbrook has formulated this well: "South Asian economic and social history was written more to explain why the region did not develop like Europe, or perhaps did not develop at all, rather than to account for the changes and developments which did actually take place" (1988: 62). I may certainly be unaware of important recent work, but it seems that a preemptive European conceptual framework of analysis has disabled us from probing central features of South Asian life, from pre-western forms of "national" (or feminist, or communalist, or ethnic) identity or consciousness, premodern forms of cultural "modernism," precolonial forms of colonialism.

3. In rejecting Eurocentrism, we have to be particularly watchful of its mirror image, "third-worldism" (as it is usually termed especially in discussions of the fate of the Iranian revolution). This seems to me a decided danger in some of the reformulations of colonial transformation now in vogue (and of the more commonplace naive image of spiritual, quietisitic India), and appeal to a largely unproblematized concept of "tradition," whether from a secularist or revivalist position, has become a standard feature of discourse in the public sphere in India. As I try to argue above, domination did not enter India with European colonialism. Quite the contrary, gross asymmetries of power—the systematic exclusion from access to material and nonmaterial resources of large sectors of the population—appear to have characterized India in particular times and places over the last three millennia and have formed the background against which ideological power, intellectual and spiritual resistence, and many forms of physical and psychological violence crystallized.

This violence is the great absent center of classical Indian studies, the subject over which a deafening silence is maintained. One task of postorientalist Indology has to be to exhume, isolate, analyze, theorize, and at the very least talk about the different modalities of domination in traditional India. By all means one is eager to help in the project of reclaiming "traditions, histories, and cultures from imperialism" (Said 1989: 219), but can we forget that most of the traditions and cultures in question have been empires of oppression in their own right—against women, above all, but also against other domestic communities? Perhaps the western Sanskritist feels this most acutely, given that Sanskrit was the principal discursive instrument of domination in premodern India and that, in addition, it has been continuously reappropriated in modern India by many of the most reactionary and communalist sectors of the population. It is a perilous enterprise for the western scholar to thematize the violence in the traditions of others, especially when they are others who have been the victims of violence from the West (though a culture's failure to play by its own rules, and evidence of internal opposition to its domination, are two conditions that certainly lessen this peril). Yet can one avoid it and still practice an Indology that is critical, responsible, and self-aware?

4. This critique of domination should be coupled with an awareness of the penetration of the present by the past—with an awareness of forms of traditional social and cultural violence sedimented in contemporary India—which in turn should entail solidarity with its contemporary victims. Here I would point to a key issue raised in perhaps the most significant confrontation with the public role of history in recent years, the *Historikerstreit* in Germany. In that controversy, a major critique was developed against "historicization," defined in the specific context of the *Streit* as an attempt to reduce a matter of historic significance, the Holocaust, to a matter of only historiographical significance, with all the consequences that making something "academic" implies (Diner 1987: 10–11). I bring this issue up here because it prompts the question why we should not resist any such "historicization" that serves to normalize or trivialize domination, not only in the egregious case of the NS state, but wherever traditional forms of oppression have perdured into the present.

Traditional domination as coded in Sanskrit is not "past history" in India, to be sure. Partly by reason of the stored energy of an insufficiently critiqued and thus untranscended past, it survives in various harsh forms (intensified by the added toxins of capitalist exploitation by twice-born classes) despite legislation designed to weaken the economic and institutional framework associated with it. When, for example, we are told by a contemporary Indian woman that she submits to the economic, social, and emotional violence of Indian widowhood because, in her words, "According to the shastras I had to do it"; when we read in a recent Dalit manifesto that "The first and foremost object of this [cultural revolution] should be to free every man and woman from the thraldom of the Shastras," we catch a glimpse not only of the actualization in consciousness of Sanskrit discourses of power, but of their continued vigor.[86]

5. It may be, to conclude on a major chord, that a transformed and transformative, an emancipatory Indology can exist only within the framework of an emancipatory domestic culture and politics. Moving beyond orientalism finally presupposes moving beyond the culture of domination and the politics of coercion that have nurtured orientalism in all its varieties, and been nurtured by it in turn.

Several friends commented on earlier drafts of this essay and attempted to check my excesses. I thank David Lorenzen (Mexico City), David Ludden (Philadelphia), Peter van der Veer (Utrecht/Philadelphia), Mitchell Ash, Christiana Hartnack, and Paul Greenough (Iowa City), and the students, particularly Thomas Friedrich, in the "Autonom Seminar: Deutsche Indologie zur Zeit des Faschismus" at Freie Universität Berlin (Winter, 1988ff.), to whom I presented my work at different stages. In preparing the first half of this essay, I profited from discussions with Wolfgang Morgenroth (Berlin [East]), Klaus Mylius (Leipzig), Gustav Roth (Göttingen), and especially Friedrich Wilhelm (Munich); thanks also to Herbert Guenther (Saskatoon) for sharing his memories with me. A fellowship from the Deutsche Akademische Austauschdienst enabled me to examine additional archives and conduct further interviews in the summer of 1989. I wrote this essay in 1989 and with only a few exceptions could not take into account work published thereafter.

Notes

1. My thinking about "power" and its maintenance has been informed by Giddens's analysis of power as the control of both "allocative" (material) resources and "authoritative" (including informational) resources. When below I focus on traditional *vaidika* India, I have in mind specifically Giddens 1979: 94ff., especially p. 162, where he argues for the primacy of "authority" over "allocation" in precapitalist societies, and 1985: 258ff., especially p. 261, where he discusses the distribution of "life chances," as for instance literacy, as one form of "authoritative" resource.

2. See now Said 1989: 207.

3. The complexity of this tie may be illustrated by Warren Hastings's preface to the first English translation of a Sanskrit text, Wilkins's *Bhagavadgītā:*

> Every accumulation of knowledge, and especially such as it obtained by social communication with people over whom we exercise a dominion founded on the right of conquest, is useful to the state; it is the gain of humanity; in the specific instance which I have stated, it attracts and conciliates distant affections; it lessens the weight of the chain by which the natives are held in subjection; and it imprints on the hearts of our own countrymen the sense and obligation of benevolence. Even in England, this effect of it is greatly wanting. It is not very long since the inhabitants of India were considered by many as creatures scarce elevated above the degree of savage life; nor, I fear, is that prejudice yet wholly eradicated, though surely abated. Every instance which brings their real character home to observation will impress us with a more generous sense of feeling for their natural rights, and teach us to estimate them by the measure of our own. But such instances can only be obtained in their writings; and these will survive when the British dominion in India shall have long ceased to exist, and when the sources which it once yielded of wealth and power are lost to rememberance. (1785: 13)

A more exquisite expression of liberal imperialism would be hard to find.

4. As widely remarked, and acknowledged, 1985: 1.

5. See the table prepared by Rhys Davids, which shows for the year 1903 a total of 47 professors (26 of them full professors) for "Aryan" orientalism in Germany (Rhys Davids, 1903–04, which he juxtaposes to the four professorships in England, the colonial metropole). For the years around 1933 that more centrally concern me in these "Notes," the *Minerva Jahrbuch* shows substantial programs in Indology at 13 German universities. The important question of the political economy of Indology in Germany in the period 1800–1945 awaits serious analysis.

6. Edward Augustus Freeman, 1879. A prescient document, widely disseminated in its reprinted form in the Harvard Classics, vol. 28.

7. Leopold 1974 provides a good survey. A number of these representations, in particular India as the cradle of Aryan civilization, have lived on in British (and Indian) discourse well into the twentieth century, often taking on a particularly local political inflection. Compare Annie Besant's remarks to the Indian National Congress in 1917: "The Aryan emigrants, who spread over the lands of Europe, carried with them the seeds of liberty sown in their blood in their Asian cradleland. Western historians [I believe she is referring in the first instance to H. S. Maine] trace the self-rule of the Saxon villages to their earlier prototypes in the East and see the growth of English liberty as up-springing from the Aryan root of the free and self-contained village communities . . . ". This was recently cited by (then) Vice President R. Venkatraman of India in his Centenary address at the Adyar Library (1988: 198).

8. A third moment is worth noting: National Socialism made Germany safe again for the open expression of a racism that, while generally accepted in nineteenth-century European scholarship—and indeed, constitutive of orientalism—had largely been excluded from the scholarly sphere for half a century (cf. Laurens

1988; the new freedom to hate publicly is brought out clearly in an early tract on the "worldview" of National Socialism by Karl Zimmerman (1933: 20–22). One might well speculate as to what degree other European scholarship would have differed had its political idiom permitted unconstrained public expression. For the notion of an "inner colonization" of Europe, I now see that I have to some degree been anticipated by the fascism critique of Césaire and Fanon, who regarded it as European colonialism brought home (see most recently Young 1990: 8).

9. For the intellectual-historical appropriation of Bopp—who would certainly have resisted it—in the NS period, see Richard Harder 1942.

10. Jeffrey Herf 1984.

11. It is thus, ultimately, against the values of the November Revolution that Weber counterposes the values of value-free science; his earlier adumbrations of this topic ("On Objectivity," etc.) thus may be thought to be superseded by his formulation here. A memorable eyewitness account of Weber's presentation and its backdrop can be found in Löwith 1986: 15–17.

12. Ringer 1969: 352ff.

13. The idea of an engaged, anti-objectivist Indology finds expression frequently in the period (e.g., in the introduction to Lommel 1935, or Güntert 1938, especially p. 11). Position papers on the question more broadly viewed were prepared by the Hauptamt Wissenschaft (e.g., "Weltanschauung und Wissenschaft," MA-608 [H.W. VortragsMsk 1938], 55672–99, in the archives of the Institut für Zeitgeschichte, Munich).

14. Güntert 1938: 6–7 (here and throughout the essay all translations are my own unless otherwise indicated); Güntert 1932, especially p. 115. The logical extrapolation of such a position is found in the demands raised by the German Student Union's campaign against "Un-German Spirit" during their book burnings of April–May 1933 (e.g., No. 5: "The Jew can only think jewishly. If he writes in German, he lies"; No. 7: "We demand of the state censor that Jewish works be published only in Hebrew. If they be published in German, they should be characterized as translations" [document published in Poliakov and Wulf 1983: 117–18]). The control of language itself is an elementary form of social power, as will be apparent in the case of India.

15. I believe I now see why: " . . . racism always tends to function *in reverse* . . . : the racial-cultural identity of the 'true nationals' remains invisible, but it is inferred from (and assured by) its opposite, the alleged, quasi-hallucinatory visibility of the 'false nationals': Jews, 'wops,' immigrants . . . " (Balibar 1990: 285).

16. As of April, 1933, 800 professors (out of a total of 7,000) had lost their positions; 85 percent of these were Jews. By 1937, 1684 professors had been dismissed. The Jewish student population dropped from 4,382 in 1933 to 812 in 1938 and zero after November 1938. See Jurt 1991: 125.

17. On the whole question, see, most recently, Sieferle 1987, who is useful principally for his analysis of nineteenth-century theories of race but is otherwise insufficient and sometimes misleading. He also incomprehensibly ignores altogether the work of professional Indologists, Iranists, and Indo-Europeanists during the NS period on the question of "Arier" (as on attitudes toward the Indian Freedom Movement).

18. There are two key figures here. The first is Egon Frhr. von Eickstedt, professor at Breslau. Much of his work focused on the racial history of South Asia: cf. *Rassenkunde und Rassengeschichte der Menschheit*, 1934 (note the encomium in Alsdorf 1942: 4) and the journal he founded in 1935, *Zeitschrift für Rassenkunde und ihre Nachbargebiete*, which carried substantial articles of his own and of others who worked in South Asia, e.g., Heine-Geldern. The second, better known, is Hans F. K. Günther, professor at Jena, later Berlin, who also had a basic subcontinental orientation: cf. especially *Die nordische Rasse bei den Indogermanen Asiens*, 1934, as well as his own journal, *Rasse*, 1934ff. A separate study could be devoted to the "orientalist" dimension of "race-science," in particular its interpreting Indian "caste law" as an expression of racial "hygiene," and adducing India as a warning of the dangers of the "blood chaos" that National Socialism prevented at the eleventh hour (for both themes, see Günther 1936). The ratio *ārya : caṇḍāla* [outcaste, untouchable] :: German : Jew was made already by Nietzsche, cited in Alsdorf 1942: 85.

19. The first, in all its confusion, reads as follows: "'Aryan' (also known as Indo-Germans or Japhites) includes the three branches of the Caucasian (white) race; these may be divided into the western (European), i.e., the Germans, Romans, Greeks, Slavs, Latvians, Celts, Albanians, and the eastern (Asiatic) Aryans, i.e., the Indians (Hindus) and Iranians (Persians, Afghans, Armenians, Georgians, Kurds). 'Non-aryans' are therefore 1) members of the two other races, namely, the Mongolian (yellow) and the Negro (black) races; 2) members of the two other branches of the Caucasian race, namely, the Semites (Jews, Arabs) and Hamites (Berbers). The Finns and Hungarians belong to the Mongolian race, but it is hardly the intention of this law to treat them as non-aryans" (cf. also Sieferle 1987: 461–62). The confusion in the popular mind, however, continued; see for example the article "Nichtarisch oder Jüdisch?" in the anti-Semitic journal *Hammer* (No. 799/800 (1935), pp. 376–77), prompted by the "Wehrgesetz" of 1935, which prohibited non-Aryans from joining the army (the author was worried about the potential exclusion of such "loyal" and "martial" non-Aryans as Finns, Hungarians, and "Moors"). I have looked in vain for any detailed social-historical analysis of the term "Arier" in the NS period. (I would add that it appears incorrect to claim that "Arier," etc. had ceased to be meaningful on the juridical plane after 1935 [Sieferle 1987: 462], though the question requires specialist adjudication. Certainly the process of expropriating Jewish businesses, which begins in earnest after Crystal Night [November 9, 1938], was referred to as "Arisierung," and laws so formulated seem to have been passed as late as September 1941 [Walk 1981: 348]. Anyway, the terminology remained a potent racist shibboleth and constantly appears in official and private documents until the end of the regime.)

20. For an example of this recentering of the notional, see Tal 1980, 1981, and Lacoue-Labarthe and Nancy 1990.

21. This paper was later presented again as a speech before the German Academy at the University of Munich on December 6, 1939, and reprinted in Wüst 1942: 33ff. (the latter collection was favorably reviewed by Frauwallner [1943: "Let us hope . . . that (the book) has the desired effect in scholarly circles and wins as many adherents as possible"]). Some scholars of the period do seem to raise the

issue of the historical validity of the term "arisch" as used in contemporary discourse (for instance Lommel 1934; Krahe 1935), but avoid, or cannot conceive of, any critique.

22. For the contemporary resonance of the term cf. Klemperer 1987: 151–57.

23. According to additional documents from the BDC, the speech was printed and distributed to the SS. Wüst was later to be named director of the SS's research institute "Das 'Ahnenerbe'" (Kater 1974).

24. Especially notable is his drive for institutional dominance in the Indological and Indo-European studies establishment. Wüst for instance got himself appointed—or appointed himself—to the editorship of a number of important journals in these fields including *Wörter und Sachen* (1938), *Wiener Zeitschrift für die Kunde des Morgenlandes* (1939), *Archiv für Religionswissenschaft* (1939). This is of a piece with his attempt to institutionalize and direct popular media coverage of scholarship in general through his short-lived "Deutscher Wissenschaftlicher Dienst" (1940: cf. MA-116/18 HA Wiss. S. 75 in the archives of the Institut für Zeitgeschichte, Munich). His more practical contributions to the NS regime include consultation in the creation of "scientific research institutes" exploiting Hungarian Jewish prisoners in concentration camps; see the memo from Himmler of May 26, 1944 reprinted in Poliakov and Wulf 1983: 319.

25. However we may wish to define "the ideology of the Third Reich"—whether as *völkisch* doctrine or as the strategy of the state for world domination—in neither case would it be correct to say that Alsdorf made no "concessions" to it (Bruhn et al. 1990: ix).

26. "A product of the most serious scholarly research, which is meant to serve contemporary life as well," Richard Schmidt 1939: 546.

27. (1936): *Germanen und Indogermanen: Volkstum, Sprache, Heimat, Kultur. Festschrift für Herman Hirt*, two volumes (with contributions by, among others, von Eickstedt, H. F. K. Günther, Hauer, Reche, and Dumézil but also by Benveniste and Meillet).

28. Contrast Wilhelm Schmidt's claim (in Scherer 1968: 314) that "East-thesis" submissions (placing the *Urheimat* in Asia or Russia, as opposed to Northern Europe) were rejected (p. 313).

29. Koppers et al. 1936. Cf. the review by Otto Reche ("Professor für Rassen- und Völkerkunde, Leipzig"): "This entire edifice of notions is tied up with church dogma [Koppers, a priest, was affiliated with Societas verbi divini in Mödling] and thus assuredly in no way scholarship . . . " (Reche 1940: 17).

30. "The homeland, the race and the culture of a supposed Proto-Indo-German population have been discussed, but this is a population that may never have existed"; "the only thing these people [i.e., speakers of IE] have in common is the fact that their languages belong to the same family . . . " since "'Indo-Germanic' is a purely linguistic notion" (1936: 81, 83; cf. Renfrew 1987: 108–9). Speaking of improbable coincidences and the politics of the *Urheitmatfrage*, I would call attention to the hypothesis recently presented, on the eve of continental unification in the European community, that lays "less emphasis on specific ethnic groups and their supposed migrations," and instead imagines peaceful Indo-European farmers spreading in a gradual, egalitarian, and what seems to be an eth-

nically almost homogeneous "wave of advance" throughout Europe (Renfrew 1987: 288).

31. Schlegel's image did live on, however; the Münster Sanskritist Richard Schmidt could still speak, in a learned journal in 1939, of the ancient Indians as "our ancestors" ("unsere Urahnen," *Wiener Zeitschrift für die Kunde des Morgenlandes* 46: 157; cf. Schmidt 1939: 548, where he refers to Meister Eckhart and Śaṅkara as "race-comrades" [*Rassengenossen*]). The myth of origins still carries on a twilight career among adherents of the new "conservatism," especially on the French right. See especially Jean Haudry, 1981, along with the review that puts this work into perspective, Bernard Sargent 1982. (The intellectual wing of the French right involved here—G.R.E.C.E. *Nouvelle École*, Alain de Benoist—is situated by d'Appollonia 1983).

32. In the most recent reconsideration of the German "intellectual quest" for India, D. Rothermund asserts that "In the Nazi period [German Indology] could survive by virtue of the esoteric character it had acquired. . . . This type of 'inner emigration' was, in fact, the only saving grace for Indologists, because the tradition of the German quest for India was perverted at that time by being pressed into the service of Hitler's ill-conceived racial theory . . . " (1986: 17). I see little evidence of this "esoteric" dimension in the NS period, or of "inner emigration," nor is it in the least self-evident that the racial theory of the NS state constituted a "perversion" of the romantic/idealist quest (rather than, say, its telos).

33. Losemann 1977: 108; see also Kater 1974: 193ff.

34. See *Zeitschrift der deutschen morgenländischen Gesellschaft* 96 (1942): *12ff. The process of *Gleichschaltung* in the German Oriental Society awaits study. It was only in 1938 that the organization actually passed a by-law whereby Orientals, Jews, and anyone else ineligible for "imperial citizenship" were denied membership (*ZDMG* 94 [1940]: *7–8). As far as I know, no history of the DMG exists, and this is a real desideratum for the study of institutional orientalism, especially in the NS and postwar years. Worth noting is the reappearance in the society's postwar membership list of people like Wüst (*ZDMG* 100 [1950] *23), despite apparent "de-Nazification" (cf. *ZDMG* 99 [1950]: 295).

35. At least in view of the generalizations of Kater 1983: 110.

36. This list could probably be expanded with further archival search, to include, for instance, the already mentioned Hermann Güntert, professor of Sanskrit and comparative philology, who according to Maas (1988: 279n.) was installed as a dean in Heidelberg (1933–37) by the "political leadership" (this certainly harmonizes with the essay of his excerpted above, as does Wüst's approval of his editorship of *Wörter u. Sachen* from 1938 on. (Incidentally, locating the Indo-German "Urheimat" in the east was not necessarily a sign of anti-Nazism, as Wolfgang Meid implies [1974: 520].) Also excluded are Indo-Europeanists strictly speaking, who merit a list of their own, starting with W. Porzig (dismissed from the University of Bern for Nazi activities already in the 1920s, he exchanged positions with Debrunner in Jena; he was banned from teaching after the war but rehabilitated in 1951 [Maas 1988: 270n.]).

37. The event that led to this awaits clarification, but for now consult with due caution Alsdorf 1960: 577 (and cf. Morgenroth 1978: 54–55). Lüders continued,

however, to sit on the board of the DMG. It may be noted that the aged Geiger, according to personal papers consulted by Bechert, objected privately to the behavior of Wüst.

38. On the former, see Kater 1974; for the latter, see the documents reproduced in Poliakov and Wulf 1983: 133ff.

39. Von Schroeder, familiar to Indologists as the punctilious editor of the *Kāṭhakasaṃhitā* and *Maitrāyaṇī Saṃhitā*, is also the author of the *The Culmination of the Aryan Mystery in Bayreuth* (Von Schroeder 1911) and of *Houston Stewart Chamberlain, A Life Sketch* (Von Schroeder 1918). His book on aryan religion (Von Schroeder 1914–16), above all the chapter entitled "Die Arier," is a summa of the racialist topoi that were to become staples of NS discourse.

40. In the sense of "ideology" powerfully argued by Thompson 1984.

41. There are exceptions; Guha 1986 is a fine example of sensitivity toward continuities or homologies in colonial and precolonial idioms of domination.

42. A form of Orientalist critique of colonialism in Indian scholarship has produced similar, and in some ways more important repercussions, given their immediacy to political actuality. See for instance Chandra 1984, on the claim that colonialism generated communalism; this is an axiom for Mani (1987: 154, the "emergence [of communalism] is inextricably linked with coloialism"), cf. Dirks (1989: 47–48), and for the most sophisticated and sustained historical argument, Pandey 1990. To a degree Bayly 1985 provides a historical counterargument. His article begins with ca. 1700, the era of Mughal decline; pre-Mughal communalism or religiously coded political mobilization—as evidenced, say, in the Coḷa extirpation of the Jains or in what appears to have been massive destruction of Buddhist sites by Pāñcarātra Vaiṣṇavas in the Kathmandu valley in the eighth century—seems not to have been much studied. I am presently exploring to what degree the *Rāmāyaṇa* can be said to have been constituted as a proto-"communal" text in twelfth-century North India (operationalized via the demonization of the Central Asian invaders).

43. I take it what is meant are not "*Brahmana* texts" in the strict sense but Brahmanical texts, the *dharmasūtras* and so on ("*varṇāshramadharma*" is hardly discussed in the former).

44. These are all in fact components in a very ancient taxonomy of *vyavahāra* (the *vyavahārapadas* or eighteen titles of law), though not all *smṛti* writers include *sahamaraṇa*.

45. Had Lakṣmīdhara dwelt long on the topic, it is likely that we would have encountered also the interpretative principles used by the pro-*sati* faction in Calcutta in the 1820s; for all of them—the hierarchy of texts, the priority of "scripture" to "usage," even the specific axioms that "order of meaning has preference over order of reading"; "non-prohibition constitutes sanction" (pp. 142, 145)—are "traditional," in fact Mīmāṃsā in origin. Whether this makes them less "disingenuous" or "facile" (p. 143), I do not know, but it certainly makes them less colonial.

46. *sahamaraṇānumaraṇayor adhikāraḥ*, p. 635.

47. Washbrook 1988: 83. This article, especially pp. 81–83, effectively summarizes the postcolonial analysis.

48. On the "absolute truth" of the *Rāmāyaṇa* see for example the sixteenth-

century commentator Maheśvaratīrtha ad 2.41.10 vulg. The poem's vision of stratification is reproduced in normative texts continuously at least from the time of the *Āpastambadharmasūtra* 1.1.5-7, "There are four *varṇas*, the brāhmaṇa, kṣatriya, vaiśya, and śūdra; of these, each succeeding is better [*śreyān*] by reason of birth; all but the śūdra . . . are to be initiated and are to study the Veda . . . ; a śūdra is to serve the other *varṇas*."

49. The distinction is usefully drawn and discussed by LaCapra 1983: 30ff., 339ff.

50. Though there seems to be a definite consensus against my view: The new multivolume history of India currently under publication from Cambridge University Press, for example, choses to ignore the problem entirely and begin—Stein's brief monograph on Vijayanagar aside—with the Mughals.

51. Thus also, from a comparative perspective, Mann 1986: 348ff.

52. For an elaboration of this argument, see Pollock 1989.

53. The dedicatory and *praśasti* verses are collected in Vol. I, 47ff. See especially the one that introduces the *Vyavahārakāṇḍa*, 51.

54. The precise nature of the *turuṣkadaṇḍa* remains problematic; most likely it was either a tax levied to defend against Afghan invasions (Smith 1924: 400) or a tax levied on the Afghan settlers in the Gāhaḍavāla dominions (cf. Sten Konow, *Epigraphia Indica* 9: 321).

55. *Epigraphia Indica* 9: 324.

56. I find myself in broad if tentative agreement with the view of the editor of the *nibandha*, K. V. Rangaswami Aiyangar (*Dānakāṇḍa*, Introduction: 16). I don't know enough about the prehistory of the *nibandha* genre to be fully convinced of the adequacy of this explanation, however. Lakṣmīdhara himself cites six earlier compendia, but these are no longer extant.

57. The Mīmāṃsā *nyāya* runs *aprāpte śāstram arthavat* ("Holy word pertains to, communicates, what is not otherwise available, knowable"), and would comprise such things as sacrificing in order to attain heaven.

58. See the elaboration in Pollock 1990.

59. Āpastamba, for example, is very clear about denying Vedic status to injunctions derived from memory or custom that reveal some motive—*karaṇa, hetu* (e.g., 1.4.9)—but at the same time encodes as *rule*-bound action that "A servant who refuses to do the tilling is to be beaten" (2.11.2).

60. Vol. I, Chapter 1, p. 5, citing *Viśvāmitra* (= *Āpastamba* 1.20.7).

61. I now find that W. Halbfass's magnum opus inaugurates just such an analysis (Halbfass 1988: 172ff.). Additional materials are collected in Thapar 1978: 152—92. For the important Buddhist (and Jain) transvaluation of the term *ārya*, see the preliminary remarks in Deshpande 1979: 40ff.; p. 10 and n. 29.

62. Compare Parasher 1983. That such bipolar visions of *ārya* and *mleccha* were actualized in conceptualizing real contacts with others is suggests by the almost contemporaneous Delhi-Siwalik pillar inscription of Vīsaladeva of the Chāhamāna dynasty of Śākambharī (A.D. 1164), which, referring (probably) to the defeat of Khusru Shah, describes the king Vīsaladeva "the god who made Āryāvarta once again true to its name by extirpating the *mlecchas*" (19, 218; cf. *Journal of Indian History* 15 [1936]: 171).

63. Vol. I, p. 49. *Viṣṇu Smṛti* 84.1–2. The same energy vibrates in late medieval representations of the monstrous races, where, for example "Yavanas," that is, Muslims, are viewed as the "*rākṣasas* of the Kali age" (see the Decannese commentators Kataka and Tilaka on *Rām.* 3.3.24 crit. ed.). The plastic arts, especially epic miniatures, provide a visual map of the demonization of various tribal cultures, it may be argued, though detailed analysis in this area remains to be done.

64. *RV* 10.90 is the locus classicus in the Veda; it is explicated in *Manusmṛti* 1.87ff. *Bhagavadgītā* 18.41–42 (cited Vol. 1, p. 9) provides the biology, which is also of course latent in the *RV* passage.

65. This paradigm is elaborated elsewhere by Lakṣmīdhara in his review of *pratiloma* (hypogamous) marriages: the impurity of such a marriage is perpetuated in the offspring; the offspring of a Brahman woman and śūdra man, for instance, exist in a permanent state of impurity, i.e., they are untouchable (*Śuddhikāṇḍa*, p. 28 and introduction p. 14). The genealogy of untouchability needs far more detailed reconsideration; see for now Jha 1986–87.

66. For instance, Dumont 1961, or Delacampagne 1983: 150–58. The best essay to date is Washbrook 1982. (I do not see, however, how one can argue that it is irrelevant whether "race" is defined culturally or biologically—the defining characteristic of "racialism" is its "legitimating social inequality by reference to qualities inherent in different ascriptive communities" [p. 145]—and still go on to claim that traditional Indian society "was not structured around principles . . . of racial domination" [p. 51]. The diachronic base of the essay is also too narrow for so weighty a topic.) There is no necessary causal dependency of racism on nationalism; Balibar points out that the classical racial myths "refer initially not to the nation but to the class, in an aristocratic perspective" (1990: 286).

67. Vol. 2, ch. 16, pp. 265ff.

68. There exist an array of texts treating of *śūdradharma* (e.g., *Śūdrācāraśiromaṇi* of Śeṣa Krishna, *Śūdrakṛtyatattva* of Raghunandana Bhaṭṭācāryya, *Śūdrakamalākara*, etc.), which to my knowledge have received no systematic (or other) analysis. The *Arthaśāstra* excludes caṇḍālas even from *śūdradharma* (3.7.37).

69. *Mati*, that is, "knowledge pertaining to duties and prohibitions with otherworldly ends," according to Lakṣmīdhara.

70. Pp. 380ff.; *Manusmṛti* 4.80–81, Yama and Vasiṣṭa (not traced).

71. The *apaśūdrādhikaraṇa*, *Pūrvamīmāṃsāsūtra* 6.1.25ff., similar but with interesting variations is *Brahmasūtra* 1.3.34ff.

72. *Mīmāṃsānyāyaprakāśa* p. 193.10ff. See also Lariviere 1988, who with some justice wants to extend the meaning of the term to include "responsibility."

73. And they must be built according to ritual injunction, being ritual fires (*Tuptīkā*, pp. 208–9).

74. In technical terminology, the injunction is conditional, not constitutive (*nimittārtha* rather than *prāpika*), 6.1.27.

75. *Pūrvapakṣa* in Śabara ad 6.1.32.

76. "The śūdra shall not recite the Veda" (6.1.29–36). The *Brahmasūtra* seamlessly extends the Mīmāṃsā argument from the prohibition for the śūdra to sacrifice to the prohibition to acquire "sacred knowledge" (*vidyā*) in general. Here the

"right" of the śūdra to have access to "sacred knowledge" is denied on the grounds that this presupposes the right to recite the Veda (*adhyayana*), which in turn presupposes the right to initiation (*upanayana*), something reserved by Vedic injunction to the first three *varṇas*.

77. According to Vācaspati (*Bhāmatī* ad *Brahmasūtra* 1.3.34) and Kumārila (*Tantravārttika* ad 1.3.9, pp. 143.9–10) respectively.

78. Consider the following discussion by the tenth-century Kashmiri logician Bhāsarvajña on the origins of the Jaina scriptures:

"Objection: the scriptures of the Jains and the rest [i.e., the Buddhists] have no instrumental purpose and are accepted by many people, too [two arguments use to support the transcendence-claim of the Veda], and so should be valid as scripture. Answer: Not so, because they were accepted for other reasons. Some śūdras once heard about the great good fortune of learning and teaching the Vedas, and they became desirous of learning the Vedas. But of course they had no authorization to learn the Vedas, and consequently had no chance of doing so. Then certain ambitious people like the Jina convinced these śūdras that there was great benefit to be had in learning the "scriptures" that they themselves had composed, and the śūdras accordingly did so. They encouraged other śūdras to the same end, and these others, including some brahmins and the other [higher social orders] who, being both stupid and crushed by poverty, were deluded into thinking they could thereby end their troubles. That is how such "scriptures" achieved prominence—not, like the Vedas, by being committed to memory even by people [who have no material interests whatever and so] live in the forest, and who are not excluded from participating in any scriptural tradition; by being taught by brahmans and brahmans alone, and learned only by the three higher social orders. Consequently the question of the authority of the "scriptures" of the Jains and the others simply does not arise (*Nyāyasārabhūṣaṇa*, p. 393).

79. See for instance the "*vidhi*" cited by Vedāntadeśika ad *Bhagavadgītā* 18.44 (hemānte śūdram eva ca [dīkṣayet], " . . . and one should initiate a śūdra in the winter").

80. A further useful comparison is with the slave codes of the U. S. South, which also included antiliteracy laws and substantial inequalities of criminal sanctions. These codes also provide us with a sobering reminder of how difficult it is to distinguish "actuality" from "sentiment" in legal materials only five generations removed from us. See Tushnet 1981: esp. 18ff.

81. In the course of the recent *Historikerstreit* in West Germany, Joachim Fest argued that the category "high culture" itself (as a condition of the singularity of the Holocaust) is inadmissible because, "taken strictly, it perpetuates the old Nazi distinction that there are higher and lower peoples" (1987: 104–5). What Fest calls "die alte Nazi-Unterscheidung" is in fact the belief that knowledge and truth are valuable for human existence, the very belief behind Fest's own intervention. For if the relationship of NS state terror and German high culture is not a real problem for us to study—if knowledge and truth are not somehow meaningful values for

life—then there is no point to any reevaluation of the Nazi state, let alone to Fest's particular argument.

82. Among only the most recent: the revelations about Paul de Man should require no reference; for Eliade, see Berger 1989; for Dumézil, Ginzburg 1985 is the first installment in a history that others are now writing. As for the standard fall-back position that seeks to draw a boundary marker between life and work, Marcuse's letter to Heidegger merits citing: "But we cannot make the separation between Heidegger the philosopher and Heidegger the man, for it contradicts your own philosophy" (Wolin 1991: 29; letter dated 1947). This may easily be extrapolated to other humanistic enterprises.

83. This is perfectly well known to us all at the theoretical level. So too is the danger of self-cancellation of rhetorical or ideology critique, or of reducing history to sheer textuality. But what, then, do we do in the practice of our own work? How many of us can follow through on the implications of all this in the execution of our own scholarship? How many confront the interests that inform our own analysis of interests, or disinter the master trope buried within our own historiography? It is one thing to acclaim White's work (for "dislodg[ing] the primacy both of the real and of the ideal") at the level of theory (Said 1989: 221), but quite another to live out its consequences in the practical task of writing a history of, say, orientalism (or "deep orientalism"). Discontinuity between the two is rather the rule.

84. See Silbey and Sarat 1987, and Trubek and Esser forthcoming (especially pp. 71ff.)

85. British colonialism gave a hearing to voices of the despised in a way pre-British colonialism did not, thus enabling the sort of recuperation that Guha performs for the Doms on the basis of Brigg's ethnography (Guha 1985).

86. The quotes are found in *India Today*, November 15, 1987: 75 and Joshi 1986: 151 respectively.

References

SANSKRIT TEXTS

Kṛtyakalpataru of Bhaṭṭa Lakṣmīdhara. Ed. K. V. Rangaswami Aiyangar. Baroda: Oriental Institute, 1941–1979.
Manusmṛtir Medhātithibhāṣyālaṃkṛtā. Ed. M. Mor. Calcutta: Udayacal Press, 1967. Gurumandala Series.
Mīmāṃsādarśanam. Ed. K. V. Abhyankar: Pune: Anandasrama Press, 1970. Anandasrama Sanskrit Series (*sūtras* cited by number; *Tantravārttika* and *Tuptīkā* by page and line number).
Mīmāṃsānyāyaprakāśa. Ed. V. S. Abhyankar. Pune: Bhandarkar Oriental Research Institute, 1972.

Nyāyasārabhūṣaṇa of Bhāsarvajña. Ed. Swami Yogindrananda. Banaras: Saddarsana Prakasan Pratisthan, 1968.

TEXTS OF THE NATIONAL SOCIALIST PERIOD

Alsdorf, Ludwig. 1942. *Deutsch-Indische Geistesbeziehungen*. Heidelberg, Berlin, Magdeburg: Kurt Vowinckel Verlag. Vol. 7 of *Indien Handbuch*, ed. Kurt Vowinckel.

Frauwallner, Erich. 1939. "Der arische Anteil an der indischen Philosophie." *Wiener Zeitschrift für die Kunde des Morgenlands* 46: 267–91

———. 1943. Review of Wüst 1942. *Orientalistische Literaturzeitung* 7/8: 269–70.

———. 1944. "Die Bedeutung der indischen Philosophie." In Schaeder 1944, pp. 158–69.

Günther, Hans, F. K. 1936. "Indogermanentum und Germanentum, rassenkundlich betrachtet." In *Germanen und Indogermanen: Volkstum, Sprache, Heimat, Kultur*. Festschrift für Herman Hirt, ed. H. Arntz. Heidelberg: Winter: 317–40.

Güntert, Hermann. 1932. *Deutscher Geist: Drei Vorträge*. Buhl-Baden: Konkordia.

———. 1938. "Neue Zeit—neues Ziel." *Wörter und Sachen* I (Vol. 19): 1–11.

Harder, Richard. 1942. "Franz Bopp und die Indogermanistik." *Nationalsozialistische Monatshefte* 13: 751–61.

Hauer, J. Wilhelm. 1934. *Eine indo-arische Metaphysik des Kampfes und der Tat: Die Bhagavad Gita in neuer Sicht*. Stuttgart: Kohlhammer.

———. 1937. *Glaubensgeschichte der Indogermanen*. Vol. 1. Stuttgart: Kohlhammer.

Koppers, Wilhelm et al., eds. 1936. *Die Indogermanen- und Germanenfrage: Neue Wege zu ihrer Lösung*. Salzburg: Anton Pustet. Institut für Völkerkunde an der Universität Wien. Weiner Beiträge zur Kulturgeschichte und Linguistik (with contributions by W. V. Brandenstein, V. Gordon Childe, and others).

Krahe, Hans. 1935. "Die alten Arier." *Geistige Arbeit* 2, 23: 6.

Lommel, Hermann. 1934. "Von arischer Religion." *Geistige Arbeit* 2, 23: 5–6.

———. 1935. *Die Alten Arier: Von Art und Adel Ihrer Götter*. Frankfurt a.M.: Klostermann.

———. 1939. *Der arische Kriegsgott*. Frankfurt a.M.: Klostermann.

Reche, Otto. 1940. Review of Koppers et al. 1936. *Orientalistische Literaturzeitung* 1/2: 11–18.

Schaeder, Hans Heinrich, ed., 1944. *Der Orient in Deutscher Forschung*. Vorträge der Berliner Orientalistentagung. Herbst 1942. Leipzig: Harrassowitz, 1944.

Schmidt, Richard. 1939. Review of Hauer 1937. *Orientalistische Literaturzeitung* 8/9: 546–48.

Schroeder, Leopold von. 1911. *Die Vollendung des arischen Mysteriums in Bayreuth*. Munich: Lehmann.

———. 1914–16. *Arische Religion*. Leipzig: Hässel.

———. 1918. *Houston Stewart Chamberlain: Ein Abriss seines Lebens auf Grund eigener Mitteilungen*. Munich: Lehmann.

Thieme, Paul. 1938. *Der Fremdling im Rigveda*. Leipzig: Brockhaus.

Wüst, Walther. 1934. "Deutsche Frühzeit und arische Geistesgeschichte." *Süddeutsche Monatshefte* 31, 12: 697–739.

———. 1937. "Des Führers Buch 'Mein Kampf' als Spiegel arischer Weltanschauung." Typescript, Berlin Document Center.

———. 1942. *Indogermanisches Bekenntnis*. Berlin-Dahlem: Das Ahnenerbe.

Zimmerman, Karl. 1933. *Die geistigen Grundlagen des Nationalsozialismus*. Leipzig: Quelle und Mayer (n.d.).

OTHER TEXTS

Alsdorf, Ludwig. 1960. "Die Indologie in Berlin von 1821–1945." *Studium berolinense*. Berlin: de Gruyter, 567–80.

d'Appollonia, Ariane Chebel. 1988. *L'Extrême-droite en France: de Maurras à Le Pen*. Brussels: Éditions Complèxe. "Questions au XXᵉ siècle."

Balibar, Étienne. 1990. "Paradoxes of Universality." In David Theo Goldberg, ed., *Anatomy of Racism*. Minneapolis: University of Minnesota Press, 283–94.

Bayly, Christopher A. 1985. "The Pre-History of 'Communalism'? Religious Conflict in India, 1700–1860." *Modern Asian Studies* 19: 177–203.

Berger, Adriana. 1989. "Fascism and Religion in Rumania." *Annals of Scholarship* 6,4: 455–65 (cf. also *Estudios de Asia y Africa* 85 [1991]: 345–58).

Bruhn, Klaus et al. 1990. *Ludwig Alsdorf and Indian Studies*. Delhi: Motilal Banarsidass.

Cannon, Garland. 1970. *The Letters of Sir William Jones*. Oxford: Clarendon Press.

Carey, William and Joshua Marshman. 1806–10. *The Ramayana of Valmeeki*. 3 vols. Serampore: Baptist Mission Press.

Chandra, Bipan. 1984. *Communalism in Modern India*. New Delhi: Vikas.

Cohn, Bernard S. 1987. *An Anthropologist Among the Historians and Other Essays*. Delhi/New York: Oxford University Press.

Delacampagne, Christian. 1983. *L'Invention du racisme: Antiquité et Moyen Âge*. Paris: Fayard.

Deshpande, Madhav. 1979. *Sociolinguistic Attitudes in India*. Ann Arbor, MI: Karoma.

Diner, Dan, ed. 1987. *Ist der Nationalsozialismus Geschichte? Zur Historisierung und Historikerstreit*. Frankfurt: Fischer.

Dirks, Nicholas B. 1987. *The Hollow Crown: Ethnohistory of an Indian Kingdom*. Cambridge: Cambridge University Press.

———. 1989. "The Invention of Caste: Civil Society in Colonial India." *Social Analysis* 25: 42–52.

Duby, Georges. 1974. "Histoire sociale et idéologies des sociétés." Jacques le Goff and Pierre Nora, eds. *Faire de l'histoire, I: Nouveaux problèmes*, Paris: Gallimard, 203–30.

Dumont, Louis. 1961. "Caste, Racism and 'Stratification': Reflections of a Social Anthropologist." *Contributions to Indian Sociology* 5: 20–43.

Fest, Joachim. 1987. "Die geschuldete Erinnerung." In *Historikerstreit*. Munich: Piper, 100–112.

Fox, Richard. 1985. *Lions of the Punjab: Culture in the Making.* Berkeley: University of California Press.

Freeman, Edward Augustus. 1879. "Race and Language." In Freeman, *Historical Essays.* Third Series. London: Macmillan, 173–226.

Geissen, I. 1988. *Geschichte des Rassismus.* Frankfurt: Suhrkamp.

Giddens, Anthony. 1979. *Central Problems in Social Theory: Action, Structure, and Contradiction in Social Analysis.* Berkeley: University of California Press.

———. 1985. *The Constitution of Society: Outline of the Theory of Structuration.* Berkeley: University of California Press.

Ginzburg, Carlo. 1985. "Mythologie germanique et Nazisme: Sur un ancien livre de Georges Dumézil." *Annales: ESC:* 695–715.

Guha, Ranajit. 1985. "The Career of an Anti-God in Heaven and on Earth." In Asok Mitra, ed., *The Truth Unites: Essays in Tribute to Samar Sen.* Calcutta: Subarnarekha.

———. 1986. "Idioms of Dominance and Subordination in Colonial India." Paper written for the Second Subaltern Studies Conference. Cf. Ranajit Guha, ed., *Subaltern Studies: Writings on South Asian History and Society,* vol. IV. New Delhi: Oxford University Press, 1989, 232ff.

Halbfass, Wilhelm. 1988. *India and Europe: An Essay in Understanding.* Albany: State University of New York Press.

Haudry, Jean. 1981. *Les Indo-Européens.* Paris: P.U.F., "Que sais-je?"

Haug, W. F., ed. 1989. *Deutsche Philosophen 1933.* Berlin: Argument. Sonderband 165.

Heesterman, Jan. 1978. "Veda and Dharma." In Wendy Doniger O'Flaherty and J. Duncan M. Derrett, eds., *The Concept of Duty in South Asia.* Delhi: Vikas, 80–94.

———. 1981. "Veda and Society." *Studia Orientalia* 50: 50–64.

Herf, Jeffrey. 1984. *Reactionary Modernism.* Cambridge: Cambridge University Press.

Jay, Martin. 1988. *Fin-de-Siècle Socialism.* New York: Routledge.

Jha, Vivekanand. 1986–87. "Caṇḍāla and the Origin of Untouchability." *Indian Historical Review* 13,1–2: 1–36.

Johnson, Richard. 1986. "What Is Cultural Studies Anyway?" *Social Text* 16: 38–80.

Joshi, Barbara, ed. 1986. *Untouchable: Voices of the Dalit Liberation Movement.* London: Zed Books.

Jurt, Joseph. 1991. "La Romanistique allemande sous le Troisième Reich: attentistes, résistants, émigrés." *Actes de la Recherche en Sciences Sociales* 86/87 (March): 135–28.

Kater, Michael. 1974. *Das "Ahnenerbe" der SS 1933–1945.* Stuttgart: DVA.

———. 1983. *The Nazi Party: A Social Profile of Members and Leaders, 1919–45.* Cambridge, MA: Harvard University Press.

Klemperer, Victor. 1987. *LTI: Notizbuch eines Philologen.* Leipzig: Reclam. (First published 1947).

Lacoue-Labarthe, Philippe and Jean-Luc Nancy. 1990. "The Nazi Myth." *Critical Inquiry* 16,2: 291–312.

LaCapra, Dominick. 1983. *Rethinking Intellectual History: Texts, Contexts, Language.* Ithaca, NY: Cornell University Press.

Lariviere, Richard. 1988. "Adhikāra—Right and Responsibility." In M. A. Jazayery et al., eds., *Languages and Cultures: Studies in Honor of Edgar C. Polomé*. Berlin, New York: De Gruyter.

Laurens, Henri. 1988. "Le Concept de race dans le *Journal Asiatique* du XIXe siècle." *Journal Asiatique* 276: 371–81.

Leopold, Joan. 1974. "British Applications of the Aryan Theory of Race to India, 1850–1870." *English Historical Review* 89: 578–603.

Losemann, Volker. 1977. *Nationalsozialismus und Antike: Studien zur Entwicklung des Faches alte Geschichte 1933–45*. Hamburg: Hoffmann u. Campe.

Löwith, Karl. 1986. *Mein Leben in Deutschland vor und nach 1933: Ein Bericht*. Stuttgart: Metzler.

Lyotard, Jean-François. 1987. "Notes on Legitimation." *Oxford Literary Review* 9: 106–18.

Maas, Utz. 1988. "Die Entwicklung der deutschsprachigen Sprachwissenschaft von 1900 bis 1950. Zwischen Professionalisierung und Politisierung." *Zeitschrift für Germanistische Linguistik* 6: 253–90.

Mani, Lata. 1987. "Contentious Traditions: The Debate on SATI in Colonial India." *Cultural Critique*: 119–56.

Mann, Michael. 1986. *The Sources of Social Power*, Vol. 1: *A History of Power from the Beginning to A.D. 1760*. Cambridge: Cambridge University Press.

Meid, Wolfgang. 1974. "Hermann Güntert: Leben und Werk." In *Antiquitatis Indogermanicae, Gedenkschrift für Hermann Güntert*. Innsbruck: Innsbrucker Beiträge zur Sprachwissenschaft.

Morgenroth, Wolfgang. 1978. "Sanskrit Studies in Berlin." In *Sanskrit Studies in the G.D.R.* Edited by the Centre of Sanskrit Studies in the G.D.R. Berlin: Humboldt University, Institute of Asian Sciences.

Oppenberg, Ursula. 1965. *Quellenstudien zu Friedrich Schlegels Übersetzungen aus dem Sanskrit*. Marburg: Elwert. Marburger Beiträge zur Germanistik, 7.

Pandey, Gyanendra. 1990. *The Construction of Communalism in Colonial North India*. New Delhi: Oxford University Press.

Parasher, Aloka. 1983. "Attitudes Towards the Mleccha in Early Northern India—up to ca. A.D. 600." *Indian Historical Review* 9,1–2,: 1–30.

Perlin, Frank. 1983. "Proto-Industrialization and Pre-Colonial South Asia." *Past and Present* 98: 30–95.

Poliakov, Léon and Joseph Wulf. 1983. *Das Dritte Reich und seine Denker*. Berlin: Ullstein. (First published 1959.)

Pollock, Sheldon. 1989. "Mīmāṃsā and the Problem of History in Traditional India." *Journal of the American Oriental Society* 109,3: 603–11.

———. 1990. "From Discourse of Ritual to Discourse of Power in Traditional India." *Journal of Ritual Studies* 4,2: 291–320.

Raheja, Gloria Goodwin. 1988. "India: Caste, Kingship, and Dominance Reconsidered." *Annual Review of Anthropology* 17: 497–523.

Renfrew, Colin. 1987. *Archaeology and Language: The Puzzle of Indo-European Origins*. Cambridge: Cambridge University Press.

Rhys Davids, T. W. 1903–4. "Oriental Studies in England and Abroad." *Proceedings of the British Academy*: 183–97.

Ringer, Fritz. 1969. *Decline of the German Mandarins*. Cambridge, MA: Harvard University Press.

Rocher, Rosane. 1968. *Alexander Hamilton 1762–1824: A Chapter in the Early History of Sanskrit Philology*. New Haven, CT: American Oriental Society.

Römer, Ruth. 1985. *Sprachwissenschaft und Rassenideologie in Deutschland*. Munich: Fink.

Roth, Fr. Heinrich. 1988. *The Sanskrit Grammar and Manuscripts of Fr. Heinrich Roth* [1620–1668]. Ed. Arnulf Camps and Jean-Claude Muller. Leiden: J. R. Brill.

Rothermund, Dietmar. 1986. *The German Intellectual Quest for India*. Delhi: Manohar.

Said, Edward. 1982. "Opponents, Audiences, Constituencies and Community." *Critical Inquiry* 9; reprinted in H. Foster, ed., *The Anti-Aesthetic*, Port Townsend, WA: Bay Press, 135–59.

———. 1985. "Orientalism Reconsidered." *Race and Class* 27: 1–15. Reprinted in Francis Barker, P. Hulme, M. Iversen, and D. Loxley, eds., *Literature, Philosophy, and Theory. Papers from the Essex Conference, 1976–84*. London: Methuen.

———. 1989. "Representing the Colonized: Anthropology's Interlocutors." *Critical Inquiry* 15,2: 205–25.

Sargent, Bernard. 1982. "Penser—et mal penser—les Indo-Européens." *Annales: ESC* 37: 669–81.

Scherer, Anton, ed. 1988. *Die Urheimat der Indogermanen*. Darmstadt: Wissenschaftliche Buchgesellschaft.

Schwab, Raymond. 1950. *La Renaissance orientale*. Paris: Payot.

von See, Klaus. 1970. *Deutsche Germanen-Ideologie*. Frankfurt: Athenaum.

Sieferle, Rolf Peter. 1987. "Indien und die Arier in der Rassentheorie." *Zeitschrift für Kulturaustausch* 37: 444–67.

Silbey, Susan S. and Austin Sarat. 1987. "Critical Traditions in Law and Society Research." *Law and Society Review* 21: 165–74.

Smith, Vincent A. [1924]. *Early history of India from 600 BC to the Muhammedan Conquest Including the Invasion of Alexander the Great*. 4th ed. Oxford: Clarendon Press, 1957: reprint 1984.

Stein, Burton. 1985. "Reapproaching Vijayanagara." In Robert E. Frykenberg and Pauline Kolenda, eds., *Studies of South India: An Anthology of Recent Research and Scholarship*. Madras/New Delhi: New Era/AIIS.

Steiner, George. 1971. *In Bluebeard's Castle: Some Notes Towards the Redefinition of Culture*. New Haven, CT: Yale University Press.

Stern, Fritz (1961). *The Politics of Cultural Despair: A Study in the Rise of the Germanic Ideology*. Berkeley: University of California Press.

Tal, Uriel. 1981. "On Structures of Political Theology and Myth in Germany Prior to the Holocaust." In Yehuda Bauer and Nathan Rosenstreich, eds., *The Holocaust as Historical Experience*, 43–74. New York and London: Holmes and Meier.

———. "Nazism as a 'Political Faith'." *Jerusalem Quarterly* 15 (1980): 70–90.

Thapar, Romila. 1975. "Ethics, Religion, and Social Protest in the First Millennium B.C. in Northern India." *Daedalus* 104.2.

———. 1978. *Ancient Indian Social History: Some Interpretations*. Delhi: Orient Longman.

Thompson, John B. 1984. *Studies in the Theory of Ideology*. Berkeley: University of California Press.

Trubek, David M. and John Esser. Forthcoming. "'Critical Empiricism' in American Legal Studiese: Paradox, Program, or Pandora's Box?" *Law and Social Inquiry*.

Trubetskoy, Nikolai S. 1939. "Gedanken über das Indogermanenproblem." *Acta Linguistica* 1: 81–89.

Tushnet, Mark. 1981. *The American Law of Slavery, 1810–1860: Considerations of Humanity and Interest*. Princeton, NJ: Princeton University Press.

Venkatraman, R. 1988. Centenary address at Adyar Library. *Adyar Library Bulletin* 52.

Verpoorten, Jean-Marie. 1987. "Le Droit de l'Adhyayana selon la Mīmāṃsā." *Indo-Iranian Journal* 30: 23–30.

Walk, Joseph, ed. 1981. *Das Sonderrecht für die Juden im NS-Staat*. Heidelberg: Mueller.

Washbrook, D. A. 1982. "Ethnicity and Racialism in Colonial Indian Society." In Robert Ross, ed., *Racism and Colonialism: Essays on Ideology and Social Structure*. The Hague: Nijhoff.

———. 1988. "Progress and Problems: South Asian Economic and Social History c. 1720–1860." *Modern Asian Studies* 22: 57–96.

Weber, Max. 1984. *Wissenschaft als Beruf*. 7th ed. Berlin: Duncker and Humbolt.

Wilkins, Charles, trans. 1785. *The Bhagavat-Geeta or Dialogues of Kreeshna and Arjoon*. London: C. Nourse. Facsimile reprint Gainesville, FL: Scholars' Facsimiles and Reprints, 1959.

Willson, A. Leslie. 1964. *A Mythical Image: The Ideal of India in German Romanticism*. Durham, NC: Duke University Press.

Wolin, Richard, trans. 1991. "Herbert Marcuse and Martin Heidegger: An Exchange of Letters." *New German Critique* 53: 28–32.

Young, Robert. 1990. *White Mythologies: Writing History and the West*. London and New York: Routledge.

Gayatri Chakravorty Spivak

4. The Burden of English

What I have called a "new orientalism" in the discipline of English constructs an object of study called "third world" or "postcolonial" literature. In this essay I suggest some ways in which this interested construction can be actively undone in the teaching of English—the "burden" of English—in India.

I use the word "burden" in at least its two chief senses. First, as the content of a song or account: in this case, expanding the metaphor, the import of the task of teaching and studying English in the colonies. And, second, as a singular load to carry, in a special way.

I am speaking not of English language policy but of the teaching, specifically, of English literature. Let me start with a passage from *Decolonizing the Mind* by the Kenyan writer Ngugi wa Th'iongo to show how much, in spite of obvious differences, the predicament of the teaching of English literature in postcolonial India has in common with the situation, say, in postcolonial Kenya:[1]

> [A] lot of good work on Kenyan and African languages has been done at the Department of Linguistics and African languages at the University of Nairobi. . . . They . . . acknowledge the reality of there being three languages for each child in Kenya, a reality which many patriotic and democratic Kenyans would not argue should be translated into social and official policy. Kiswahili would be the all-Kenya national and official language; the other nationality languages would have their rightful places in the schools; and English would remain Kenya people's language of international communication. But . . . I am not dealing so much with the language policies as with the language practice of African writers.[2]

I, too, am dealing with practice, not policies. But I am not dealing with the language practice of Indian writers either. To repeat, my topic here is the situation of the Indian teachers of English.

What is the basic difference between teaching a second language as an instrument of communication and teaching the same language so that the student can appreciate literature? It is certainly possible to argue that in the most successful cases the difference is not easy to discern. But there is a certain difference in orientation between the language classroom and the literature classroom. In the former, the goal is an active and reflexive use of the mechanics of the language. In the latter, the goal is at least to shape the mind of the student so that it can resemble the mind of the so-called implied reader of the literary text, even when that is a historically distanced cultural fiction.

The figure of an implied reader is constructed within a consolidated system of cultural representation. The appropriate culture in this context is the one supposedly indigenous to the literature under consideration. In our case, the culture of a vague space called Britain, even England, in its transaction with Europeanness (meaning, of course, *western* Europe), Hellenism and Hebraism, the advent of Euramericanism, the trendiness of Commonwealth literature, and the like. Our ideal student of British literature must so internalize this play of culturel self-representation that she can, to use the terms of the most naive kind of literary pedagogy, "relate to the text," "identify" with it. However naive these terms, they describe the subtlest kind of cultural and epistemic transformation, a kind of upward race mobility, an entry, however remote, into a geopolitical rather than merely national "Indian"-ness. It is from this base that R. K. Narayan can speak of "English In India" as if it were a jolly safari arranged by some better-bred version of the India Tourist Board; conversely, it is also on this base that a critical study of colonial discourse can be built.[3]

It is with this in mind that many decolonized intellectuals feel that the straightforward ideal of teaching English literature in the theater of decolonization continues the process of producing an out-of-date British Council style colonial bourgeoisie in a changed global context.

I am not suggesting for a moment that, given the type of student who chooses English as a field of study in the general Indian context of social opportunity (whatever that might be), this kind of ideological production is successfully achieved. The demand for a "general cultural participant" in the colonies has at any rate changed with the dismantling of actual territorial imperialism. Today, the student of English literature who is there because no other more potentially lucrative course of study is open to him is alienated from his work in a particular way.

It cannot be ignored that there is a class argument lurking here, although it is considerably changed from my student days in the mid- to late 1950s. The reasons why a person who obviously takes no pleasure in

English texts chooses English Honors are too complex to explore here. At any rate, the class value of the choice of English Honors is gendered, and is different according to the hierarchy of institutions—in the metropolitan, urban, suburban, and rural centers. The same taxonomy as it operates among students of English literature as a Pass subject, and the teacher's accommodation within it as Brit. Lit. becomes less and less normative, are much more demographically and politically interesting. I have not the skills to study this area and so will turn to a more literary-critical topic and return to the "implied reader."

The implied reader is imagined, even in the most simple reading, according to rudimentary or sophisticated hypotheses about persons, places, and times. You cannot make sense of anything written or spoken without at least implicitly assuming that it was destined for you, that you are its implied reader. When this sense of latent destiny of the texts of a literary tradition is developed along disciplinary lines, even the students (mostly women) who come to English studies in a self-consciously purposive way—all students at elite institutions would have to be included here—might still be open, under the best circumstances, to an alienating cultural indoctrination that is out of step with the historical moment. This becomes all the more dubious when the best of them become purveyors of native culture abroad.

I should like to look first at a few literary figurations of this alienation. I want next to plot some ways of negotiating with the phenomenon. As I have already suggested, this alienation is a poison *and* a medicine, a base on which both elitism and critique can be built. The institutional curriculum can attempt to regulate its use and abuse.

I will discuss a few literary figurations of the gradual cultural alienation that might become a persistent accompaniment to the successful teaching of English literature in India. I employ the word "figure" here from the word "figurative" as opposed to "literal." When a piece of prose reasonably argues a point, we understand this as its *literal* message. When it advances ths point through its form, images, and metaphors, and indeed its general rhetoricity, we call it figuration or figuring forth. Rhetoric in this view is not mere *alamkāra*. The literal and the figurative depend on each other even as they interrupt each other. They can be defined apart but they make each other operate.

Indeed, literature might be the best complement to ideological transformation. The successful reader learns to identify implicitly with the value system figured forth by literature through learning to manipulate the figures, rather than through (or in addition to) working out the argument explicitly and literally, with a view to reasonable consent. Literature buys your assent in an almost clandestine way, and therefore it is an excellent instrument for a slow transformation of the mind, for good or for ill, as medicine or as poison, perhaps always a bit of both. The teacher must negotiate and make visible what is merely clandestine.

To emphasize my point that the assent the implied reader gives to literature is more than merely reasonable, indeed perhaps clandestine, my first example is a text where I am perhaps myself the type-case. To make of "myself," written into a cultural text, the example of alienating assent is a direct challenge to the hegemonic notion of the "willing suspension of disbelief," still an active orthodoxy coming via such influential figures as the Anglo-American T. S. Eliot and I. A. Richards, and the Euramerican Herbert Marcuse.

The text is the short story "Didi" (1895) or "The Elder Sister" by Rabindranath Tagore.[4] It is not a text written in English, although many of you have read it in a rather indifferent English translation. My point here is to illustrate how the implied reader is drawn into patterns of cultural value as she assents to a text and says "yes" to its judgments, in other words, as she reads it with pleasure. When we teach our students to read with pleasure texts where the implied reader is culturally alien and hegemonic, the assent might bring a degree of alienation.[5]

It is a simple story. Shoshi was the only daughter of an elderly couple. Her husband Joygopal was hoping to inherit their property. The elderly couple had a son in late middle age. After their death, Shoshi takes her orphaned infant brother to her bosom almost in preference to her own sons. Joygopal, enraged by the loss of his inheritance, does everything to take it away from the orphan boy and indeed tries to precipitate his death by neglecting a serious illness. At this point, the English magistrate for the area comes on tour. Shoshi delivers her brother over to the magistrate. She soon dies mysteriously and is cremated overnight.

I have read this story many times. I am not only its implied reader, but its *successful* implied reader. Even after all these readings, my throat catches at the superb sentimental ending: "Shoshi had given her word to her brother at parting, we will meet again. I don't know where the word was kept" (p. 290). This assent is so strong that the analysis of it that I will now begin and that I have performed before cannot seriously interfere with it. This is why literature is such an excellent vehicle of ideological transformation—for good or for ill, as medicine or as poison.

Literature, for women of any class and inclination (*pravritti*), is a major ingredient in the centering of the subject that says "yes," first to reading, and then to reading something, so that more of that subject can be consolidated and sedimented; so that it can go on saying "yes" indefinitely. (There are different systems of representation that facilitate this centering for different classes or *varnas*, different inclinations. And the weave—the *text*-ile—of the system is interrupted with the patchwork of intervention and contingency. To give an example of a different class, a different history, a different set of inclinations: it is "religion" thrown into the potential sign-system of "citizenship" as concept and metaphor that wins the assent of the young woman whose class-family *pravritti* insert her into the Rashtriya Sevika Samiti.)

How then is my assent given to this story? To what do I assent? How am I, or indeed how *was* I, historically constructed as its implied reader so that I was able to read it with pleasure within my cultural self-representation?

Many of Tagore's short stories are *about* emancipated women. This story is about a village woman whose love for her brother emancipates her to the extent that she can see that the impartial white colonial administrator will be a better *ma-baap* than her self-interested Indian kin. Yet, as a woman, she cannot choose to give herself over to him. Does she choose to remain behind? Or is she, for herself, a prisoner of the patriarchal system from which she delivers her brother by assigning the Englishman as his father? (This is, of course, a central patriarchal theme, this giving of the name of the father to the Englishman, for the issue is inheritance and the passage of property.) At any rate, the implied reader, whose position I occupy for the moment as the daughter of upper middle-class female emancipation in urban Bengal, cannot be sure whether Shoshi chooses to remain with or is a prisoner of patriarchy, and, indeed, still cannot be sure where she stand within this situation. This must remain what Meenakshi Mukherjee has called an "interesting but elusive and unverifiable statement" for the moment. I will speak of the thrill of ambivalence later. Here all I need to say is that, in order to assent to the story, to derive pleasure from a proper reading, one must somehow see the entire colonial system as a way out of indigenous patriarchy.[6] I have written elsewhere about the cultural politics of this conviction in the matter of the abolition of the self-immolation of widows in 1829.[7]

In most of his prose writing, Rabindranath Tagore is not simply telling a story or making a point but also fashioning a new Bengali prose. You will therefore accept the suggestion that the texture of the levels of prose plays a strong part in the fabrication of the implied reader's assent. In "Didi," Tagore endows only Shoshi with full-fledged subjectivity. It is in the service of building that subject that Tagore deploys that stunning mixture of Sanskritized and colloquial Bengali that marks his writing of this period.

There is some cultural discrepancy in creating Shoshi as the subject-agent of a romantic love or *prem* that is still not the legitimate model of the cementing emotion of the institution of the Indian marriage. Rabindranath brings this about through an expert manipulation of the model of *biraho* or love-in-absence abundantly available in classical Sanskrit. Any careful reader will see the marks of this in the construction of Shoshi's subjectivity.

The discrepancy involved in the Sanskritization of Shoshi's subjectivity as the agent of *prem* is never treated ironically by Tagore. It is in the interest of constructing Shoshi as the subject or agent of *sneho* or affection that a benevolent irony makes its appearance, but always only at the expense of her brother Nilmoni. There are many instances of this. I will quote a tiny fragment simply to remind myself of the pleasure of the text:

কুশকায় রুংসমুখ গম্ভীরমুখ শ্যামবর্ণ (ছেলেটী)

This fantastic collection of epithets, reading which it is almost impossible to depart from pure Sanskrit phonetics, is a measure of the registers of irony and seriousness with which Tagore can play the instrument of his prose. The available English translation, "the heavy-pated, grave-faced, dusky child," is, of course, hopeless at catching these mechanics.

Why read a high-culture vernacular text as we think of the burden of teaching English? Let us backtrack. The goal of *teaching* such a thing as literature is epistemic: transforming the way in which objects of knowledge are constructed. One such object, perhaps the chief object, is the human being, inevitably gendered. It is always through such epistemic transformations that we begin to approximate the implied reader. In our case, the approximation is mediated by the new vernacular literatures secreted by the encounter described, for this writer with a profound imperialist irony, as "the Bengal Renaissance." That particular mediation has been commented on ad nauseam and is indeed a cliché of Indian cultural history. Like most clichés, this one has become part of the "truth," of Indian cultural self-representation. And in the fabrication of this truth, Tagore's role is crucial.

Some of Tagore's most significant epistemic meddling is with women.

Women constituted by, and constituting, such "minds" become the culturally representative "implied reader." Therefore the problem of the teaching of English literature is not separated from the development of the colonial subject. And as women are notoriously the unfixed part of cultural subjectivity as it is represented by men, the construction of the feminine subject in colonial vernacular literature can give us a sense of the classroom molding of minds preserved in literary form. To read vernacular colonial literature in this way, as preparing the ground for, as it is prepared by, British literature in the colonies, is to challenge the contrast often made, in "western" colonial discourse studies, between western literature as "central" and third world literature—in this case "Indian" (!)—as "marginal" or "emergent." Expanding Ashis Nandy's idea of the "intimate enemy," or my own notion of "violating enablement," it seems more productive to consider the heterogeneity on both sides.[8]

In order to make systemic changes we need systemic taxonomies. It bears repeating here that two discontinuous ways in which the opposition center/margin or dominant/emergent is undone are gender and class. Thus it seems important to look at Tagore's participation in the project of epistemic transformation by way of a rural woman. This is more interesting in this business of the construction of the implied reader precisely because Shoshi, the central character, does not belong to the class of women who will read the story felicitously, "in its own time." This class separation allows for a feeling of identity-in-difference that seems a much more flexible instrument of epistemic transformation as a site of negotiations. What happens when an exceptional underclass woman is herself a creative reader of British literature will be considered in the next section.

Shoshi is developed as an agent of romantic love in elegant Sanskritic prose in descriptive third person with no hint of indirect free style.[9] In other words, rhetorically she is given no access to a Sanskritized subjectivity. In her case, what will be shown is the subordination of love or *prem* for her husband to affection or *sneho* for her orphan brother. The entire network of *Indian* patriarchy, including colonial functionaries, would like to keep Shoshi in the gendered private sphere, as her husband's adjunct. Shoshi enters the public sphere by establishing direct contact with the British colonial authority and *chooses* to reenter the patriarchal enclosure. She is destroyed by this choice, since the story strongly suggests that she dies by foul play and is therefore cremated as quickly as possible.

Keeping within the allegory of the production of the colonial subject, with something like a relationship with the implied reader of British literature, we see the orphaned brother as the full-fledged future colonial subject, mourning his sister—his personal past—but encircled by the sahib's left arm, the right implicitly pointing to a historical future. But it is Shoshi who supplements the picture, choosing to remain in the static culture, while sending the young unformed male into the dynamic colonial future. A gendered model, this, of the colonial reader, not quite identical with the "real" reader and therefore, in a patriarchal system of reckoning, more like a "woman."

How, then, can we construct a model of the woman and man of the urban middle class, themselves woven and patched as well by the same strands, of the same stuff, reading, in the exciting identity-in-difference frame of mind, the subject laid out in the pages of the story? A richly constructed, richly praised female subject chooses to remain within the indigenous patriarchal structure; she places her confidence in the Magistrate as foster-father, another mark of her heroism. This is the complex of attitudes that is the condition and effect of any appropriate reading of the story. The structure survives; Madhu Kishwar of the *Manushi* collective will not call herself a "feminist" because the word is too much marked by the West, but will work for (other) women's rights.[10]

The Magistrate is constructed as a subject who might be privy to the thrill of this ambivalence. The possibility is lodged in this exchange: "The saheb asked, 'Where will you go.' Shoshi said, 'I will return to my husband's house, I have nothing to worry about.' The saheb smiled a little and, seeing no way out . . . ." By contrast, the neighbor Tara, who opposes husbands if they are scoundrels at the beginning of the story, and roars out her rage at the end, is displeased when Shoshi leaves her husband's house to look after her sick brother: "If you have to fight your husband why not sit at home and do it; what's the point in leaving home? A husband, after all" (p. 288).

The Magistrate (Brit Lit)(perhaps) understands best of all that Shoshi must sacrifice herself to her own culture, but takes charge of Nilmoni (the indefinite future): a crude but recognizable model of what the "best" students manage—saying "yes" and "no" to the Shoshi-function, as it were—in our Brit Lit classes.

I want now to show how this necessarily limited and divided assent to implied readership is parodied in Kipling's *Kim*, published within five years of the publication of "Didi." Thus it is particularly necessary today not to differentiate British and Indian literatures as "central" and "marginal" in a benevolent spirit; that differentiation is a mere legitimation by reversal of the colonial cliché whose real displacement is seen in the turbulent mockery of migrant literature—Desani or Rushdie. Here is Kipling's

> Hurree Chunder Mookerjee, . . . an M.A. of Calcutta University, [who] would explain the advantages of education. There were marks to be gained by due attention to Latin and Wordsworth's *Excursion*. . . . also a man might go far, as he himself had done, by strict attention to plays called *Lear* and *Julius Caesar;* the book cost four annas, but could be bought second-hand in Bow Bazar for two. Still more important than Wordsworth, or the eminent authors Burke and Hare, was the art and science of mensuration. . . . "How am I to fear the absolutely non-existent?" said Hurree Babu, talking English to reassure himself. It is an awful thing still to dread the magic that you contemptuously investigate—to collect folklore for the Royal Society with a lively belief in all the Powers of Darkness.[11]

What Tagore is performing in the narrative, through the epistemic transformation of the central *female* character, is a productive and chosen contradiction: a self-sacrifice to culture while bequeathing the future to the colonist *in loco parentis*. Kipling describes an identical phenomenon in this minor male character as an unproductive contradiction: a bondage to a superstitious and mercenary indigenous culture while mouthing sublime doctrine, the distinctive failure of the colonial subject. (We know that Kipling understood the good Indian within an earlier, feudal, semiotic system and was incapable of bringing to life an Indian woman as subject or agent of profound inner change.)

At least two kinds of point can be made here. By contrast to Kipling— of course Kipling is an interested choice on my part—Tagore's complicated and complicit structure remains preferable as a mode of assent in the colonies. In the frame of indigenous class alliances and gendering the Tagorean structure becomes dubious. The activist teacher of English can negotiate this only if she works to undo the divide between English and vernacular literatures laid down in our institutions. The teacher can use her own native language skills and draw on the multilingual skills of the students. More important, departments of Modern Indian Literatures, of Literature in the State Vernacular, of Comparative Literature must work together so that the artificial divide between British and Native is undone.

I should like to make clear that I am not *conflating* British and colonial/Commonwealth literatures. Nor am I suggesting a collapsing of boundaries. I am proposing rather that the complexity of their relationship, collaborative/parasitical/contrary/resistant, be allowed to surface in literary pedagogy. They are different but complicit. I will recite this refrain again, for it is a common misunderstanding.[12]

As contrast to Tagore's class-divisive gendering I will draw on Binodini Dasi's *Amar Katha* (*My Story*).[13] First, to contrast Kipling's dismissal of the agency of a productive contradiction in the colonial subject, I will point at Tagore's *Gora* as a counter to *Kim*.[14]

Gora ("Whitey"—the word applied to the British tommy is here a perfectly acceptable diminutive from Gaurmohan) appeared five years after the publication of *Kim*. The heroes of both novels are Irish orphans of the Indian Mutiny, turned Indian. But there the resemblance ends. Gora becomes both a nationalist Indian and a tremendously orthodox Brahman. At the end of the novel he finds out that he is not only not a Brahman, but not even a Hindu or an Indian by birth. It is then that he realizes that he is most truly Indian, because he chooses to be so. His realization is embedded in a discourse of woman. First his identification of India with his (foster) mother who, unlike his (foster) father, did not observe caste difference: "Ma, you have no caste rules, no loathing, no contempt. You are my India." Then the summons to the hitherto spurned untouchable servant: "Now call your Lachchmia. Ask her to bring me a glass of water." And finally the Mother's request to him to acknowledge the love of the emancipated Brahmo heroine, expressed obliquely as a request to summon a male friend: "Gora, now send for Binoy" (p. 572).[15] This ending is rather different in historical "feel" from *Kim*, (which ends with Kim O'Hara and the Lama on a hilltop.

If I were commenting on the thematics of the half-caste as "true" Indian, I should contrast Gora with Mahasweta Devi's Mary Oraon, and again the registers of class and gender (and of course coloniality and *post*coloniality) would come into play.[16] In contrasting it to Kipling's Irish-as-Indian hero, however, one would have to notice there the feudal and here the nationalist axiomatic: the codified past as opposed to a possible dynamic future. Kim's return is acted out again by E. M. Forster's Fielding; their futures are not seriously marked by the colonies. For Gora, agency is bestowed by the colony as nation. The theme of choice is important here as well.

But Gora is not a divided subject in the same way as Shoshi is; if he chooses a return to culture, he is also the inheritor of the future. The theme of sacrifice is less ambivalent and therefore less interesting in *Gora*. The colonial reader is as race- and gender-divided from Gora as she would be class-divided from Shoshi. And from that race- and gender-distanced position, the system of representations the reader assents to is again not quite accessible to the staging of her own identity, but this time "from below," not, as in the case of the indigenous woman, "from above." [17] The cultural choice and bequest of the future can inhere in the same fantasmatic character: the white man turned Indian by choice. [18] The development of readership thrives in the difference and deferment staged between hero and reader, whether from above or below. In a former colony, the institutional teacher of imperialist and colonial literature can open this space of difference only by way of persistently undoing the institutional difference between that literature and the literature(s) in the mother tongue(s). It is then that the active vectors of these differences, negotiating gender, class, and race, would begin to appear. [19]

Let us now consider a performance of this undoing, in the very house of performance, during the colonial era. I am referring to the Calcutta professional theater at the end of the nineteenth century. To give an example of the undoing of institutional difference, I will quote from Binodini's *Amar Katha* at length:

> Girishbabu [the eminent actor Girishchandra Ghosh (1844–1912)] taught me with great care the performance of parts. His teaching method was superb. First he explained the essence [*bhab—bhava*] of the part. Then he would ask us to memorize it. Then when he had time he would sit in our house, with Amrita Mitra, Amritababu and others, and tell us the writings of many different British actresses, of eminent British poets such as Shakespeare, Milton, Byron, Pope, as if they were stories. Sometimes he would read the books aloud and explain. He taught various moves and gestures [*hab-bhab*] one by one. Because of this care I started learning the work of acting with knowledge and intelligence. What I had learnt before was like the cleverness of parrots, I had experienced little. I had not been able to say or understand anything with argument or reasoning. From now on I could understand my own performance-selected part. When big British *actors* or *actresses* came I would be eager to see their acting. And the directors of the theatre would accompany me with infinite care to see English theatre. When we returned home Girishbabu would ask, "How was it?" (p. 33–34).

Here indeed is teaching to perform. Men teaching women the trick of the "inside" of their captors, as the captors themselves code that "inside," with instruments supposedly generated in a deeper "inside," for general decipherment in an "outside," the British audience, who supposedly possess "insides" that are resolutely considered quite different from those held by these men and women. But the devout colonial subject, decent dupe of univeralism, thinks to learn the trick perfectly. The performance of the teaching and of the learning is not mere mimicry. Deliberate, canny,

wholesale epistemic transformation is what we are witnessing here. This is
not the *Natya Sastra* warmed over. The idea that apprenticeship with the
West introduces analytic learning in place of rote learning is a sentiment
that thoroughly informed the debates on education in the nineteenth century and continues to this day: it was heard in February 1991 from an
Indian woman dancer who learnt her stuff from an old-fashioned Indian
male master but went on to collaborate with a European male director
whose method was not unlike Girishbabu's.[20]

A later passage allows us to sense how completely the principle of
reasonable learning affected the episteme:

> I had no taste for other topics of conversation. I liked only the accounts of
> the great British actors and actresses that respected Girishbabu gave me, the
> books he read to me. When Mrs. Sidnis [Siddons?] left theatre work, spent
> ten years in the married state and then returned to the stage, where in her
> acting the critics noticed what fault, where she was excellent, where lacking,
> all this he read and explained to me from books. He would also tell me which
> British actress practised her voice by mingling it with birdsong in the woods,
> this too he would tell me. How Ellen Terry dressed, how Bandman made
> himself up as Hamlet, how Ophelia dressed in flowers, what book Bankim-
> chandra's *Durgeshnandini* imitated, in what English book *Rajani* found its
> idea [*bhab* = thoughts], so many things of this nature, I do not know where
> to begin. Thanks to the loving care of respected Girishbabu and other affec-
> tionate friends, I cannot recount how many tales by what great English,
> Greek, French, and German authors I have heard. I did not only listen, I
> collected ideas [*bhab* = mood] from them and reflected upon them cease-
> lessly. As a result of this my nature [*shabhab—swabhava*] became such that,
> when I went to visit a garden, I did not like the buildings there, I would
> search out the secluded spots resplendent with wild flowers. I would feel that
> perhaps I lived in those woods, ever-nurtured by them! My heart would
> throw itself down as it witnessed beauty so intimately mingled with every
> plant and bud. It was as if my soul would start to dance with joy! When I
> sometimes went to a riverbank it would seem as if my heart would fill with
> waves, I would feel as if I had played in the waves of this river forever. Now
> these waves have left my heart and are throwing themselves about. The sand
> on the banks of the river at Kuchbihar is full of mica, most lovely, I would
> often go alone to the riverbank, which was quite far from my living quarters,
> lie down on the sand and watch the waves. I would feel as if they spoke to
> me. (p. 35–36)

The rhetoric of this extended passage lays out the construction of the
colonial subject as contradictory implied reader of the imperial text. Binodini was indeed receiving an education in English and European literature in a way that no university student does. To be sure, to learn to read
well is to say "yes, yes" to the text, if only in order to say "no," in other

words to perform it, if only against the grain. But between that general sense of performance and the narrow sense of performing in order to simulate there is an immense difference in degree. Binodini was not obliged to get her information right; the proper names are often askew. (Ellen Terry comes out "Ellentarry" in Bengali, a single word; and "Ophelia" inhabits the same register of reality as Mr. Bandman and Mrs. Sidnis.) Yet here we see the difference between knowing and learning. Binodini identifies with Bankim, the master-creator recognized as the successful colonial subject by the very *babu*-culture of Bengal that Kipling mocks. If Bankim had taken the *bhab* of British Literature, so would she; he to write, she to interpret through performance. Reading-in-performance *is* a species of writing, as Bankim himself recognized:

> One day Bankimbabu came to see the performance of his *Mrinalini*, and I was playing the part of "Manorama" at that time. Having seen the part of Manorama being played Bankimbabu said: "I only wrote the character of Manorama in a book, I had never thought to see it with my own eyes, seeing Manorama today I thought I was seeing my Manorama in front of me." (p. 36) [21]

The public sphere of professional theater and the private sphere of the self interpenetrate in the longer passage in a clearer and more intense model of what *can* happen in the classroom. In the consummate rhetoric of this gifted craftswoman, the epistemic simulacrum is obstinately sustained. The translator has taken care to preserve every "as if," every "perhaps." (It would have been possible to construct the Bengali sentences without them.) It is not a "real" nature that Binodini imagines as the place of eternal nurture. It is rather the planted woods in a garden house. In the passage about the waves, the *location* of the waves is made nicely indeterminate; but in fact the waves, ostensibly the vehicle of union, preserve separation between river and heart, displacing it from figure to figure. This rhetorical effusion does not break step with the ritual language celebrating her dead protector within which the autobiography is framed. It seems appropriate that we, in search of a model for the colonial subject as implied reader, should be implicated in the reader function of this thoroughly benevolent and utterly dominant male.

Binodini was no rural subaltern. In her own words: "I was born in this great city of Calcutta, in a family without resource and property. But not to be called poverty-stricken, for, however painfully, we scratched together a living. . . . My grandmother, my mother, and the two of us, brother and sister" (p. 14). Binodini is in a family of women, quite within the other discursive formation that can look upon marriage as a socio-economic institution of exchange for consumption.

> But with our sentience our sufferings from poverty increased, and then our grandmother perpetrated a marriage between my infant brother of five years and a girl of two and a half [the play between infant *shishu*—and girl—*balika*—is her own] and brought home a negligible quantity of ornaments. Then our livelihood was earned through the sale of ornaments.

It is not only the play between *shishu* and *balika* that signals that Binodini, writing at the age of forty-seven, after her brilliant and thwarted attempt at staging herself, in every sense, as female individualist, is still unemphatically at ease with the pragmatic patriarchal culture that thwarted her; although her expressed sentiments will not draw from it. The next few sentences quietly emphasize this, for it is the love [*sneho*] of the older women rather than the unconsummated child marriage that remains in memory: "My grandmother and respected Mother were most affectionate [*snehomoyee*]. They would sell the ornaments one by one at the goldsmith's shop and give us all kinds of food stuff. They never regretted the ornaments."

The brother died soon after the marriage. What happened to the child bride deprived of her ornaments for the subsistence of the other women? We cannot know. But there can be no doubt that the tragedy of feminism is played out not only in the obvious and visible masculist suppression of Binodini's ambitions but also in the widening gap between the obscurity of the unremembered child widow and the subtle and layered memoir of the autobiographer.[22]

The male suppression of the competitive female is a poignant story, where the politically correct judgment is trivially obvious, but it is not the only story in coloniality. The feminist has the dubious task of marking the division in womanspace. Tagore may have found it difficult to stage the estranged wife Shoshi as the full-fledged colonial subject, insert her fully into the contradiction of implied readership, make her the agent of both *sneho* and *prem*, but the prostitute-performer Binodini straddles the gap with ease. In prostitution, sublated through performance on the colonially fractured stage, the old lesson in *lasya* is destroyed and preserved on another register as *prem*.[24] Although Binodini is bitter and contemptuous about the men's refusal to let her own a part of her beloved Star Theatre, and indeed to keep their promise of preserving her proper name by naming it "B-Theatre"—curious synecdoche, known only to the knowing—her extraordinary language of exalted devotion to her dead protector, her companion in the long years after her departure from the stage, rings with greater affect, as does the explicit (auto-)eroticism of her singular love poems, where the agency of the male lover is only present to the extent that it is necessary for the topos of male inconstancy. Marriage may be an institution that crumples when the woman is epistemically fractured, but residential (rather than itinerant) prostitution can be recoded as a peculiar liberty. How far do we want to take this as an allegory of colonial reading?

In the Brit. Lit. classroom today, an answer might be concocted in terms of Hanif Kureishi's *The Buddha of Suburbia*.[24] The shifts are: a century in time, coloniality through postcoloniality to migrancy, a literary representation by a male author who "read philosophy at King's College, London" (jacket blurb). Here too an uncomfortable opposition between native and migrant can be undone or put under erasure (crossed out while leaving visible.)[25] Again, this is not conflation; perhaps the very shock of the reconstellation lets "truth"(s) flash forth.

The central character Karim will not be allowed to be English, even as Binodini was not allowed to be entrepreneurial professional individualist, although she carried bricks on her head for the building of the theater, he is

> Englishman born and bred, almost. . . . Englishman I am (though not proud of it), from the South London suburbs and going somewhere. Perhaps it is the odd mixture of continents and blood, of here and there, of belonging and not, that makes me restless and easily bored. (p. 3)

This is the flip side of Binodini's restless self-separation on the glittering sand of the Kuchbihar river; the style difference may be that between Romanticism (capital R) and existentialist modernism (small e, small m: *Catcher in the Rye, Under the Net*), rather than only that between India and Britain. Let the student notice that Karim, as he learns performance from British and American directors, is being asked to be "Indian," or to portray migrants favorably. He must dye his skin browner (his mother is working class English) as he is given Mowgli's part in Kipling's *The Jungle Book*, and produce "an Indian accent," which he finally, during performance, begins to "send up" with occasional lapses into Cockney. Yet outside the theater, he lives in the incredible violence of racism in contemporary London, which is also vividly described in the novel.

Karim's father, a Muslim, becomes a Buddhist from do-it-yourself books and finds fulfillment with an "artist" woman. Yet there is real good sense in him, real unworldliness, and there is love between them, however sweetly sexist.

Dominant British society shuttles between racist violence and approval of the "real" Indian. Once again, it is the productive epistemic fracture of the colonial, postcolonial, hybrid subject that is denied. The benevolent expectations are Kipling's Mowgli, or the Buddha of Suburbia. The transformation of the father is given in the third person. Let us consider what the son says, in the first person, about learning to act.

"India" is an imagined ingredient with material vestiges in the son's account, important in the survival technique of the fabrication of a hybrid identity. With a different political impulse from the malevolent racist British underclass, or the benevolent racist British artist, we too would like to keep alive the divide between "real" Indian and migrant "Indian." Without collapsing the difference, what if we attended to the fact that Binodini's imagined "England" and the representation of Karim's imagined "India" are both "created" under duress? We would begin, then, to plot an alternative literary historiography. Binodini thought of the duress as imaginative freedom. We are not surprised that Karim is represented as creatively happy when he puts together his stage Indian. Both are the intimate enemy, a violation that enables. The teacher of British literature in the former colonies must look at this phenomenon carefully, to let the differences appear in their entanglements.

Here, then, are the passages from *The Buddha of Suburbia*. Karim is rethinking the Indian character, having been criticized for his initial negative representation of an Indian immigrant: [26]

> At night, at home, I was working on Changez's shambolic walk and crippled hand, and on the accent, which I knew would sound, to white ears, funny and characteristic of India. (p. 188)

He is at his father's best friend Anwar's funeral (the two had come to Britain from Bombay many years ago):

> There was a minor row when one of the Indians pulled out a handy compass and announced that the hole hadn't been dug facing in the right direction, towards Mecca. . . . But I did feel, looking at these strange creatures now—the Indians—that in some way these were my people, and that I'd spent my life denying or avoiding that fact. I felt ashamed and incomplete at the same time, as if half of me were missing, and as if I'd been colluding with my enemies, those whites who wanted Indians to be like them. Partly I

blamed Dad for this. After all, like Anwar, for most of his life he'd never shown any interest in going back to India. He was always honest about this: he preferred England in every way. Things worked; it wasn't hot; you didn't see terrible things on the street that you could do nothing about [this is contradicted by the graphic descriptions of racist violence in London]. He wasn't proud of his past, but he wasn't unproud of it either; it just existed, and there wasn't any point in fetishizing it, as some liberals and Asian radicals like to do. So if I wanted the additional personality bonus of an Indian past, I would have to create it. (p. 212–13)

How very different from the "uncreative" sacrificial choice thrust on the rural woman or the unfetishized choice of a culture without the bonus of a past accessible to the "white migrant" imagined in the colonial context! Again, leisurely classroom consideration of the difference will show how the representation of "race," of "gendering," of "religion/culture" construct the chain of displacements on which these examples may be plotted. "Nation" and "class" relate to these links on other levels of abstraction.

For Binodini, the professional theater had promised an access to feminist individualism that residential prostitution denied. Along a chain of displacements, casual prostitution and the stage have become confused for Kureishi's character Karim, although in the "real" world, professional prostitution still has a confining relationship to the media. At any rate, the identity forged in the theater had come to organize Binodini's own staging of her identity in honorable residential prostitution recalled in later life. "The acting bit of her lost its moorings and drifted out into real life."[27] There is no such bleeding over in the representation of Karim. The character who plays the sexual field is the Paki. When he "wants the additional personality bonus of an Indian past," he reverses the demands of his protector, and "creates":

> There were few jobs I relished as much as the invention of Changez/
> Tariq. . . . I uncovered notions, connections, initiatives I didn't even know
> were present in my mind. . . . I worked regularly and kept a journal [*Amar
> Katha?*]; . . . I felt more solid myself, and not as if my mind were just a kind
> of cinema for myriad impressions and emotions to flicker through. This was
> worth doing, this had meaning, this added up the elements of my life. And
> it was this that Pyke [the director] had taught me: what a creative life could
> be. . . . I was prepared to pay the price for his being a romantic, an experi-
> menter. He had to pursue what he wanted to know and follow his feelings
> wherever they went, even as far as my arse and my girlfriend's cunt. (p. 217)

Karim is a character in a book. The fact that this passage about creativity and the discovery of a coherent identity is much less gripping than

Binodini's passage about divided self-creation cannot be taken as representative of the differenc between the colonial reader's longing for the metropolis and the migrant's fancy for his roots. It is simply that our students might be encouraged to place it on that chain of displacements that will include *Gora* and *Kim* and *The Jungle Book*. Through attention to the rhetorical conduct of each link on the chain, the student might be encouraged, to belabor the by now obvious, neither to conflate nor oppose, but to figure out gender and class difference in complicity. I draw attention, again, to the moment when the half-caste tribal woman in "The Hunt" fabricates identity for the object (rather than the individualist subject) by intoning a word that would allow the indigenous exploiter to be constructed within the script of Oraon performance. Mahasweta offers a link in the chain away from migrancy into subalternity.

What I am suggesting, then, is that, in the postcolonial context, the teaching of English literature can become critical only if it is intimately yoked to the teaching of the literary or cultural production in the mother tongue(s). In that persistently asymmetrical intimacy, the *topos* of language learning, in its various forms, can become a particularly productive site. I am not speaking here of becoming an "expert" of the mother tongue, for the benefit of those who are thoroughly ignorant of it in the metropolis, a temptation to which many of us have given in. I am speaking of a much less practical thing: becoming "inter-literary," not "Comparative," in the presence of long-established institutional divides and examination requirements. It is a kind of homoeopathic gesture: scratching at the epistemic fracture by awkwardly assuming a language to be an "epistemic system" and staging a collision between Kipling and Tagore, "Didi" and Binodini, "Mary Oraon" and "Karim." The authority of cultivating the felicitous implied readership is questioned in such teaching and learning. Any number of "correct" readings can be scrupulously taught here, with some degree of assurance that the reader's space of the mother tongue will secure the quotation marks by way of repeated colonial and postcolonial encounters, among them the one in the classroom.

Great clumps of topics are pulled up with this style of teaching: access to subjectivity, access to the other's language are among them. Such topics allow us to float into Commonwealth Literature, even without access to the various native traditions or emergences. The peculiar authority in this floating reading is of the contingent reader who *might* have that access. An interruptive authority, for the text is in English.

Let us consider an example: the last scene of Nadine Gordimer's *July's People*.[28]

Successful black insurgency in South Africa. A family being protectively steered into the village of their former servant, July. Barriers falling, people learning about being human, the nature of power, being gendered, the master-servant dialectic. The emergence of July's proper name—Mwawate—in itself the kind of topic that rocks the centralized place of the "implied reader." As if Man Friday should have a history. When people have been pared down a good bit, we encounter an event impossible to conceive earlier in the book. Mwawate speaks to his former mistress, the central character in the book, in his own language, with authority, dignity, and irritation. I will first quote the preparatory moments: "She knew those widened nostrils. Go, he willed, go up the hill to the hut; as he would to his wife. . . . The only way to get away from her was . . . to give up to her this place that was his own . . . " (p. 152).

Then a furious exchange in English about why had he stolen little things; why had she given him only rubbish; why had he accepted rubbish; almost frantically resembling what Jan Nederveen Pieterse has called "the dialects of terror": "*Not* discussed is the *initial* . . . terror, which includes the institutional violence of the denial of . . . human rights and [of imperialist] occupation."[29]

It is in response to this frustrating exchange that Mwawate speaks:

You—He spread his knees and put an open hand on each. Suddenly he began to talk at her in his own language, his face flickering powerfully. The heavy cadences surrounded her; the earth was fading and a thin, far radiance from the moon was faintly pinkening parachute-silk hazes stretched over the sky. She understood although she knew no word. Understood everything: what he had had to be, how she had covered up to herself for him, in order for him to be her idea of him. But for himself—to be intelligent, honest, dignified for *her* was nothing; his measure as a man was taken elsewhere and by others. She was not his mother, his wife, his sister, his friend, his people. He spoke in English what belonged in English—Daniel he's go with those ones like in town. He's join.—The verb, unqualified, did for every kind of commitment: to a burial society, a hire purchase agreement, their thumbprints put to a labour contract for the mines or sugar plantations. (p. 152)

Gordimer is playing a whole set of variations on the topos of languages as epistemes. To begin with, the imperious gesture of the pronominal address as imperative: "You." But even before that, and surreptitiously, the sudden incursion of Mwawate's "inside" into the novel: "Go, *he willed*" (emphasis mine). It remains paratactic—cannot be staged as becoming syntactic in the hands of this white author woman writing about a female white protagonist, precisely because both are painfully politically correct. The sentences can start only after that enabling shifter, "you," (staged by the writer as) pronounced by the imperfect speaker of English. Put this on a spectrum of contemporary artists using this topos in many different ways: Toni Morrison, J. M. Coetzee, Guillermo Gomes-Pena, Jamelie Hassan.[30]

In the hands of a radial Creole writer like Gordimer, the implied black reader of a white text cannot be in a subject position, not even a compromised one like Shoshi's. The text belongs to the native speaker. But the rhetorical conduct of the text undermines and complicates this. The desire of the radical native speaker of English is in the sentence: "She understood although she knew no word." How fragile the logic of that sentence is; there are no guarantees. It is as if the white magistrate in "The Elder Sister" should enunciate the desire for understanding Shoshi's ambivalence, which the writer as classed male colonial subject articulates by way of the representation of his slight smile. And, in Gordimer's text there is the strong suggestion that rather than understand the "burden" of Mwawate's words, the peculiar situation of being addressed by him in his tongue produces in her an understanding of a narrative of, precisely, the infelicity of their communication. His utilization of this uneven bilinguality was elsewhere. "He spoke in English what belonged in English."

Just as Mwawate's subject space is syntactically inaccessible in the rhetoric of the novel, so is the dubious assertion of "understanding" unmoored from the passage that tells you *what* she understood. In addition, the man speaking his mother tongue—the other tongue from English—is deliberately distanced by a metonym with nature: Mwawate flickering, adjacent to the moon and the parachute silk clouds. Put this on a spectrum with the neat divisive locatives of nature and mind in Binodini's *self-staging*!

What is it that Mwawate says in English? It is the matter of public organizations: "he's join." This is not a "mistake," just as Dopdi Mejhen's "counter" is not.[31] In its profound ungrammaticality, it undoes the dominant language and pushes its frontiers as only pidgin can. Put this calm approach on a spectrum with Kipling's mockery, Rushdie's teratology, and Tagore's colonial prose.

It is not possible for an "expatriate English Professor," as Madhu Jain described me in a December 1990 issue of *India Today,* to produce a thick analysis of the burden of English teaching in India. Let me remind my readers that I have not attempted to comment on the importance of English as an international medium of exchange. (For the record, the proportion of Honors to Pass students in English at Delhi University is 602/ 13,900, 580/15,700, 660/17,300, 748/18,800 and 845/19,800—for 1986–1990 respectively.) [32] All I seem to have done is offered impractical suggestions: to undo the imported distinction between center and periphery as well as some indigenous institutional divisions by looking at literature as the staged battleground of epistemes.

These suggestions may not be altogether as impractical as they seem, at first glance, to the embattled local teacher. I am speaking, after all, of disturbing the arrangement of classroom material as well as our approach to it. Predictably, this would be against the interest of the student, who would have to sit for an examination that expects ferocious loyalty to a colonial curricular arrangement. (This is an argument we daily face, mutatis mutandis, in terms of bilingualism in the United States; in the 1960s and 1970s it was black English.) Can one share the dilemma with the students while preparing them for the regular exam papers? We have a time-honored strategy of politicization through pedagogy. The counterargument here is the cynicism of students in a demoralized society, where English learning does not occupy center stage; also the difficulty of learning the language for those students who would be most susceptible to such politicization. (In the United States, this translates, as imperfectly as all translations, to the justified cynicism of the urban underclass student toward the smorgasbord of Cultural Studies.) Alas, the answers to that one are lost or found, lost *and* found, in the transactions in the classroom. It is to the most practical aspect of our trade that I dedicate these ruminations.

Would such a technique of teaching work outside of modern literature? And if so, with Adivasi creation-myths and the reclaiming of "African" mythic traditions by writers and filmmakers of contemporary Africa? Or only with *Beowulf* and the *Mahabharata*? One looks forward to an alternative literary historiography of postcoloniality critical of the hierarchical imprint of "the Commonwealth."

This paper was delivered in a shorter form at Miranda House on February 13, 1987. I thank Gyan Pandey for giving the present version of the paper a first reading.

Notes

1. Ngugi wa Th'iongo, *Decolonizing the Mind: The Politics of Language in African Literature* (Portsmouth, NH: Heinemann, 1986).

2. Ngugi, *Decolonizing the Mind*, xi.

3. R. K. Narayan, "English in India," in *A Story-Teller's World* (New Delhi: Penguin India, 1989), 20–23.

4. Rabindranath Tagore, "Didi," in *Galpaguchchha* (Calcutta: Visva-Bharati, 1975), vol. 2. Translations are my own.

5. I have given a historical account of this alienation outside of the classroom in "Once Again a Leap into the Post-Colonial Banal," *Differences* III, 3 (Fall 1991): 139–70.

6. David Hardiman comments on the peasants' misplaced belief that the British would give them direct access to vengeance as justice (discussion after "The Peasant Experience of Usury: Western India in the Nineteenth Century," paper delivered at the Davis Center for Historical Studies, Princeton University, April 12, 1991). In response to my query to Hardiman as to whether there is any documentary evidence that indigenous collaborators with the colonial authorities saw through this peasant belief, Gyan Prakash advises me to look in Bengali tract literature. Until I can undertake that research, I mark this place with the question: what are the cultural politics of Tagore's rhetorical representation of this belief or faith, at a later date, and on the woman's part?

7. Spivak, "Can the Subaltern Speak?" in Cary Nelson and Lawrence Grossberg, eds., *Marxism and the Interpretation of Culture: Limits, Boundaries, Frontiers* (Urbana: University of Illinois Press, 1988).

8. Ashis Nandy, *The Intimate Enemy: Loss and Recovery of the Self Under Colonialism* (Delhi: Oxford University Press, 1983).

9. For the importance of the assignment of reported, direct, and indirect speech and style, see V. N. Volosinov, *Marxism and the Philosophy of Language*, tr. Ladislav Matejka and I. R. Titunik (Cambridge, MA: Harvard University Press, 1986), Part III.

10. Madhu Kishwar, "Why I Do Not Call Myself a Feminist," *Manushi* 61 (Nov –Dec 1990).

11. Rudyard Kipling, *Kim* (reprint New York: Viking Penguin, 1987), pp. 210–11.

12. For an example of such a misunderstanding, with reference to the relationship between philosophy and literature, and based on minimal documentation, see the chapter on Derrida in Jurgen Habermas, *The Philosophical Discourse of Modernity: Twelve Lectures* (Cambridge, MA: MIT Press, 1987).

13. Binodini Dasi, *Amar Katha o Anyanyo Rachona*, ed. Saumitra Chattopadhyaya et al. (Calcutta: Subarnorekha, 1988). Translations mine. For a reading of this text in the context of women's autobiographies, see Partha Chatterjee, "In Their Own Words? Women's Autobiographies in Nineteenth-Century Bengal" (forthcoming).

14. Rabindranath Tagore, *Gora*, in *Rabindra Rachanabali* (Calcutta: Biswa-Bharati, 1955), vol. 6. Sujit Mukherjee is supervising a new translation of *Gora*.

15. I am grateful to Ranes Chakravorty for reading this paragraph to me, when my own *Gora* was inaccessible and the library did not have one.

16. Mahasweta Devi, "The Hunt," *Women in Performance* V, 1 (1990): 80–92.

17. The elegantly staged representation of Sarada Devi as the rural woman denoting cultural choice and victory in the general text of imperialist seduction is a complex variation on the thematics we are discussing (Swami Gambhirananda, *Srima Sarada Devi* [Calcutta: Udbodhan, 1st ed., 1954], pp. 1–6).

18. There are a handful of prominent whites of this genre who receive a great deal of publicity (on a less exalted register, like middle class husbands who cook). They offer an eagerly grasped standby for cultural representation as alibi. One thinks of their role in Richard Attenborough's film *Gandhi* and, more recently, in the conception of the hero of *Dances with Wolves*.

19. The artificial separation between colonial (roughly British) and neocolonial (roughly U.S.), migrant and postcolonial, covers a wide field. Howard Winant, for example, makes the claim that "*in the postmodern political framework of the contemporary United States, hegemony is determined by the articulation of race and class*" (Howard Winant, "Postmodern Racial Politics in the United States: Difference and Inequality," *Socialist Review* XX,1 (Jan–Mar 1990): 137; emphasis author's. "Postmodern" is used here in the to me unsatisfactory sense of neocolonialism as being not only after the phase of modernization but also entering a phase after orthodox socialist radicalism.) A curricular reconstellation as is being proposed here might have broader implications than one imagines.

20. For a sober accounting of the debates, see J. P. Naik and Syed Nurullah, *A History of Education in India* (2d rev. ed., London: Macmillan, 1951). The recent reference is to Samjukta Panigrahi, discussion after lecture demonstration with Eugenio Barba, at a Conference on Inter-Cultural Performance, Bellagio, February 20, 1991. The denigration of "rote" learning as opposed to "analytic" knowing is no longer as clearly on the agenda and shows evidence of an unquestioning ideological (and therefore often unwitting) acceptance of nineteenth-century imperialist universalism. The project would be to reinscribe the presuppositions—of knowledge before understanding—proposed in some Indian Speech Act linguistics that challenge British speech act theory (Bimal Krishna Matilal, "Knowledge from Linguistic Utterances," in *The Word and the World* (Delhi: Oxford University Press, 1990).

21. For the contrast between Binodini's testimonial and Tagore's literary representation of the insulted wife playing, precisely, Manorama, see "Giribala " (see note 4, above).

22. It is not to denigrate feminism to point out that feminist ambition in the colonial nineteenth century must involve competition and class ambition. For a discussion of this in the western context, see Elizabeth Fox-Genovese, *Feminism Without Illusions: A Critique of Individualism* (Chapel Hill: University of North Carolina Press, 1991). Here too the relationship between colony and the West is complex, not merely oppositional. The fact that powerful men suppressed Binodini's ambition points at another complex relationship between feminism and the critique of capitalism.

23. The connection between the dramatic representation of lust and drama

proper is available in reverse in Damodargupta's *Kuttinimatam* (see Mandakranta Basu, "*Lasya*: A Dramatic Art?" in Bimal Krishna Matilal and Bilimoriya, eds., *Sanskrit and Related Studies* (Albany: State University of New York Press, 1992).

24. Hanif Kureishi, *The Buddha of Suburbia* (New York: Viking Penguin, 1991).

25. Sensitively argued in "Location, Intervention, Incommensurability: A Conversation with Homi Bhabha," *Emergences* I (1989).

26. The criticism comes from Tracey, a politically mature African-British woman. In our classroom, we would have to develop the point of this criticism, significantly different from the desire of the white.

27. Martin Amis, *London Fields* (New York: Harmony Books, 1989). I quote this from a trendy English novelist somewhat bloody-mindedly, because Amis too is in a world transformed by migrants. His villain is "multiracial" in his choice of women. But the staging of identity in migrancy is not Amis's burden. Hence this sentence about life and acting does not attach to a multiracial character. They remain victims. Our best students will have to come to grip with the fact that the epistemic fracturing of the colonial reader is no longer a marginal event. . . .

28. Nadine Gordimer, *July's People* (New York: Viking Penguin, 1981).

29. Jan Nederveen Pieterse, *Israel's State Terrorism and Counterinsurgency in the Third World* (Kingston: NECEF Publications, 1986), 4. My extrapolations refer to the specific case of Israel and Palestine. Again, the student can link the international press with autobiography, Brit. Lit. and vernacular literature if the teacher fills in Pieterse's passage. The pedagogic interest is, always, to globalize and politicize the burden by pointing at linked differences rather than divisive turf battles.

30. I have discussed this cluster in Spivak, "Acting Bits/Identity Talk," *Critical Inquiry* XVIII, 4 (1992): 770–803. Lars Engle makes a persuasive case for this passage as the characteristic irruption of the Freudian "uncanny" (Lars Engle, "The Political Uncanny: The Novels of Nadine Gordimer," *Yale Journal of Criticism* II,2 (1989): 120–21). I think, however, it is more fruitful to consider the "uncanny" as inhabiting the past and the present and the future—always under the skin of the familiar everyday—rather than only a "postrevolutionary" future conceived as a future present in sequential narrative time. I also think that we should take note of "July"'s real name. The uncanny lurks under the skin of the everyday as Mwawate always lives in the skin that is always called July by his masters.

31. See Spivak, "'Draupadi' by Mahasveta Devi," in *In Other Worlds: Essays in Cultural Politics* (New York: Routledge, 1987).

32. Figures received from University Grants Commission, May 9, 1991. For an excellent analysis of who studies English, see Yasmeen Lukmani, "Attitudinal Orientation Toward Studying English Literature in India" and Lola Chatterji, "Landmarks in Official Educational Policy" in Rajeswari Sunder Rajan, ed., *The Lie of the Land: English Literary Studies in India* (Delhi: Oxford University Press, 1992), pp. 156–86, 300–308.

Vinay Dharwadker

5. Orientalism and the Study of Indian Literatures

1. Introduction

In *Orientalism* (1978), his classic critique of European imperialism, Edward Said argued that if we take the late eighteenth century as an approximate starting point we can dissect and expose orientalism as "the corporate institution of dealing with the Orient—dealing with it by making statements about it, authorizing views of it, describing it, by teaching it, settling it, ruling over it: in short [we can treat] Orientalism as a western style for dominating, restructuring, and having authority over the Orient" (Said 1978: 3). Although Said focused much of his polemical energy on European representations of what is now called the Middle East, his strategic orientation and location with respect to the texts, procedures, and institutions of Orientalism were clearly applicable in productive ways to a range of other historical and political situations. In "Orientalist Constructions of India" (1986) Ronald Inden successfully exploited the potential of Said's critique for an attack on Indology and South Asian studies, by directly confronting "the central questions of knowledge and its multiple relations to power in Orientalist representations" of India and Indians, in contexts that Said himself could not explore with comparable expertise. Inden ambitiously aimed at "deconstructing" orientalist discourse in the disciplinary fields controlled by "Indologists, . . . sociologists, historians, political scientists, anthropologists, and historians of religion," and hoped that his critique would be useful for the study of South Asia "in the other human sciences as well" (Inden 1986: 411, 401).

Said's general insights into orientalism and Inden's specific suggestions regarding South Asia need to be extended to a phenomenon that has not yet been subjected to a sustained critique of this kind, namely, the longstanding British, European, and North American engagement with Indian literatures and literary histories, which occupy such a prominent place in the orientalist enterprise. In this essay I would like to attempt such an extension (without adopting either Inden's analytical framework or his particular political position) by grappling with a very specific question: within the networks of power relating Europe and India and the multiple relations of knowledge to power in the British-Indian colonial context, how precisely did the orientalists treat the "native" literatures of the subcontinent? Instead of approaching issues of "power" directly (which would lead me to reproduce abstractions that have already been reproduced too often), I will concentrate on the particulars of theory and practice that emerged over a period of about two hundred years in the orientalists' encounters with the various Indian languages and literatures and their histories. As my exploratory discussion should demonstrate, for all practical purposes these particulars constitute the field of orientalist Indian literary studies rather differently from such other, even closely related fields of inquiry as those analyzed by Inden (1986, 1990).

In keeping with these objectives, I begin my discussion in section 2 by examining the conception of "literature" itself as the dominant orientalists employed it in their studies of Indian materials between the mid-eighteenth and mid-twentieth centuries. In section 3 I situate the orientalist conception of literature within a history of post-Renaissance European thought, recounting several of its well-known and some of its relatively unknown moments of theory and practice. Such a contextualization reveals that the orientalists developed an apparently coherent, yet changing, heterogeneous, and curiously inconsistent discourse about the various literatures of India, different parts of which seem (at least in retrospect) to stand in different relations to the institutions of British colonial power.

In the rest of the essay I use historical, institutional, disciplinary, and methodological arguments and analyses to explain the interconnectedness and especially the heterogeneity of orientalist discourse about the Indian literatures. This portion of my discussion is itself divided into two unequal parts, one of which consists of section 4, where I approach the "double standard" of literary orientalism by examining the methodological rift between "Sanskrit literature" and the literatures of the "vernaculars," connecting the divergence in the treatment of the two domains to the institutional trajectory of British colonial literary studies in the nineteenth and early twentieth centuries, as well as to some features of what I characterize tentatively as post-orientalist literary studies in the post-Independence decades. The larger part of my analysis consists of sections 5 through 7, where I argue in much greater detail that the apparent coherence and internal heterogeneity of the orientalists' discourse are consequences not only of their conceptions of literature, but also crucially of their conceptions of the discipline of philology. I move into my discussion of philology by outlining a history of the discipline in Europe, which shaped orientalist practice in relation to Indian-language materials between the late eighteenth and early twentieth centuries and later (section 5). I follow this up by analyzing the philological theories and practices of two major European Indologists—Friedrich Max Müller and Moritz Winternitz—which begin to explain why Indian "literatures" were defined, studied, and represented the way they were at the height of colonial dominance (section 6). I close my historical, institutional, and methodological analysis of philology by showing how early twentieth-century reorientations with respect to the literatures and literary histories of India—in the influential work of A. Berridale Keith—generate further internal divisions within orientalist discourse (section 7).

The main portions of my essay thus sketch a "crooked path of development" in British and European representations of literary India during the late eighteenth, nineteenth, and early twentieth centuries, suggesting quite simply that the reasons why those representations emerged lie not so much in the "nature" of the Indian materials as in the intellectual contexts of European disciplinary thought before, during, and after the Enlightenment, within which the orientalists received their training, pursued their careers, and circulated their discourse.

Finally, in section 8 I conclude my essay by bringing together some of the general implications of my analysis and relating them summarily to questions of British colonial power on the subcontinent. While the overall shape of my argument is thus quite predictable (given Said and Inden's antecedent critiques), its substance in the particulars of literary orientalism and Indian literatures ought to provide some fresh insights into the European "imperial project" as a whole.

2. The Orientalist Conception of Literature

One of the most familiar facts about orientalist discourse on the various Indian literatures is that, from its beginnings in the third quarter of the eighteenth century, it employed a very broad conception of what constitutes "literature." When Sir William Jones used phrases like "Indian literature" (Jones 1784: 200), "the literature of Asia" (Jones 1786: 246), and

"Sanscrit literature" (Jones 1786: 261) in his lectures and essays, by literature he meant something like "all the known and existing texts" in a specified language (such as Sanskrit) or from a specified region (such as Asia or India). This was and still is clear from his materials and references: under the category of Indian, Hindu, or Sanskrit "literature" he variously mentioned or discussed the Vedas, the Upaniṣads, the *Mahābhārata* and the *Rāmāyaṇa*, the *Bhagavad-gītā*, the *Manusmṛti*, the *śilpīśāstra* (sculpture), *nītiśāstra* (ethics) and Advaita-Vedānta texts, the *Hitopadeśa*, several Purāṇas (*Sakanda, Bhāgavata, Matsya,* and so on), Caraka's second-century medical treatise, the *Yavanajātaka* and the *Sūrya-siddhānta* (astronomy), the *dharmaśāstras* in general, Kālidāsa's *Abhijñānaśākuntala*, Māgha's *Śiśupālavadha,* Jayadeva's *Gīta-govinda,* Rūpa Gosvāmī's *Bhāgavatāmṛta,* and even (in an Italian summary) what may have been a version of Tulsīdās's *Rāmacaritmānas* in Hindi (Jones 1784, 1786, 1788).

Jones was not unique among his immediate predecessors or contemporaries in this latitude of reference, which turns "literature" into an umbrella term for a wide range of ritual, philosophical, religious, social-theoretical, didactic, scientific, and poetic texts. We find, for example, a similar (though not so impressively articulated) breadth of meaning in Alexander Dow's use of the terms "literary" and "literature" (Dow 1768: 108) and in Warren Hastings's references to "the Literature, the Mythology, and Morality of the ancient Hindoos," "the ancient and modern literature of Europe," and "Hindoo literature" (Hastings 1785: 6, 7, 14). In fact, the late-eighteenth-century British-Indian orientalists consciously and repeatedly used the word "literature" in a sense that, almost two hundred years later, corresponds exactly to Northrop Frye's quasi-structuralist definition of literature as "the total order of words" in a given language, period, country, or continent (Frye 1957). It is also remarkably close to the generalized conceptions of "text" and "discourse" that, elaborated to include "all forms and mediums of representation," now stand at the center of contemporary cultural studies (Bathrick 1992). Although a post-orientalist scholar like Edwin Gerow finds that the early orientalist conception of literature has become "trivial" in our times (Gerow 1977: 219), the fact remains that it dominated Indological literary studies for nearly two centuries.

We see the same latitude of meaning at play, for instance, in the major orientalist efforts to write a history of "Indian literature" or "Sanskrit literature" during the second half of the nineteenth century and the first half of the twentieth. This is true whether we consider classic studies like Albrecht Weber's *The History of Indian Literature* (1852), Friedrich Max Müller's *A History of Ancient Sanskrit Literature* (1859), and Moritz Winternitz's *A History of Indian Literature* (1907), or more derivative works like Robert W. Frazer's *A Literary History of India* (1898) and Herbert H. Gowen's *A History of Indian Literature: From Vedic Times to the Present Day* (1931). Winternitz made the all-encompassing orientalist meaning of "literature" explicit when he observed that, as far as the "contents" of his multivolume project were concerned, "Indian literature embraces everything which the word 'literature' comprises in its widest sense: religious and secular, epic, lyric, dramatic and didactic poetry, as well as narrative and scientific prose" (Winternitz 1907: 1). Like most other orientalists before and after him, Winternitz included literary theory and criticism, for example, as well as scholarly discourse in general, in the category of literature, placing them under the label of "scientific discourse."

The paradigmatic articulations and applications of the inclusive orientalist conception of literature, of course, are Arthur A. Macdonnell's *A History of Sanskrit Literature* (1900) and A. Berridale Keith's *A History of Sanskrit Literature* (1928). Macdonnell's work was the first short but "complete" account in English of its subject, historically tracing all the known and extant texts and genres in Sanskrit: from the Vedic Saṃhitas, the Brāhmaṇas, and the Sūtras through the epics, the various kinds of *kāvya*, and the varieties of classical drama to "fairy tales and fables" and the major philosophical systems, with notes on the "technical literature" on law, history, grammar, poetics, mathematics, astronomy, medicine, and the arts included in the appendix. Keith's longer work, though confined to "the field of Classical Sanskrit Literature, as opposed to the Vedic Literature, the epics, and the Purāṇas" (Keith 1928: vii), similarly convered not only "The Language" (Sanskrit, the Prākrits, the Apabhraṃśas) and "Belles-Lettres and Poetics" (all the varieties of classical literary practice and theory) but also in great detail the entire "Scientific Literature" from lexicography and metrics to the science of love, medicine, astronomy, astrology, and mathematics.

Much of this is familiar to historians of orientalism and scholars of Indian literatures, but it is worth summarizing here because it frames a simple yet all-important question: Why did the British orientalist dealing with India employ such a broad conception of literature for so long? Their reasons for doing so clearly did not lie in the Indian-language materials they had to deal with. After all, Sanskritists at least from Weber and Max Müller to Macdonnell and Keith knew (or ought to have known) from their readings in Indian sources that the ancient and "medieval" theorists in Sanskrit did not accept a totalizing concept of "literature," but rather insisted on a series of vital distinctions. The series included the typical distinctions between *śruti* (what is heard, revelation) and *smṛti* (recollection, what is remembered, the received tradition); *kāvya* (poetry) and *itihāsa* (history); *śāstra* (science) and *purāṇa* (ancient lore, legend, mythology, theology); *itihāsa* (history) and *kathā* (story, narrative); *kāvya* (poetry) and *nāṭya* (drama, theater); and so on (Lienhard 1984). Moreover, each of the distinctions in the Indian taxonomy was based on complex criteria of difference (*viśeṣaṇa*), which were not always consistent or unambiguous but nevertheless did prepare the ground for a composite Indian theory of discourse that the orientalists could have used. Since ancient Indian works and literatures tend to be self-conscious about their "positionality" in "the total order of words" and are attached to substantial quantities of contextualizing commentary, an explanation for the orientalists' persistence with an "alien" conception of literature over such a long period (from the 1760s to at least the 1930s) has to be sought outside the materials they studied.

3. Literature in European Contexts

The reason why the British orientalists and, following them, their Continental and American counterparts used a broad, alien conception of literature in the Indian case lies, at least partly, in the fact that they were all working within a specifically European intellectual context (see the introduction in Marshall 1970). As a matter of fact, the history of the concept of "literature" in Europe reveals that what the orientalists did with the concept in their Indian studies was tied very closely to what western scholars were doing with it at about the same time, especially in dealing with the ancient and modern discursive and cultural traditions of Europe. It is consequently possible to argue that, during the late eighteenth century and a substantial part of the nineteenth, the literary orientalists working on India were at the forefront of European scholarly thought about the category of "literature."

If we follow René Wellek's unusual comparative account of the European history of the idea of literature (Wellek 1974), and Raymond Williams's more analytical and critical discussion on the subject (Williams 1977: 45–54), we find that the words "literature" in English, *littérature* in

French, and *Litteratur* in German acquire the meaning of "a body of writing" for the first time between the 1730s and 1760s. From the late seventeenth century to about the middle of the eighteenth century, "literature" and *littérature* had meant "knowledge of literature," "literary culture," or, even in Samuel Johnson's *Dictionary* definition, "learning; skill in letters," thus referring back to, say, Quintilian's use of *literatura* as simply "a knowledge of writing and reading" (our modern sense of the word "literacy") and Cicero's use of the Latin word to imply something like "erudition, literary culture" (Wellek 1974: 81). As Wellek goes on to state, the new sense of literature as a body of writing, rather than as a quality or ability in a person, appears as a novelty in Voltaire's phrase *les genres de littératur* in 1751, in Lessing's display of *Litteratur* in the title of his *Briefe die neueste Litteratur betreffend* (1759–), and in Herder's similar strategy in his *Über die neuere deustche Litteratur* (1767). From our vantage point, it is not an insignificant fact that Herder's classic work appears less than two decades before Sir William Jones begins to apply the term "literature" to the whole body of works composed in Sanskrit.

Jones's use of the new concept of literature (and, before that, Alexander Dow's in 1768) is all the more remarkable because, according to Wellek, the common circulation of the word "literature" as designating the general body of written works begins in England in the early 1760s. The phrase "History of Literature" appears for the first time in Adam Ferguson's *Essay on the History of Civil Society* in 1767, and the canonical Dr. Johnson himself inscribes a phrase like "our antiquated literature" only in 1774, instituting a meaning that he was to employ more often in his *Lives of the Poets* at the end of the decade. What comes as something of a shock in this context is particularly the fact that "the first book in English called *A History of English Language and Literature* by Robert Chambers dates from as late as 1836" (Wellek 1974: 82). As Williams corroborates more generally, one of our commonplace modern conceptions of "literature," as referring to all written and printed works, is thus not very old at all, being specifically a product of the English, Scottish, and European Enlightenment (Williams 1977: 46–48)

How much the early British orientalists in India, including their first East India Company patron, Warren Hastings, were ahead of the times in England is perhaps best gauged by a related set of facts. Fort William College, the principal research and teaching institution of the British Empire under the East India Company, established professorships in the ancient and modern Indian languages at its inception in 1800, so that Sanskrit and Bengali, for example, had their own professors in Henry Thomas Colebrooke and William Carey at the beginning of the nineteenth century. Something similar had happened in Scotland, as part of the Scottish Enlightenment, a little earlier. As Franklin E. Court observes, "University courses in English had been taught at Edinburgh and other universities in Scotland in the eighteenth century," and Adam Smith's lectures on rhetoric and belles letters between 1748 and 1751, as well as Hugh Blair's similarly constituted courses at Edinburgh between 1759 and 1784, had covered "distinctly literary subjects and used selections from English literature extensively" (Court 1988: 796). In contrast, Oxford and Cambridge did not formally recognize England's own "vernacular literature" as a subject suitable for teaching until long into the nineteenth century. In fact, the first professor of English literature in England, the undistinguished Reverend Thomas Dale, was appointed to his position at University College, London, only in 1828. Even after Dale's appointment, the study of English literature—as distinguished from classical studies, and from rhetoric and composition—did not take off properly "until R. G. Latham assumed the University College professorship in 1839" (Court 1988: 806). Furthermore, academic literary studies in English were institutionalized in the United States just as belatedly, if not even more so (Graff 1987; Graff and Warner 1989).

The significant point, however, is that in the English and European usages cited above—in Voltaire, Lessing, and Herder, in Ferguson and Johnson—the category of literature was very inclusive: "It obviously refers to all kinds of writings, including those of an erudite nature, history, philosophy, theology, etc." (Wellek 1974: 81; see also Williams 1977: 47–48). In this the term "literature" and its equivalents in French and German introduced a major shift (and historical repetition) in European thinking about the classification of texts. As Wellek and Williams in their different ways inform us, around the beginning of the Christian era and for a few centuries after that, Latin writers had used *litterae*, meaning "letters," to denote a general body or kind of writing, thus referring to what we now call Greek literature as *Graecae litterae*, or to "divine literature" as *divinarum litterarum*. European Renaissance writers revived this usage when, in order to distinguish "secular literature" from scripture, theological writing, and the erudite writing of the Latin schoolmen, they coined terms like *litterae humanae*, *lettres humanis* (both meaning humane or humanistic letters), and *bonnes lettres* (which we find in Rabelais and Montaigne, among others). The more restricted and familiar form, *belles lettres* (fine letters), appeared in the middle of the seventeenth century and gained currency across Europe, including England, in the eighth century. When the Enlightenment thinkers devised a term like *littérature*, *Litteratur*, or "literature" in the middle of that century, they in effect made it a "new or alternate term" for the old Latin *litterae*, a comprehensive designation for texts and textuality of all kinds. The terms were much wider in scope than *belles letters*, which had already come to mean what the *American Heritage Dictionary* today specifies as "literature regarded for its aesthetic value rather than for its didactic [function] or informative content," though it did not yet carry the pejorative connotations that have become common in the twentieth century (Wellek 1974: 82–83). In short, Alexander Dow (1768), Sir William Jones (1784, 1786, 1788), Warren Hastings (1785), Charles Wilkins (1785), Henry Thomas Colebrooke, and Horace Hayman Wilson, and even their hostile nineteenth-century critics James Mill (1820) and Thomas Babbington Macaulay, were working with a rather new and radical European concept when they applied the word "literature" to Sanskrit, Bengali, Hindi, and other Indian languages. The novelty of the Enlightenment conception of literature as an all-inclusive body of writing persisted long into the nineteenth century, for in 1868 as distinguished a philogist and cosmopolitan an intellectual as Ernest Renan complained that "The group of works that used to be called 'works of the mind' . . . are now designated as 'literature'" (Wellek 1974: 82). Significantly enough, the British-Indian orientalists pushed the word precisely in the direction that allows us today to insert it comfortably and freely in phrases like "Tagalog literature," "Nigerian literature," "Sikh literature," "scientific literature," "popular literature," and "world literature."

To broaden the analysis of the orientalists' conception of literature, it is useful to recapitulate two other points in Wellek's and Williams's respective accounts. One is that the more modern notion of literature as consisting of works of poetry, prose fiction, drama, and nonfictional prose (autobiographies, literary and personal essays, certain kinds of diaries and letters, and so on) that are valued for their aesthetic qualities grew very slowly out of the intersection of the idea of belles lettres and the Enlightenment and orientalist idea of literature as "the total order of words," becoming canonical in western universities only after the end of the nineteenth century (Williams 1977: 49–52). As a matter of fact, the relatively narrow, exclusive, and exclusionary aesthetic conception of literature that has dominated much of this century is largely the product of late-nine-teenth-century symbolism and early-twentieth-century modernism and formalism, especially as these movements emerged in Moscow, Prague, Vienna, Berlin, Zurich, Triéste, Paris, London, Dublin, New York, and Chicago (Bradbury and McFarlane 1976; Calinescu 1987; Karl 1988).

The other important point is that, even as they formulated an all-encompassing definition of literature, late-eighteenth-century European thinkers started to conceive of literature

> as a particular national possession, as an expression of the national mind, as a means toward the nation's self definition. The Germans were particularly conscious of their nationality and in German the term "Nationalliteratur" began to be used widely [in the last quarter of the eighteenth century]. (Wellek 1974: 83)

One of the origins of the powerful link between nation and literature, which still controls our thought, of course lies in Herder's work in Germany between the 1760s and 1780s, and in the writings of the historians Wellek mentions—Ernst Wachler, August Koberstein, G. G. Gervinus, August Vilmar, Rudolf Gottschall—who developed German nationalist literary historiography in the nineteenth century. But another, largely un-acknowledged origin lies in the discourse of the British orientalists dealing with Indian literature, who were influential figures in an international community of orientalists and Europeanists and helped lay the ground-work for the "tradition" of national literary histories that became a world-wide phenomenon in the twentieth century, particularly after the breakup of the empire (for other views on colonial Indian cultural nationalism, see Kopf 1979: chaps. 5–7; Raychaudhuri 1990). In the work of the orientalists on India, as in that of other kinds of European scholars on other subjects, a broad definition of literature was part of a larger theory about the collec-tive shape and substance of a national culture or civilization as a whole.

In other words, the European contexts I have outlined above suggest that the literary orientalists concerned with India adopted an all-inclusive conception of literature, not because their Indian materials demanded or gave rise to it, but because it was the radical new conception that had begun transforming Europe's self-definition and self-understanding in their times. They also adopted such a conception because it enabled them to treat literature as a complete (totalized, totalizable) expression of the "character," "spirit," or racial and cultural identity of a nation. Moreover, it allowed them to occupy the typical site of cross-cultural encounter within the institutional framework of colonialism, in which "literature" and its study defined the European self and the oriental other in the same discursive space, at the same moment. As I shall suggest at the end of the essay, such factors are implicated in the process by which Europeans established and exercized their power over their colonial subjects in Asia.

4. Institutional Inconsistencies in Orientalism

To understand how the three divergent factors mentioned above came together in the orientalists' overall enterprise, it is important to remind ourselves that their discourse about the Indian literatures did not remain conceptually, methodologically, or even ideologically consistent in the course of its history. Over time, orientalist discourse shifted its ground, broke with its own past, expanded in new directions, and repeated itself in unexpected ways. One of its surprising historical features, which emerged clearly by the end of the nineteenth century, was that the orientalists did *not* apply the broad concept of literature, which they had adopted at the beginning of their enterprise, to *all* the Indian languages and traditions. In fact, they reserved the comprehensive definition of literature for very specific cases: the ancient Hindu-Sanskrit world, and the Sanskrit-Pali-Tibetan Buddhist world. In retrospect, the orientalists therefore seem methodologically and even ideologically inconsistent. For, if all their literary and historical efforts were geared to the colonial machine, and directed toward the practical fulfilment of the imperial dream, then they ought to have "mastered" the "living literatures" of India with as much thoroughness as they had covered the ancient literatures. If orientalism was primarily the discursive-disciplinary arm of the colonial state, then a knowledge of the newer bodies of writing would have enabled the orientalists, and their policy making and administrative colleagues, to control their colonial subjects (reduced epistemologically to the status of objects) to an even greater degree in the present. Why, then, did the orientalists adopt a disciplinary double standard?

To answer this crucial question, it is useful first to examine (in this section) how the orientalists actually handled the postclassical literatures of India, and then to turn (in the next three sections) to their own definitions of disciplinary methods and purposes. If we go beyond the account I have provided so far, we find that when literary orientalists started charting out the "other" major Indian literatures, they applied either an attenuated or an alternative conception of literature. This move frequently enabled them to exclude large quantities of existing texts from their historical and critical accounts of the literatures in the various Dravidian and modern Indo-Aryan languages. The result is very evident in the new literary histories of "Indian literature" that began to appear at the end of the nineteenth century and subsequently influenced many common western perceptions of India.

Robert W. Frazer, for example, devoted about two thirds of his *A Literary History of India* (1898) to the discussion of the full range of Sanskrit literature, along the lines Weber (1852) had drawn nearly half a century earlier and Macdonell (1900) was to extend quite rigorously about two years later. But Frazer then used the remaining one third of his book to offer a composite account of Tamil, Hindi, Bengali, Marathi, Panjabi, and Indian Islamic literatures (the last confined to Turkish and Persian sources) in the so-called medieval period, with a final chapter on the British colonization of India and nineteenth-century Bengal, and some modern fiction and poetry by Bengalis in English and in Bengali. He reduced each of the postclassical Indian-language literatures to a few examples of (religious) poetry and their related hagiographic traditions and to a series of selected historical documents, some of which were quite irrelevant to the poetic material under discussion. In his *A History of Indian Literature* (1931), Herbert H. Gowen essentially followed Frazer's pattern and strategy, except for two significant modifications. He offered a more inclusive chapter on nineteenth- and early-twentieth-century Bengali fiction, poetry, and drama (mainly in order to concentrate on Nobel prize winner Rabindranath Tagore), and added a short chapter on the colonial "Anglo-Indian" writers, from Sir William Jones and Bishop Reginald Heber (a friend and minor collaborator of Samuel Taylor Coleridge in England), through Sir Alfred Lyall, Henri Derozio, and Sir Edwin Arnold, to Rudyard Kipling, Meadows Taylor, and Flora Annie Steel.

Within their common framework, Frazer and Gowen followed their Sanskritist precursors in effectively treating Sanskrit literature as literature in the broadest possible sense of the term. For the "medieval" Indian literatures in half a dozen languages, however, they employed a romantic conception of literature as consisting primarily of "expressive" works in prose and verse. They were thus able to read *bhakti* texts—the poems attributed to, and the hagiographic traditions centered around, Caitanya in Bengali, Kabīr in Hindi, Tukārām in Marathi, the Sikh *gurus* and *bhagats* in Panjabi, and the Vaiṣṇava and Śaiva saint-poets in Tamil and Kannada—in a highly restricted way. Correspondingly, in the case of the modern Indian literatures, produced in the colonial period under the "influence" of English, European, or western norms and conventions, they conceived of literature as a body of imaginative and aesthetically oriented poetry, short and long fiction, and drama, largely to the exclusion of other varieties of discourse.

From these instances it is clear that, once the literary orientalists step outside "ancient India" and especially "Sanskrit literature," they tend to reject or replace their own initial conception of literature as the entire body of known and existing texts. One practical reason for such a shift is that, by the turn of the century, literary orientalism as an enterprise of the Raj had reached a moment of collective exhaustion. The progressive mastery of Sanskrit and the ancient Indian traditions had drained several institutions (such as Fort William College and Sanskrit College in Calcutta), as well as the best minds of four or five successive generations of Englishmen, Germans, and Frenchmen. In Europe and in America, a "Eurocentric" reaction had set in against the constant "selling" of Sanskrit by the orientalists and comparatists (Jespersen 1922: chap. 4), and in India the prospect of redoing the project of Sanskrit orientalism a dozen or more times in order to successively cover the most important Dravidian and modern Indo-Aryan languages must have seemed colossal, redundant, wasteful, and even pointless. India was no longer a "theoretical" puzzle of the kind the first orientalists had set out to solve: it was now overwhelmingly a "practical" problem for the British colonial state, to be tackled by administrators, bureaucrats, accountants, policemen, generals, judges, negotiators, and members of Parliament. Max Müller actually recorded the change well before the end of the nineteenth century, when he complained quite bitterly about the new breed of Indian civil service recruits who came to him at Oxford for a "quick fix" introduction to Indian culture (Max Müller 1883: 5–6). In such a situation, even an exhaustive understanding of "the total order of words" in Bengali, the westerners' favorite postclassical Indian language, would have served no discernible colonial purpose.

It has taken more than three decades in a "post-orientalist" age of Indian and South Asian studies (with new transnational networks of political, economic, and cultural interests, postcolonial institutions and sources of funding, and newly immigrant and migrating scholars) to begin the process of dealing with the postclassical languages and literatures of India as inclusively as the orientalists had covered the ancient traditions centered around Sanskrit. The massive post-orientalist shift in the conception of what "literature" is, or might have been, in the cultures of the Dravidian and Indo-Aryan languages of the past one thousand years and more is already perceptible in a number of recent works in Indian literary studies published mainly in the West. To cite examples very selectively from work on five important languages, A. K. Ramanujan (1968, 1981, 1985), George L. Hart III (1975, 1979), David Shulman (1989), Norman Cutler (1987), and Indira Peterson (1989) have mapped out a whole alternative "classical culture" in Tamil, as well as its manifold and gradual shift "from classicism to *bhakti.*" For the cluster of literary languages we call Hindi, Charlotte Vaudeville (1974), Ronald Stuart McGreggor (1984), John Stratton Hawley (1983, 1984), Hawley and Mark Jurgensmeyer (1988), Kenneth Bryant (1978), Linda Hess and Shukdev Singh (1983), and Philip Lutgendorf (1991), among others, have collectively explored a wide range of texts, textual traditions, and performance traditions in the "medieval" period, establishing a new set of interconnections among these traditions and between them and the traditions of the ancient period. Similarly, McGreggor (1974), Peter Gaeffke (1978), Karine Schomer (1983), David Rubin (1977), and Gordon Roadarmel (1974), again among others, have comprehensively opened up the multiform modern literature in Hindi, substantially revising the existing orientalist stereotypes about Indian literary modernity.

On a comparable scale, Shanker Gopal Tulpule (1979), Dilip Chitre (1967), Ian Raeside (1966), Eleanor Zelliot (1976a, 1976b, 1981), Philip Engblom (1987), Zelliot and Engblom (1982), and Ann Feldhaus (1983) have altered our understanding of the multiple traditions of Marathi literature in this millennium. On a more limited but nevertheless significant scale, V. Narayana Rao and Hank Heifetz (1987) and Rao and Gene H. Roghair (1990) have started to compensate for the orientalists' regrettable neglect of the extensive literatures of Telugu. In a different set of instances, Edward C. Dimock, Jr. (1963, 1967, 1986, 1989), David Kopf (1969, 1979), Tapan Raychaudhuri (1990), and Clinton B. Seely (1990) have accomplished an extensive revision of the old orientalist views of premodern and modern Bengali life, literature, and culture. An analysis of the theories, methods, interpretations, and historical and literary insights generated by these scholars will have to await another occasion, but even a quick survey of the works cited above should show that they have systematically "restored the balance" with respect to their orientalist predecessors.

5. The Conception of Philology

As I have suggested in the preceding section, a practical reason for incon-sistencies in the orientalist treatment of the Indian literatures is that of diminishing institutional resources and energy. Another, more theoretical reason why the orientalists by and large concetrated their full powers on Sanskrit, rather than on the postclassical Indian languages, is simply that the most rigorous and influential among them were trained, and regarded themselves professionally, as philologists (see Said 1978; Schwab 1984; Graff 1987). Like the conception of literature, the conception of philology that the literary orientalists brought to their work on Indian materials was related closely to their European intellectual contexts. In fact, the two con-ceptions—one of the subject matter of the field, the other of the discipline that gives shape and substance to the field—are themselves intricately in-terconnected, and exploring the links clarifies the orientalists' conception and treatment of Indian literatures.

Since about the middle of the seventeenth century, the European conception of philology has undergone several crucial changes, and philo-logical practice has acquired fairly distinctive national characteristics, particularly in England, France, Germany, and the United States. Never-theless, over the last four hundred years or so, the word "philology" has quite consistently meant "love of learning and literature" (*OED*). Its prac-tice has been pursued by writers as well as readers and has generally in-volved the systematic and often technical study of words and languages, mainly in the form of grammar and, through it, of rhetoric and poetics, or of literary theory and criticism in general (Graff 1987: chaps. 4–5; Graff and Warner 1989: 1–14).

In England, however, around the middle of the seventeenth century philology was understood in two contrasting ways: relatively narrowly as "Terse and Polite Learning, *melior literatura*," and more broadly "in the larger notion, as inclusive of all human liberal studies" (*OED*). At this point in time, philology was evidently quite close in meaning to the word "literature" itself that, as I suggested earlier, until the last quarter of the eighteenth century designated an individual's skill and interest in writing and in written works, especially "humane letters." The principal difference between philology and literature at this juncture seems to have been the difference we now postulate between an academic, scholarly, or profes-sional interest in literature, and a nonacademic, literary, or amateur one:

in the eighteenth century, "philology" was an erudite scholar's love for learning and literature (as represented in, say, Hugh Blair, professor of rhetoric and belles lettres at Edinburgh), while "literature" was a gentleman's or writer's love for the written word (as represented in, for example, Samuel Johnson and James Boswell; see Graff and Warner 1989: 4–10).

In the case of philology, between the middle of the seventeenth and the middle of the eighteenth centuries the more inclusive and academic meaning of the term won out, so that just before the time of Sir William Jones it designated a master discipline that had several branches of learning, such as "history, civil, ecclesiastic, and literary: grammar, languages, jurisprudence, and criticism" (*OED*). It is quite amazing how literally some of the British orientalists embody this late eighteenth-century definition of philology in their professional careers. Jones, for example, was educated at Harrow and University College, Oxford, and then

> quickly distinguished himself as a poet, critic and linguist, built up a successful practice as a barrister and made a name as a radical pamphleteer. . . . His contribution to the understanding of Hinduism and Sanskrit literature only represents a part of his work as an Orientalist, and his achievement as an Orientalist is only a part of his wider scholarly interests: he was also a classical scholar of very high standing, a historian, and a distinguished academic lawyer, as well as being able to write with authority on astronomy, botany and the theory of music. He was an exceptionally gifted linguist, who mastered both European and Asian languages with great facility. He learnt Arabic and Persian while at Oxford and made his early reputation as an Orientalist with a Persian grammar, essays on Persian and Arabic literature and adaptations from Persian and Arabic poetry. In 1783 after much solicitation he was appointed a puisine judge of the Supreme Court at Calcutta, and went to India for the first time. (Marshall 1970: 14)

The combination of training and interest in law, classics, languages, history, science, and literature we find in Jones remains typical of Indological scholars for nearly one and a half centuries after him. Early in the twentieth century, for example, A. Berridale Keith, "Of the Inner Temple, Barrister-at-law, and Advocate," became the Regius Professor of Sanskrit and Comparative Philology and Lecturer on the Constitution of the British Empire at the University of Edinburgh, producing not only his masterful *History of Sanskrit Literature* (1928), but also a series of authoritative books on the legislative, legal, and administrative workings of the worldwide British imperial system. Clearly, to be a serious or professional scholar (as against a dilettante belleslettrist or a Grub Street hack) in the

Enlightenment and post-Enlightenment world was to be a philologist with a wide-ranging mastery of several "liberal arts" disciplines.

In the nineteenth century, broadly speaking, philology passed out of the hands of philosophers and rhetoricians of the generalist variety (Nietzsche on the art of "slow reading" notwithstanding), and into the hands of new kinds of specialists. It developed into at least three subdisciplines, each of which was to grow into a more or less independent field of study in the twentieth century. The first was classical philology, which was concerned exclusively with the study of the Greek and Latin languages and civilizations in European antiquity and placed great emphasis on a "totalized" knowledge of its object of study. The second was comparative philology, which involved the study of the world's major languages (as in its "founding text," Franz Bopp's *A Comparative Grammar of the Sanscrit, Zend, Greek, Latin, Lithuanian, Gothic, German, and Slavonic Languages* [1833–1849]) and developed a version of historical and cultural relativism as well as a universalist framework for cross-cultural comparisons. The third subdiscipline was what might be called general philology, the "loving" study of any one or more of various languages and literatures, focused in the final analysis on the national traditions of the European vernaculars. In retrospect, it seems that general philology at this time had no particularly strong methodological agenda or investment in subject matter which it could use to compete with classical philology or comparative philology for attention.

By the end of the nineteenth century, stimulated especially by the exciting new Mediterranean archaeology of the period, classical philology had turned into the highly rigorous and well-defined discipline we now recognize as the canonical core of classics departments in twentieth-century universities. Comparative philology had begun metamorphosing itself into modern linguistics (Jespersen 1922: chaps. 3–4) and into smaller fields like romance philology (as practiced by, say, Eric Auerbach 1953 and Ernst Robert Curtius 1953), which were dominated by comparative interests within Europe as a self-contained cultural whole. In England as well as in the United States, general philology had become indistinguishable from modern "literary studies" in the English language, the slightly mysterious business that departments of English still conduct on a daily basis. General philology, in fact, had held on to the least specialized meaning of the word throughout the long transformation, making it possible for *The Yale Review*, for instance, to assert as recently as 1980 that "Philology meant, and still ought to mean, the general study of literature" (*OED*).

6. Philology and Nineteenth-Century Orientalists

Toward the end of the eighteenth century, the literary orientalists who came out to India were trained as classical philologists and explicitly addressed themselves—like Jones in his various lectures and essays, especially pieces like "On the Chronology of the Hindus" (1784) and "On Hindu Gods" (1786)—to fellow classicists back home and abroad, who at that time had wide-ranging interests. By the middle of the next century, however, the world of European classicists had shrunk down to the trivialities and niceties of Greek and Latin, as Max Müller (1859: 1–16) complained, and the orientalists concerned with India found themselves working increasingly as comparative philologists and, more narrowly, as Sanskritists or Indologists. Despite this shift, however, they saw themselves as practitioners of philology, now a transcultural "science" of language, mind, and civilization.

This science could be conceived in several different, even apparently conflicting, ways. The *Athaeneum* of June 25, 1892, for example, Eurocentrically and synecdochically collapsed all of philology into classical philology, claiming that "philology is not a mere matter of grammar, but is in the largest sense a master-science, whose duty is to present to us the whole of ancient life, and to give archaeology its just place by the side of literature" (*OED*). In spite of its prejudicial and perhaps provincial note, however, this statement did capture very suggestively the combination of ingredients that had emerged at the practical level of academic life in the course of the nineteenth century. If we look closely at this combination, we find that philology as a discipline is concerned principally with the past, and not with just any portion of the past but specifically with the earliest period in recorded history. The discipline conceives of the ancient world as the source, beginning, or origin of a civilization, race, people, or nation, and hence also as the explanatory frame of reference for its entire subsequent historical development, evolution, or descent. In effect, philology constitutes itself as a comprehensive historical discipline, by assuming that the present condition of a society or civilization can be understood only as the outcome of its past. In the regress of successively "past" moments that constitute a particular people's history, the "first moment of true civilization" is historically and historiographically the master moment: if that epoch can be understood in its totality, then everything subsequent in time can be understood or explained by working out the requisite facts and principles of change. At the same time, philology constitutes itself as a textual discipline, practicing and perfecting the art of "slowly reading" words, documents, languages—the whole web of verbal significations that, in the first place, provides access to the past, any past. Moreover, in this perspective, since language and thought are inseparable, and language and civilization, history and human beings, documents and societies, are all the intertwined means and ends of philological investigation, philology ultimately also calls itself a master-science of the human mind.

For the nineteenth-century orientalists concerned with India, this was the disciplinary reality of philology, and in keeping with its imperatives they concentrated heavily on a totalized reconstruction of "ancient India," from the Vedic period to the end of the so-called classical age (roughly 1200 B.C. to A.D. 1200). But following Sir William Jones's discovery of the unmistakable connections between Sanskrit, Persian, Greek, and Latin, the "roots" of ancient Indian civilization had become inseparable from the whole theory of an antecedent "Indo-European" civilization, the origin of all origins. The study of Sanskrit thus became central to any understanding of the Occident or the Orient: the orientalist, a white male, could not conceive of defining his self without defining it in the same discursive space as his dark other. As Max Müller argued from within this tradition in 1859, "The object and aim of philology, in the highest sense, is but one,—to learn what man is, by learning what man has been." In order to learn what human beings are and have been, the philologist has to enter the world of Sanskrit.

> In little more than half a century, Sanskrit has gained its proper place in the republic of learning, side by side with Greek and Latin. The privileges which these two languages enjoy in the educational system of modern Europe will scarecely ever be shared by Sanskrit. But no one who wishes to acquire a thorough knowledge of these or any other of the Indo-European languages,—no one who takes an interest in the philosophy and the historical growth of human speech,—no one who desires to study the history of that branch of mankind to which we ourselves belong, and to discover in the first germs of the language, the religion, and mythology of our forefathers, the wisdom of Him who is not the God of the Jews only,—can, for the future, dispense with some knowledge of the language and ancient literature of India. (Max Müller 1859: 2–3)

Between the middle of the nineteenth century and the middle of the twentieth, Anglo-American and European Indologists provided massive evidence to support this overall position. Albrecht Weber, working independently around 1850 (a little before Max Müller), effectively constructed a methodologically "complete" history of Indian literature, in which "Indian literature divides itself into two great periods, the Vedic and the Sanskrit," and ended it around A.D. 1000, thus defining the philological "founding moment" of Indian civilization. Moritz Winternitz, bringing together more than a century and a quarter of intensive Indological research on the literatures of the subcontinent, argued in 1907 that even though it is

> more than doubtful whether the peoples which speak Indo-European languages are all descended from a common origin, still it must not be doubted that a common language, this most important instrument of all mental activity, implies a relationship of mind and a common culture. Though the Indians are not flesh of our flesh, or bone of our bone, we may yet discover mind of our mind in the world of Indian thought. In order, however, to attain to a knowledge of the "Indo-European mind", *i.e.* of that which may be called the Indo-European peculiarity in thought, reflection and poetry of these peoples, it is absolutely essential for the one-sided knowledge of the Indo-European character, which we have acquired by the study of European literatures, to be completed by an acquaintance with the Indo-European mind as evidenced in the distant East. It is for this reason that Indian literature, more especially, forms a necessary complement to the classical literature of Ancient Greece and Rome for all who would guard themselves against a one-sided view of the Indo-European character. Indian literature cannot, indeed, be compared with Greek literature in regard to artistic merit. The world of Indian thought has not, it is true, exercised by any means such an influence over modern European ideas as did Greek and Roman culture. But if we wish to learn to understand the beginnings of our own culture, we must go to India, where the oldest literature of an Indo-European people is preserved. For whatever view we may adopt on the problem of the antiquity of Indian literature, we can safely say that the oldest monument of the literature of the Indians is at the same time the oldest monument of Indo-European literature which we possess. (Winternitz 1907: 5)

As this long passage makes amply clear, for Winternitz, too, "Indian literature" in this context meant largely the "great, original, an ancient literature" of the subcontinent, captured in its essence by the entire surviving web of textuality in Sanskrit.

7. Philology and Early Twentieth-Century Indologists

However, as I remarked earlier, orientalist discourse cannot be treated as a homogeneous formation or a seamless whole. In the 1920s, for instance, the general emphasis on the primacy of Sanskrit in Indian literary history and culture entered a new phase. This shift precipitated itself in A. Berri-dale Keith's equation of "Sanskrit literature," not with "the total order of words" in the language, but with that portion of it which we call the "classical," which is centered in turn around the still smaller portion known as *kāvya* ("poetry," an aesthetically defined variety of verbal com-position and performance). Keith's equation was based on the judgment that Sanskrit *kāvya*—the poetry especially of Kālidāsa and his successors in the second half of the first millennium A.D.—constitutes the permanent master-paradigm of Indian poetry, across most languages, regions, and historical situations on the subcontinent as a whole.

Keith's canonization of *kāvya*—as a body of works, a set of inter-related genres, a well-defined common style, and a bundle of poetic qualities—was in several ways a limited modification of the philological position articulated by Max Müller and Winternitz. It was limited in the sense that it did not reject the basic historical and cultural logic of phi-lology but simply altered the criteria for choosing the "founding moment" of Indian civilization. Instead of valorizing the *earliest* moment of Indian civilization—the literature of the Vedas—as Max Müller, for example, had done in his *A History of Ancient Sanskrit Literature* (1859), Keith val-orized its *best* moment within the ancient period as a whole. It is impor-tant to note that, contrary to some recent anthropological and historical arguments in cases of this kind, Keith's valorization of *kāvya* was not a "construction" of his own making. He critically articulated an already well-defined Indian canonization of *kāvya* that had occurred over one thousand years or more, even as he added a new, complex perspective to it in the European cultural context, and put it to radical uses within the history of Europe and its colonial empires.

The many-layered process of recuperating *kāvya* as the paradigm of Indian poetry, in fact, is not Keith's invention even within the orientalist tradition. It goes back to Sir William Jones's translation of Kalidasa's *Abhijñānaśākuntala* in 1789 and its enthusiastic reception by the romantics in Europe, including Goethe, Herder, Friedrich Schlegel, Chateaubriand, and Hugo. That reception, occurring about one hundred and twenty-five years before Keith, was based not on an Enlightenment-style all-encompassing conception of "literature," but specifically on a nationalist theory of literature. In this romantic theory, a literature is a select body of aesthetically produced verbal compositions, which constitutes the deepest and most valuable "expression" of the spirit of a race, people, society, or nation, or of a national character. As Herder put it in a letter to a friend, commenting on Jones's version of Kālidāsa's play:

Do you not wish with me, that instead of these endless religious books of the Vedas, Upavedas and Upangas, they [the orientalists] would give us the more useful and more agreeable works of the Indians, and especially their best poetry of every kind? It is here the mind and character of a nation is best brought to life before us, and I gladly admit, that I have received a truer and more real notion of the manner of thinking among the ancient Indians from this one Sakuntala, than from all their Upnekats [Upanisads] and Bhagavedams [*Bhagavatpuranas*]. (Quoted in Max Müller 1859: 4–5)

This passage helps us to realize that when, in the 1920s, Keith moved away from his predecessors' obsession with the "Indo-European" theme, he basically chose a more romantic-nationalistic conception of literature over the all-inclusive Enlightenment one. This choice introduced a whole new range of interrealted assumptions and judgments into the argument for the canonicity of classical Sanskrit poetry. If we analyze Keith's position in some detail, we find that *kāvya* is paradigmatic for Indian literature because, in the eyes of European and American philologists as well as certain kinds of Indian *paṇḍits* and common readers, it is the most beautiful, technically accomplished, and emotionally pleasing variety of poetry in Indian literary history. Writing in the mid-1920s, Keith himself makes the case as follows:

The great poets of India wrote for audiences of experts; they were masters of the learning of their day, long trained in the use of language, and they aim to please by subtlety, not simplicity of effect. They had at their disposal a singularly beautiful speech, and they commanded elaborate and most effective metres. . . . It is in the great writers of Kavya alone, headed by Kalidasa, that we find depth of feeling for life and nature matched with perfection of expression and rhythm. The Kavya literature includes some of the great poetry of the world, but it can never expect to attain wide popularity in the West, for it is essentially untranslatable; German poets like Rückert can, indeed, base excellent work on Sanskrit originals, but the effects produced are achieved by wholly different means, while English efforts at verse translation fall invariably below a tolerable mediocrity, their diffuse tepidity contrasting painfully with the brilliant condensation of style, the elegance of metre, and the close adaptation of sound to sense of the originals. (Keith 1928: vii–viii)

As the claim goes at the level of unstated assumptions and premises, since *kāvya* marks the highest point of poetic achievement among the Indian literary genres, it serves, or ought to serve, as a touchstone or norm against which all comparable kinds of literary composition are to be judged. Despite the focus on Indian details, however, the orientalist argument here evidently runs parallel to the classicist argument in European literature—explicit, for example, in the classicism or neoclassicism that runs in English from Ben Jonson and John Dryden to Samuel Johnson, and then through Matthew Arnold, W. B. Yeats, Ezra Pound, and T. S. Eliot—in which the classics of Greek and Latin function as the norms for all or most literary evaluation for a very long time.

Moreover, from the new orientalists' point of view, classical Sanskrit poetry serves as a touchstone because it is a body of writing which generated, late in its own period (especially A.D. 700–1200 or so), the most complex and general of Indian literary and aesthetic theories, which we associate with the concepts of *rasa* (essence, poetic emotion, affect), *dhvani* (sound, suggestion), and *vakrokti* (obliqueness, defamiliarization) [discussed in Dimock et al. (1974)]. As a consequence, *kāvya* is a body of Indian literary texts for which we have a comprehensive criticism and metacriticism that originate entirely on the subcontinent, enabling us to arrive at a "truly relativistic" assessment of native practice in terms of native theory (this relativism, of course, is tied very closely to Herder's romantic-nationalistic conception of literature and culture). In addition, the preeminence of *kāvya* in Indian literature is reinforced by the commonplace late-orientalist judgment that the verse and prose texts of the Vedas, which ancient and modern Indian theorists do *not* classify as "poetry," are canonical for their cosmology and their social, religious, and ritual prescriptions, but fall short of "aesthetic refinement." It is also reinforced by the determination that a text like the *Bhagavad-gītā*, which (as part of the *Mahābhārata*) simultaneously occupies the generic categories of *itihāsa* (history) and *kāvya* (poetry), is a touchstone for religious and philosophical literature rather than for imaginative poetic expression. In other words, to echo the passage from Keith quoted above, among the major genres or style of world literature, Sanskrit *kāvya* is extremely distinctive in its aesthetic framework as well as technical articulation and hence stands out forcefully as a poetic and critical standard. By the time we have reached this point, however, we have replaced the original Enlightenment and orientalist conception of "literature," as "the total order of words" in the language, with a highly restrictive (and, in the Indian case, largely "elitist") conception based on aesthetic and nationalistic canons.

8. Conclusion

From the foregoing exploratory analysis, it should be clear that the orientalists concerned with Indian literatures exercised variable intellectual and political control over their materials, and that their discourse was therefore implicated in differential relationships between knowledge and power. The heterogeneity of the orientalists' discourse, however, was constantly framed and undercut by various continuities and consistencies. At one level, for almost two hundred years the orientalists consistently used an all-inclusive Enlightenment conception of literature (as the total order of words and works in a given language) to define their subject matter and field of expertise, and thus brought an immense quantity and variety of Indian discourse within the range of their investigations, speculations, interpretations, explanations, and representations. At a second level, they consistently operated according to the "imperatives" of their European or Western intellectaul contexts (rather than the pressures exerted on concepts, methods, and expository practices by their Indian materials), defining "literature" as it was defined by the European thought of their day and developing philology within European institutions of legitimate and authoritative disciplinary activity. At both these (sometimes mutually-conflicting) levels the orientalists, in effect, strongly aligned their production of knowledge and their collective representation of Indian literatures with Europe's assertions of political dominance and claims to cultural superiority over the colony on the subcontinent.

At the same time and at a third level, however, the orientalists also used Romantic expressivist, nationalist, and aesthetic criteria to exclude a large number of languages and varieties of literature from their consideration, thus quite deliberately exercising little or no discursive power over substantial portions of Indian literary production. This heterogeneity of orientalist discourse, which was developed over time and articulated within different linguistic, literary, and cultural spaces, clearly made a simple one-directional alignment between knowledge and power impossible. But the orientalists implicitly justified this institutional and methodological inconsistency in their work—between the totalization of Sanskrit and the ancient period, and the partial treatment or neglect of the vernaculars in the middle and modern periods—by arguing that philology as a discipline enabled them to completely understand the founding moment of Indian civilization. Once they had produced such an understanding or knowledge their intellectual task was over, because the study of languages, literatures, and histories outside the founding moment could not seriously displace, question, or alter that knowledge. In proposing such an argument the orientalists used the disciplinary formation of philology simultaneously to accommodate and contain methodological and institutional double standards within their discourse, thus reaffirming European political and cultural dominance at "deeper" or "higher" levels of rationality and coherence.

References

Auerbach, Eric. 1953. *Mimesis: The Representation of Reality in Western Literature.* Trans. by Willard R. Trask. Princeton, NJ: Princeton University Press.

Bathrick, David. 1992. "Cultural Studies." In Joseph Gibaldi, ed., *Introduction to Scholarship in Modern Languages and Literatures.* 2nd ed. New York: Modern Language Association of America, 320–40.

Bopp, Franz. 1833–1849. *A Comparative Grammar of the Sanscrit, Zend, Greek, Latin, Lithuanian, Gothic, German, and Slavonic Languages.* Trans. by Lieutenant Eastwick. Ed. by Horace Hayman Wilson. 4 vols. London: Madden, 1845–1853.

Bradbury, Malcolm and James McFarlane, eds. 1976. *Modernism 1890–1930.* Harmondsworth: Penguin.

Bryant, Kenneth E. 1978. *Poems to the Child-God: Structures and Strategies in the Poetry of Sūrdās.* Berkeley: University of California Press.

Calinescu, Matei. 1987. *Five Faces of Modernity.* Durham, NC: Duke University Press.

Chitre, Dilip, trans. 1967. *An Anthology of Modern Marathi Poetry, 1945–65.* Bombay: Nirmala Sadanand.

Court, Franklin E. 1988. "The Social and Historical Significance of the First English Professorship in England." *PMLA* 103, 5: 796–807.

Curtius, Ernst Robert. 1953. *European Literature and the Latin Middle Ages.* Trans. by Willard R. Trask. Reprint New York: Harper and Row, 1963.

Cutler, Norman J. 1987. *Songs of Experience: The Poetics of Tamil Devotion.* Bloomington: Indiana University Press.

Dimock, Edward C., Jr., trans. 1963. *The Thief of Love: Bengali Tales from Court and Village.* Chicago: University of Chicago Press.

Dimock, Edward C., Jr. 1986. *The Sound of Silent Guns and Other Essays.* New Delhi/London: Oxford University Press.

———. 1989. *The Place of the Hidden Moon: Erotic Mysticism in the Vaisnava-Sahajīya Cult of Bengal.* Chicago: University of Chicago Press.

Dimock, Edward C., Jr. and Denise Levertov, trans. 1967. *In Praise of Krishna: Songs from the Bengali.* Garden City, NY: Anchor Books.

Dimock, Edward C., Jr. et al. 1974. *The Literatures of India: An Introduction.* Chicago: University of Chicago Press.

Dow, Alexander. 1778. "A Dissertation Concerning the Hindoos." In Marshall (1970): 107–39.

Engblom, Philip C., trans. 1987. *Pālkhī: An Indian Pilgrimage.* By D. B. Mokashi. Albany: State University of New York Press.

Feldhaus, Anne. 1983. *The Religious System of the Mahānubhāva Sect: The Mahānubhāva Sūtrapāṭha.* New Delhi: Manohar.

Frazer, Robert W. 1898. *A Literary History of India*. New York: Charles Scribner's Sons.

Frye, Northrop. 1957. *Anatomy of Criticism: Four Essays*. Princeton, NJ: Princeton University Press.

Gaeffke, Peter. 1978. *Hindi Literature in the Twentieth Century*. Vol. 8, Fasc. 5 of *A History of Indian Literature*. Ed. by Jan Gonda. Wiesbaden: Otto Harrassowitz.

Gerow, Edwin. 1977. *Indian Poetics*. Vol. 5, Fasc. 3 of *A History of Indian Literature*. Ed. by Jan Gonda. Wiesbaden: Otto Harrassowitz.

Gowen, Herbert H. 1931. *A History of Indian Literature: From Vedic Times to the Present Day*. Reprint. New York: Greenwood Press, 1968.

Graff, Gerald. 1987. *Professing Literature: An Institutional History*. Chicago: University of Chicago Press.

Graff, Gerald and Michael Warner, eds. 1989. *The Origins of Literary Studies in America: A Documentary Anthology*. New York: Routledge.

Hart, George L., trans. 1975. *The Poems of the Tamil Anthologies*. Berkeley: University of California Press.

———. 1979. *Poets of the Tamil Anthologies*. Berkeley: University of California Press.

Hastings, Warren. 1785. "To Nathaniel Smith, Esquire." In Wilkins (1785): 5–16.

Hawley, John S. 1983. *Krishna, the Butter Thief*. Princeton, NJ: Princeton University Press.

———. 1984. *Sūr Dās: Poet, Singer, Saint*. Seattle: University of Washington Press.

Hawley, John S. and Mark Jurgensmeyer, trans. 1988. *Songs of the Saints of India*. New York: Oxford University Press.

Hess, Linda and Shukdev Singh, trans. 1983. *The Bījak of Kabīr*. San Francisco: Northpoint Press.

Inden, Ronald. 1986. "Orientalist Constructions of India." *Modern Asian Studies* 20, 3: 401–46.

———. 1990. *Imagining India*. Oxford: Blackwell.

Jespersen, Otto. 1922. *Language: Its Nature, Development and Origin*. London: George Allen and Unwin. Reprint. 1969.

Jones, Sir William. 1784. "On the Gods of Greece, Italy and India." In Marshall (1970): 196–245.

———. 1786. "On the Hindus." In Marshall (1970): 246–61.

———. 1788. "On the Chronology of the Hindus." In Marshall (1970): 262–90.

Karl, Frederick R. 1988. *Modern and Modernism: The Sovereignty of the Artist 1885–1925*. New York: Atheneum.

Keith, Arthur Berridale. 1928. *A History of Sanskrit Literature*. London: Oxford University Press. Reprint. 1956.

Kopf, David. 1969. *British Orientalists and the Bengal Renaissance*. Berkeley: University of California Press.

———. 1979. *The Brahmo Samaj and the Shaping of the Modern Indian Mind*. Princeton, NJ: Princeton University Press.

Lienhard, S. 1984. *A History of Classical Poetry: Sanskrit, Pali, Prakrit*. Vol. 3, Fasc. 1 of *A History of Indian Literature*. Ed. by Jan Gonda. Wiesbaden: Otto Harrassowitz.

Lutgendorf, Philip. 1990. *The Life of a Text: Performing the Rāmacaritmānas of Tulsīdās*. Berkeley: University of California Press.

Macdonell, Arthur A. 1900. *A History of Sanskrit Literature*. London: William Heinemann.

Marshall, Peter J., ed. 1970. *The British Discovery of Hinduism in the Eighteenth Century*. Cambridge: Cambridge University Press.

McGregor, Ronald Stuart. 1974. *Hindi Literature in the Nineteenth and Early Twentieth Centuries*. Vol. 8, Fasc. 2 of *A History of Indian Literature*. Ed. by Jan Gonda. Wiesbaden: Otto Harrassowitz.

———. 1984. *Hindi Literature from Its Beginnings to the Nineteenth Century*. Vol. 8, Fasc. 6 of *A History of Indian Literature*. Ed. by Jan Gonda. Wiesbaden: Otto Harrassowitz.

Mill, James. 1820. *The History of British India*. 6 vols. London. Reprint New York: Chelsea House, 1968.

Müller, Friedrich Max. 1859. *A History of Ancient Sanskrit Literature*. Oxford: Oxford University Press. Reprint 1956.

———. 1883. *India: What Can It Teach Us?* London: Longmans, Green, and Co.

The Oxford English Dictionary. 1989. 2d ed. 20 vols. Oxford: Clarendon Press.

Peterson, Indira V. 1989. *Poems to Śiva: The Hymns of the Tamil Saints*. Princeton, NJ: Princeton University Press.

Raeside, Ian, trans. 1966. *The Rough and the Smooth: Short Stories Translated from the Marathi*. Bombay: Asia Publishing House.

Ramanujan, A. K. 1968. *The Interior Landscape: Love Poems from a Classical Tamil Anthology*. Bloomington: Indiana University Press.

———. 1981. *Hymns for the Drowning: Poems for Viṣṇu by Nammāḻvār*. Princeton, NJ: Princeton University Press.

———. 1985. *Poems of Love and War: From the Eight Anthologies and the Ten Long Poems of Classical Tamil*. New York: Columbia University Press.

Rao, Velcheru Narayana and Gene H. Roghair, trans. 1990. *Śiva's Warriors: The Basava Purāṇa of Palkuriki Samanatha*. Princeton, NJ: Princeton University Press.

Rao, Velcheru Narayana and Hank Heifetz, trans. 1987. *The Lord of the Animals— Poems from the Telugu: The Kalahastīśvara Satakamu of Dhurjati*. Berkeley: University of California Press.

Raychaudhuri, Tapan. 1990. *Europe Reconsidered: Perceptions of the West in Nineteenth Century Bengal*. New York: Oxford University Press.

Roadarmel, Gordon. 1974. "The Modern Hindi Short Story and Modern Hindi Criticism." In Dimock et al. (1974): 239–48.

Rubin, David G., trans. 1977. *A Season on the Earth: Selected Poems of Nirala*. New York: Columbia University Press.

Said, Edward. 1978. *Orientalism*. New York: Pantheon Books.

Schomer, Karine. 1983. *Mahadevi Varma and the Chhayavad Age of Modern Hindi Poetry*. Berkeley: University of California Press.

Schwab, Raymond. 1984. *The Oriental Renaissance: Europe's Rediscovery of India and the East, 1680–1880*. Trans. Gene Patterson-Black and Victor Reinking. New York: Columbia University Press.

Seely, Clinton B. 1990. *A Poet Apart: A Literary Biography of the Bengali Poet Jiban-ananda Das (1899–1954)*. Newark: University of Delaware Press.

Shulman, David D. 1989. *The King and the Clown in South Indian Myth and Poetry*. Princeton, NJ: Princeton University Press.

Tulpule, Shanker Gopal. 1979. *Classical Marathi Literature: From the Beginning to A.D. 1818*. Vol. 9, fasc. 4 of *A History of Indian Literature*. Ed. by Jan Gonda. Wiesbaden: Otto Harrassowitz.

Vaudeville, Charlotte. 1974. *Kabir*. Vol. 1. Oxford: Clarendon Press.

Weber, Albrecht. 1852. *The History of Indian Literature*. London: 1878.

Wellek, Rene. 1974. "Literature and Its Cognates." In *Dictionary of the History of Ideas*. Ed. by Philip P. Wiener. New York: Charles Scribner's Sons. Vol. 3: 81–89.

Wilkins, Charles, trans. 1785. *The Bhagavat-Geeta or Dialogues of Kreeshna and Arjoon*. London: C. Nourse. Facsimile reprint. Gainesville, FL: Scholars' Facsimiles and Reprints, 1959.

Williams, Raymond. 1977. *Marxism and Literature*. Oxford: Oxford University Press.

Winternitz, Moritz. 1907. *A History of Indian Literature*. 3d ed. Vol. 1, pt. 1. Trans. S. Ketkar. Reprint. Calcutta: University of Calcutta, 1962.

Zelliot, Eleanor. 1976a. "Dalit Sahitya: The Historical Background." *Vagartha* 12: 1–10.

———. 1976b. "The Medieval Bhakti Movement in History: An Essay on the Literature in English." In Bardwell L. Smith, ed., *Hinduism: New Essays in the History of Religions*. Leiden: E. J. Brill, 143–68.

———. 1981. "Chokhamela and Eknath: Two *Bhakti* Modes of Legitimacy for Modern Change." In Jayant Lele, ed., *Tradition and Modernity in Bhakti Movements*. Leiden: E. J. Brill, 136–56.

Zelliot, Eleanor and Philip Engblom, eds. 1982. "A Marathi Sampler: Varied Voices in Contemporary Marathi Short Stories and Poetry." *Journal of South Asian Literature* 17, 1: 1–169.

Part II

The Genealogy of the Postcolonial

David Lelyveld

6. The Fate of Hindustani: Colonial Knowledge and the Project of a National Language

A well-known episode in the life of Mahatma Gandhi—it provides the occasion for the handsome travelogue that is the only tolerable portion of Richard Attenborough's excruciating film—is the promise he made to G. K. Gokhale when he returned to India in January 1915, after having spent nearly his entire adult life to that point, some twenty-five years, abroad, first in Britain and then in South Africa, to keep his ears open and his mouth shut for a year while he learned anew about his country.[1]

Predictably, Gandhi broke his silence on political issues almost exactly twelve months after his arrival. The occasion was the inauguration of a new university, Banaras Hindu University, India's first national as opposed to provincial one, twinned with what was to become a few years later a Muslim counterpart in Aligarh. Gandhi's speech on that occasion was a remarkable one even though, or maybe because, he didn't get to finish it. Shouted down by Annie Besant, the Irish Theosophist, the speech came to a close when all the maharajas who were benefactors of the university, including the one who was presiding over the gathering, walked off the stage in protest for what they took to be Gandhi's altogether too friendly words for Indian bomb throwers and assassins and their devotion to the cause of Indian freedom. Before he reached that point, however, Gandhi had already been sufficiently provocative: for example, he denounced "the gorgeous show of . . . jewellery" that those same benefactors were wearing in the midst of the squalor and poverty of Banaras.

Gandhi started the speech by apologizing for the fact that he and all the other speakers were conducting the whole proceeding in a foreign language, English. His reasons, for opposing English, he said, were practical: India as a whole would never learn English, and India could never be free unless its leaders could "[speak] to the heart of the nation . . .

working among the poorest of the poor." Otherwise Indian leaders would be "foreigners in their own land." As he had said while still in South Africa, a freedom under such circumstances would just be "English rule without the Englishman."[2] Even for the few who could afford to learn English, their education wasted six years by being conducted in that language. What he now called for was a new generation of "educated" Indians, that is, educated according to European standards, who were prepared to go out to the people throughout the country and serve them in a number of ways, including the spread of a national language. But the issue was not just a matter of practical communication:

> Our language is the reflection of ourselves, and if you tell me that our languages are too poor to express the best thought then I say that the sooner we are wiped out of existence, the better for us.[3]

Over the next thirty-one years, Gandhi returned again and again to the question of language, searching for an inclusive linguistic formula for the "people," that fundamental nationalist concept, to participate in public life and the exercise of power. Real freedom for India required linguistic autonomy, freedom from the domination of the English language. Beyond that, one of the central projects of Gandhi's life was a unifying language for India, one that would overarch the diversities of region and religion and other lines of cultural and linguistic division.

Gandhi's point of departure in the Banaras speech was hardly original. He appears to accept colonial notions, going back to Macaulay, of an "educated" elite, educated initially in English, but now ready to transmit that knowledge to a larger public and to future generations in Indian languages. There is no apparent challenge to colonial institutions and concepts in the construction of an Indian nation, the model of an Indian nation constructed under British tutelage and then transferred to a suitably prepared political leadership in 1947. Or one might put that in a seemingly less imperialistic sense by saying that Indians would be able to take over the institutions of the modern nation state—with or without the consent of their colonial rulers. Gandhi had already developed a radical critique of modernity while still in South Africa, but he was not prepared to carry the full measure of such ideals forward into a practical political program for India.[4]

There is also a concern here, however, with language as a matter of self-identity, of self-defined difference from the ruler, a society to be created by Indians within Indian cultural space. Gandhi says that our language is the reflection of ourselves, and here he seems to mean not only that he wishes to mark off a boundary with the colonial culture, but also that there is something characteristically Indian that is not available in English. Only in an Indian language can a speaker reach "the heart of the nation."

The Banaras incident serves to introduce three themes for the present discussion: the colonial model of language, counter-claims that there is a separate, indigenous character to Indian languages, and the politics of identifying language with political empowerment for a total Indian populace, that is, for a nation—or, on the other hand, for particular populations within India. This will serve as an occasion to consider some of the central questions of modern historiography of South Asia: The centrality of the colonial state and its ideology and the effort to create a nation state, or more than one, by the political mobilization of cultural loyalties. Another way of approaching these matters is to consider the ways both colonial knowledge and nationalist ideology sought to define and fix what were thought to be indigenous, precolonial cultural models. But one would hope to reach beyond these colonial and nationalist perspectives to a more complex historical understanding of how people in India, in many domains of life and not just the grand political narrative, were able to create, change, or resist their institutions and ideologies of communication.

Gandhi is typically vague about what language other than English he might have preferred to use and why, as a matter of fact, he was not using it. He refers to "our language" as well as "our languages." He notes that in the city of Banaras it would have been appropriate to use "Hindi," and he praises the speakers at the recent Indian National Congress who had spoken in "Hindustani." He himself had frequently spoken and written in Gujarati and had ventured a few brief speeches in a very elementary Hindi—or was it Hindustani—at other occasions, nonpolitical ones, over the previous year. Three years later, at the height of the first great India-wide noncooperation campaign, Gandhi was reported to be spending every spare moment, at meals and even in the lavatory, studying a Hindustani primer. Could there in fact be a national language usable or at least understandable to most Indians, and if so what would that language be and how would it relate to other languages, such as Gujarati or Bengali or Tamil and so on? Speaking in Banaras, Gandhi was comfortable enough referring to the language as Hindi, but on other occasions he realized that the definition of Hindi was in dispute—a dispute, most simply stated, first about vocabulary and, second, about what script it should be written in. To the extent that the vocabulary used Sanskrit words, one would tend to call it Hindi; to the extent that it used Persian and Arabic words, one would call it Urdu. Hindi was associated with the *devanāgarī* script, the most common script used for Sanskrit and related, if sometimes distantly, to most of the other written languages of India. Urdu was associated with Persian and ultimately Arabic. Other differences, of syntax and phonology, were slight, some would say almost nonexistent, although there was a much more complex question of the separateness of literary traditions in Hindi and Urdu and how they related to other linguistic varieties past or present. It would be debatable in 1916 to say that Hindi was Hindu and Urdu was Muslim, but there were certainly grounds and occasion for relating language and religion in this way. It was one of the central projects of Gandhi's life, and a tenet of the Indian National Congress after 1920, that the national language must overarch this distinction, that instead of being Hindi or Urdu, it should be Hindustani.

What were the political and social circumstances by which people came to bracket or divide Hindi and Urdu, to associate language with certain social roles and group identities? How were such associations contested or ratified by further political processes? It is important to see these as questions with a history, to consider this defining as a social action, not a matter of fixed abstract categories, and to locate the act of marking boundaries in a narrative of events in the lives of specified persons. Being religious and speaking a language are things that people do over time and according to circumstance. If we remember that in talking about language we are not only dealing with a label or symbolic abstraction but with the actualities of communication—who gets to speak, who is allowed to listen, which topics and settings are appropriate to which linguistic codes— we may be able to find a meeting place between self-conscious cultural identity and the facts of power, competition, and exploitation.[5] We may also find a place to look for the strategic role of British rule in setting down, in significant domains of Indian life, the relevant rules of communicative competence and the categories of people who qualified to participate in public discourse.

Eventually, by the early twentieth century, the question of Hindi-Urdu-Hindustani was placed on the nationalist agenda, particularly by Gandhi. Language was a matter of national unity and the empowerment of the popular will. The British colonial regime—bureaucratic, commercial, and military—had developed new technologies of communication and promoted a repertoire of linguistic competences among a limited class of its subjects. At the higher levels the language of public business was English. But with the important exception of the military, the colonial state made no effort to promote an indigenous Indian language beyond the provincial level. The provincial level, however, was a very wide domain; and by the end of the nineteenth century the modern standard languages of India, including Hindi and Urdu, had been institutionalized in schools, courts, and government offices as well as in books, periodicals, and public meetings. Hindi, Urdu, or both, were official languages in U.P., Bihar, the Central Provinces, Punjab, and many princely states, subsuming beneath them, at least for public purposes, numerous languages and linguistic varieties. That process was by no means finished, for access to the standard was severely limited and the advocates of some languages, notably Punjabi, had rescued them from substandard oblivion.

Hindi and Urdu, however, occupied a special position both in relation to each other and, at least in the minds of some, in relation to all the languages of India as a possible national language. The advocates of one denied the very existence of the other, saw the other as a conspiracy to monopolize participation in the public life of India on the basis of religion. Although many of the languages of India had their "Mussalmani" varieties, texts written in a script derived from Arabic, Persian and Arabic words, poetic meters, and literary genres shared with the wider Islamic world, it was only Urdu that had achieved the status of a standard language in British India.[6] Whether the language was by definition "Mussalmani" or the confluence of all Indian history, whether it was Urdu or Hindustani, came to have much bearing on the definition of India as a national community and the place of Muslims within it.

Colonial Knowledge and the Languages of India[7]

In recent years, a number of scholars, most prominently Edward Said, have addressed the ways in which the European and American study of the rest of the world has been entangled with the goals of political and economic domination.[8] Said has emphasized the encapsulation of colonized others in static notions of tradition designed to deny them control of the conditions of their own lives, but there is a countermovement among colonialists that has sought to transform societies under their control to supposedly universal models of history, to make them full participants, producers, and consumers in a world system of exchange. In either mode, and in actual practice they were often mixed and self-contradictory, the gathering and analysis of information of dominated peoples was not just a piece of intellectual history, although that too was important both for the rulers and the ruled. What characterized this knowledge was that it was institutionalized, it set down the lines for what older style historians called "constitutional" arrangements in the relations between state and society. The partition of India and the boundary lines of states within the federal systems of India and Pakistan are perhaps the most dramatic examples of how cultural categories as construed by the colonial regime became fundamental political facts.

The belated British discovery of India's languages, as Bernard Cohn has shown, was bound up with the acquisition and exercise of territorial domination.[9] For over a century and a half, British traders and soldiers had been content to rely on interpreters and some knowledge of Portuguese or Persian; what they knew of "Hindustani" was that it was a "jargon" associated with Muslims and useful for giving orders to soldiers and servants. Only after taking on direct political authority in 1772 did the British look about them and start to study Sanskrit, Bengali, and "Hindustani" seriously. Starting with William Jones, however, they developed from their study of Indian languages not only practical advantage but an ideology of languages as separate, autonomous objects in the world, things that could be classified, arranged, and deployed as media of exchange. Different languages had different histories, the histories of the people who spoke them or used them to create literatures, and these could be studied comparatively and used to make sense of the advantages that some nations had gained over others in the course of history.[10] India now became a rich field for philological enterprise, just as it was beginning to wane as an exporter of textiles.

It was in this entrepreneurial spirit that a Scottish physician, sometime indigo planter, determined to corner the vernacular market. John Gilchrist arrived in Bombay in 1782 and secured a post as assistant surgeon in the company army. For two years he was posted at Fatehgarh, a small military outpost in the Mughal heartland, not far from Agra. There he decided that the language he had been learning, "Hindustani," was not a jargon at all; it was, in fact, "the grand, popular and military language of all India."[11] With an admirable literature—Gilchrist had started with the *Kulliyāt* of Sauda, a contemporary poet who is still honored—the language deserved far more respect than Gilchrist's European predecessors had accorded it. He believed that by composing a proper lexicon and grammar he would be performing a highly useful service for the Europeans in India, in other words, there was a market. Persuading the governor general in council at Calcutta to give him a year's leave, Gilchrist set about raising a subscription to support his project. He then grew a long black beard, put on Indian clothes, and traveled through the major cities of the Gangetic plains, finally settling in Faizabad, a center of Urdu literature, where he gathered together "learned Hindoostanees," both Hindu and Muslim, and employed them as paid informants.[12]

According to Gilchrist, the Indians he approached "stared with astonishment" when he asked if there were any indigenous dictionaries that he might consult and asked him in turn "if it was yet every known in any country, that men had to consult vocabularies, and rudiments for their own vernacular speech." Nevertheless, Gilchrist set about to prepare an English-Hindustani dictionary, starting with Samuel Johnson's and, like Johnson, using literary quotations, supplied by his informants, to go along with the translated words. But here too he couldn't count on his informants. They kept straying beyond the boundaries of Hindustani:

> . . . my learned associates, were some of them with their mind's eye roaming for far-fetched expressions on the deserts of Arabia, others were beating each bush and scampering over every mountain of Persia, while the rest were groping to the dark intricate mines and caverns of Sunskrit lexicography.[13]

It was not, however, Gilchrist's intention to purify the language. Instead, he considered Hindustani as historically analogous to English with its accumulation of Saxon, Celtic, Latin, French, and other languages, all the result of migrations and conquests.[14] As with English, it was a necessary task to liberate the language, to advance its cause in opposition to the languages of priests and aristocrats. In particular, he considered Sanskrit "a cunning fabrication . . . by the insidious Bruhmuns."[15] Gilchrist now saw it as his task to advance the historical progress of Hindustani by discovering for it new uses. After setting up a proprietary language school in Calcutta, he was appointed in 1800 to become professor of Hindustani at the newly established College of Fort William. Over the next four years he brought together a staff of Indian literati and set them to the task of inventing a Hindustani prose. Intended initially for the instruction of company servants, now required to study Indian languages, the books Gilchrist had printed, some in Persian script, a few in the *nāgarī* script associated with Sanskrit, as many as sixty in all, inaugurated the print revolution in Hindi-Urdu.

The tendency of John Gilchrist's enterprise was to define Hindustani as a unified language that extended over the whole of India. He identified three major varieties according to the extent that they used Sanskrit, Persian, and Arabic, or unmarked Hindi words. He did not explicitly divide the language variations on Hindu-Muslim lines, though he recognized that Brahmans, maulavis, and members of the Mughal ruling class would have varying lexical repertoires. He was prepared to publish in Persian script or *nāgarī*, and he also developed a system of Roman transliteration.[16]

What is striking here is Gilchrist's sheer entrepreneurship. Anything but a bureaucrat, during his relatively brief interludes of employment in the East India Company service he was continually falling out with his supervisors. Instead, through most of his long career in both India and Britain, he operated by seeking investments and partnerships; by hiring informants, teachers, and writers as employees; by "extracting" the raw linguistic material from a wide variety of sources; and by selling his product, as best he could, to a general public. The cause of his schools and his books were advanced by advertisement.

Like so many philologists and lexicographers of his time, Gilchrist had objectified the language, made it an object of study, and developed new possibilities, especially printing, for its use and diffusion. He demonstrated that the "vernacular" could be taught in school. When he wasn't doing language, he was growing indigo, usually with considerably more financial success. In all these respects, Gilchrist would seem to be the model representative of the "print-capitalism" that Benedict Anderson, following Febvre and Martin, associates with the rise of national communities and the nation-state.[17] The difference between them, of course, is the colonial situation. For the audience, the clientele for all these efforts, was exclusively British, by and large officers of the East India Company.

It is worth noting that Gilchrist was an active radical in politics and that his ideas about language were antiauthoritarian in the context of British thought.[18] In Britain, language was a profoundly contested issue, with figures like Tom Paine, William Cobbett, and Horne Tooke placing it at the center of their challenge to established authority. Aarsleff has shown that the comparative philology that grew out of William Jones's Enlightenment classicism was of little influence in Britain until the middle of the nineteenth century. Seeking to undermine the mystification of priests and philosophers, radicals like Gilchrist demonstrated that vernacular language was valid and legitimate for the exercise of power.[19]

By the middle of the nineteenth century, however, British authorities had formulated a very different analysis of the languages of India from the ones developed by their predecessors in Gilchrist's time. The earlier grammars and dictionaries had made it possible for the British government to replace Persian with "vernacular" languages at the lower levels of judicial and revenue administration in 1837, that is, to standardize and index terminology for official use and provide for its translation to the language of ultimate ruling authority, English. For such purposes Hindustani was equated with Urdu, as opposed to any geographically defined "dialect" of Hindi, and was given official status through large parts of North India. Written in the Persian script with a largely Persian and, via Persian, Arabic vocabulary, Urdu stood at the shortest distance from the previous language of official business and was easily attainable by the same personnel. In the wake of this official transformation, the British government began to make its first significant efforts on behalf of vernacular education. The earliest Hindi-Urdu controversies appear to have taken place among the British, with some officials anxious to uproot the old establishment by replacing Urdu with what was still an unformulated standard Hindi.[20]

The colonial analysis of Indian languages was brought to elaborate fruition at the end of the nineteenth century. In September 1886, two official representatives of India, both British, presented a proposal to the Aryan section of the Seventh International Oriental Congress at Vienna for "a deliberate systematic survey of the languages of India, nearer and farther," past and present. Noting that the government of the United States was at that very moment conducting a similar survey of the languages of North American Indians, the orientalists extended their enthusiastic support. G. A. Grierson, one of the officials from India, then presented his research on "Bihari" to "show how radically the real language—the mother tongue of all classes, rich and poor, educated and uneducated alike in Bihar, differs from the so-called Hindi and Hindustani languages." He himself had "attended at the birth" of Bihari, which persuaded him that further research would uncover new languages all over India, buried beneath "the literary or Government language." Grierson dismissed Hindustani—"a camp jargon"—which he differentiated from Urdu, the language of "Mussalman pedants," and "Pundit-ridden" Hindi, both "mere inventions of the closet." Someday, perhaps, the railway and the printing press might establish this official language as "the norm of half-conversation," but for now it was an imposition. "Before a poor man can sue his neighbor in the court he has to learn a foreign language, or to trust to interpreters, who fleece him at every step." It was therefore desirable for British officials to learn the local spoken languages.[21]

In Bihar Grierson had already developed his methodology: to get some "village Gurus," give them some model sentences in Hindi, and have them write the corresponding words in their own "*bôle*." They would have to be supervised by "a couple of sharp Sub-Inspectors of Schools." Sir Monier Monier-Williams, Boden Professor of Sanskrit at Oxford, proposed that each language and dialect be given a translation of the Sermon on the Mount. Later, it was decided to use the Tale of the Prodigal Son instead, though there was some difficulty about the swine and the kine upsetting religious sensibilities. The fatted calf had to be turned into a goat.[22] When all this was done it would be possible to prepare a grammar and dictionary. Grierson expected that the work for the whole of India would take three years.[23]

The work took many more years than that because a reluctant government was at first disinclined to give Grierson the time, money, or power to carry it out and his fellow scholar officials were less than supportive. Eventually, with some government and voluntary assistance, although largely although his own efforts, Grierson brought out the monumental *Linguistic Survey of India (LSI)*. By 1902 the first volumes were ready to go to press. Volume IX, Part I, *Specimens of Western Hindi and Panjabi*, did not get published until 1916. In the *LSI* "Western Hindi" was bracketed with Panjabi, and Rajasthani with Gujarati. "Eastern Hindi" was a separate category altogether, not to be confused with Bihari, which belonged with Oriya, Bengali, and Assamese.

Each language was a contained entity with a demarcated geographic identity—as determined from administrative headquarters. The exception was what Grierson now called "Literary Hindostani," in its Urdu and Hindi versions and their varying literary styles. His attitude to these languages was hardly more positive than it had been twenty years before.[24] Grierson believed that every individual in a population had a single "mother tongue" and that it was possible to locate and count the speakers of each language and represent them on maps and statistical charts. This was, of course, the work of the Census of India, started in 1881 after some censuses at the provincial level in the previous decade.[25] Grierson became involved with the census operations in 1901, and his analysis of India's languages prevailed over the 1911 report.[26]

For Herbert Risley, the director of the 1901 census, there was an additional consideration, the relation of the biological evolution of identifiable social groups to language: "all languages may be regarded as true genera and species from which no hybrid progeny can arise." While conceding an analytic distinction between "race" and "language," he placed emphasis, for example, on the "differences of phonetic capacity among the Indian races." Groups differed in their ability to pronounce /v/ as opposed to /w/ or /s/ as opposed to /sh/, just as it was impossible for Europeans to make certain non-European sounds like the click in Xhosa or the guttural /gh/ in Arabic (and Urdu). The relation between linguistic shifts and migrations of racial groups were matters for serious "ethnological" research.[27] In contrast to Gilchrist's entrepreneurial enterprise, which saw Hindustani as an Indian language that could be used in the same sorts of ways as its European counterparts, the later colonial analysis of language tended to fix boundaries and limits and to associate them with similarly bounded populations that could be counted and located for the purposes of administrative control.

Indigenous Formulations of Hindi and Urdu

One body of nationalist writing on the history of language explicitly denies the relevance of colonial knowledge to the contested terrain of Hindi/Urdu/Hindustani. Recently, Amrit Rai has identified some traditions of devotional poetry from the eleventh to the seventeenth century as evidence of a far-flung linguistic unity reaching through the whole of northern India and well into the south.[28] The proper name, according to Rai, for this various but unified language, often used at the time, is Hindi.

Amrit Rai's account of "the origin and development of Hindi-Urdu" is above all an impassioned polemic that urges writers of both Hindi and Urdu to draw on the widest possible concept of the Hindi-Urdu past as a literary heritage. To put this another way, Rai's study is a contribution to the narrative of the nation, with special emphasis on what is perceived to be the tragedy of Hindu-Muslim division and the calamity of partition. In this account the formation of Urdu as language, literature, and community was a highly regrettable event, and the villains of the piece, the agents of the bifurcation of a unified linguistic entity, properly called Hindi, are to be found not among the British colonizers but rather among people associated with the Mughal court in the eighteenth century, its period of decline.

Rai's history repeats and elaborates on an older book by a distinguished linguist, Suniti Kumar Chatterji.[29] According to so-called genetic linguistics, the philological tradition that Chatterji belonged to, languages are natural, organic systems whose synchronic features and diachronic developments are to be understood according to scientific principles. The component subsystems of any language, particularly phonology, morphology, and syntax, but also a core lexicon and, for Rai, even the script, all exist and change according to the internal dynamics of what is essentially a self-contained entity. Both Chatterji and Rai rely on literary texts, above all *bhaktī* poetry, as the data for their historical reconstructions, but these are taken as just that, data, evidence of what is referred to as natural language and how it has varied over time and space. Poets, or anyone else for that matter, are at most agents of diffusion, moving linguistic features from one territory to another. In this process whatever variation one finds remains constrained by the underlying structures of the language. What is unnatural, according to this theoretical position, is for an event to take place, for conscious human agents to intrude on this linguistic aquarium, motivated by considerations that are extraneous to the internal principles of language in itself.[30]

The crucial turning point in Rai's narrative, the founding event in what he calls "the cultural divide," is the familiar story of the poet Vali arriving in Delhi from Aurangabad in about 1702. Although Emperor Aurangzeb had long established his imperial headquarters in Aurangabad, Delhi remained the cultural capital of the empire. At this point, Vali's poetry, like that of his Dakhani predecessors, drew freely on Indic sounds, words, and to some extent, themes. Rai makes a point of arguing that Dakhani, often called Hindi at the time, was indeed part of the unified field of language and literature that he has demarcated for the previous centuries. But in Delhi, so the story goes, Vali was taken aside by Shah Gulshan and told to change his poetry to make the language conform to the language of the Urdu-i Mu'alla, the exalted cantonment of Shahjahanabad, that is, Delhi. Shah Gulshan also advised him to confine himself to themes and images of the Persian literary tradition.

What follows is what Rai calls, in capital letters, "the Language Reform movement," led by an "Irani lobby" in Delhi. Vali returned to Delhi about 1720, a few years after the Mughal court had shifted back from the South. By all accounts his new poems created immense excitement and stimulated much imitation. There were numerous *musha'iras*, poems were memorized, copied, widely dispersed. The institution of *ustād* and *shāgird* was extended to the new style of poetry: teachers corrected the work of their pupils, schools of poets engaged in controversies over matters of imagery and diction. Shah Hatim, who according to Garçin de Tassy wrote out a list of his numerous disciples, including Sauda,[31] purged his earlier *divān* of "all indigenous Hindi and Braj Bhaka words." His revised *divān*, called *divānzāda*, son of *divān*, included rules that Arabic and Persian words, if "near to comprehension," should always be used in preference to "Hindavi" or "Bhaka" ones. Poetic language should conform to "the usages of Delhi, which are the idiom of the Mirzas of India and the pleasure-seeking men of culture." Rai then jumps ahead to a later generation and quotes Nāsi̱kh, "As long as you find Persian and Arabic words that serve the purpose, do not use Hindi words." Nāsi̱kh represents a further development, according to Rai, because as a resident of Lucknow, not of Delhi, he had to compensate all the more for his unfamiliarity with the ways of the Mughal court.

The final stage in this narrative of linguistic conspiracy is Insha's *Daryā-i Laṭāfat,* written in 1808, a work in Persian on the grammar and diction of what he calls, simply, Urdu. Insha starts out by asserting that any country has a center that sets cultural standards and that the center of Hindustan is Delhi under the auspices of the royal court.[32] From this Rai arrives at the clincher of his argument, a quotation from the Babi-i Urdu, Abdul Haq, in 1961 after he had moved to Pakistan: "It was Urdu," he said, "that created Pakistan."

Although Amrit Rai effectively undermines a cultural history of India founded only on the dominance of colonial theories and practices, his narrative of elite Muslim conspiracy exemplifies Partha Chatterjee's description of Indian nationalism as a "derivative discourse" based on colonial prototypes.[33] It also falls into the elementary historical fallacy of seeking "origins" in the context of anachronistic assumptions.[34] Identifying a language as a bounded entity to be located in dictionaries, grammar books, a literary canon and, most important, a "community" of human beings who can be counted and located on a map—all these are developments that emerged in nineteenth-century India and distort our understanding of earlier times.

There was, of course, a precolonial history to the languages and literatures of India, which continued sometimes in response to and sometimes in spite of British ideas and institutions. But such long and various language histories need not be construed in terms of bounded linguistic communities or, indeed, bounded bodies of linguistic behavior called "languages." Although Sanskrit (and for Muslims, Arabic), as codified by the classical grammarians, stood apart as a perfected entity, the languages people actually spoke, like their *jātī* identities, were believed to be the result of mixing over time and were situationally variable. Languages were not so much associated with place as with function, and in many cases the naming of a language—for the directors of British census operations and more elaborately for the *Linguistic Survey of India*—was problematic. People didn't have languages; they had linguistic repertoires that varied even within a single household, let alone the marketplace, school, temple, court, or devotional circle. These codes of linguistic behavior took on the same characteristics of hierarchy that other sorts of human interaction did; they were after all the most common medium of interaction. In that sense Sanskrit could stand as the primal whole to which all speech had ultimate reference. Recitation, conversation, and other modes of linguistic expression were exchanges of physical substance that continually altered what a person was as a moral being, creating new combinations, new social collectivities. Language then was part of a flexible ideology of occasion and identity.[35] In Sanskrit drama and also in a good deal of the courtly literature of the later Muslim sultanats there is often a deliberate use of multilingual variation in a single text, and many wrote in more than one language.[36]

In the eighteenth century, before Europeans knew of it, there had already developed a canon of Urdu literature as defined by a number of *tazkiras*, biographical dictionaries, of poets, as well as prescriptive guidelines for judging the correctness and aesthetic status of the language. There was a literary world sufficiently wide for controversies about metaphor and diction to reach well beyond Delhi to other outposts of Mughal culture.[37]

But Hindi and Urdu did not get into print until the early nineteenth century. Gilchrist and the missionaries may not have reached a wide audience in India, but at least they had solved some of the problems of printing Hindi and Urdu with movable type and lithography. In the first decades of the nineteenth century, there emerged an indigenous public for printed material, in particular lyric poetry, prose narratives, religious texts, and newspapers. The earliest printed works were published in Calcutta. These, along with a new development of popular religious oratory, appear to establish a new public sphere in which Hindi and Urdu were to develop and to change the nature of the Hindi or Urdu text as a social object.[38] As a modern standard language, Urdu tended to lead the way, while in the later decades of the nineteenth century Hindi drew on Bengali as well as Urdu models in the formation of new forms and uses. Not only in rules of syntax and morphology but in matters of rhetoric and genre this new Hindi was in many respects closer to Urdu than it was to Braj, Avadhi, and other, older literary languages it purported to encompass.[39]

Printed texts in Hindi and Urdu were distributed by sale or prior subscription to a general public, and it was within this new social space that new genres of Hindi-Urdu utterance developed and old ones were transformed. The source and recipients of a printed text were not bound by complex social relations that entailed authority or obligation. The book or newspaper could have an autonomous existence as a commodity. On the other hand, it was still possible for published books to be exchanged in the same way as manuscripts had been.[40]

It would be a mistake to look for the development of a public language only in the written word, especially in a society in which access to reading and writing was so limited and oral performance loomed so large. Manuscript or printed, texts were often aids to recitation. There were certainly preachers and storytellers in India long before the British came, although evidence about the languages they used is thin. But in the nineteenth century we encounter great popular orators, such as Sayyid Ahmad Barelvi and Shah Muhammad Isma'il, who toured North India in the 1820s. Their sermons, like the translation of the Qur'an into Urdu in the 1790s and its publication (as an interlinear text with the Arabic) in 1829, may mark the transition from the global community of believers to an Urdu-knowing South Asian Muslim public. The audience for these preachers was formally inducted into Sufi discipleship, and the ultimate aim of the movement was to reestablish India as an abode of Islam; but in the context of British rule we may begin to see the formation of a mobilized opposition. The language of these preachers, from Peshawar to east Bengal, was Urdu. It was filled with scriptural quotations in Arabic but avoided the Persianized diction of courtly literature. There appears to have been a good deal of such oratory in the 1857 Revolt.[41] From the 1870s Dayananda Saraswati and others established a Hindu oratorical counterpart in Hindi.[42]

The book, the oration, and the poetic recitation all find new institutional settings in the course of the nineteenth century, moving into new regions of style and subject matter while retaining features and conventions of earlier periods. Starting in the 1830s, Urdu became a subject to be learned in school and not merely a matter of extrapolating what one had learned of Persian writing on to the language one already knew through speech. The slow spread of western-style education and the concurrent establishment of new maktabs and madrasas both involved the preparation of printed textbooks—from Arabic and Persian in one case, from English in the other. Such translations from such diverse sources left their mark in a multiplicity of Hindi and Urdu prose styles. The same was true of journalism, with newspapers and magazines often relying on translation.[43] The British, both government and missionary, had considerable influence here, both in their patronage of schools and books and in the ability of the government to define opportunities for literate employment in official service, but the public for Urdu or Hindi, or both, appears to have run well ahead of the meager stimulus that the British provided.[44] With the increasing availability of models to cover a wide variety of uses, writers had many options in deciding with words to use, how to construct a sentence, how to organize a text. Out of these choices emerged a multiplicity of Urdu and Hindi audiences, some of which were religious in their orientation, but not necessarily Muslim for Urdu or Hindu for Hindi.

The rise of voluntary associations and the public meeting after 1857, gatherings outside the *darbar* of a ruler or a religious assemblage, created new arenas for the oration and the poetic recitation. Admission tickets or memberships, published verbatim proceedings after the event, lists of the people who came and how much they donated to the cause—all this was new to India. The great Urdu orators of the late nineteenth century, such as Sayyid Ahmad Khan, Nazir Ahmad, and Muhsin ul-Mulk, did not offer mystic discipleship. They spoke on behalf of social causes. Such meetings usually had poetry, often on current political themes or what was called "naichar." One special type of public meeting was the religious disputation, first brought on by Christian street preaching, later in orderly debates. The proceedings were often published.[45]

Another new setting for the use of Hindi and Urdu was theater, starting at the court of the Nawab of Avadh in 1853 but soon expanding out to traveling companies, often Parsis based in Bombay. The writers for this "Parsi theatre," like Agha Hashr Kashmiri, were usually North Indian Muslims. The conventions of Urdu poetry were suitable to courtly and chivalrous themes, but the plays apparently appealed to a diverse audience whose understanding of the finer points might have been limited.[46] The more popular *nautanki* theater drew freely on both Hindi and Urdu diction, metrical forms, and literary conventions.[47]

From Language Controversy to the Politics of Partition

The combination of new public uses of the spoken languages of India and their administrative role in the colonial regime was a recipe for political controversy starting in the late 1860s.[48] A representative example of the early Hindi-Urdu debate occured when the Indian Education Commission came to Aligarh in August 1882 and its chairman, W. W. Hunter, received a deputation of fifteen Muslim notables from four adjoining districts. Hunter, perhaps the supreme "expert" of the Indian Civil Service, having served as Director-General of Statistics and presided over *The Imperial Gazetteer*, had lived in India for twenty years. But the members of the deputation still felt it necessary to tell him what language people spoke in India. That language, they claimed, was Urdu. They weren't speaking as Muslims, they assured the British official. "Urdu is not our religious or national [*qaumi*] tongue. . . . It is a product of India itself."

> We are zamindars, often frequent our villages, talk with every description of cultivators [*kashtkār*] of both sexes, see and hear them converse with each other, and find that it is Urdu which is the mother tongue [*mutanaffis kī zubān*] of them all.[49]

Unfortunately, there is no record of the conversations that the zamindars had overheard in the villages they owned. The text that we do have is a "memorial" (*yād dāsht*) of some wealthy Indian landholders, men with considerable power over a fair number of people, presented to an official British commission of enquiry. Its purpose was to contest other "memorials" and "evidence," presented on the same occasion, which made sharply conflicting linguistic claims.[50] At issue was what the British government should or should not do to encourage education, or rather, schooling: what kind, how much, and for whom.

The use of the word *mutanaffis* (having breath, being animate), morphologically unmodified from the Arabic and inaccurately translated at the time in the phrase "mother tongue," was just the sort of thing the opponents of Urdu objected to. Aside from its form, the word carried heavy ideological baggage that reached beyond India to a widely shared Islamic vocabulary: the contrast between *nafs*, the "lower soul," and *'aql*, the intellect.[51] *'Aql* draws on the energy of *nafs*, but it is the power of reason and spiritual enlightenment that must control and channel mere biology toward higher purposes, for example, in the forms and uses of language. Richard Kurin has identified this opposition in contemporary Pakistani Punjab, where Urdu "may be associated with the cultivation and control of *'aql*" and Punjabi, "with the immanence and immediacy of *nafs*." Another way to characterize the "earthiness" of a language in Punjab or northern India is to call it *theth*, which means genuine, idiomatic, and rural.[52] A word that has the virtue of being neither Sanskrit, Arabic, or

Persian, *theth* usually characterizes Punjabi and non-Sanskritized Hindi, not Urdu. But by calling Urdu *mutanaffis kī zubān*, the members of the Muslim deputation were claiming for it that same homegrown authenticity—and distancing themselves from it. From one point of view, the choice of vocabulary undermines their argument. But from another, it is a way of asserting, at least to their own satisfaction, the authority of their greater knowledge and discernment, that is, their *'aql*.

The major figure of Hindi literature in the nineteenth century, Bharatendu Harishchandra, also met the education commission, when it came to Banaras. The problem with Muslims, he told them, in English, was that they have "a sharp and oily tongue" and try to "overpower other people." The reason they wanted to retain Urdu was that it gave them a monopoly of the clerical and subordinate administrative posts in government and enabled them to dominate the legal profession. Aside from that, it was the language of prostitutes. Urdu was just a device for cheating people. Take away the chicanery, he said, and it was the same as the most widespread form of Hindi, Khari Boli.

As part of his testimony, Harishchandra explained in some detail the linguistic variety of northern India, where the language changes every eight miles. In his own writing he drew on a literary tradition that played on linguistic diversity. He adapted into modern language plays from Sanskrit and Prakrit, which themselves had characters speaking different languages according to their status and situation. If Sanskrit was the eternal and perfect foundation of being and knowledge, the languages of ordinary life, like the circumstances of real human beings, were various and unequal. Aside from the Khari Boli, Harishchandra himself wrote in several varieties, especially Braj, but sometimes even Urdu.[53]

The trouble with Urdu was not only in its vocabulary; even more relevant to the matters at hand was the Persian script, especially when it was written in *shikast*, its shorthand style. Ever since 1868 the educationist Siva Prasad had led a campaign to replace this script with *nāgarī*. Testifying before the commission, Siva Prasad reiterated his arguments by giving examples of the ambiguity and deception possible in the Persian script.[54] The Muslim deputation in Aligarh, on the other hand, claimed that *nāgarī* was inappropriate for government records because it took too long to write and took up too much space. It was the script of shopkeepers.[55]

In these early examples of the Hindi-Urdu controversy, the spokesmen for either side spoke with clear, well-formulated authority. It is important to recall, however, that it was the commission that had set the agenda, chosen the participants, and dictated the form of their testimony. There appears to be a shared assumption, for example, that the language of education and government ought to be the common language of everyday life as spoken by the population at large. In fact, the predominance of English at the higher levels of both domains is not called into question, and the population at large remains an abstraction. The enquiry also rests on the assumption that once the British government is persuaded of the true nature of language in India it will take appropriate steps. It was W. W. Hunter, after all, who wrote the final report. In this particular case, it was the conclusion of the panel—announced before the proceedings even started—that schooling ought to be a matter of "free enterprise" : Indians could run their own schools and choose the language of instruction.[56] The government would continue to provide "grants-in-aid," but would close down all but a handful of government schools. As for the language of official business, that was not part of the commission's writ.

It was this sort of controversy between Hindi and Urdu that Gandhi sought to address in his campaign for an overarching Hindustani in the early twentieth century. Although he argued that all Indian languages, even his own Gujarati, ought to be written in the same script, he made a special exception for Urdu. It could continue in *nastalīq* derived from Arabic via Persian. But what was more important was the spoken language, and here all that was at issue was the lexicon: a Hindustani that would avoid words that were strongly marked as Sanskrit or Arabic, that would seek neutral words as much as possible, and that would give no premium to words of a particular derivation at the cost of common usage.

One of the final arenas for this controversy came with the development of radio broadcasting under strict colonial control but for that very reason subject to intense political demands in the final ten years of British rule.[57] Film, on the other hand, was a creature of the market—during this period a largely urban one—and made somewhat different linguistic decisions. The policy of the authorities in charge of broadcasting was to formulate an acceptable lexicon that would bridge the gap between Hindi and Urdu, not necessarily at the expense of other Indian languages or English. Although there were a few points of morphology, phonology, syntax, and genre that marked a distinction between Hindi and Urdu, vocabulary was the main issue of public controversy, particularly with respect to newscasts. Eventually, the concern broadened to include statistical tabulations of the extent to which poetry readings, radio dramas, and talks, the standard BBC-style fare that All-India Radio (AIR) provided, could be counted as one or the other. As a spoken medium, radio would not seem to raise the question of *nāgarī* versus Persian script, but it did. Because of strict censorship rules and the absence of recording technology, everything that was said had to be written out in advance. As a result, radio texts were closely tied to established literary language.

Designs for All-India Radio were developed at the same time as the major constitutional reforms that brought popularly elected provincial governments, mostly under the Congress, in 1937. For this reason, British authorities were careful to keep control of broadcasting as a central power. All news broadcasts were prepared in English, translated into selected Indian languages, and transmitted from Delhi. That left little room for linguistic variation. But centralized control of language was also the result of a deliberate cultural policy promoted by Lord Reith of the BBC: the idea that each language had a single standard of clarity and aesthetic perfection and that it was the business of broadcasting to exemplify that standard. With certain specified exceptions, radio was designed for a literate audience.

The most important figure in the leadership of AIR in the preindependence years, especially with regard to language policy, was Ahmad Shah Bukhari, who joined in 1935 as station director in Delhi and served as Director-General from 1939 to 1947. The authorities of All-India Radio faced a continual barrage of protests about the details of language.[58] Their policy was entirely consistent with the ideas of Gandhi, Nehru, and the Indian National Congress, but that didn't protect them from parliamentary questions, budget resolutions, public meetings, petitions, and boycotts from all sides of the dispute. The advocates of Hindi were the most seriously dissatisfied, but every gesture of concession in their direction inspired an equally angry response from the Urdu side.

In 1940, Bukhari appointed S. H. Vatsyayan "Ageya" and Chaudhuri Hassan Hasrat, well-known writers in Hindi and Urdu respectively, to prepare an authoritative lexicon for Hindustani news broadcasts. The procedure was to list English words from the original news copy from which the vernacular translations were prepared. The Hindi poet then made a list of Hindi equivalents, the Urdu essayist set down his Urdu counterparts; then the two sat down and worked out a compromise based on what they considered most common, precise, and, if possible, neutral. The lexicon took five years to complete and was then submitted to influential political and literary figures for comment.[59] By then, Hindustani was already a lost cause and separate Hindi and Urdu broadcasts were about to start.

Having failed to establish a unified language, Bukhari and AIR's chief engineer, C. W. Goyder, conceived of another strategy in a plan for post-war broadcasting development. In 1944, they undertook "to formulate a scheme by which every person in India, wherever he is situated, is provided with a broadcast programme in his own language. . . ." By that time, All-India Radio was broadcast from nine cities to about 90,000 licensed radio receivers. Relying on the *Linguistic Survey of India*, somewhat revised by S. K. Chatterji, and the 1931 and 1941 censuses, including a set of maps charting population densities and urban-rural distributions, they set out to establish the most rational distribution of transmitter locations, broadcasting studios, and listening areas within the constraints of ninety-five possible wavelengths. On such a map there was no place for either Hindustani or Urdu.[60]

Language, Culture, and the Nation-State

Like Borges's tale of an imperial map that was the same scale as the empire itself, the pre-independence plan for radio broadcasting stands for the ambition and futility of colonial knowledge and its nationalist derivative.[61] Since Partition, neither Hindi nor Urdu as separate national languages of India and Pakistan respectively have had more than qualified success. In official hands, including radio, television, and the sponsored textbooks of the schools, standard Hindi emphasizes Sanskrit vocabulary that is supposed to link it to similarly Sanskritized styles of most, but not all, of India's other standard languages, the languages of the states. It is in six North Indian states with over forty percent of the Indian population that modern standard Hindi prevails.[62] For the rest of India, however, Hindi has failed to establish itself as the national language. The Hindi film industry is still largely Hindustani, but it has been surpassed in production and audience by three regional languages of South India. In Pakistan, on the other hand, Urdu has no regional base, though it has become identified with a rapidly forming ethnicity of North Indians and their descendants who migrated in the wake of partition. Throughout South Asia it is English that still dominates the highest levels of power and privilege, because no South Asian can compete with an English already in place as a language of official business and transregional communication, to say nothing of the advantages of English in international communication and for the purposes of emigration to richer countries. Even where Indian languages are used, as in the news broadcasts on radio and television, they are translated from English originals.

It is clear that the history of Hindi and Urdu and the fate of Hindustani does not lend itself to a linear narrative or a clear identification of either colonial knowledge or indigenous cultures as explanatory of how languages have come to be bounded from each other and associated with particular populations. One aspect of the distinction of modern standard Hindi from modern standard Urdu can be associated with markers of Hindu or Muslim identity, but the considerable overlap between them, the Hindustani remnant, includes also the influence of English models, along with the kinds of uses to which standard languages are put in modern India and Pakistan. And it remains the case that the languages used by most South Asians for most purposes are neither Hindi nor Urdu.

Perhaps because poetry is less translatable than journalism, for example, it has remained in the minds of many the core marker of linguistic difference. But the considerable realm of interchangeability among the standard South Asian languages emphasizes the paradox of nationalism, that the marking of boundaries does not necessarily entail significant cultural difference. As Benedict Anderson and others have taught us, claims of national distinctiveness are often relatively vacuous in comparison to the "modular" uniformity of the nation as a system of institutions. But for this very reason Anderson overestimates the power of nationalism to overawe other forms of emotional commitment, including religion. What may count as matters of national, religious, or some other identity, ideology, or institutional system are subject to mutual influence and continuing change. There is no evidence that this history has come to an end.

Notes

1. *The Collected Works of Mahatma Gandhi* (New Delhi: Publications Division, 1958–) XIII, 16.

2. *Hind Swaraj* in *The Collected Works*, X, 15.

3. Speech at Benares Hindu University, February 6, 1916, in *The Collected Works*, XIII, 211.

4. Cf. Partha Chatterjee, *Nationalist Thought and the Colonial World: A Derivative Discourse* (London: Zed Books, 1986), 85–130.

5. Cf. Raymond Williams, *Marxism and Literature* (Oxford: Oxford University Press, 1977), 21–44.

6. This was pointed out by Rajendralala Mitra in "On the Origins of the

Hindvi Language and its Relation to the Urdu Dialect," *Journal of the Asiatic Society*, 33 (1865): 513–18. See David Shulman, "Muslim Popular Literature in Tamil: the Tamimancari Malai," in Yohanan Friedmann, ed., *Islam in Asia* (Boulder, CO: Westview Press, 1984), 174–207; Asim Roy, *The Islamic Syncretist Tradition in Bengal* (Princeton, NJ: Princeton University Press, 1983), 8–15.

7. For an expanded version of this section see my "Colonial Knowledge and the Fate of Hindustani," *Comparative Studies in Society and History* (forthcoming).

8. Edward W. Said, *Orientalism* (New York: Pantheon, 1978).

9. Bernard S. Cohn, "The Command of Language and the Language of Command," in Ranajit Guha, ed., *Subaltern Studies: Writings on South Asian History and Society* IV (Delhi: Oxford University Press, 1985), 276–329. I am of course heavily indebted to Cohn, but I will briefly go over the same ground to make some additional points.

10. See Michel Foucault, *The Order of Things: An Archaeology of the Human Sciences* (New York: Vintage, 1973), 294–300.

11. This is part of the lengthy subtitle of Gilchrist, *The Stranger's Infallible East-Indian Guide,* third ed. (London: Kingsbury, Parbury, and Allen, 1820).

12. Quoted in M. Atique Siddiqi, *Origins of Modern Hindustani Literature* (Aligarh: Naya Kitab Garh, 1963), 49. See also Sadiq-ur-Rahman Kidwai, *Gilchrist and the "Language of Hindoostan"* (New Delhi: Rachna Prakashan, 1972), 37–43.

13. Siddiqi, *Origins*, 63.

14. Ibid., 154

15. Quoted in Kidwai, *Gilchrist*, 90–91.

16. Kidwai, *Gilchrist*, 89–96; Siddiqi, *Origins*, 153–55; Sisir Kumar Das, *Sahibs and Munshis: An Account of the College at Fort William* (New Delhi: Orion, 1978), 65, 82–84.

17. Benedict Anderson, *Imagined Communities: Reflections on the Origin and Spread of Nationalism* (London: Verso, 1983); Lucien Febvre and Henri-Jean Martin, *The Coming of the Book: The Impact of Printing 1450–1800* (London: New Left Books, 1976).

18. [Gordon Goodwin], "John Borthwick Gilchrist," *The Dictionary of National Biography*, reprint ed. (Oxford: Oxford University Press, 1917) VII, 1221–23.

19. Hans Aarsleff, *The Study of Language in England, 1780–1860* (Princeton, NJ: Princeton University Press, 1967), 44–72; Olivia Smith, *The Politics of Language, 1791–1819* (Oxford: Clarendon Press, 1984), 110–53.

20. Christopher Rolland King, "The Nagari Pracharini Sabha (Society for the Promotion of the Nagari Script and Language) of Benares, 1893–1914," Ph.D. dissertation, University of Wisconsin, 1974, 66–105.

21. GOI Home/Political 311–29, 1887; reprinted in R. A. Singh, *Inquiries into the Spoken Languages, Census of India, 1961* I, 124–25.

22. GOI Home/Public A, 43–54, 1886, in Singh, *Inquiries into the Spoken Languages,* 126; see also 267–71.

23. GOI, Finance and Commerce/Bonuses and Honorariums 143, 1887, in Singh, *Inquiries into the Spoken Languages*, 133.

24. *Linguistic Survey of India* IX, Part I (Calcutta: Superintendent of Government Printing, 1916), 42–56. For a critique of the methodology of the *LSI* see John

J. Gumperz, *Language in Social Groups* (Stanford, CA: Stanford University Press, 1971), 1–11.

25. Singh, *Inquiries into the Spoken Languages*, 107–14.

26. See Grierson, *The Linguistic Survey of India and the Census of 1911* (Calcutta: Superintendent of Government Printing, 1919); his *Index of Language Names* (Calcutta: Superintendent of Government Printing, 1920) and the General Reports in the 1901, 1911, and 1921 censuses. For an excellent discussion of the British colonial project with regard to language, see David Washbrook, "'To Each a Language of His Own': Language, Culture and Society in Colonial India," in Penelope J. Corfield, ed., *Language, History and Class* (Oxford: Basil Blackwell, 1991), 179–203.

27. Herbert Risley, *The People of India* (Calcutta: Thacker, Spink & Co., 1915), 8–10.

28. Amrit Rai, *A House Divided: the Origins and Development of Hindi-Urdu*, reprint ed. (Delhi: Oxford University Press, 1991). My discussion here draws from my paper, "*Zubān-i urdu-i mu'alla* and the Idol of Linguistic Origins," *Annual of Urdu Studies* (forthcoming).

29. Suniti Kumar Chatterji, *Indo-Aryan and Hindi* (Ahmedabad: Gujarat Vernacular Society, 1942), 131–197.

30. Sarah Grey Thomason and Terrence Kaufman, *Language Contact, Creolization, and Genetic Linguistics* (Berkeley: University of California Press, 1988).

31. Garçin de Tassy, *Histoire de la litterature hindouie et hindoustani*, reprint of second ed. (New York: Burt Franklin, 1968) II, 588–98; cf. Ralph Russell and Khurshidul Islam, *Three Mughal Poets* (Cambridge, MA: Harvard University Press, 1968), 37–38.

32. Saiyad Insha' Allah K̲h̲an Insha', *Daryā-i Laṭāfat*, trans. into Urdu by 'Abd ur-Ra'ūf 'Uruq, reprint ed. (Karachi: Aftāb Academy, 1962), 22.

33. Partha Chatterjee, *Nationalist Thought* (note 4).

34. Marc Bloch, *The Historian's Craft*, trans. Peter Putnam (New York: Vintage, 1964), 29–35.

35. See Gumperz, *Language in Social Groups* (note 24); Michael C. Shapiro and Harold F. Schiffman, *Language and Society in South Asia: Motilal Banarsidas*, (Delhi; Columbia, MO: South Asia Books, 1981).

36. Late Luigia Nitti-Dolci, *The Prakrita Grammarians*, trans. P. Jha (Delhi: Motilal Banarsidas, 1972); 'Abd u'l Ghani, *A History of Persian Language and Literature at the Mughal Court* (Allahabad: The Indian Press, 1926, 1930), Part II, 116–120.

37. For example, see Sarfarāz K̲h̲ān K̲h̲atak, *Shaikh Muhammad 'Ali Hazīn* (Lahore: Sh. Muhammad Ashraf, 1944). See my "Eloquence and Authority in Urdu: Poetry, Oratory and Film," in Katherine P. Ewing, ed., *Shari'at and Ambiguity in South Asian Islam* (Berkeley: University of California Press, 1988), 98–106. For a classic comparative study see Eric Auerbach, *Literary Language and its Public in Late Latin Antiquity and in the Middle Ages* (Princeton, NJ: Princeton University Press, 1965), 237–238.

38. Frances W. Pritchett, *Marvelous Encounters* (Riverdale, MD: Riverdale Co., 1985), 20–29; Muhammad 'Atīq Siddiqi, *Hindūstāni Ak̲h̲bārnavīsi (Kampanī kē ahd mē)* (Aligarh: Anjuman-i Taraqqī-i Urdū [Hind], 1957), 262–63; Krishna

Kumar, "Quest for Self-Identity: Cultural Consciousness and Education in Hindi Region, 1880–1959," *Economic and Political Weekly* 225, 23 (June 9, 1900): 1247–55.

39. See Ronald Stuart McGregor, *Hindi Literature of the Nineteenth and Early Twentieth Centuries*, vol. 8, fasc. 2 of *A History of Indian Literature*, ed. Jan Gonda (Wiesbaden: Otto Harassowitz, 1974); Christopher Shackle and Rupert Snell, *Hindi and Urdu Since 1800: A Common Reader* (London: School of Oriental and African Studies, 1990).

40. Barbara Daly Metcalf, *Islamic Revival in British India: Deoband, 1860–1900* (Princeton, NJ: Princeton University Press, 1982), 201.

41. Harlan Pearson, "Islamic Reform and Revival in the Nineteenth Century: the 'Tariqah-i Muhammadiyya,' " Ph.D. dissertation, Duke University, 1979.

42. Kenneth W. Jones, *Arya Dharm: Hindu Consciousness in 19th-century Punjab* (Berkeley: University of California Press, 1976), 34–35.

43. Mīr Hassan, *Maghribi Tasanīf kē Urdū Tarājim* (Hyderabad: Daftar Idarah-i Adabiyat-i Urdū, 1939); Muhammad Sadiq, *A History of Urdu Literature*, 2nd ed. (Delhi: Oxford University Press, 1984), 342–43.

44. See my *Aligarh's First Generation: Muslim Solidarity in British India* Princeton, NJ: Princeton University Press, 1978), 68–92. For British literary patronage see C. M. Naim, "Prize-Winning *Adab*: A Study of Five Urdu Books Written in Response to the Allahabad Government Gazette notification," in Barbara Daly Metcalf, ed., *Moral Conduct and Authority: The Place of Adab in South Asian Islam* (Berkeley: University of California Press, 1984), 290–314.

45. Metcalf, *Islamic Revival in British India* (see note 40), 215–34.

46. Sayyid Viqar 'Azim, *Agha Hashr aur un ke dramā* (Delhi: A'tiqad Publishing House, 1978).

47. Kathryn Hansen, *Grounds for Play: The Nautanki Theatre in North India* (Berkeley: University of California Press, 1992), 38.

48. See my *Aligarh's First Generation*, 97–99. For major studies of the politics of Hindi versus Urdu see Kerrin Dittmer, *Die Indischen Muslims und die Hindi-Urdu-Kontroverse in den United Provinces* (Wiesbaden: Otto Harrasowitz, 1972); King, "The Nagari Pracharini Sabha" (note 20).

49. *Aligarh Institute Gazette* XVII, 64 (August 12, 1882), where the text is presented in both English and Urdu. The statement says that none of the members of the deputation could read English.

50. Indian Education Commission, *Report by the North-Western Provinces and Oudh Provincial Committee* (Calcutta: Superintendent of Government Printing, 1984). Hereafter EC/NWP.

51. The word *mutanaffis* derives most immediately from *nafas*, breath, related to but separate from *nafs*, soul. It is reasonable to associate the two words with *mutanaffis*, not only in etymology but in the usage of late-nineteenth-century Urdu.

52. Richard Kurin, "The Culture of Ethnicity in Pakistan," in Ewing, ed., *Shari'at and Ambiguity* (note 37), 223–25, 235–38.

53. EC/NWP, 195–211. See McGregor, *Hindi Literature* (note 39), 75–83; Madan Gopal, *The Bharatendu: His Life and Times* (New Delhi: Sagar Publications, 1972).

54. EC/NWP, 312–29. See King, "The Nagari Pracharini Sabha" (note 20 above), 106–14.

55. *Aligarh Institute Gazette* XVII, 64 (August 12, 1882). Harishchandra and Siva Prasad were both, by caste designation and family background, identified with merchants.

56. *Aligarh Institute Gazette* (August 22, 1882).

57. See my "Transmitters and Culture: The Colonial Roots of India Broadcasting," *South Asia Research* 10, 1 (Spring 1990).

58. Ravi Shanker Shukla, *Language Policy of A.I.R. (Atrocities of the A.I.R. on Hindi and Hindu Culture)* (Allahabad: Provincial Hindi Sahitya Sammelan, n.d. [1944]).

59. *A.I.R. Lexicon* (New Delhi: All-India Radio, 1946) [Library of Congress]; PZ-3/42 (Coll I), 1942; P(1)Z-2/46-II, 1946 (AIR Archives); interview with Vatsyayan in Bombay, 1982.

60. Directorate-General, All-India Radio, "Basic Plan for the Development of Broadcasting in India" (first draft November 1944; revised September 1945) in Home-Public 179/1946 (National Archives of India).

61. Jorge Luis Borges, "Of Exactitude in Science," in *The Universal History of Infamy*, trans. N. di Giovanni (New York: Dutton, 1972), 141.

62. Baldev Raj Nayar, *National Communication and Language Policy in India* (New York: Frederick A. Praeger, 1969), 72; for recent critical comments on the politics of Hindi see Ashis Nandy, "The Political Culture of the Indian State," *Daedalus* 118, 4 (Fall, 1989): 6–7.

Rosane Rocher

7. British Orientalism in the Eighteenth Century: The Dialectics of Knowledge and Government

Introduction

Edward Said's sweeping and passionate indictment of orientalist scholarship as part and parcel of an imperialist, subjugating enterprise does to orientalist scholarship what it accuses orientalist scholarship of having done to the countries east of Europe; it creates a single discourse, undifferentiated in space and time and across political, social, and intellectual identities. Written primarily with the Middle East and Islam in view, it includes India and Hinduism by a dittoing procedure founded on sparse documentation. By failing to examine German scholarship—the predominant branch of Indology through much of the nineteenth and twentieth centuries—it shies away from confronting the crucial issue of what may be attributable to colonial conditions and what may not. By collapsing the entire history of orientalism into a consistent discourse, it leaves in the shadows the precise relations between the genesis and uses of particular forms of knowledge and their immediate historical environments. In doing so, it obscures the more central issue of the intricate dialectics between the pursuit of knowledge and governmental pursuits, an issue that is not restricted to orientalist knowledge and imperial governments, but one that every scholar must face. Examining closely the connections of political and intellectual concerns at given points in history and in different milieus may serve to identify the multiple processes that come into play.

The period between 1772 and 1794 in Bengal affords a particularly apt opportunity to analyze the articulation of orientalist knowledge with a colonial government in the making. The year 1772 marked the assumption of the governorship by Warren Hastings and his implementation of the East India Company's decision to exercise direct administrative control

over Bengal, which heralded the transformation of what had been a private
trading company into a colonial power. Hastings's governmental policies
were the most orientalist any British governor in India ever enacted. He
was also a scholar of Persian and a patron of oriental scholarship (Marshall
1973). The orientalist knowledge the production of which he fostered
served as a foundation both for modern Indological scholarship and for
government policies that withstood later, Anglicist administrations. By
1794, when Sir William Jones died, the system of justice that Hastings had
decreed and that Jones consolidated was firmly entrenched, and Indological knowledge produced in Bengal was institutionalized in the Asiatic Society, from which it was beamed to Europe. As such, this period represents
a singularly important as well as intimate concatenation of political and
intellectual concerns.

As one of the foremost scholars of East India Companies has observed, "in considering what we should now do to learn more from the
history of East India Companies, we must never forget that the men who
directed and served them hardly knew what imperialism was. They knew
what trade was. . . . Even toward the end of the eighteenth century when
the rule of the English and Dutch Companies over large populations was
becoming clearly apparent, contemporaries were not thinking in terms of
Kipling's 'White Man's Burden'" (Furber 1970: 415–16). Hutchins (1967)
and A. Nandy (1983), who do not focus on trade, also note that the prevailing ethos was not yet imperialist in this period. Yet, a colonial government
was being introduced in India. These years were rife with ambiguities and
changing perceptions.

Initially, the British East India Company had not been eager to assume the direct administration of its possessions in Bengal. After the
Moghul emperor ceded the Diwani of the three provinces of Bengal,
Bihar, and Orissa in August 1765, it took six years and a devastating famine
that disrupted the collection of revenue for the home administration to
decide to "stand forth as Diwan by the agency of the Company's servants"
(August 28, 1771, quoted in Misra 1961: 153). Until the 1790s the home administration of the Company and the British public at large remained opposed to expansionist wars and the further annexation of territories. Yet,
sentiments changed in the waning years of the century. Whereas the wars
Hastings waged in the 1770s and 1780s were severely censured at home,
the Third Mysore War in 1790–92 earned his successor Cornwallis official
commendation and popular adulation (Marshall 1992). This changing
mood is documented pictorially, with the emergency of a heroic, jingoistic
style in British portraiture relative to India (Archer 1979: 417–35).

When Company servants were beginning to wrestle with issues of colonial administration and increasingly complex relations with other Indian powers, the primary object of the home administration of the Company remained trade, and it was a commercial training it expected of, and provided to, its civil servants. Not until Governor Wellesley founded the College of Fort William in 1800 did the Company provide formal instruction to its personnel. Until then the only qualification that was required of the young men it sent to India at an average age of sixteen was a certificate in accounting, and the only education it offered them was on-the-job training. New writers were sent to up-country factories to learn about trade and to pick up local languages.[1] These factories were manned by a handful of Europeans—in 1783 the total number of British civil servants in Bengal was still below three hundred.[2] The Europeans' world in the *mofussil* was primarily made of native trading partners and native assistants in the midst of native populations. Many lived openly with native women and some wore native dress.[3] At least until the newly arrived mastered oriental languages—Persian for official correspondence and the local vernacular for trade—they were managed by their *banians* or native factotums. These *banians* were or became men of great wealth and consequence,[4] and Europeans often remained dependent on them through their entire stay, all the more so when they had taken out sizeable loans from them to get started on their private business ventures or to indulge in one or another luxury. These middlemen were crucial for the Europeans' private trade, which throughout the eighteenth century remained the main avenue to amassing a competence, in spite of a steady increase in official salaries intended to stem predatory personal ventures.

Until the end of the eighteenth century the Company did not feel compelled to train its servants in the duties of colonial administrators, and it did little more than attempt to set limits to their activities from afar and from above. The most notable attempt at control occurred when Lord Cornwallis was pointedly chosen from outside the ranks of Company servants to succeed Hastings as governor-general. By and large, the rank and file of eighteenth-century civil servants, from which most orientalist scholars came, behaved like bees in a garden, come to collect honey from bush to bush, with little sense of responsibility toward their surroundings, save for their determination to preserve optimal conditions for their harvest. As Hutchins (1967: chapter 1) has shown, they did not yet view the British presence in India as either permanent or inherently just. In that and other respects they were very different from their successors in the nineteenth century, who, though nominated at the same age, were not sent out into the field, but were detained in Calcutta at the College of Fort William for some two years of language instruction and indoctrination in the duties of colonial officers. Nineteenth-century civil servants enjoyed better formal instruction in oriental languages than their eighteenth-century predecessors, but that instruction was part and parcel of the training of imperialist officers. The tenor of that educational philosophy is evident in the titles of the students' disputations and declamations in oriental languages held at the College. In March 1803, for example, the future cadres of the British government in India addressed the following propositions:

> in Persian:
>> The natives of India under the British Government enjoy a greater degree of tranquility, security and happiness than under any former government.
>
> in Hindustani:
>> The suicide of Hindoo widows by burning themselves with the bodies of their deceased husbands is a practice repugnant to the natural feelings, and inconsistent with moral duty.
>
> in Bengali:
>> The distribution of Hindoos into customs [castes?] retard[s] their progress in improvement. (Das 1978: 150)

What developed among those who sat together in classes at Fort William, and even more so later on at Haileybury, was a class spirit, an esprit de corps which bonded them together and segregated them from those they were being trained to rule. For all its emphasis on oriental languages, Fort William College was a training school for imperial-minded administrators, and its imperial founder acknowledged it when he stated "the College must stand or the Empire must fall" (quoted Kopf 1969: 131). Eighteenth-century civil servants had a very different training, and their attitudes reflected it. Servants of the Hastings circle scoffed at Wellesley's love of pomp and at his posturing as a great proconsul (R. Rocher 1983: 213). The different conceptions which Hastings, who rose through the ranks of civil servants in India in the 1750s to 70s, and Wellesley, the aristocrat sent from home in 1797 to extend the British possessions in India into an empire, had of their own roles and of the British presence in India are evident even from their sartorial styles (Archer 1979: compare plates 47, 72, 164 and 219–20).

When appreciating the attitude of those of the Company's servants who searched for orientalist knowledge, it is also necessary to take into account the intellectual climate of the times. As Halbfass (1988) has made clear, dogmatic Eurocentric attitudes were not yet the norm in the eighteenth century. Those British civil servants who had an intellectual bent were men of the Enlightenment and leaned toward deism, as has been documented both in a general way (Marshall 1970: introduction; Halbfass 1990: chapter 4) and with special reference to Jones (Mukherjee 1968: 42–43, 96–97). This did not make them free from cultural and other blinders; it did not exempt them from experiencing difficulties in understanding foreign concepts and from interpreting them through the lens of their own culture and of the dominant thought processes of their times. Yet the prevailing attitude, the general will, among them was one of tolerance and of purposeful, if not always successful, attempt at learning and at understanding. Though statistical data are hardly available, it is evident that a higher proportion of civil servants were aficionados of Indian culture in the eighteenth century than was the case in later times. We know primarily those who published the results of their studies, but there were a vast number of Europeans who collected manuscripts, particularly of Persian texts and of Persian translations of Sanskrit texts, since Persian was then the administrative language and the one most Europeans knew best. Hastings himself and Chief Justice Sir Robert Chambers as well as lower-rung servants such as Richard Johnson had large collections of manuscripts.[5] Even John Shore, the future Lord Teignmouth, who was to join the Clapham Saints and give support to the Anglicist and missionary cause in later life, labored in 1784, when a young civil servant, on a translation of the Vedantic text *Yogavāsiṣṭha* in Persian translation (Teignmouth 1843: 1: 110–11). Interest in Indian culture was not confined to those projects that were motivated by or applicable to governmental concerns.

It is the purpose of the following pages to illustrate some of the diverse motivations for and consequences of the production of orientalist knowledge in the late eighteenth century. At one extreme of the spectrum were some projects that were conducted at governmental behest and for governmental purposes; at the other were some that had neither such origin nor such potential use. Most interesting are those for which connections with governmental concerns were neither straightforward nor always planned.

As the agenda for the production of oriental knowledge was complex, so was the situation of the British government in India, which wrestled with establishing the foundations of a colonial administration while often being at odds, and always fearing it might be at odds, with the home administration of the Company, with Parliament and the Crown, and with a growing segment of the British public that took interest in Indian affairs. Some steps taken by the British government in India that impinged on the production and dissemination of orientalist knowledge were rooted in its tussle with the metropolis more than in local, colonial circumstances. They are by no means reducible to a dichotomy of ruler and ruled.

We will begin with an example of orientalist knowledge that was entirely determined by government concerns, both within India and with regard to Britain.

Orientalist Knowledge and the Enfranchisement of Hindus

Foremost in the production of orientalist knowledge for governmental purposes were two treatises on Hindu law, the first commissioned by Hastings in 1773 and published in English translation by Nathaniel Brassey Halhed (1776) under the title *A Code of Gentoo Laws* (henceforth *Code*); the second proposed to Cornwallis in 1788 by Sir William Jones and published in English translation by Henry Thomas Colebrooke (1796–98) after Jones's death under the title *A Digest of Hindu Law on Contracts and Successions* (henceforth *Digest*).[6] Both were produced at government expense from composition to publication.[7]

In the famed Judicial Plan of 1772 Hastings resolved that "in all suits regarding inheritance, marriage, caste, and other religious usages, or institutions, the laws of the Koran with respect to Mahometans and those of the *Shaster* with respect to Gentoos shall be invariably adhered to" (quoted Acharyya 1914: 153). This statement of intent coalesced a number of discrete decisions.

A first decision was to have Indian, not common, law administered to Indians. This was a fundamental principle of orientalist government and stemmed from the conviction Hastings and his associates had that "it would be a grievance to deprive the people of the protection of their own laws, but it would be a wanton tyranny to require their obedience to others of which they are wholly ignorant, and of which they have no possible means of acquiring a knowledge" (Gleig 1841: 1: 400).

A second decision inherent in Hastings's plan was to have native laws apply only to what was then perceived to be religious usages or institutions, that is, usages and institutions that corresponded to subjects that in Britain fell then under the purview of ecclesiastical law and the Bishops' courts (Derrett 1968: 233–35). Thus Hastings's resolve not to impose foreign laws on Indians was less categorical than his stated rationale. It still placed most of what was then perceived to be lay matters squarely under the purview of British laws and regulations. Its consequence was that it set the British on the dangerous course of having to discriminate the religious from the lay under changing conditions both in Britain and in India. It was an issue they were to prove notoriously unable to solve and that they were often prone to manipulate in later times (examples in Mani 1986 and 1987, Dirks 1989).

A third decision subsumed in the Judicial Plan was to find the source of laws in books rather than in local customs. With the benefit of hindsight, scholars of Hindu law now consider this to have been a mistake, though an understandable one (Derrett 1968: 292–93; L. Rocher 1972). All Hindus would have claimed that their religious—if the term made sense—usages and institutions were founded on *dharma*, and some, although by no means all, were aware that there was a body of texts on the subject, even if few knew much about their contents. If Hastings considered at all applying local customs, he must have feared that collecting them would take time and that Anglicist sentiment in Britain might mistake these customs for, and dismiss them as, the product of an illiterate, uncivilized people; he was intent on providing documentary proof that "the inhabitants of this land are not in the savage state in which they have been unfairly represented" and that they "do not require our aid to furnish them with a rule for their conduct, or a standard for their property" (letters of March 1774 to Lord Chief Justice Mansfield and the Court of Directors of the East India Company, quoted R. Rocher 1983: 53). The principal consequence of the decision to found Hindu law on the Sanskrit *śāstras* was to have Hindu law defined by Brahmanical norms, but, as Derrett (1968: 234–35) has shown, the fact that the British confused Brahmans with priests made it all the more natural for them to vest what was then conceived as ecclesiastical law in Brahmans, just as it was in Bishops' Officials in Britain. This decision also had a deep effect on Sanskrit scholarship, in that it led to a renaissance in *dharmaśāstra* literature. The specially commissioned *Code* and *Digest* were only two of a considerable number of legal treatises eighteenth-century pandits composed at the instance of the British (list in Derrett 1968: 270–73). At the same time this decision made of *dharmaśāstra* texts, both ancient and modern, one of the branches of literature most studied by early British Sanskritists.

An underlying assumption of Hastings's Judicial Plan was that the multiplicity of cultural and religious traditions in India was reducible to a dichotomy: Muslim and Hindu. It showed no awareness or recognition of Jains, Sikhs, Parsis, or tribals, who, for the purpose of personal laws, were made to be subsets of Hindus—only Parsis have since had their separate identity recognized (Derrett 1968: chapter 1). Hastings's decision also implicitly condemned Indian Christians to being governed by nonindigenous laws and hence to being treated as if they had exited Indian society to join that of foreigners.[8] The lumping together of different groups under the label "Hindu" for the purpose of personal laws led to much confusion (Derrett 1968: 542–45), all the more since for other purposes, such as caste, a narrower definition of "Hindu" has been used (Galanter 1989: chapter 7). The net effect, however, of categorizing most non-Muslims as Hindus was to make the Hindu majority appear yet more overwhelming than it was, and they were precisely the people whom Hastings sought to enfranchise. Indeed, the most important yet unstated decision that underlay the Judicial Plan was to discontinue the official monopoly Muslim law had enjoyed in civil courts under the regime the British were displacing. For all its simplicity and for its stated purpose of upholding local norms with minimal intrusion from the foreign power, it was a radical act.

British sympathies tended to be on the side of Hindus against Muslims in the eighteenth century. There were evident political reasons for this. Not only had Europeans a heavy baggage of fear of, and hostility toward, Muslims that went back to the struggle for Spain and the Crusades, in India the British were primarily displacing Muslim powers. The two great villains of eighteenth-century British India from the perspective of the British public were both Muslims: Suraj-ud-Daula, of the infamous Black Hole of Calcutta, and Tipu Sultan, whose fall was the object of novel and massive public celebrations (Marshall 1992). It was natural that the British try to recruit Hindus to their side, all the more since Hindus constituted a majority of the people. The British cast themselves as the protectors of a vast and suppliant majority that had been held under the thumb of Muslim oppressors.[9] None was more eloquent on this subject than the translator of the *Code* Hastings had commissioned. While engaged in this translation, Halhed wrote a rousing panegyric of Hastings as the savior of Hindus from "each prostitute decree, each venal law the pliant Coran sold" and the restorer of "[their] country's laws, . . . the moral system of the slighted Vedes" (poem titled "The Bramin and the River Ganges," dated May 22, 1774, quoted R. Rocher 1979: 217–19). The "Preliminary Discourse" of the pandits who composed the *Code* voiced the same sentiments:

And whereas, this kingdom was the long residence of Hindoos, and was governed by many powerful Roys and Rajahs, the Gentoo religion became catholick and universal here; but when it was afterwards ravaged, in several parts, by the armies of Mahomedanism, a change of religion took place, and a contrariety of customs arose, and all affairs were transacted, according to the principles of faith in the conquering party, upon which perpetual oppositions were engendered, and continual differences in the decrees of justice; so that in every place the immediate magistrate decided all causes according to his own religion; and the Laws of Mahomed were the standard of judgment for the Hindoos. Hence terror and confusion found a way to all the people, and justice was not impartially administered; wherefore a thought suggested itself to the Governor General, the Honourable Warren Hastings, to investigate the customs of the Hindoos, and to procure a translation of them in the Persian language, that they might become universally known by the perspicuity of that idiom, and that a book might be compiled to preclude all such contradictory decrees in future, and that, by a proper attention to each religion, justice might take place impartially, according to the tenets of every sect. (Reprinted Marshall 1970: 183)

Although this document shows strong evidence of British inspiration and is not included in any of the manuscripts of the original Sanskrit text of the *Code*, it has a parallel in a dedication to Hastings by the pandit author of another treatise he commissioned. The compendium of *Purāṇas* by Rādhākānta Tarkavāgīśa hails the governor-general as superior to Hindu and Muslim kings, in that he sought to protect the laws of each community, not just his own:

Hindu and Muslim kings of this earth are well versed in the principles of their own canonical texts (*śāstras*), but are hostile to each other's. There is no ruler on earth other than Hastings who, like the lord of the universe, in his wisdom upholds all canonical texts, he who assembled the best of pandits to compose the *Code of Gentoo Laws* for the welfare of his subjects. (Translated from the Sanskrit manuscript of the *Purāṇārthaprakāśa*, 1783, British Library Or. Ms. 1124)

The same notion is also pictorially represented in the lithograph that adorns the *Map of Hindoostan* of James Rennell (1783)—a friend of Hastings who had served as surveyor-general in Bengal—, which shows Britannia bestowing on deeply beholden Hindus a document labeled "Shaster."[10]

In spite of this rhetoric, Hastings's policies were not strikingly pro-Hindu. All the Judicial Plan of 1772 did was to make Hindu law the standard for civil cases between Hindus in British courts. If the pay scales of pandits and maulavis, Hindu and Muslim assistants to the courts are to be taken as indicative of the relative value given to their work, Hindu civil law was valued at only about two thirds of its Islamic twin: in the 1790s, when figures become available, the monthly salaries of pandits were 40 rupees versus 60 rupees for maulavis in the appellate courts, and 25 versus 35 in the lower courts (India Office Records P/147/25, November 6, 1795, No. 22). In criminal cases Islamic law remained in force, and Hastings did not try to reverse the tradition of a Muslim-dominated administration. In the realm of education he founded in 1781 the Calcutta Madrassa, an educational establishment for Muslims. A government-sponsored educational institution for Hindus was not to come about until ten years later, in Banaras, as the creation of another orientalist administrator, Jonathan Duncan (Narain 1959: 170–73). It is also indicative of what Hastings held to be of the highest importance that, when proposing in 1769 the creation of a chair at Oxford, it was Persian, not Sanskrit, he had in mind (Marshall 1973).

There are, therefore, several aspects to the impact of governmental concerns on the search for knowledge involved in the *Code* and in the *Digest*, beyond the obvious fact that they were sponsored by government for administrative reasons. As the lithograph in Rennell's *Map* makes clear, the *Code* was also used for governmental propaganda, as a prime symbol of the British intention to enfranchise Hindus. Its English translation was intended for yet a different kind of propaganda: Hastings used it as a proof of the advanced state of Indian civilization in his efforts to stem any attempt on the part of the home administration of the Company to usher in common law and thwart his orientalist philosophy of government. The primary motivation behind the composition and translation of the *Digest*, on the other hand, as Jones stated and as will be discussed further below, was to have a readily available source book that would allow British judges to verify or dismiss the opinions rendered by the pandits who assisted the courts. The *Digest* was later given preeminence among sources and raised to the status of "the book of authority for determining legal questions and consequently to attain the desirable object of introducing uniformity in the Decisions of the Courts" (India Office Records P/128/15, 10 Oct. 1794, Civil Nos. 15–16). What the *Digest* was promoting then was the expectation that the British could and should know better than what they might be told by the living sources of the law. There is an issue of yet greater significance, a more pervasive process at work both in the *Code* and in the *Digest* that affected not only the uses made of knowledge but its very genesis: the fact that the intellectual enterprise proceeded on the basis of a political definition of "Hindu" and validated it, and that it accepted and affirmed that Hindu law was vested in the *dharmaśāstras*. We thus have in this case an example not only of what Said defines as orientalism, but, more fundamentally, of the insidious way in which unwary scholars may have the object of their research first framed by governmental planning. Further knowledge has since exposed the false premises under which the *Code* and the *Digest* were undertaken. Their example makes patent the vulnerability of incipient government-sponsored research.

Orientalist Knowledge and Pristine Hinduism

Contrary to what happened in the legal sphere, attempts at unraveling the complexities of Hindu religious beliefs and rites did not stem from a mandate issued by government. Yet, they proceeded on strikingly similar assumptions. One was the premise that the ultimate source of, and rationale for, religious beliefs and practices is to be sought in scriptures, a presumption that a great religion, as opposed to a set of superstitions, ought to be a religion of the book—or of many books, as soon became apparent in the case of Hindus. A second postulate was that the best, if not the only, way to disentangle complexity is to reduce it to essentially binary oppositions.

Many of the early aficionados of Indian culture, Halhed, Jones, and Hastings among others, had had a classical education. They knew, from the accounts of India given in the Greek and Latin classics, of the existence in ancient times of what the Greeks called gymnosophists, or naked philosophers. They knew that Indian culture had a long and distinguished tradition (Marshall 1973; Halbfass 1990: chapter 1). Their estimate of the antiquity of Indian civilization was extended further by the Indian texts they read. Among the texts that first became accessible to them, because several existed in Persian translations, were *Purāṇas*, the reputed repositories of India's ancient lore (Gorekar 1965; Shukla 1974; Mujtabai 1978: 68–91). So popular were they that Hastings commissioned a compendium of them, the *Purāṇārthaprakāśa*, which Jones called "a treasure" (R. Rocher 1989: 628–29) and of which Halhed prepared a translation, as he did of Persian versions of older *Purāṇas* (R. Rocher 1983: 137–38). The *Purāṇas* presented the first British orientalists with records, or so they were accepted, of vast expanses of time, with a claim of Hindu civilization to unfathomable antiquity—some did not hesitate to claim it antedated the deluge (R. Rocher 1984). They featured prominently a theory of the ages of the world, familiar on a lower scale and hence legitimated by ancient Greek lore, which posited the existence of a golden age (*kṛta-* or *satya-yuga*) in a remote antiquity, and a gradual deterioration through later ages, till the present age (*kali-yuga*), of utmost depravity. Though eighteenth-century accounts of India were not generally marked by the gory displays of revulsion at modern conditions that became all too characteristic of later times, it is evident that orientalists considered the religious rites and practices they observed to fall far short of the philosophy of the ancient gymnosophists. The indigenous outline of steadily worsening conditions through India's history provided a particularly inviting interpretive framework since it corresponded with a theme of the Enlightenment. India came to illustrate what Halbfass has called "the theme of the eclipse and suppression of the 'natural light' through superstition and ritualism, a theme that enjoyed great popularity among thinkers of the Enlightenment" (1990: 60). Thus, textual sources, western and Indian, and the dominant intellectual trend of the times conjoined begged eighteenth-century orientalists to organize their mixed feelings about Hinduism on two sides of a temporal divide.

The Persian translations of Sanskrit works that originated from Akbar's and Dārā Shikoh's attempts at syncretism and systematic investigation of Hinduism included *Upaniṣads* and other Vedantic texts as well as the two great epics (Halbfass 1990: chapter 2). Examples of what was then called "philosophical Hinduism" were, therefore, readily available. The crowning piece was Charles Wilkins's (1785) translation of the *Bhagavadgītā* directly from Sanskrit. Reading Wilkins's manuscript translation in Banaras—a city the scenes of which have been particularly hard on European sensibilities—his fellow orientalist Halhed was prompted to voice an exemplary description of the orientalists' divided judgment of Hinduism arrayed on either side of a temporal divide: in the hallowed past, the sublime, pristine, deist Hinduism of the *Bhagavadgītā* and the *Upaniṣads*, and now, in this cursed age, the corrupt, debased, and polytheistic practices they found repulsive. He did so in deist terms and in the vocabulary of the Enlightenment:

> Om! Veeshnu! Brahm! or by whatever name
> Primeval Reshees have thy power ador'd:
> They worshipp'd thee, they knew thee still *the same*,
> One great eternal, undivided lord!
> Tho' now, in these worn days, obscur'd thy light,
> (Worn days, alas, and crazy wane of time!)

Tho' priest-craft's puppets cheat man's bigot sight
   With hell-born mockeries of things sublime.
Ages *have* been, when thy refulgent beam
   Shone with full vigour on the mental gaze:
When doting superstition dar'd not dream,
   And folly's phantoms perish'd in thy rays.
          ("An Ode on Leaving Banaras,"
        quoted in R. Rocher 1979: 224–25)

This view of deist primeval rishis was, of course, made possible by the fact that the *Veda*s were yet unknown. No Persian translations of the Vedic *saṃhitās* were available,[11] and manuscripts of the Sanskrit texts were hard to come by. Eighteenth-century orientalists were not aware that the most ancient of Indian texts were hardly deist in nature. When the *Veda*s first became known, they failed to elicit much enthusiasm. Colebrooke was to conclude a first survey of the *Veda*s with the judgment, "what they contain, would hardly reward the labour of the reader; much less that of the translator," though he conceded that "they well deserve to be occasionally consulted by the oriental scholar" (1805: 497). It was not until German romanticism and nineteenth-century German philology, with their emphasis on *Ur-literatur*, the very first and original sources, that the Vedic *saṃhitās* became a primary focus of interest.

The orientalists found traces in modern times of the pure, deist Hinduism they thought prevailed in ancient times. In 1768 Alexander Dow already voiced the notion that "in India, as well as in many other counties, . . . [some] look up to the divinity, through the medium of reason and philosophy" (reprinted Marshall 1970: 139). The translator of the *Gītā* ventured in his preface the thought that "the most learned *Brāhmans* of the present times are Unitarians . . . but, at the same time that they believe but in one God, an universal spirit, they so far comply with the prejudices of the vulgar, as outwardly to perform all the ceremonies . . . [since] these ceremonies, are as much the bread of the *Brāhmans*, as the superstition of the vulgar is the support of the priesthood in other countries" (reprinted Marshall 1970: 194). Jones similarly stated, "with all my admiration of the truly learned Brahmens, I abhor the sordid priestcraft of Durgā's ministers, but such fraud no more affects the sound religion of the Hindus, than the lady of Loretto and the Romish impositions affect our own rational faith" (Cannon 1970: 856). For these orientalists the light of deism and of rational religion still glimmered in contemporary Hinduism, even though much obscured by superstition and ritualism, and Hinduism was not different on this score from other religions such as Christianity. That the first text translated directly from Sanskrit into English was the *Bhagavadgītā* is a direct reflection of the intellectual climate of the times. Its tenor could be interpreted in deist terms, and the "many precepts of fine morality" that Hastings found this "most wonderful work of antiquity" contained, and which he quoted in letters to his wife (Grier 1905: 365), coincided with the principal concerns of liberal, undogmatic Anglicans.

Yet, even works that owed their origin to intellectual attitudes could be used to political advantage. As soon as Hastings read Wilkins's draft translation, he realized that it was an ideal propaganda tool in his battle with the home administration for an orientalist form of government. The *Code*, which had been his first documentary proof of the high level Indian civilization had reached, had been an imperfect tool, in that it contained a number of provisions that were bound to be adversely received. No one, however, could fail to be impressed by the lofty message of the *Gītā*. Thus Hastings took the extraordinary step of forwarding to England, for publication under the direct sponsorship of the East India Company, a document that had no possible application in any branch of government. As his prefatory letter stated, this was to serve as an advertisement for Indian culture:

> It is not very long since the inhabitants of India were considered by many, as creatures scarce elevated above the degree of savage life; nor, I fear, is that prejudice yet wholly eradicated, though surely abated. Every instance which brings their real character home to observation will impress us with a more generous sense of feeling for their natural rights, and teach us to estimate them by the measure of our own.(reprinted Marshall 1970: 189)

By having the *Gītā* published in England in English translation Hastings intended to influence the British public. Yet, the privileging of the *Gītā* and of *Vedānta* by the British was to have a profound effect in India itself. Kopf (1969) in a positive mode and A. Nandy (1983) in a negative mode tell the same story, how Hindus from Rammohan Roy to Gandhi came to adopt and adapt the appreciation that the British orientalists had of their scriptures.[12] Hindus came to view the *Gītā* as the Hindu text par excellence, to be placed—in English translation by their president-philosopher Radhakrishnan—next to the Gideon bible in the nightstands of modern western-style hotels.

It is probably not coincidental that it was when Jones visited Banaras, where he met Wilkins, and after Hastings had given him "a taste" of the *Gītā*, that he "left orders at Benares and Gaya, both holy cities, for the oldest book on the *Hindu* laws to be translated from the *Shanscrit*," and that it was on receipt of the *Manusmṛti* as a result of this search that he resolved to learn Sanskrit (Cannon 1970: 658–64). Though the *Manusmṛti* was not the oldest source on Hindu law, it was old as well as prestigious. Jones was impressed by the fact that modern law treatises such as Halhed's *Code* and the *Digest* on which he was working offered quotations of the *Manusmṛti* and other early texts as the authoritative pronouncements of ancient sages, and he and others increasingly put the accent on texts of high antiquity, favoring them over more recent treatises that might have been expected to be more representative of current legal practices. The British orientalists' infatuation with the ancient was legitimized by the fact that the indigenous scholarly tradition presented itself as derivative and commentarial. It would have taken a much greater knowledge of that tradition than early orientalists had to appreciate its unadvertised, even disclaimed, creativity. Thus, in spite of continuing work on a modern *Digest*, the focus shifted to ancient texts, all the more when they became easily accessible in translation. The fact that the *Manusmṛti* was the first ancient "lawbook" to be translated (Jones 1794) and the fact that it was translated by the most eminent scholar of Hindu law of his time endowed the *Manusmṛti* with a reputation that was to withstand the discovery of other texts, ancient and modern, that were much more useful from a legal standpoint. Later scholarship was unable to reverse, either in the West or in an India that accepted British views, the privileging of the *Manusmṛti* as the premier book on Hindu law.[13]

The notion that contemporary India was steeped in medieval darkness, fallen from a glorious past, not only led orientalists to pay scant attention to later treatises, but also convinced them that a renaissance, a return to pristine sources, could be stimulated from within the culture. This applied even to linguistic concerns. Halhed recommended in his *Grammar of the Bengal Language* that Bengali be cleansed of the foreign— Persian, Portuguese, and English—accretions that marred its purity, and that Sanskrit be made the fountainhead for any needed innovations (1778: xx–xxii, 138, 178). For scholars nourished in the classics, who measured linguistic refinement by reference to Greek and Latin, Sanskrit represented an object proof of the superiority of the ancient over the modern. Before Jones's famous pronouncement of 1785, Halhed already voiced the opinion that Sanskrit was a paragon language, "equally refined with either the Arabic or the Greek" and "more copious than either [Latin or Greek]"

(R. Rocher 1980). This aesthetic appreciation of Sanskrit was again legitimized by the prestige the native tradition gave to what it termed *gīrvāṇa* "the language of the gods." As with the *Gītā* and the *Manusmṛti*, western standards of linguistic purity were to be adopted by Indian elites and to have a profound influence on the development of Bengali and other modern Indian languages.

The religious and cultural renaissance and the linguistic purism British orientalists favored did not stem from government concerns, nor were they directly enforced by government. They came to be adopted by Indians primarily because of the prestige British approval conferred on them. Yet, orientalist knowledge produced in this context was susceptible to being used as a tool of government. Jonathan Duncan, the orientalist Resident in Banaras, marshaled ancient Sanskrit texts that condemned as the worst of crimes the killing of a woman and the killing of an embryo when he lobbied with the heads of Rajput groups in 1789 to discontinue female infanticide (Narain 1959: 176–78). In the case of an eighteenth-century orientalist administrator like Duncan, this was merely an attempt at persuasion, but nineteenth-century Anglicist reformers were to take great pains to argue in an orientalist idiom their case for an outright prohibition of practices they wished to suppress. As Mani (1986, 1987) amply illustrates, Anglicist reformers tried hard to prove that *satī* was not countenanced by the authoritative texts on *dharma*. Eighteenth-century orientalist scholars such as Halhed and Wilkins and orientalist administrators such as Hastings and Duncan were satisfied that the custom of *satī* had ancient and religious sanction, and Colebrooke went so far as to publish a collection of passages from Sanskrit texts that countenanced the practice (Colebrooke 1794; Marshall 1970: 179; Lloyd 1979: 18).[14] Horace Hayman Wilson, the orientalist scholar who was the primary standard-bearer for a continued orientalist form of government in the nineteenth century, felt likewise (Philips 1977: 337–39, 377). By couching their arguments for a ban on *satī* in an orientalist idiom, the opposing Anglicist faction implicitly recognized and attempted to twist to its advantage the hegemony of the orientalist discourse.[15] By denying that there was scriptural authority for *satī*, the reformers hoped to establish that *satī* was not a matter of time-honored religion, which even Anglicist administrators claimed to be pledged to respect, but that it was nothing more than a modern aberration that could and should be made illegal. Thus, an orientalist scholarship that had its twin roots in the *Purāṇas*' tradition of increasingly worsening conditions through the world's ages and in the Enlightenment's view of a pristine religion later debased by obscurantism eventually allowed Anglicist administrators to encapsulate religion in ancient texts and to draw in its perimeter, while conversely expanding the realm of social concerns, in which Anglicist and evangelical reformers increasingly convinced government that it was not only its right, but also its duty to intervene by executive decree.

Orientalist Knowledge and Literary Delights

A recent history of the Asiatic Society founded by Jones in Calcutta in 1784 claims that "the world of scholarship and the world of administration during this period were worlds apart" (Kejariwal 1988: 226). That this cannot be maintained has been illustrated in the preceding two sections of this essay. It is now necessary to controvert the opposite and equally summary claim, made in a study of Jones's attitudes, to the effect that "all Oriental Studies in the eighteenth century had a political slant," a statement that the author, however, immediately tempers with the observation that "early Orientalists were not an isolated group. They were involved in the political conflicts of the time and their 'theories' about Indian history and culture were influenced by their respective political *and intellectual* convictions" (Mukherjee 1968: 2, emphasis added).

While it is the case that Jones's decision to learn Sanskrit was motivated by his perceived need to access sources on Hindu law as a judge charged with applying it in court, and while his translation of the *Manusmṛti* and his other work on both Muslim and Hindu law digests are to be viewed in that context, there were other dimensions to his orientalist scholarship which were not connected with his public duties. Jones took up law relatively late in life, for the purpose of gainful employment. As he stated, in Latin, to the Dutch Arabic scholar Henry Albert Schultens, "it would not be reprehensible of [him] if [he] preferred the fruitful and useful olive to the sterile laurel," all the more since he could not "stomach the arrogance of princes and nobles, which has to be swallowed by poets and lovers of literature" (Cannon 1970: 167)—a bitter memory of his dealings with the king of Denmark for his translation of the Persian history of Nadir Shah. Though Jones took law seriously, both in its practice and in its scholarly aspects, he could not, in the end, cease to be a man of letters.

Jones made a clear distinction between his avocations and his professional projects, even when both were scholarly: "my principal amusement is botany, and the conversation of the pundits, with whom I talk fluently in the language of the *Gods*; and my business, besides the discharge of my public duties, is the translation of Menu, and of the digest which has been compiled at my instance" (letter of October 20, 1791, Cannon 1970: 900). In earlier letters he similarly and repeatedly placed them in contrast: "the discharge of my public duty, and the studies which are connected with that duty, such as the Indian and Arabic laws in their several different languages" versus "my present study . . . the original of Bidpa's fables, called Hitopadesa, which is a charming book"; "the difficult study of Hindu and Mohammedan laws, in two copious languages, Sanscrit and Arabic, which studies are inseparably connected with my public duty" versus "(though rather an amusement than a duty) my pursuit of general literature, which I have here an opportunity of doing from the fountain head, an opportunity, which, if lost, may never be recovered"; and "the Sanskrit and Arabick law, which I find it necessary to study" versus "literature being only an amusement" (Cannon 1970: 706, 714–15, 717).

Jones's delight at translating the *Abhijñānaśākuntala* stemmed from his appreciation of Kālidāsa as "the Indian Shakespeare" and of his play as a literary jewel, the plot of which he related at length in letters to his former pupil, the second Earl Spencer (Cannon 1970: 766–68, 792). He felt almost guilty and definitely defensive about indulging in literary pastimes instead of devoting all his energy to projects that were directly connected with his official duties. He had not been able to maintain his resolve of 1774, "to work hard for at least twenty years at only legal or political studies" (Cannon 1970: 166). In the preface to his translation of Kālidāsa's play, published fifteen years later, he vowed that there would be no more such literary interludes (reprinted Jones 1807: 9: 372). Yet, he could not refrain from undertaking further literary projects. Three years after his translation of the *Abhijñānaśākuntala*, he offered the first printed edition ever of a Sanskrit text. That text, the *Ṛtusaṃhāra*, a poetic description of seasons attributed to Kālidāsa, was as far removed as could be from the political realm. Its "advertisement" noted,

> This book is the first ever printed in *Sanscrit*; and it is by the press alone, that the ancient literature of *India* can long be preserved: a learner of that most interesting language who had carefully perused one of the popular grammars, could hardly begin his course of study with an easier or more elegant work, than the *Ritusanhāra*, or *Assemblage of Seasons*. Every line composed by CĀLIDĀS is exquisitely polished; and every couplet in the poem exhibits an *Indian* landscape, always beautiful, sometimes highly coloured, but never beyond nature. (Reprinted in Jones 1807: 13: 386)

In Jones's opinion Indian literature was on a par with Greek literature, in that it was not only "sublime and beautiful in a high degree," but also "perfectly original," whereas Latin literature was derivative from the Greek (Cannon 1970: 716). To his correspondents in Britain he tried to convey the thrill of his intellectual quest:

> To what shall I compare my literary pursuits in India? Suppose Greek literature to be known in modern Greece only, and there to be in the hands of priests and philosophers; and suppose them to be still worshippers of Jupiter and Apollo: suppose Greece to have been conquered successively by Goths, Huns, Vandals, Tartars, and lastly by the English; then suppose a court of judicature to be established by the British parliament, at Athens, and an inquisitive Englishman to be one of the judges; suppose him to learn Greek there, which none of his countrymen knew, and to read Homer, Pindar, Plato, which no other Europeans had even heard of. Such am I in this country; substituting Sanscrit for Greek, the *Brahmans*, for the priests of *Jupiter*, and *Vālmic*, *Vyāsa*, *Cālidāsa*, for Homer, Plato, Pindar. Need I say what exquisite pleasure I receive from conversing easily with that class of men, who conversed with Pythagoras, Thales and Solon, but with this advantage over the Grecian travellers, that I have no need of an interpreter. (Cannon 1970: 755–56)

He enumerated branches of Sanskrit literature in which he and the Asiatic Society he had founded were interested:

> *Sanscrit* literature is, indeed, a new world. . . . In Sanscrit are written half a million of Stanzas on sacred history & literature, Epick and Lyrick poems innumerable, and (what is wonderful) Tragedies and Comedies not to be counted, above 2000 years old, besides works on Law (my great object), on Medicine, on Theology, on Arithmetick, on Ethicks, and so on to infinity. (Cannon 1970: 747)

He listed the literary projects on which he was spending his vacation in the summer of 1787: not only the *Manusmṛti* "a noble Sanscrit work on Hindu Law," but also the *Hitopadeśa* "the original Sanscrit of those charming Indian fables, which we read in French 20 years ago," centuries-old Sanscrit dictionaries, "a very ancient Sanscrit book on Musick in beautiful verse; but very concise; and, therefore, obscure," besides his avocation to botany (Cannon 1970: 747–59).

The fables of the *Hitopadeśa* and Kālidāsa's lyrical description of the seasons and his play *Abhijñānaśākuntala*—which Jones likened to Shakespeare's fairy-pieces—had, unlike the *Manusmṛti*, no application in government, any more than Jones's studies of Indian music or of the game of chess could have. Nor, and differently from the *Bhagavadgītā*, were they susceptible of becoming normative for Indian religion. Like the *Manu-smṛti* and the *Bhagavadgītā*, the *Abhijñānaśākuntala* became a paragon of Indian high culture, lauded by Goethe and other poets, but, unlike these texts, it was not liable to provide standards by which to judge the social or religious behavior of Hindus. It added to the documentation of India's brilliant cultural past, but, unlike the *Manusmṛti* and the *Bhagavadgītā*, it did not provide tools by which later to define, contain, curb, or mold current beliefs and practices.

Orientalist Knowledge and Indigenous Scholarship

In India the British encountered not only a great and ancient culture but also a brilliant and enduring tradition of indigenous scholarship. The way British orientalists related to pandits was highly ambiguous: they initially depended entirely on pandits for information and for instruction in Sanskrit, yet they sought to exercise control over them. This relationship was all the more complicated since the pandits themselves were uncertain of how to respond to this new breed of rulers. Bengali pandits did not respond immediately to British requests for instruction in Sanskrit and information about Indian culture, nor to offers of employment with the courts. Both Hastings and Halhed met with refusals, and Wilkins found it necessary to go to Banaras (R. Rocher 1983: 79; 1989: 628). The first British orientalist who obtained the cooperation of, was in a position to offer employment to, and lived in daily intercourse with a multiplicity of pandits was Jones, whose attitude vis-à-vis these pandits was divided. In many ways Jones's divided attitude with regard to pandits parallels the ambiguity of his position as a staunch Whig and supporter of the American Revolution serving in a colonial administration, which constitutes the fundamental tension Mukherjee (1968) has analyzed.

Jones entertained suspicions about the reliability of pandit assistants to the courts. These suspicions were fundamentally institutional and antedated his familiarity with learned pandits. His plan for the British administration of justice in India, submitted to Edmund Burke barely six months after Jones took office, stated as principles that "*native interpreters* of the respective laws must be duly selected and appointed with such stipends, as will entitle them to respect, and raise them above temptation . . . but the learning and vigilance of the *English* judge must be a check on the native interpreters" (April 1784, Cannon 1970: 643). His conviction that it was necessary to monitor closely the pandits of the Supreme Court was the single cause that drove him to learn Sanskrit. As of February 1785, he admitted only to being "almost tempted to learn [Sanskrit, so that he might] be a check on the Pundits of the court" (Cannon 1970: 664). Soon, however, knowing Sanskrit became an imperative, and his distrust of the pandit assistants to the courts became more pointedly expressed: "I am proceeding . . . in the study of Sanskrit; for I can no longer bear to be at the mercy of our pandits, who deal out Hindu law as they please, and make it at reasonable rates, when they cannot find it ready made" (September 28, 1785, Cannon 1970: 683–84; also 686, 720, 742, 762, 795). "Pure Integrity," he said, "is hardly to be found among the Pandits and Maulavis, few of whom give opinions without a culpable bias, if the parties can have access to them" (October 24, 1786, Cannon 1970: 720–21).

A first visit to the traditional seat of Sanskrit learning at Nadiya, in September 1785, when most of the pandits were unfortunately absent, failed to change Jones's views. On his return to Calcutta, accompanied by the Vaidya pandit Rāmalocana, he declared, "I have brought with me the father of the university of Nadya, who, though not a Brahmin, has taught grammar and ethics to the most learned Brahmins, and has no priestly pride, with which his pupils in general abound" (Cannon 1970: 687). Yet, less than two years later, he happily reported that the Raja of Nadiya and his court pandits, with whom he conversed in Sanskrit, had coopted him as "a Hindu of the *Military* tribe, which is next in rank to the Brahmanical," and he proudly named Nadiya, near which he first rented and later bought a summer cottage, "the third university of which [he had] been a member" (August 1787, Cannon 1970: 748, 754). He took naive pride in the fact that the pandits seemed to find the Sanskrit verses he composed good enough to be learned by their children (Cannon 1970: 784, 828). The *Asiatick Researches*, the journal of the Asiatic Society he founded and for which he served as single editor, published, with due acknowledgments, translations of papers he solicited from learned pandits. His own publications credited his pandit teachers and assistants for their instruction in the Sanskrit language and for literary information supplied. His letters to friends brimmed with expressions of deep appreciation as well as of warm friendship for learned pandits. He described Jagannātha Tarkapañcānana as "a prodigy of learning, virtue, memory, and health," a "venerable sage" (September–November 1793, Cannon 1970: 923). Rādhākānta Tarkavāgīśa, the "honest pandit" he was to choose to head the composition of the *Digest*, elicited as early as May 1787 the remark, "need I say, that I shall ever be happy in the conversation of so learned a man" (R. Rocher 1989). As quoted above, he delighted in personal intercourse with pandits, in whom he saw the heirs to the gymnosophists who had influenced Greek philosophers.

One could view Jones's praise for individual pandits he knew and his expressed distrust of pandits as a class as an instance of the kind of double-talk that all too often characterizes prejudicial statements and racial slurs. Yet the fact remains that Jones and the pandits engaged one another on two different levels. As a judge, Jones was a member of the colonial establishment. Not only could British judges hire and fire pandits who served as assistants to the courts, but they were also charged with the ultimate responsibility of passing judgment and hence of ascertaining the facts and their due interpretation. As such, Jones was bound to be frustrated by his inability to ascertain the validity of the pandits' opinions, and hence he was likely to be led to question their motives. As an orientalist scholar, as a searcher for knowledge, on the other hand, Jones was, and acknowledged he was, a student of the pandits, and he developed a profound appreciation for their learning. Both modes of relationship represented powerful forces on his perceptions. Rather than dismiss Jones's divided attitude as a predictable, automatic, mindless case of double-talk of a discriminatory nature, it is of interest to deaggregate the two sets of forces at work. This will allow us to examine how, for Jones and for others who were both administrators and scholars, a more intimate acquaintance with panditic learning failed to dispel the suspicion with which pandits were viewed as sources of the law, and how, to the contrary, frustration and suspicion spread to the sphere of scholarship.

Hastings's simple, yet radical decision to have Hindu law apply to Hindus can profitably be viewed in the light of Cohn's statement to the effect that "the history of British rule in India is to some extent to be seen in the unanticipated consequences of its actions" (1968: 17). This decision made the administration of justice depend on a legal corpus as yet unknown and on native interpreters whose knowledge of the law the British had initially no means to assess. All British administrators had to go by at first was the pandits' reputation. In the best of cases, they appointed as assistants to the courts pandits who had repeatedly been called on by parties to settle disputes as private arbitrators, more often simply old men who seemed to command the respect of their local communities, or sometimes *purohitas* of prominent families that sponsored their candidacy. Such, indeed, were the primary rationales for the appointment of pandit incumbents identified in a series of reports that followed the British administration's decision of January 3, 1794, to review and rationalize the appointment of pandit assistants to the courts (India Office Records P/128/9–15).

Granted that the possibility of bribery or favoritism existed, the British would have done well to question whether the learning of the pandit assistants to the courts was up to the task they were expected to fulfill, before they doubted their integrity. Even if we assume that all the Brahmans whom the British appointed were well versed in Sanskrit—by no means a safe assumption—it would not follow that they were specialists in *dharmaśāstra*. All the evidence we have on panditic scholarship in Bengal in the period that immediately preceded the advent of the British points to the fact that the primary school of learning was logic (*navya-nyāya*), and that the renaissance of *dharmaśāstra* studies in the late eighteenth and early nineteenth centuries was the direct result of a new demand created by the British decision to apply Hindu law in the courts (Derrett 1968: 230–31). Of the eleven pandits who coauthored the *Code*, several were logicians and poets of note, but only two seem to have written on *dharma* prior to their involvement with the British (R. Rocher 1983: 49). For all their good intentions, Hastings and his acolytes were naive about Hindu law. They thought, in western fashion, that it was possible to consult a code and to pick out the law that was applicable to a particular case. What *dharmaśāstra* offered instead was a multiplicity of authoritative texts and a variety of commentaries that, in Indian fashion, sought to integrate and reconcile conflicting statements by the application of interpretory rules of *mīmāṃsā* and the entire array of panditic learning and skill. Not all pandits may have been capable of doing or even of following this arcane style of argumentation. And Jones, when he happily reported that he had reached the point where he could singlehandedly translate *dharma* rules from Sanskrit, was not better placed to appreciate and unravel the maze of rules, exceptions, and counterexceptions that it was necessary to control for the panditic processing of these texts.

The British also thought, in western fashion, that for a single problem there was only one solution that could be right. When they suspected pandits of rendering biased or just erroneous opinions, they were not aware that different solutions could be right, depending on which source was relied on generally and which were made to apply to particular cases. Commentators had immemorially handled divergent statements in the *smṛtis* by privileging some as leading rules, while reducing the compass of others to more strictly defined circumstances. It was perfectly legitimate for the eighteenth-century pandits who were heirs to, and participants in, this tradition to do likewise, and for each of them to choose for himself in each case which of the commentarial traditions he thought best to follow and further to elaborate.[16] Matters were further complicated by the fact that, until 1794, even pandits of the appellate court, the Sadar Diwani Adalat, were not made privy to the evidence in the cases about which they wrote opinions (India Office Records P/152/47: September 18, 1794, No. 4). The judge heard the case, then formulated a number of questions that he thought bore on the case. These questions were translated into Persian, then into Bengali or Sanskrit. Then the pandit or pandits consulted their Sanskrit sources and wrote an opinion (*vyavasthā*) that was translated into Persian and into English, on the basis of which the judge rendered his judgment. Even if all important points remained intact through this tortuous process of translation, the questions the British judge formulated did not necessarily elicit the most relevant information. It is evident from the law reports that these questions could be too broad, or miss altogether the types of distinctions that are important in the dialectics of *dharma-śāstra*. The different ways in which they were couched could precipitate different opinions, and sometimes it must have been hard for pandits to figure out how to answer them at all. As apparent contradictory opinions continued to be rendered over time and at different levels of the court hierarchy, the British administrators' paramount consideration shifted from discovering the true sources of Hindu law to insuring consistency in the courts' decrees. This, it was first hoped toward the end of the eighteenth century, could be achieved by appointing to the courts pandits who had been trained in a common mode, in a common norm, at the Sanskrit College in Banaras. As part of the reform of 1794, the Head of the Sanskrit College in Banaras was asked to forward rank-ordered lists of graduates from which appointments to the courts might be made (India Office Records P/128/13: August 15, 1794, Civil No. 3). This attempt failed to a large extent, when pandits balked at being posted at a long distance from their homes and when the pressures of patronage persisted. This situation eventually led, in the nineteenth century, to judgments being rendered by precedent, and ultimately, in 1864, to dispensing with pandit assistants to the courts (Derrett 1968: chapter 9).

Though some of the pandits who served as assistants to the courts, particularly at the appellate level and in the Supreme Court, were well known and highly respected,[17] most were obscure and were viewed like clerical workers, particularly by those British administrators who had no scholarly interests. For a vast majority of pandits employed with British courts in Bengal, Bihar, and Orissa up to 1805, of whom I have culled a file from judicial records of the East India Company, little more than their assignments appears to be known. Summary dismissals were not uncommon. Most were probably a far cry from the learned teachers of Nadiya whose company and conversation Jones sought, nor did every *mofussil* judge have the intellectual curiosity of a Jones. Yet even Jones ultimately found it desirable that British orientalist scholars as well as judges be independent from pandits. He was alive to the possibility of forgeries, whether for legal or for literary purposes. His insistence on finding forms for oaths—almost an obsession—caused a pandit to comply with a forgery (Cannon 1970: 677–78, 684, 685, 838). Two years later Jones rightly suspected that Francis Wilford's startling materials on ancient geography stemmed from a forged Puranic text (Fall 1791, Cannon 1970: 888, 889, 900). He eventually published them, adding, however, a note of his own to the effect that he had "at length abandoned the greatest part of that natural distrust, and incredulity, which had taken possession of [his] mind, . . . [since he had] lately read, again and again, both alone, and with a *Pandit*, the numerous original passages in the *Purānas*, and other *Sanscrit* books, which the writer of the dissertation adduces in support of his assertion" (*Asiatick Researches* 3: 463). According to Jones the scholar as well as according to Jones the judge, accurate knowledge could be obtained only by a dual process, consultation with a pandit and independent, unmediated reading of the texts, and he so advised fellow scholars. Thus, he wrote Samuel Davis, who studied Indian sciences, and particularly astronomy, "I am very anxious, that (if you do not already read Sanscrit with ease) you will learn enough of it to be in great measure independent of the Pandits" (January 6, 1791, Cannon 1970: 879).

Even if Jones's attitude may have had less to do with colonial arrogance than with the fundamental reluctance a scholar has to accept unchecked the evidence adduced by other scholars, there is no denying the fact that the status of pandits declined rapidly. They ceased to be considered the living guardians and interpretors of the indigenous tradition and were downgraded to assistants to, and employees of, the British. Parallel to the traditional panditic establishments such as Nadiya, and ultimately leading to their downfall, a British-sponsored system of panditic education was initiated with the founding in 1791 of the Sanskrit College in Banaras. For all the eminence of its head, the learned Kāśīnātha who had been

Wilkins's teacher, and for all the orthodoxy of the rules under which it operated, the British ran it as a training school for future employees and were ultimately in charge of the curriculum (Narain 1959: 170–73).

The value of panditic instruction and mediation to western orientalist scholarship was to remain a hotly debated issue. Jones may have wished to be sufficiently independent of pandits to check their assertions, but he would not have dispensed with their help and advice, for he held them to be the contemporary practitioners of an unbroken scholarly tradition that went back to the gymnosophists of old. Indeed, he kept lists of learned pandits at several locations (Cannon 1990: 225). In the nineteenth century, however, the predominant orientalist school was no longer to be vested in British scholars on Indian soil, but in German cabinet scholars most of whom neither visited India nor thought there was an advantage to doing so. For them Indology was to be just another form of classical philology, in no way different from the study of dead Greek and Latin. For such a study the panditic tradition was not so much distrusted as judged to be irrelevant. The tension between this new type of philology and the still enduring British school in India found its first expression in 1832 in the dispute that opposed H. H. Wilson to A. W. Schlegel on the qualifications required of the first incumbent of the Boden chair of Sanskrit at Oxford (reprinted Schlegel 1846: 3: 212–41, 269–73). It was later to be fully articulated in the criticisms Böhtlingk and Roth (1855–75: 1: iii–vii) leveled at Wilson's continuing reliance on the indigenous scholarly tradition.

Conclusions

The orientalist projects discussed above are only samples of the areas of knowledge the British pursued in Bengal between 1772 and 1794. They were selected because they represent a range of interactions between intellectual and governmental concerns. My point in analyzing them has been to highlight the multiplicity of factors that bore on them and the diversity and occasionally unintended nature of the outcomes of this interplay. My method is purposely disaggregative, for I subscribe to the view that "with a totalizing theoretical discourse of superstructures, representational systems, mediation and methodological attitudes, everything is bound to become incriminating evidence of complicity and hegemonic activity if you assume it is" (King 1991: 324). Knowledge and governmental objectives were often, but not always, related, and their relationship was not unidirectional. While a political agenda can corrupt, drive, or even define the production of knowledge, intellectual trends also impinge on government.

As illustrated in the beginning of the chapter, orientalist projects such as the *Code* and the *Digest* were government projects from conception to consumption. Knowledge was generated on government premises for government use. Yet, government is not to be equated with colonial rule in every aspect of these projects. The publication and distribution in Britain of the English translation of the *Code* was not intended as a tool of law enforcement but as an advertisement for Indian culture. Its targeted audience was neither the rulers nor the ruled in India but the home administration of the East India Company and the British public at large. Whereas the parties in the composition of the Sanskrit law texts were the British orientalist administrators, the pandits, and the Hindus to be governed, for the translation of the *Code* the parties were orientalist administrators in India and their masters in Britain. A similarly vivid case of multiple discourses built around a common issue was to take place in the first half of the nineteenth century with regard to *satī*, when divergent arguments were made for audiences in India and in Britain. In India the focus was on regulation (Mani 1986 and 1987), while the missionaries' message to Britain aimed primarily at rallying support and boosting fund-raising activities (Mani 1989).

Orientalist projects such as the translation of the *Bhagavadgītā* did not stem from administrative concerns, yet were used for political purposes. As with the translation of the *Code*, the targeted audience was not in India, but in Britain. Diffusing a knowledge of the *Gītā* in Britain was a second installment in the advertising campaign Hastings waged on behalf of Indian culture as the legitimizing foundation for his orientalist form of government. Neither Hastings nor Wilkins could have anticipated that the admiration for Indian culture, as represented in the *Gītā*, that they sought to inspire in the British public would influence the perception Indians had of their own culture. The privileging of the *Gītā* and of *Vedānta* by the British and by reform movements within Hinduism appears to be an accident of intellectual history. The spirit of the Age of the Enlightenment is so intimately involved in the enthusiastic response these texts elicited from orientalist scholars and in the positive reception they received in Britain that one may doubt that they would have met with a like fate in Europe—and ultimately in India—if they had been published a decade later, in the changed intellectual climate that followed the French revolution. Whatever factors may have been at work—intellectual trends in the case of the *Gītā*, perhaps only relative date of publication in the case of the *Manusmṛti*—, the adoption of British standards and preferences by Indians is only partly a matter of intellectual history. While there was a measure of direct enforcement of the privileging of the *Manusmṛti* by the British, there was none in the case of the *Gītā*. Yet, the selective approval of representative texts in the Indian tradition by the foreign ruling power had potent implications, which are as much part of political as of intellectual history. Such were the more insidious consequences of colonialism.

A feature of orientalist scholarship that had a profound impact on government was its promotion of the distant past as normative. This notion was born of the coincidence of two distinct strands, the European Enlightenment and the Indian Puranic tradition, both of which conceived the world to have undergone a progressive deterioration. The fact that the indigenous scholastic tradition presented itself as derivative and commentarial of ancient statements that were attributed to inspired seers added apparent justification to this view. Thus, society was made to conform to ancient *dharmaśāstra* texts, in spite of those texts' insistence that they were overridden by local and group custom. It eventually allowed Anglicist administrators to manipulate the porous boundary between religion as defined by texts and customs they wished to ban. Yet, as indicated in the section "Literary Delights," there were other orientalist projects, such as Jones's translation of the play *Abhijñānaśākuntala*, his edition of the lyrical *Ṛtusaṃhāra*, and his studies of music and of chess, which were unrelated to governmental concerns and without governmental application.

The indigenous scholarly tradition discussed next was the key to instruction in Sanskrit and to information on the extant literary corpus as well as to expert opinions on points of the *dharmaśāstra* tradition that bore on law cases. From the start, orientalist scholars had a dual identity, as scholars and as members of a colonial administration. Pandits developed similarly dual roles. Although not all pandits accepted to serve the British either in their official or private capacity, a significant and growing number did, so that by the turn of the century, it had become "a way of life" (R. Rocher 1989: 633). The esteem in which pandits were held could only suffer from their transformation from sought-out keepers of the indigenous tradition into hired government employees and paid informants for foreign scholars. Yet, what rendered their position most precarious was, in their official capacity, the lack of consistency in the opinions they delivered and the refuge British judges sought in case law, and, in their role as private tutors, the yearning western scholars of any nationality had to access texts unmediated.

The challenge for modern scholars is to draw from a critique of prior forms of scholarship lessons that remain of enduring value. One such lesson is the multiplicity of ways in which the pursuit of knowledge can be warped by government concerns. This danger persists. It is not specific to colonial governments.

Another lesson is the need for vigilance against purism in new forms. While acknowledging the profound impact the colonial period had on present Indian culture and society, it is important that current scholarship not appear to promote a return to a pristine precolonial past. As Galanter (1989: chapter 5) aptly points out, Anglo-Indian law has now become an indigenous conceptual system, the legitimacy of which does not depend on the correctness of the principles on which it was first elaborated, but stems exclusively from the general acceptance it currently enjoys. Scholars, least of all western scholars, neither could nor should seek now to unprivilege texts modern Indian reform movements hold fundamental to their mission. If scholars are to draw any lesson from the predicament of scholarship in the colonial age, it should be the necessity of looking at contemporary culture as normative, whatever attraction ancient and pristine traditions may have.

Yet another salutary course is to question the legitimacy of unstated, yet recurrent, approaches to knowledge that have led to questionable results in the past, but to which we may still be unwittingly prone. A review of the ways orientalists organized complex Indian realities in the eighteenth century uncovers a pattern of dichotomies: Hindu versus Muslim, ancient versus modern, philosophical versus vulgar, right versus wrong. To a large extent the dichotomy philosophical versus vulgar was but a variant of the dichotomy ancient versus modern. It has since been reworked in further dichotomies such as great versus little tradition, precept versus practice, text versus context. The persistence of these binary oppositions, when the lives of Indians patently incorporate elements on either side of the presumed boundary, is a fundamental blinder of western modes of thought. Yet students of India ought to have been sensitized to the possibility of other interpretive schemes, since the culture they study offers alternative models. Besides traditional divisions in sets of eighteen, Indian culture shows a fondness for classifications in 3 + 1 schemes: three Vedas that are recited in the sacrifice, and a fourth that is not; three castes that are twice-born, and a fourth that is not; three purposes to this life, and a fourth out of this life;[18] three stages in this life, and a fourth out of this life; three stages of sleep, and yet another, named "the fourth"; and so forth. My point here is not to argue for a Dumézilian view of Indian or Indo-European society and culture (Dumézil 1958), but, on the contrary, to suggest that classificatory schemes in traditional numbers of constituent elements, such as binary oppositions, ought to be examined more critically than is generally the case. In particular, it is to be hoped that postcolonial scholarship will not resort to yet another Procrustean dichotomy that would treat the study of colonial India, including orientalist scholarship during that period, as reducible to the binary opposition of rulers and ruled.

Notes

1. For accounts of the in-country training in the 1770s of two young Company servants who became orientalist scholars, see Lloyd 1979: 11 and R. Rocher 1983: 38–39.

2. For this and for documentation on the commercial and other activities of Europeans in eighteenth-century Bengal see Marshall 1976.

3. Though keeping Indian mistresses was not uncommon in later times, it became frowned on and ceased to be openly acknowledged. The *bibi*s of eighteenth-century European men were publicly acknowledged and sat for formal portraits by British artists (Archer 1979: 52, 207–08, 286, 291–92, and plates VIII, XII, XIII, 198–99, 202). The two Muslim ladies of William Palmer, Hastings's favorite agent, came from royal families, and he, they, and their children posed unabashedly as a family (282–84 and plates 196–97). Some European men, with or without native families, posed in native dress (84, 293–94, and plates 39, 203). See also A. Nandy 1983: 5.

4. The rise of Hastings's *banian* has been chronicled by one of his descendants, S. C. Nandy (1978–81).

5. Part of Hastings's collection is now in the British Library, part in the India Office Library; Johnson's is in the India Office Library; Chambers's is in Berlin.

6. The change in title from *Code* to *Digest* and from *Laws* to *Law* reflects the greater familiarity the British acquired with Hindu law in the intervening period. From the naive expectation they had of being able to collect and codify legal statutes, they came to realize that *dharmaśāstra* was a body of literature. The narrowed scope on contracts and successions in the *Digest* reflects their estimate of what kind of information was most needed for the courts, as opposed to the open-ended investigative aim of the *Code*.

7. On the *Code* see chapter 4 in the biography of its English translator (R. Rocher 1983), on the *Digest* see the biography of the pandit who supervised its composition (R. Rocher 1989). For general discussions of the issues involved see Derrett 1968: chapters 8–9 and Cohn 1989. Both the *Code* and the *Digest* had Islamic counterparts, which, however, did not require the composition of new treatises, but only the translation of existing texts: Charles Hamilton's *Hedāya, or Guide; a Commentary on the Mussulman Laws* (1791) and Jones's *Al-Sirajjiyah: or the Mohammedan Law of Inheritance* (1792).

8. Hastings and his associates remained forever opposed to missionary activities, which they were convinced would generate resentment and be destabilizing for Company rule (see, for example, R. Rocher 1983: 213, 216–17, 230 n. 13).

9. How, from this early sympathy for mild, meek, downtrodden Hindus, the British went on, in Victorian times, to favor virile, fearless Muslims, provides much of the texture for Hutchins 1967 and A. Nandy 1983.

10. I am indebted to David Ludden for pointing out this illustration. My interpretation of it differs from his (this volume).

11. There appears to be no extant copy of a Persian translation of the *Atharvaveda* mentioned in the *Ā'īn-i Akbarī* (Mujtabai 1978: 80–81).

12. Sharpe's (1985) bicentenary survey of *Western* images of the *Gītā* not inappropriately features a chapter on "Gandhi's Gita."

13. See, for example, the early nineteenth-century debate on *satī*, in which both the abolitionist and the anti-abolitionist sides accepted the privileging of the *Manusmṛti* among *dharmaśāstra* texts (Mani 1987: 142–45).

14. Eighteenth-century writers and painters commonly portrayed *satī* scenes in a positive light (Irwin 1776; Archer 1979: 72, 156, and plates VII, 27).

15. By stressing the commonalities in the arguments proffered by both sides and construing them into a single discourse, Mani (1986) attempts to establish that they were not as different as they have generally been held to be. I do not share this totalizing approach.

16. Mani (1986: 36–39, 1987: 130–35) notes that the opinions on *satī* given by nineteenth-century pandit assistants to the British courts attested to their interpretive rather than authoritative character. In that pandits were entirely consistent with the tradition of the writers of *nibandhas* (interpretive digests) of prior centuries.

17. The exceptional career of a prominent pandit with the Sadar Diwani Adalat is sketched in R. Rocher 1989.

18. In the words of the *Mahābhārata* (12.59.30), duty (*dharma*), material gain (*artha*), and pleasures of the senses (*kāma*) "are termed the triad; a fourth is release (*mokṣa*), which is distinct in goal and distinct in nature."

References

MANUSCRIPT SOURCES

British Library: Oriental Ms. 1124. *Purāṇārthaprakāśa* by Rādhākānta Tarkavāgīśa. 1783.
India Office Records: P/128/9–15. Bengal Criminal and Civil Judicial Consultations. 1794.
———— P/147/25. Bengal Civil Judicial Consultations. 1795.

PRINTED SOURCES

Acharyya, Bijay Kisor. 1914. *Codification in British India*. Calcutta: Thacker, Spink.
Archer, Mildred. 1979. *India and British Portraiture 1770–1825*. London: Sotheby Parke Bernet.
Asiatick Researches: Comprising History and Antiquities, the Arts, Sciences, and Literature of Asia. 4 vols. 1788–94. Calcutta: Asiatic Society. Reprint Delhi: Cosmo Publications. 1979.
Böhtlingk, Otto and Rudolph Roth. 1855–75. *Sanskrit-Wörterbuch*. 7 vol. St. Petersburg: Kaiserliche Akademie der Wissenschaften.
Cannon, Garland, ed. 1970. *The Letters of Sir William Jones*. 2 vols. Oxford: Clarendon Press.
————. 1990. *The Life and Mind of Oriental Jones: Sir William Jones, the Father of Modern Linguistics*. Cambridge: Cambridge University Press.
Cohn, Bernard S. 1968. "Notes on the History of the Study of Indian Society and Culture." In Milton Singer and Bernard S. Cohn, eds., *Structure and Change in Indian Society*. Chicago: Aldine, 3–28.
————. 1989. "Law and the Colonial State in India." In June Starr and Jane F. Collier, eds., *History and Power in the Study of the Law*, Ithaca and London: Cornell University Press, 131–52.
Colebrooke, Henry Thomas. 1794. "On the Duties of a Faithful Hindu Widow." *Asiatick Researches* 4. Reprint Delhi: Cosmo Publications, 1979, 205–15.
————, transl. 1797–98. *A Digest of Hindu Law on Contracts and Successions*. 4 vols. Calcutta: Honourable Company's Press.
————. 1805. "On the Védas, or Sacred Writings of the Hindus." *Asiatick Researches* 8. Reprint Delhi: Cosmo Publications, 1979, 377–497.
Das, Sisir Kumar. 1978. *Sahibs and Munshis: An Account of the College of Fort William*. New Delhi: Orion Publications.
Derrett, J. Duncan M. 1968. *Religion, Law and the State in India*. London: Faber and Faber.
Dirks, Nicholas B. 1989. "The Policing of Tradition in Colonial South India." Presented at the Ethnohistory Workshop, University of Pennsylvania.
Dumézil, Georges. 1958. *L'Idéologie tripartie des Indo-Européens*. Brussels: Latomus.
Furber, Holden. 1970. "The History of East India Companies: General Problems."

In Michel Mollat, ed., *Sociétés et Compagnies de Commerce en Orient et dans l'Océan Indien*. Paris: S.E.V.P.E.N., 415–18.

Galanter, Marc. 1989. *Law and Society in Modern India*. Delhi: Oxford University Press.

Gleig, George Robert. 1841. *Memoirs of the Life of the Right Hon. Warren Hastings*. 3 vols. London: Richard Bentley.

Gorekar, N. S. 1965. "Persian Language and Sanskritic Lore." *Indica* 2: 107–19.

Grier, Sidney C., ed. 1905. *Letters of Warren Hastings to His Wife*. Edinburgh: William Blackwood and Sons.

Halbfass, Wilhelm. 1988. "Hegel, India, and the Europeanization of the Earth." Presented at the South Asia Seminar, University of Pennsylvania.

———. 1990. *India and Europe. An Essay in Understanding*. 2d ed., Albany: State University of New York Press.

Halhed, Nathaniel Brassey, transl. 1776. *A Code of Gentoo Laws, or, Ordinations of the Pundits, from a Persian Translation Made from the Original, Written in the Shanscrit Language*. London: East India Company.

———. 1778. *A Grammar of the Bengal Language*. Hoogly in Bengal: East India Company Press.

Hamilton, Charles, transl. 1791. *Hedāya, or Guide; A Commentary on the Mussulman Laws*. 4 vols. London: T. Bensley.

Hutchins, Francis G. 1967. *The Illusion of Permanence: British Imperialism in India*. Princeton, NJ: Princeton University Press.

Irwin, Eyles. 1776. *Bedukah or the Self-Devoted. An Indian Pastoral*. London: J. Dodsley.

Jones, Sir William, transl. 1792. *Al-Sirajjiyah; or the Mohammedan Law of Inheritance*. Calcutta: Joseph Cooper for the benefit of insolvent debtors.

———, transl. 1794. *Institutes of Hindu Law or, the Ordinances of Menu, according to the Gloss of Cullūca, Comprising the Indian System of Duties, Religious and Civil*. Calcutta: Honourable Company's Press.

———. 1807. *The Works of Sir William Jones*. 13 vols. Reprint Delhi: Agam Prakashan, 1976–80.

Kejariwal, O. P. 1988. *The Asiatic Society of Bengal and the Discovery of India's Past 1784–1838*. Delhi: Oxford University Press.

King, Bruce. 1991. Review of *Masks of Conquest. Literary Study and British Rule in India* by Gauri Viswanathan. *Comparative Literature Studies* 28: 322–26.

Kopf, David. 1969. *British Orientalism and the Bengal Renaissance. The Dynamics of Indian Modernization, 1773–1835*. Berkeley: University of California Press.

Lloyd, Mary. 1979. "Sir Charles Wilkins, 1749–1836," *India Office Library & Records: Report for the Year 1978*, 8–39.

Mani, Lata. 1986. "Production of an Official Discourse on *Sati* in Early Nineteenth Century Bengal." *Economic and Political Weekly* 31, 17: 32–40.

———. 1987. "Contentious Traditions: The Debate on *Sati* in Colonial India," *Cultural Critique* 7: 119–56.

———. 1989. "Writing History after *Orientalism*." Presented at the South Asia Seminar, University of Pennsylvania.

Marshall, Peter J. 1970. *The British Discovery of Hinduism in the Eighteenth Century.* Cambridge: Cambridge University Press.

———. 1973. "Warren Hastings as Scholar and Patron." In Anne Whitman, J. S. Bromley, and P. G. M. Dickson, eds., *Statesmen, Scholars and Merchants: Essays in Eighteenth-Century History Presented to Dame Lucy Sutherland.* Oxford: Clarendon Press, 242–62.

———. 1976. *East Indian Fortunes. The British in Bengal in the Eighteenth Century.* Oxford: Oxford University Press.

———. 1992. "'Cornwallis Triumphant': War in India and the British Public in the Late Eighteenth Century." In Lawrence Freedman, Paul Hayes, and Robert O'Neill, eds., *War, Strategy and International Politics: Essays in Honour of Sir Michael Howard.* Oxford: Clarendon Press, 57–74.

Misra, B. B. 1961. *The Judicial Administration of the East India Company in Bengal 1765–1782.* Delhi: Motilal Banarsidass.

Mujtabai, Fathullah. 1978. *Aspects of Hindu Muslim Cultural Relations.* Delhi: National Book Bureau.

Mukherjee, S. N. 1968. *Sir William Jones: A Study in Eighteenth-Century British Attitudes to India.* Cambridge: Cambridge University Press. Second edition reprinted Delhi: Oriental Books Reprint Corp., 1987.

Nandy, Ashis. 1983. *The Intimate Enemy: Loss and Recovery of Self Under Colonialism.* Delhi/New York: Oxford University Press.

Nandy, Somendra Chandra. 1978–81. *Life and Times of Cantoo Baboo (Krisna Kanta Nandy) the Banian of Warren Hastings.* 2 vols. Vol. 1 Bombay: Allied Publishers; vol. 2 Calcutta: Dev-all.

Narain, V. A. 1959. *Jonathan Duncan and Varanasi.* Calcutta: Firma K. L. Mukhopadhyay.

Philips, C. H., ed. 1977. *The Correspondence of Lord William Cavendish Bentinck, Governor-General of India 1828–1835.* Oxford: Oxford University Press.

Rennell, James. 1783. *Memoir of a Map of Hindoostan; or the Moghul's Empire.* London: M. Brown for the author.

Rocher, Ludo. 1972. "Schools of Hindu Law." In J. Ensink and P. Gaeffke, eds., *India Maior: Congratulatory Volume Presented to J. Gonda.* Leiden: E. J. Brill, 167–76.

Rocher, Rosane. 1979. "Alien and Empathic: The Indian Poems of N. B. Halhed." In Blair B. Kling and M. N. Pearson, eds., *The Age of Partnership: Europeans in Asia Before Dominion.* Honolulu: University of Hawaii Press, 215–35.

———. 1980. "Nathaniel Brassey Halhed, Sir William Jones, and Comparative Indo-European Linguistics." In Jean Bingen, André Coupez, and Francine Mawet, eds., *Recherches de Linguistique: Hommages à Maurice Leroy.* Brussels: Éditions de l'Université de Bruxelles, 173–80.

———. 1983. *Orientalism, Poetry, and the Millennium: The Checkered Life of Nathaniel Brassey Halhed 1751–1830.* Delhi: Motilal Banarsidass.

———. 1984. "The Early Enchantment of India's Past," *South Asian Review* 8, 5: 1–5.

———. 1989. "The Career of Rādhākānta Tarkavāgīśa, an Eighteenth-Century Pandit in British Employ." *Journal of the American Oriental Society* 109: 27–33.

Schlegel, August Wilhelm. 1832. *Réflexions sur l'étude des langues asiatiques, adressées à Sir James Mackintosh, suivies d'une lettre à M. Horace Hayman Wilson.* Reprinted in *Oeuvres écrites en français,* ed. Edouard Böcking. Leipzig: Weidmann, 1846, 3: 95–274.

Sharpe, Eric J. 1985. *The Universal Gītā: Western Images of the* Bhagavad Gītā, *A Bicentenary Survey.* La Salle, IL: Open Court.

Shukla, N. S. 1974. "Persian Translations of Sanskrit Works." *Indological Studies* 3, 1–2 (A. D. Pusalker Commemoration Volume): 175–91.

Teignmouth, Charles John, Lord. 1843. *Memoir of the Life and Correspondence of John, Lord Teignmouth.* London: Hatchard and Son.

Wilkins, Charles. 1785. *The Bhagvat-Geeta . . . Translated from the Original in the Sanskreet or Ancient Language of the Brahmans.* London: East India Company.

HINDOOSTAN
By J. Rennell *F.R.S.* 1782.

Lithograph, "James Rennell's Map of Hindoostan." From his *Memoir of a Map of Hindoostan, or the Moghul's Empire.*

Relief from monument to Sir William Jones in the chapel of University College, Oxford, depicting Jones as "the Justinian of India." The inscription reads, "He formed a digest of Hindu and Mohammedan laws."

David Ludden

8. Orientalist Empiricism: Transformations of Colonial Knowledge

Uncertainty about what constitutes truth underlies the pursuit of knowledge and logically entails critical scrutiny of the means by which some representations of reality and not others become established as true. In this endeavor, the veracity of statements about reality is not at issue so much as their epistemological authority, their power to organize understandings of the world. In this vein, I join authors in this volume to pursue a proposition derived from Edward Said: there is knowledge constituted as truthful by the authority of a system of representations called "orientalism," which arose from and bolstered European supremacy.

Michel Foucault provides a point of departure for many authors in this volume, as he does for Said (1978: 23). Said recognizes that Foucault's method is deficient for historical studies, because "the individual text or author counts for very little" (Said 1978: 23). Thus Foucault can conjure discursive formations in history but cannot write their histories, having blinded himself to dynamics of creation, tension, contest, and change. Said only partially liberates himself from Foucault (Said 1984, 1986). Seeing orientalism in descriptive, literary terms, he makes provocative associations among texts that constitute orientalism and dynamics of European power. But the particulars that connect histories of imperialism and knowledge are missing. In this essay, I consider connections between histories of political power in South Asia and knowledge about Indian tradition. Though my goal is not a critique of Said, I do conclude that by detaching his chosen texts from history, in the manner of Foucault, Said has lost sight of the politics that reproduce the epistemological authority of orientalism today.

Orientalism

Said conflates three formations of "orientalism" that have very distinct relations to colonial power. Most narrowly, orientalism is a field of scholarship with a distinct academic genealogy and tradition. I designate only specialists in this field as "orientalists." Most broadly, orientalism is a vast set of images in scholarship, painting, literature, and other media—a sprawling formation in which the works of William Jones, orientalist painters, Rudyard Kipling, and Henry Kissinger mingle in a multimedia text that conjures the essences of the East. This constitutes orientalism for Edward Said. Between these two extremes—the first formation being small and defined rigidly by scholarly norms, the other being huge and defined loosely by the implications of its imagery—there is a third formation: a venerable set of factualized statements about the Orient, which was established with authorized data and research techniques and which has become so widely accepted as true, so saturated by excess plausibility (Ludden [1988] 1990), that it determines the content of assumptions on which theory and inference can be built. This body of knowledge did originate in part in the work of orientalists, but it grew far beyond their scope by contributions from other authorities. Now shared and disseminated within a multicultural world, where many disciplines add to its authority (Abdel-Malek 1963), this last formation—orientalism as a body of knowledge—is the subject of this essay.

The three formations of orientalism overlap and share historical space. They all presume a fundamental divide between East and West and observe the East through western epistemologies in cognitive relation to the West. That they have common substance defined by a single attitude toward the East and common links to western domination is an argument Said makes but I do not. For, despite a history that unites them, they have separate histories that account for their distinctive substance and interactions with power. Orientalists, for instance, played a more distinct, powerful role in the production of official colonial knowledge about India before 1830 than after. By 1830, Parliament and political economy provided independent authority for the determination of truths about the "real" India. By 1880, imperial government and European social theory were arguably more important than were orientalists for the production of orientalist images like those in Kipling's work, as well as for the authority of conventional wisdom about India, such as that enshrined in census reports and ethnological tradition (Cohn 1983, 1989). By 1900, high imperialism, social Darwinism, and scientific racism gave orientalism meanings quite contrary to orientalist scholarship (Stepan 1982).

For Said, imperialism is inherent in orientalism. Knowledge is power. But this begs many important questions. How does orientalism support imperialism? How does imperialism explain the substance of orientalism in different world areas? How has orientalism survived and even thrived in a world of nation-states and national movements? By separating knowledge and power (which Said does not do, following Foucault), we can address issues like these and historicize orientalism more effectively. By locating forces at work in the production of orientalism, we can show how its reproduction has transformed its composition and political meanings over time. Doing so, we find orientalism much more diverse and vital than Said makes it out to be.

Orientalism as a body of knowledge about India dates back to classical antiquity and has many early-modern precursors (Halbfass 1988; O'Leary 1989). But eighteenth-century European expansion in India generated qualitatively new knowledge. Much of it served instrumental functions for capitalist, military, and administrative expansion by the English East India Company. Yet methods to produce this knowledge were not specific to India, nor was its substance understood to be dictated by utility. Even the most instrumental knowledge, produced to sustain technologies of colonial rule—what I will call colonial knowledge—was produced under the Enlightenment rubric of objective science. Additions to knowledge about India were understood as scientific discoveries whose veracity was based on methodologies authorized by scientific standards of the day. Orientalism as a body of knowledge drew material sustenance from colonialism but became objectified by the ideology of science as a set of factualized statements about a reality that existed and could be known independent of any subjective, colonizing will. Thus detached epistemologically from politics by a culture that objectivized the world as a collection of scientific observations with universal validity, orientalism floated free of its original moorings; it could therefore serve diverse political purposes and receive new sustenance from many quarters. By 1900, it was even deployed against European dominance by Indian nationalists. Its substance also changed with time: because it ordered knowledge about India in relation to the West, orientalism changed substantively through the production of new "facts," with advances in science and changing structures of world power.

Colonial Knowledge

Foundations of orientalism lie in the transition to Company rule in India, circa 1770–1820, when producing new knowledge about India was bound tightly with political patronage. As Company territory grew, centralization became a policy imperative; as the Company became a ruling power, its autonomy decreased (Spear 1978: 85–6ff). Intellectual labor became implicated in struggles to subordinate Company to Parliament, Indian provinces to Calcutta, and districts to provincial capitals. The centralization that accompanied colonial expansion involved the subordination of many intermediaries, "partners in empire," and "loose cannons" who had been critical for the Company in earlier decades but were now seen as detrimental (Furber 1948; Kling 1976; Sutherland 1952; Nightingale 1970). The fathers of orientalism in India furthered colonial centralization by subordinating the Indian intelligentsia to English epistemological authority.

Beginning in 1784, the year that Pitt's India Act was passed and the Asiatic Society of Bengal founded, and increasingly with reforms under Lord Cornwallis in the wake of Burke's denunciations of Company Raj (Furber 1987), new attention was paid to Indian intermediaries who stood between the Court of Directors and Indian subjects (Stein 1989). To subordinate these men, Europeans had to appropriate knowledge that was locked away in the minds of Indian commercial, judicial, military, and revenue specialists. By appropriating knowledge toward this end, Europeans discovered India for themselves, in their own terms, by converting knowledge from native sources into English language forms that were systematic, scientific, and accessible to means of truth-testing that were becoming the pride of European culture (Adas 1989). In addition, military operations and political centralization required that data which had never been produced by Indian rulers be generated and controlled by government; such data constituted new facts for the creation of orientalism as a body of knowledge. Colonialism reorganized India politically and empirically at the same time, and the two reorganizations supported one another.

The works of James Rennell, William Jones, and Thomas Munro show how military expansion and political centralization implicated colonial knowledge. Rennell joined the Royal Navy in 1756 at age fourteen, and went to the Philippines with Alexander Dalrymple at age twenty. He had been surveying harbors for the Royal Navy when the Company, in

1763, hired him to survey routes from Calcutta to the Bay of Bengal. He became Surveyor General of Bengal the next year; when he left India, in 1777, he literally put India on the map with his comprehensive *Map of Hindoostan*, whose accompanying *Memoir* appeared in three editions, the last in 1793. This compendium was not superseded for decades and was possible, Rennell says in the preface to his *Memoir*, because so few geographical facts were known when he began his work. He says also that he abandoned revising the *Memoir* because data multiplied too rapidly with the expansion of Company power and that the market for his work arose from public curiosity in England stimulated by Company wars.

The lithograph adorning Rennell's map (this volume: following p. 249) symbolizes the progress of geography during Rennell's career. It shows the surveyor's and map maker's tools on the ground and European civilians in the shadow of Britannia, as she receives texts from Brahmans, one text being labeled "Shastas" (Shastras), Hindu law books. The gesture linking Britannia and the central Brahman figure seems ambiguous and could be seen to depict a gift being made to him by Britannia. But Brahmans in queue with arms full of texts wait to give, not receive. And the temple tower behind Britannia presents her as a goddess/queen receiving gifts from supplicants who bear offerings/tribute. They offer knowledge, that special gift of India's literati, so critical for Britannia's transformation from conquering to ruling power (Bayly 1988; Dirks, this volume). The lithograph thus represents European merchants and surveyors dependent on Britannia's might, through which they gain knowledge from a supplicant India. The irony is that even as the lithograph represents the power of Britannia and pays homage to her from the vantage points of science and commerce, it implies that natives, especially Brahmans, hold knowledge that she needs. To loosen that grip became a political goal for Company Raj for the advancement of science and commerce. With military victories, more English surveyors marched into the interior every year. Observation and measurement by Englishmen supplanted "secondhand," "hearsay," and "traditionary" native accounts. In 1808, Rennell measured progress in surveying by looking back to the 1770s; he said to a gathering of surveyors, "At that day we were compelled to receive information from others respecting the interior of the country, but in your time you *explored* for *yourselves*" (Phillimore 1954–1956: frontispiece).

The shastras in Rennell's lithograph signify another branch of knowledge in which the Company sought to end its dependence on native experts. A letter from William Jones to Cornwallis proposing that Jones be commissioned to compile a "Digest of Hindu and Mohammadan laws" shows the importance of this project for colonialism. Penned in Calcutta in 1788, the letter reads like a grant proposal. It begins by arguing that civil law should accord with native practice, a principle enshrined in the 1781 Act of Settlement (Mukherjee [1968] 1987: 117ff.), with which Jones begins his proposal. He goes on to say that "the difficulty lies . . . in the application of the principle to practice; for the Hindu and Muselman laws are locked up for the most part in two very difficult languages, Sanscrit and Arabick, which few Europeans will ever learn." As a result, judges in Jones's day depended on native experts; and on his arrival in Calcutta as a judge, Jones "soon began to suspect the pandits and maulavis . . . ." In 1784 he wrote to Warren Hastings, "I can no longer bear to be at the mercy of our Pundits, who deal out Hindu law as they please . . ." (Mukherjee [1968] 1987: 118). His argument to Cornwallis—who once wrote, "Every native of Hindustan, I verily believe, is corrupt" (Spear 1978: 88)—proceeds accordingly.

> . . . if we give judgment only from the opinions of native lawyers and scholars, we can never be sure, that we have not been deceived by them. . . . my experience justifies me in declaring, that I could not with an easy conscience concur in a decision, merely on the written opinion of native lawyers, in any case in which they could have the remotest interest in misleading the court . . . . (Cannon 1970, II: 795)

Jones had devised "the obvious remedy for this evil" and communicated it to Burke and others before he left England. It is this plan that he submitted to Cornwallis for support.

> If we had a complete digest of Hindu and Mohammadan laws, after the model of Justinian's inestimable Pandects, compiled by the most learned of the native lawyers, with an accurate verbal translation of it into English; and if copies of the work were reposited in the proper offices of the Sedr Divani Adalat, and of the Supreme Court, that they might occasionally be consulted as a standard of justice, we should rarely be at a loss for principles at least and rules of law applicable to the cases before us, and should never perhaps, be led astray by the Pandits or Maulavi's (sic), who would hardly venture to impose on us, when their impositions might be so easily detected. (Cannon 1970, II: 795)

Jones then goes on to sketch a proper method for the project, estimate its cost, and modestly offer himself as "superintendent of such a work." His argument and offer were accepted. Jones could then seek what

S. N. Mukherjee calls "his greatest desire," to become "the legislator of the Indians" ([1967] 1987: 112). To fulfill his desire required disciplined devotion to divulging secrets buried in difficult texts in languages "few Europeans will ever learn" (see Rocher: this volume). The requisite esoteric skills became the orientalists' hallmark, which Nietzche subsequently criticized for its intellectual narrowness and which soon marginalized Indology as "it quickly became clear that the most interesting scholastic problems had no practical value at all" (Gaeffke 1990: 67, 69). But his language skill, his ability to systematize legal codes on Justinian principles, and the patronage of Cornwallis did give Jones real power in his day, enabling him to attempt a reversal of the power/knowledge relationship depicted in Rennell's lithograph. Through Jones, Britannia could generate knowledge of Hindu law that never existed before; she could give the "Shastas" to Indians who would rely on her for correct understanding of their own sacred texts and laws.

Jones saw this reversal of roles, its attendant subordination of "pandits and maulavis," and the power it gave him both as scientific achievement and as testimony to his dedication and intellect. He also saw it as a paternal generosity that would also typify orientalists, as Wilhelm Halbfass indicates when he says of J. G. Herder that, "His sympathy for the people of India became ever more apparent in his friendly and glorifying view of the 'childlike Indians'" (Halbfass 1988: 70; see Mojumdar 1976). Jones described his feelings in a letter to G. J. Spencer, in 1791:

> I speak *the language of the Gods*, as the Brahmens call it, with great fluency, and am engaged in superintending a Digest of Indian Law for the benefit of the *twenty four millions* of black British subjects in these provinces: the work is difficult & delicate in the highest degree & engages all my leisure every morning between my breakfast and the sitting of the court; the natives are charmed with the work, and the idea of making their slavery lighter by giving them their own laws, is more flattering to me than the thanks of the company and the approbation of the king, which have also been transmitted to me. (Cannon 1970, II: 885; emphasis original)

Language learning also enabled Thomas Munro to perform a special role in the production of colonial knowledge, also under the patronage of Cornwallis, who appointed him to assist another military officer, Alexander Read, in administering the Baramahal territory ceded to the Company by Tipu Sultan in 1792. Cornwallis appointed these military men to perform this critical civilian duty on the frontiers of Company expansion in order simultaneously to subordinate Madras to Calcutta and native inter-

mediaries to the Company. Cornwallis distrusted Madras civilians, because, as he reported to the Court of Directors in 1792, few men under the
governor of Madras "are acquainted with country languages," so they

> are obliged, both from habit and necessity, to allow the management of their
> official, as well as their private business, to fall into the hands of dubashes, a
> description of people in the Carnatic, who, with very few exceptions, are
> calculated for being the most cruel instruments of rapine and extortion in the
> hands of unprincipled masters, and even of rendering . . . the most upright
> and humane intentions . . . perfectly useless to the interests of the company,
> and to the unfortunate natives who happen to be within the reach of their
> power and influence. (Stein 1989: 38)

Munro, appointed as revenue administrator, advanced his career for thirty
years by applying the "political principle of destroying any and all inter-
mediary authority between the Company and the cultivator as the best
assurance of the securing of control by the Company over its new dominions." He sought "nothing less than the completion, by administrative
means, of the military conquest of the Baramahal . . ." (Stein 1989: 59–60).
From this arose the authoritative construction of village India enshrined
in the "ryotwari system," which became an essential element of orientalism
as a body of knowledge.

Politics and Empiricism

William Jones, Indologist and lawgiver, died in 1793, and Thomas Munro,
soldier and administrator, died in 1827. Their legacies grew from intellectual constructions of India relative to Britain during the institution of that
relationship as colonial. Though Munro died preoccupied by war in
Burma, the conclusion of the Maratha wars had eliminated the Company's
last major military threat. By 1820, "the acute moral crisis of a generation
before—the time of Burke's attack—had passed" (Stein 1989: 138). When
Sir Thomas was governor at Madras, fears of the French and revolution
had also passed away, which had preoccupied Wellesley when he established the College at Fort William (Kopf 1969: 46–47) and which made
Jones, whatever his own beliefs, "part of (a) revivified conservatism, which
sought to define and defend British society in the terms employed by
Burke" (Majeed 1990: 211). As the frontier days of colonial knowledge
passed away, Company Raj became secure; pathbreaking discoveries be-

came authoritative wisdom; innovative methods became systems. Jones fathered a discipline and Munro an administration.

Like Indian administrative politics, which remained split into provinces and departments but became ever more centralized, colonial knowledge remained divided into specialized compartments but became increasingly integrated as a body of knowledge by forces centered in London. Continuities across this transition and beyond reveal major political victories and long-term trends in the history of knowledge that built empirical certainty into orientalism. Among political victories, none is more critical than Munro's triumph in constructing *The Fifth Report on East India Company Affairs*, which made him an architect of the modern understanding of agrarian India (Stein 1989, 138–77). Among long-term trends, the most critical is the expanding scope of empiricism, which made colonial knowledge into a set of factualized statements about reality. Indology, revenue surveys, and commission reports came to share the same epistemological terrain with positivist knowledge about all societies, cultures, and political economies. Separate streams of knowledge about India could thus intersect and enrich one another, and facts from investigations in India could be integrated with facts from around the world in political economy and world history.

Empiricism embraced ever more of the world with the expansion of British power. Encyclopedic compendia like Malachy Postlethwayt's *The Universal Dictionary of Trade and Commerce* (1766) organized data from treaties, laws, travel accounts, histories, and technical manuals on productions and trades in one authoritative, fact-filled format; but much of the world was still missing, including India. In their day, Rennell and later surveyors like Hamilton Buchanan and Benjamin Heyne published accounts of Indian journeys, and their volumes went beside others of the same sort, like that by Joseph Townsend, a rector from Cornwall who published his account of a journey in the 1780s, in France and Spain, advertising "particular attention to the agriculture, manufacture, commerce, population, taxes, and revenue." Rennell also drew maps for Mungo Park's best-selling account of an expedition to Africa. Such works made the world visible and usable for British enterprise. They were of a piece with efforts in art and literature to render the world as a unified landscape for intellectual and material appropriation by English capitalism (Cosgrove 1984).

In the early nineteenth century, pieces of colonial knowledge generated by experts as diverse as Munro and Jones, on subjects as diverse as Hindu law and agrarian administration, became situated side-by-side within one empiricist epistemology, in which they could be integrated into a unified construction of India. Authoritative sources produced diverse types of data that became factualized and located in a unified empirical domain where they could be formed into verified statements about Indian reality. "Hindu law books" became understood as accounts of legal practice and therefore of actual law-abiding behavior and thus of religious norms that guided traditional life. These could be then combined with accounts of observed practice and of history and lore to demonstrate how Indians obeyed or violated norms in practice. In short, once the authority of colonial knowledge was established in its power over English-language understandings of India, its veracity escaped the political nexus portrayed in Rennell's lithograph. Freed from politics, authoritative knowledge about traditional India could be designed from virtually any collection of authoritative data.

The template for a lasting design was devised in Munro's time and became increasingly ornate and codified by the routinization of the colonial administration; as knowledge production was systematized, individual explorations gave way to routine reports, native informants became employees and subjects of the Raj, and journey literature gave way to official correspondence. By 1820, colonial knowledge had begun to emerge as authoritative, official wisdom, and orientalism to take definite shape as a body of knowledge.

We have no complete account of this process and I cannot attempt one here. What I can do is illustrate how colonial knowledge generated authoritative "facts" that constituted traditional India within a conceptual template that would be progressively theorized within modern world history. These factualized representations of India became official wisdom. They were conventionalized and then fixed as a factual basis for inference and theory. Two vignettes illustrate how early colonialism produced two foundational ideas about traditional India: (1) India was "from time immemorial" a land of autonomous village communities in which (2) the force sustaining tradition was Hindu religion, with its complex social prescriptions, above all those pertaining to caste.

1. When Read and Munro went to Baramahal in 1792, their purpose was revenue collection. They found that by eliminating middlemen they could contract for revenue directly with village leaders. This was a major change in Company routines, and Read had to defend it to the Board of Revenue in Madras. From experience in Bengal and in Madras territories,

the Board assumed that it would collect its revenue from zamindars and contractors who would deliver revenue from the villages; indeed, in 1801, the Board confirmed erstwhile poligar chiefs as zamindar landlords in Madras territories. But Read argued that collecting taxes directly from villagers enabled him to lower tax rates and to collect more taxes, though this raised the cost of tax collection, which led to vehement objections from the Board. Eliminating the middlemen between the Company and village taxpayers became a crusade for Munro. By 1811 he had collected revenue and information from several parts of South India, and his influence in London enabled him to organize evidence for submission to Parliament as it considered the Company's 1813 charter renewal. Evidence for the *Fifth Report*, which Munro effectively compiled, helped to prove his case, with data from Company experts, that the village had always been the basic unit of administration in India, and peasant rights in villages had been usurped by thieving middlemen and tyrants like Tipu Sultan. Thus, for its own interests and to protect the rights of the people, the Company should establish the village as the basic unit of administration.

Munro argued for and effectively proved traditions in which village headmen administered villages composed of peasant families who had always enjoyed the equivalent of private property rights, though these had been abrogated by rapacious tyrants, poligars, and renters. To accomplish his victory, Munro had to best competitors in Madras, above all Francis Ellis, who commanded evidence that might have won the day, were the matter to have been settled scholastically. But this was not to be (Stein 1989).

2. For surveyors and revenue collectors throughout South India, as for Rennell, Brahmans were the most influential native informants, and they became key figures in Company administration. Even so, until 1810, it seems that Britons in Company service viewed Brahmans essentially as specialists in a complex division of labor. Early lists of castes from southern territories normally transliterate and translate caste names with occupational labels without ranking. By 1820, this pattern has changed; why, I cannot say exactly. But it seems that as the village became for the Company the foundation of Indian society, principles were needed for ordering that society without reference to political structures larger than the village. In principle, Munro's ryotwari system proposed that all citizen taxpayers were juridically equal; in practice, however, revenue collection and Company law rested on a logic of hierarchy, with the Company at the top adjudicating disputes based on precedent (Washbrook 1981). Company

courts established precedents, but common law tradition required logical basis for precedent in Indian society itself. Though Company officials collected evidence to confirm rights on the basis of charters from precolonial kings, this evidence was often inconvenient or lacking and positivist law required logic to fill in the gaps left by its silences and exclusions.

Hindu law codes and caste prescriptions therein provided that logic. By 1820, legal and revenue proceedings are filled with cases and reports on the traditional, religiously based, social order of village society, self-regulated by caste and village panchayats, demanding recognition in Company governance and law. Caste lists by 1820 uniformly use *varna* categories to rank *jatis*. By this time, of course, the Company was deeply embroiled in the administration of Hindu temples (Appadurai 1981). Hindu religion was in the early nineteenth century very much a part of Company Raj; the colonial construction of caste society in village India needs to be seen in this light (Bayly 1988). Practical experience proved and proved again that religion was the basis of social order in India.

These early moments in the making of colonial knowledge suggest how Company Raj produced factualized formulations that would populate orientalism as a body of knowledge. They also suggest the complex and contested, shifting role of native authority for Company experts who endeavored to establish truths about India. Though the distinctions between the intellectual work of Jones and Munro suggest a division like that which would later separate humanities from social sciences, it was the combination of these two streams of learning that created colonial knowledge and orientalism, by establishing epistemological privilege for European expertise deployed to establish concurrently the essential truth about India and policies for Indian governance. The utility of ideas about India for governance and their institutionalization by the state bolstered their epistemological authority.

Orientalism began with the acquisition of the languages needed to gain reliable information about India. Indian languages became a foundation for scientific knowledge of Indian tradition built from data transmitted to Europeans by native experts. Rennell's lithograph illustrates that texts were most the valued objects of transmission: properly studied, texts would reveal the positive facts of Hindu legal doctrine. For collectors as much as judges, precedent and principles of right were essential and could be positively determined from reputable witnesses through translation. Reliable evidence with which to establish a factual basis for Company Raj thus came initially from reputable natives whose authority was rooted in their expertise and social status, as evaluated by Company authorities. Evidence from Brahman pandits and other Indian elites was essential for sound knowledge on which to base sound policies, and it established a bond between the Company and Indian elites that was used to stabilize the colonial state within a conservative mold (Bayly 1988).

Empirically sound and useful knowledge about India was not to be found only in classical texts. Even Jones himself indicates that properly constituted European expertise was required to discover the real truth in texts. For Rennell and the others, only British experts could determine veracity and therefore sound knowledge for government. Surveyors took great pains to distinguish data *gleaned* from the accounts of natives from data *produced* by direct observation; Munro necessarily used only evidence produced by collectors to establish the village as a traditional foundation of government. For Rennell and Munro, the real India experts were those scientists and trained administrators who worked and traveled in the countryside and absorbed local information and observed local conditions—those incipient social scientists who created "hard" objective data in surveys and settlements for policy decisions based on facts and political economy. A stray Sanskrit quote might be relevant here and there, but only to provide color for conclusions based on "real" data. For Munro, as for James Mill and many others to follow, skepticism about native sources combined with opposition to policies intended to preserve native elite privileges, associated with orientalists like Jones and Ellis.

My two vignettes also suggest how politics influenced not only the kind of data generated by Company expertise but also the logic of their integration into constructions of India. Colonial knowledge was seriously contested intellectual terrain. The Company collected data that could have been used to construct very different images of rural India (Ludden 1988). But alternative formations were obscured and marginalized in Munro's lifetime by the political process that wielded authority in the production of knowledge about India. This authority was centered in London. Munro worked within complex webs of influence connecting European trends, British politics, Indian administration, and orientalism. His prose shows the influence of logical positivism and utilitarianism. But his work is also tinged with conservative ideas about hierarchy and is inconsistent by standards of contemporary philosophy (Stein 1989). His victories in intellectual contests to construct rural India were not those of an ideology or philosophy. They were political. His formulations became fixed as factual knowledge about Indian reality by establishing effective official wisdom for

Company Raj. Victories in London made Munro judicial commissioner and then governor; his minutes became almost biblical in authority. His characterization of the village as "a little republic" dates from 1806. Published by Mark Wilks in 1810 during the campaign to shape *The Fifth Report*, it was by 1830 at the metaphorical heart of orientalism (Stein 1989). Its most famous formulation, in a minute by Charles Metcalfe read in 1830 as evidence for the Select Committee of the House of Commons on the Affairs of the East India Company, had a powerful influence on Karl Marx. It reads in part:

> The village communities are little republics, having nearly everything they want within themselves, and almost independent of any foreign relations. They seem to last where nothing else lasts. Dynasty after dynasty tumbles down; revolution succeeds to revolution; Hindoo, Patan, Mogul, Mahratta, Sik, English are all masters in turn; but the village communities remain the same. . . . If a country remain for a series of years the scene of continued pillage and massacre, so that villages cannot be inhabited, the scattered villagers nevertheless return whenever the power of peaceable possession revives. A generation may pass away, but the succeeding generation will return. The sons will take the place of their fathers; the same site for the village, the same position for the houses, the same lands, will be occupied by the descendants of those who were driven out when the village was depopulated . . . . (Kessinger 1974: 25)

Metcalfe, like Munro, engaged fierce debates in Britain about colonial policy that rested on disputed facts about India and policy principles for Indian governance. Science and political disputation continued to work together in the formation of orientalism and within it to fix the essentially timeless self-reproduction of village India firmly in the modern mind. Although James Mill savagely criticized the East India Company in his *History of British India*, published in 1820, his work marshaled what he believed to be all necessary facts to show the necessity of British rule as a remedy for India's traditional tyranny and chaos, which the village had survived to enjoy Company protection.

Theory and Empire

Mill's *History* represents a starting point for the theoretical repositioning of India in relation to Europe that attended the growth of industrial capitalism. India's political and cognitive relation to Europe changed dramatically in the process, and with it orientalism. Mill attacked orientalists and romantics and denied that anyone could reconstruct India's past from native myth and legend. He erased cultural traditions altogether from his understanding of India and Europe. For him the study of history and law were founded on rational philosophical principles with which both "Britain and India could be criticized and reformed" (Majeed 1990: 212). He disliked empire because it sustained aristocratic privilege, but he embarked on a systematic intellectual subordination of India to the universalist principles of European social theory that attended European imperial expansion and inscribed orientalism at the roots of modern social science. Mill—and subsequently Hegel, Marx, and Weber—did not merely elaborate orientalism as a body of knowledge; they transformed it and enhanced its vitality by theorizing India's changing relation with Europe.

Mill first theorized India within British imperial hegemony, but for him their connection was merely circumstantial: both Britain and India were places like any other for the conduct of government. India may have only suffered bad government, but this was not an explanation or a justification of empire; it was a condition to be rectified. Universal rationality, not history, put Britain and India in the same theoretical field. It just so happened that British officials could effect rational policies in India and in fact could do so more freely there than in Britain. For India was tabula rasa to be inscribed with rationality. Cultural and historical differences were irrelevant: "Indeed, it was crucial to the emergence of Utilitarianism as a rhetoric of reform to ignore any such distinction" (Majeed 1990: 222–23). Mill's *History* began the intellectual project of using orientalism to identify features of India that were necessary objects for rational policies of social reform. Just as Mill attacked orientalists for romantic attachments and for "aesthetic attitudes which underpinned . . . revitalized conservatism" (Majeed 1990: 218), he reformulated orientalism into a body of knowledge that revealed oriental irrationality, for which good government was to be the cure.

Mill's attack on orientalists, his repositioning of India as an object of reform, and his reformulation of orientalism indicate how "the emergence of new political languages in Britain in the early 19th century was closely involved with the British imperial experience" (Majeed 1990: 222). But for the history of orientalism it is also critical that shipments of colonial knowledge back to Britain were continuously reconstituted and reauthorized by European political discourse. Empirical data and factualized statements about India entered European intellectual life through Parliamentary debates, books, newspapers, pamphlets, art, and universities. Such venues for disseminating and reproducing orientalism widened the scope for participation in the history of orientalism far beyond the halls of India House. In this setting, orientalism was shaped by forces having little to do with India. For instance, Mill's India was a platform for utilitarian studies that dovetailed with his cognitive psychology. Likewise, Hegel, Marx, and Weber had preoccupations unconnected to India that conditioned their ideas about its essential character.

Orientalism became a versatile component of political discourse in Europe, as political disputes about India in relation to Britain shaped understandings of both India and Europe. Jones and Mill informed Hegel's study of India (Halbfass 1988: 87). Parliamentary evidence for the Company charter renewal and news dispatches from India informed Marx's reports for the *New York Tribune* and his sketch of an Asiatic Mode of Production (Krader 1975; O'Leary 1989). Weber's later work drew on a huge body of orientalist scholarship. As the hearth of orientalism was moving increasingly into the universities, social sciences were developing within the legacy of Hegel, Marx, and Weber, who put India and Europe side by side in universal theories of history that made sense of each in their relation to one other.

European superiority became more theoretically pronounced in Europe as European supremacy became a dominant political phenomenon in the modern world. Beginning with Hegel, Europe's dynamism and historicity expressed Europe's primacy as a force in world history and India's at best secondary stature. For Marx and Weber, capitalism revealed and contextualized India's stagnant backwardness, which they explained using facts about traditional village economy, despotic governance, religiously based social life, and sacred caste divisions. The facts behind their theoretical formulations about India were not questioned. Established as facts by colonial knowledge and by their conventional authority in European political discourse, they were there as truths for theorists to use in making sense of the world. Orientalism became the template for knowing an oriental other in contradistinction to European capitalism, rationality, historicity, modernity, and powers of self-transformation.

As it became integrated theoretically into modern discourse on Europe's place in history, orientalism as a body of knowledge became more detached epistemologically from colonialism; it wielded power over understandings of the world grounded not only in conventional wisdom but in social theory. From this position, it would inform both modernization and Marxist theory in the twentieth century. This would not have been possible had not empirical reality in India been shaped on lines consistent with orientalism, so that "facts of life" apparent to the eye and institutional practices built into social experience in India would constantly verify perceptions of India guided by social theory. Colonial governance constructed this concordance between empirical evidence and social theory by weaving orientalism as a body of knowledge into the fabric of administration and law.

That the village constituted the basic unit of Indian social life became evident beyond critical questioning as government demarcated, bounded, surveyed, and studied villages, to make the village the basic unit of data collection and administration. Property rights and social order became officially grounded legally and textually in village traditions and village records. The village officer became the "keystone of the arch" of rural administration. Whatever its status in precolonial times, the village thus became the elemental unit of empirical and theoretical reference in British India through its construction as a unit of governance. Empirical evidence about the countryside based on village data and social theory positing village autonomy "from time immemorial" harmonized completely. The origin of this concordance in a colonial politics of knowledge—which had thrust Munro's theory of village India into social theory, on the one hand, and built an Indian system of village administration, on the other—became irrelevant for the authority of ideas about the status of village society in Indian civilization. In the twentieth century, the authority of these ideas increased further as they entered social science practice: first for economics, then for anthropology, village India became the elemental unit of empirical analysis and theory alike (Ludden forthcoming).

Similarly, Indian political culture became institutionalized in religious terms that made the division of Indian society between Hindus and Muslims an iconic principle of governance. That this religious antagonism was the fundamental challenge to law and order—to the social tranquility that benefited everyone—became conventional wisdom in Munro's lifetime, in part through the work of orientalists. But routine administrative practice produced data that accumulated over decades to bolster the concordance between theory and evidence pertaining to this fundamental division. A critical site for this construction of communalism was the writing of riot reports. To represent riots as communal, pitting Hindus against Muslims, became a routine solution to administrative problems posed by urban unrest (Pandey 1990). By selecting and excluding data, and by insinuating religious motives to crowds, official observers built a descriptive genre that evidenced unitary Hindu and Muslim communities fighting each other head to head, in situations, such as the Banaras riots of 1809, where evidence abounded to show that various local groups confronted one another for various reasons and with various ends. This body of official evidence thus harmonized with the theory on which it was based and which it substantiated (Freitag 1989: 51–52). Orientalism as a body of knowledge informed this empirical genre by establishing the analytic grid for description and explanation and locating the origin of conflict in the essential character of Indian civilization.

In addition, as with the building of village India as the basic unit of social life, official evidence that substantiated India's essential communalism removed the colonial state as an explanation of realities reflected in authoritative data and empirical facts. The state could thus be represented as an impartial arbiter of communal disputes, an attitude enshrined in imperial historiography, where government always does its best to mediate conflicts between Hindus and Muslims that originate in the Muslim conquest and spoliation of Hindu India centuries before British rule (e.g., Spear 1978).

The imperial state thus represented itself both as the origin of authoritative knowledge about India and as the protector of all Indian people, striving to maintain order in the realms of knowledge and social life and to facilitate modernization in a fundamentally divided oriental society. Orientalism bolstered the authority of the state and was in turn sustained as a body of knowledge about that society that gave the imperial state confidence in selecting Indian representatives on religious grounds for inclusion in governance. That representatives should be officially recognized leaders of religious communities, and that the interests of those communities as expressed by these leaders should be balanced in government, became a natural means to articulate the state and society. It provided a logic to guide the imperial construction of local and then regional institutions of political representation after 1880 (Brown 1985). Built into institutional politics, theory and evidence of Hindu-Muslim conflict harmonized more completely and reproduced the authority of orientalism as effective knowledge in political practice.

The age of high imperialism thus transformed colonial knowledge and orientalism. Before 1850, the politics of Company Raj had turned statements about traditional India formulated in accord with British power into facts authorized by the epistemological powers of science. By

1850, factual foundations for orientalism as a body of knowledge were firm. After 1850, a second transformation involved constructions of theory and institutions on those foundations that wove orientalism deeply into social science and social experience. The ideas that the village constituted the basic unit of social order in India and that Indian civilization was built on religion became institutionalized and theorized so as to obscure their colonial origins, which became irrelevant to their authority.

In social theory, the orient served as the "other" to capitalist Europe. This defined Europe and capitalism as much as it did India. Thus, social science and political practice built on this foundation reproduced its authority without reference to its colonial origins, and did so moreover while the one theoretical principle informed actors on all sides of imperial struggles. In India, the colonial invention of tradition became irrelevant to experience of the village and communalism, once their traditionalism was built into institutions that conditioned social life. The evidentiary base for substantiating village and communal traditions arose from the same institutional practices. The empire made orientalism as a body of knowledge appear as a verified representation of reality by building it into both the construction of empirical evidence and the social experience of people in governance and education. Imperial bureaucracy produced empirical data of an ever more scientific and modern sort, a data base so vast as to describe a reality of its own. Because the imperial bureaucracy defined reliable data, reliability became based on English training and imperial credentials commanded by a mass of technical specialists who gathered facts on economy, epigraphy, tribes, castes, religious practices, language, literature, and customs (Appadurai, this volume). The reality of tradition arose from evidence, theory, administrative ideology, art, and literature that described India's subordination and England's supremacy, Europe's modernity and India's backwardness (Adas 1989; Bernal 1987; Cohn 1983; Fieldhouse 1981; Moore-Gilbert 1986; Ludden, 1987).

States and Nations

Voices articulating orientalism thus multiplied and diversified across the colonial period. Factual formulations drawn from colonial knowledge gained authority by being theorized, institutionalized, and empirically substantiated. Yet from its birth on the frontiers of empire, the empirical construction of tradition served political functions. By 1880, it was woven deeply into the ideology of empire, capturing essences of South Asia in relation to Britain, to establish the fixity and timelessness of the essential India for intellectual manipulation by the imperial ruling class. And from Rammohan Roy to Bankimchandra Chattopadhyay, Rabindranath Tagore, Mohandas Gandhi, Jawaharlal Nehru, and beyond, orientalism as a body of knowledge informed the discourse of India's nationhood. For political discourse on both sides of the colonial encounter entailed the other. The colonial divide evolved as each side defined itself in relation to its "other" (Chatterjee 1986; Ludden 1992; Prakash 1990; Raychaudhuri 1988), and orientalism became a versatile component of national discourse, an authoritative base for India's self-definition. Both sides of the colonial divide were secure in the knowledge that village India had survived into modern times from ancient days, by its autonomous reproduction within a religiously prescribed caste society.

The role of orientalism in nationalism has not been studied adequately. But it seems evident that being grounded in a formulation of India in relation to Europe, orientalism contained vital elements for constructing national identity in India and in Britain alike. Vitality came from the longevity and the empirical and theoretical depth of these ideas, but also from their versatility in political debates conducted in the context of empire. The meaning and content of Indian "otherness" would be contested by nationalists, as they had been by Jones and Mill, Munro and Ellis, so that orientalism entered political rhetoric as a venerable set of analytic oppositions between Britain and India, with dispersed, fluid implications. Intellectuals in India never confronted a unified colonial construction of India, except when they devised it; and there was never a unified nationalist construction of India, except that devised by its proponents and their adversaries. Ideological terrain inscribed by orientalism provided rich ground for invention, wide ground for maneuver and opposition.

Foundational ideas established in early colonial decades, such as the religious basis of Indian social order, could be powerfully deployed for opposing purposes. This is sharply represented in successive editions of Mill's *History*, with editorial additions by Horace Hayman Wilson, the first professor of Sanskrit at Oxford, who defended Jones and criticized Mill. Wilson's Preface to the fourth edition calls it "the most valuable work on the subject which has yet been published," but he then raves against its rash statements based on insufficient evidence and its "evil tendency" to depict Hindus as "plunged almost without exception in the lowest depths of immorality and crime," which is "calculated to destroy all sympathy between the rulers and the ruled." Wilson then ventures that "There is reason to fear that these consequences are not imaginary, and that a harsh and illiberal spirit has of late years prevailed in the conduct and councils of the rising service in India, which owes its origins to impressions imbibed in early life from the History of Mr. Mill." Wilson blames Mill for the growth among the impressionable youth who became colonial servants of feelings of "disdain, suspicion, and dislike" toward Indians "wholly incompatible with the full and faithful discharge of their obligations to Government and to the people" (Mill [1820] 1968: viii; also Majeed 1990: 222).

Students who entered the colonial service, however, did not only read Mill. Racism became science (Stepan 1982; LaCapra 1991). Social Darwinism made poverty, weakness, and technological backwardness characteristic of all nonwhite peoples, who became degraded in the eyes of Europe (Adas 1989). In the 1850s de Tocqueville "found it incomprehensible that the 18th-century Physiocrats should have had such an admiration for China" (Bernal 1987: 238). Whereas for orientalists the essence of India came from ancient family relations among the Indo-European languages, by Queen Victoria's death in 1901, the essence of India included prominently its religious irrationality and fractiousness. Thus orientalism as knowledge shifted meanings with India's changing relation to Britain, until the dominant fact, which made sense of all others—including subjective facts like imperial paternalism and liberal outrage, as well as disdain and distrust among colonial officers—ordering them all in a coherent discourse, was that India lived under the Crown.

Victorian empire also generated knowledge that could be used to defend Indian tradition in counterattacks against imperialism and its denigrations. Orientalists built a body of texts to document the grandeur of Indian culture. In the heyday of empire, Max Müller produced the *Sacred Books of the East*, which would number over fifty volumes, and argued in *India: What Can It Teach Us?* (1883) that Indian thinkers could edify all mankind. An imperial administrator, Alfred Lyall, even questioned the morality of imposing materialism on an inherently spiritual Indian people (Adas 1989: 351ff). At this juncture, Dadabhai Naoroji in the 1870s and Romesh Chandra Dutt in the 1890s began to nationalize orientalism by positing a British imperial assault on traditional India, employing colonial knowledge to criticize the Raj for impoverishing India. Like Mill, Munro, and imperial commissions, they used colonial knowledge to criticize colonial policy. As Wilson charged the liberal Mill with illiberal attitudes toward India, Naoroji castigated "un-British rule" and Dutt charged Munro with oppressive land taxation (Chandra 1966).

The nationalist critique inverted the imperialist claim to have brought India moral and material progress. Orientalism provided a framework for this effort. Dutt and Naoroji targeted oppressions heaped on formerly self-sufficient villages by imperial policy. Gandhi negated and inverted myths of western superiority with his version of traditional Truth. Ideas that Gandhi used to conjure the essential India—with its ageless rural simplicity and moral continuity—came from the treasure chest of orientalism. Gandhi concludes *Hind Swaraj* with a list of "authorities"—including Naoroji and Dutt, but also Henry Maine's *Village Communities*—and "testimonies by eminent men," quotations from the likes of from Müller, Frederick Von Schlegel, William Wedderburn, and Thomas Munro. Nehru's *Discovery of India* is a more systematic use of orientalism to craft a charter for nationhood. Nehru discovers a wise and ageless Indian nation, invaded, conquered, exploited, and divided over centuries of foreign rule, but still surviving in the essence of its traditions and still struggling for freedom. Nehru's *Discovery* is a journey toward national self-awareness; as he discovers India's identity in knowledge constituted by orientalism, he finds himself.

In nationalism we find the vitality of orientalism today. This conclusion is at odds with Said and suggests that his work inhabits a place inside the history of orientalism. For to imply, as he does, that orientalism sustains a body of false, colonial images of the East and its peoples leaves us with the implicit promise that a true image would be constructed if these peoples were free to render images of themselves. Such oppositional moments are many in the history of orientalism. Opposing claims to represent the real truth about the East and disputes over the authentic, authoritative voices and evidence that establish that truth animate orientalism historically. By presuming that there is to be found in the East a real truth about its self-existent peoples, Said employs the very positivist logic that gives orientalism life. And behind his back, nationalism has claimed authority over this truth and appropriated orientalism in the name of national self-representation. Today, orientalism is most defensible on the ground that people in India and elsewhere believe its imagery to represent the truth about themselves.

Nationalism again transformed the transaction in Rennell's lithograph: India took Britannia's place. Though orientalism did originate in colonial knowledge and did bolster European power, its epistemological authority—reproduced by its transformation in the nineteenth century—enabled orientalism as a body of knowledge to be deployed against European supremacy; thus it became ever more deeply woven into Indian politics. The continuity of Indian culture over millennia became a central theme in a national mythology that depicts India's religiously prescribed social order of self-reproducing villages as a foundation of Indian civilization. It is irrelevant that scholars dispute the truthfulness of such ideas. National culture bestows its own authority; these foundational ideas constantly emerge as pivots of debate. For some, that India was a land of self-sufficient villages signifies desirable stability; for others, it signifies backwardness and stagnation. For some, villages are ancient nodes of democracy; for others, they are sites of feudal oppression. For some, the fact that religiously prescribed social identities sustained traditional India represents India's cultural core and is a source of pride; for others, it signifies repressive coercion. Such struggles over the meanings of tradition, today as in the days of Jones, Munro, and Mill, have serious policy implications and political significance, of which the struggles over the Mandal Commission Report provide ample evidence. But above all, the unity, autonomy, and permanence of Indian tradition signify the unity, autonomy, and permanence of Indian nationhood, which defines its own context for debate, as British empire once did (Ludden 1986, 1992).

So orientalism is not the moribund legacy of colonialism that Said makes it out to be. In the transition from empire to nation, it attained new authority and vitality, to which scholars all across the spectrum have contributed. In the 1920s a brilliant administrator and historian, W. H. Moreland, took Hindu law as the basis of India's traditional agrarian system; an equally brilliant Indian nationalist historian, Surendranath Sen, pronounced that "Before the Marathas succumbed to their western rival, we find in their empire the same judicial system still in existence that prevailed in the days of Manu . . . the same village communities still flourishing that existed in the days of the Buddha" (Sen 1925: 296). In the 1980s venerable Marxist historians still based arguments on assumptions of a self-reproducing village economy (Sharma 1980; Habib 1963), and an ingenious free-marketeer from the World Bank has used algebraic equations to explain the "Hindu equilibrium" from ancient times to the present (Lal 1988). Such scholarship reinvigorates the authority of orientalism as a body of knowledge by reinvocation, as it marginalizes and obscures evidence supporting other images of precolonial India (Ludden [1988] 1990).

Orientalism as a body of knowledge is today not only embedded in a vast corpus of official wisdom, scholarship, social theory, and empirical data. It is also embedded rhetorically and institutionally in political culture, revitalized by reinvocation in national histories that show South Asian peoples struggling for freedom and progress in their own terms. Now those histories are terrain for debates about the present and future. Scholars engage politics by constructing the past in terms that call out for particular lines of political action and policy formulation. In the same way as the fate of village India signified the denigrations of empire for nationalist scholars before independence, opposing interpretations of that fate hold implications for national policy today and express political oppositions among intellectuals (Lal 1988). As it did in the opposition between the orientalist William Jones and the utilitarian James Mill, orientalism provides icons around which political oppositions form today.

Those icons are also weapons in struggles for state power. From its early days, nationalism in South Asia has been wracked by tensions wrought by the institutionalization of political representation based on the religious categories enshrined in orientalism. The authority of primordial categories like Hindu, Muslim, and Sikh in the conduct of politics has been reconstituted and reinvigorated by invocation not only by leaders of political parties but in the popular literature and consciousness of subnational groups seeking self-determination. In the same way as nationalists used orientalism against imperialism, competing nationalisms use orientalism against one another inside and across national boundaries in South Asia.

The vitality of orientalism today thus emerges from its authority as a body of knowledge in a political context that demonstrates deep institutional continuities across the divide separating colonialism and national independence. The government of India is both an imperial and a national state; and like the Raj it represents itself as impartial protector of all people, standing above conflicts among communities, maintaining law and order as it deploys modern science and technology for modernization and development. But the state must also represent the nation, not merely lord over it. So government as representative of the people strives to represent itself as the embodiment of a "real India" that has been defined from the beginning by opposition to its European "other" in a political culture of competing nationalisms. The national state has imperial instruments of power for this purpose, not only the army and bureaucracy, but also technologies that shape a political culture by media representations of "the real India."

Media image-making was politically charged long before independence (see Barrier 1974, 1976; Bhaskaran 1981). The imperial government of India must use its powers of representation to mobilize support for its constituent parties in a milieu where divisions and oppositions among communities are institutionalized as political facts. Contenders for state power are caught in a situation like that of early nationalists facing imperialism; those in control of the state inhabit a position analogous to that of imperialists. They each deploy their powers to represent themselves as the embodiment of "the real India," and in this conundrum, orientalism is reinvigorated by its utility for many sides, in contests that produce the tumultuous contradictions of contemporary Indian politics. For instance, Indira Gandhi represented an essentialized Sikh nationalism as a threat to national unity, and concurrently sought to reduce the power of Sikh separatism by supporting the rise of a Sikh zealot whose career lead ultimately to her assassination (Tully and Jacob 1985). In 1989, during the national election campaign, Congress used its control of state television simultaneously to popularize Hindu epics; to identify Rajiv Gandhi with his grandfather, and thus with the birth of the nation; to identify Nehru with progress and prosperity; and to censor opposition parties (Farmer forthcoming).

When we situate representations of India in a political history of their deployment in struggles for power, from colonial times to the present, we see that claims about Indian reality can never be adequately understood as existential self-expressions of a people or as objective descriptions by scholars. For they are political acts. Orientalism remains political hostage and weaponry. Its epistemological authority did arise from colonialism, to be sure, but it was reproduced by anti-imperial, national movements and reinvigorated by Partition, in 1947, and the reorganization of Indian states, in 1956; it thrives today on conflict expressed in religious and ethnic terms. In its reification of tradition and of oppositions between East and West, nationalized orientalism suffuses postcolonial political culture and scholarship that claims to speak for India by defining India's identity in a postcolonial world (e.g., Nandy 1983; Prakash 1990). Having helped to make nations in South Asia what they are, orientalism fuels fires that may consume them. From this it appears that only intellectual labor that demolishes the nation as a cultural formation of social being and historical becoming can challenge the authority of orientalism as a body of knowledge.

Research for this paper was funded by the American Philosophical Society and The National Endowment for the Humanities. Comments on earlier drafts by Carol A. Breckenridge, Victoria L. Farmer, and Peter van der Veer informed its revision.

References

Abdel-Malek, Anouar. 1963. "Orientalism in Crisis." *Diogenes* 44 (Winter): 103–40.

Adas, Michael. 1989. *Machines as the Measure of Men: Science, Technology, and Ideologies of Western Dominance*. Ithaca, NY: Cornell University Press.

Appadurai, Arjun. 1981. *Worship and Conflict Under Colonial Rule: A South Indian Case*, Cambridge: Cambridge University Press.

Barrier, N. Gerald. 1974. *Banned: Controversial Literature and Political Control in British India 1907–1947*. Columbia: University of Missouri Press.

———, ed. 1976. *Roots of Communal Politics*. Columbia: University of Missouri Press.

Bayly, Christopher A. 1988. *Indian Society and the Making of the British Empire*. New Cambridge History of India. II, 1. Cambridge: Cambridge University Press.

Bernal, Martin. 1987. *Black Athena: The Afro-Asiatic Origins of Classical Civilization*. Volume I, *The Fabrication of Ancient Greece, 1785–1985*, New Brunswick, NJ: Rutgers University Press.

Bhaskaran, S. Theodore. 1981. *The Message Bearers: Nationalist Politics and Entertainment Media in South India, 1880–1945*. Madras: Cre-A.

Brown, Judith. 1985. *Modern India: The Origins of An Asian Democracy*. Delhi, New York: Oxford University Press.

Cannon, Garland, ed. 1970. *The Letters of Sir William Jones*. 2 vols. Oxford: Clarendon Press.

Chandra, Bipan. 1966. *The Rise and Growth of Economic Nationalism in India: Economic Policies of the Indian National Leadership, 1880–1905*. New Delhi: People's Publishing House.

Chatterjee, Partha. 1986. *Nationalist Thought and the Colonial World: A Derivative Discourse?* London: Zed Books for the United Nations University.

Cohn, Bernard S. 1983. "Representing Authority in Victorian India." In Eric Hobsbawm and Terence Ranger, eds., *The Invention of Tradition*. Cambridge: Cambridge University Press, 165–209.

———. 1989. "Cloth, Clothes, and Colonialism." In Annette B. Weiner and Jane Schneider, eds., *Cloth and Human Experience*. Washington: Smithsonian Institution Press, 303–53.

Cosgrove, Denis. 1984. *Social Formation and Symbolic Landscape*. London: Croom Helm; Totowa, NJ: Barnes and Noble, 1985.

Farmer, Victoria L. Forthcoming. "The Limits of Image-Making: Doordarshan and the 1989 Lok Sabha Elections." In Ayesha Jalal and Sugata Bose, eds., *Democracy and Development in South Asia*. Delhi.

Fieldhouse, D. K. 1981. *Colonialism, 1870–1945: An Introduction*. New York: St. Martin's Press.

Freitag, Sandria. 1989. *Collective Action and Community: Public Arenas and the Emergence of Communalism in North India, 1870–1940*. Berkeley: University of California Press.

Furber, Holden. 1987. "Edmund Burke and India." *Bengal Past and Present* 56, (I–II), 202–3, pp. 163–175.

———. 1948. *John Company at Work: A Study of European Expansion in India in the Late Eighteenth Century*. Cambridge, MA: Harvard University Press. Reprint New York: Octagon Books, 1970.

Gaeffke, Peter. 1990. "A Rock in the Tides of Time: Oriental Studies Then and Now." *Academic Questions* 3, 2: 67–74.

Habib, Irfan. 1963. *The Agrarian System of Mughal India (1556–1707)*. Bombay: Published for the Department of History, Aligarh Muslim University, by Asia Publishing House.

Halbfass, Wilhelm. 1988. *India and Europe: An Essay in Understanding*. Albany: State University of New York Press.

Kessinger, Tom G. 1974. *Vilyatpur 1848–1968: Social and Economic Change in a North Indian Village*. Berkeley: University of California Press.

Kling, Blair. 1976. *Partner in Empire: Dwarkanath Tagore and the Age of Enterprise in Eastern India*. Berkeley: University of California Press.

Kopf, David. 1969. *British Orientalism and the Bengal Renaissance: The Dynamics of Indian Modernization, 1773–1835*. Berkeley: University of California Press.

Krader, Lawrence. 1975. *The Asiatic Mode of Production: The Sources, Development and Critique in the Writings of Karl Marx*. Assen: Van Gorcum.

LaCapra, Dominick, ed. 1991. *The Bounds of Race: Perspectives on Hegemony and Resistance*. Ithaca, NY: Cornell University Press.

Lal, Deepak. 1988. *The Hindu Equilibrium*. Vol. I. *Cultural Stability and Economic Stagnation, India, c. 1500 BC–AD 1980*. Oxford: Clarendon Press.

Ludden, David. 1986. "Historians and Nation States." *Perspectives*, The American Historical Association Newsletter 24, 4, (April): 12–14.

———. 1987. "World Economy and Village India, 1600–1900: Exploring the Agrarian History of Capitalism." In Sugata Bose, ed., *South Asia and World Capitalism*. Delhi: Oxford University Press.

———. 1988. "Agrarian Commercialism in Eighteenth Century South India: Evidence from the 1823 Tirunelveli Census." *Indian Economic and Social History Review* 25, 4: 493–519. Reprinted in Sanjay Subrahmanyam, ed., *Merchants, Markets and the State in Early Modern India*. Delhi: Oxford University Press, 1990, pp. 215–41.

———. 1992. "India's Development Regime." In Nicholas B. Dirks, ed., *Colonialism and Culture*. Ann Arbor: University of Michigan Press.

———. Forthcoming. "Introduction." In David Ludden, ed., *Agricultural Production Regimes*. Delhi: Oxford University Press. *Themes in Indian History*, general editors Christopher A. Bayly, N. Bhattacharya, and B. Chatterjee.

Majeed, J. 1990. "James Mill's 'The History of British India' and Utilitarianism as a Rhetoric of Reform." *Modern Asian Studies* 24, 2: 209–24.

Mill, James. 1820. *The History of British India*. 9 vols. Ed. Horace H. Wilson. Reprint New York: Chelsea House, 1968.

Mojumdar, M. A. T. 1976. *Sir William Jones, the Romantics, and the Victorians*, Dacca: Zakia Sultana.

Moore-Gilbert, B. J. 1986. *Kipling and "Orientalism"*. New York: St. Martin's Press.

Moreland, William H. 1929. *The Agrarian System of Moslem India*. Second edition reprinted Delhi: Oriental Books Reprint Corp.

Mukherjee, S. N. 1968. *Sir William Jones: A Study in Eighteenth-Century British Attitudes to India*. Cambridge: Cambridge University Press. Second edition Hyderabad: Orient Longman, 1987.

Müller, Friedrich Max. 1883. *India: What Can It Teach Us?* London: Longmans, Green.

Nandy, Ashis. 1983. *The Intimate Enemy: Loss and Recovery of Self Under Colonialism*, Delhi/New York: Oxford University Press.

Nehru, Jawaharlal. 1959. *The Discovery of India*. Ed. Robert I. Crane. Garden City, NY: Anchor Books.

Nightingale, Pamela. 1970. *Trade and Empire in Western India, 1784–1806*. Cambridge: Cambridge University Press.

O'Leary, Brendan. 1989. *The Asiatic Mode of Production: Oriental Despotism, Historical Materialism, and Indian History*. Oxford: Basil Blackwell.

Pandey, Gyanendra. 1990. *The Construction of Communalism in Colonial North India*. Delhi: Oxford University Press.

Parenti, Michael. 1986. *Inventing Reality: The Politics of the Mass Media*. New York: St. Martin's Press.

Phillimore, R. H. 1954–56. *Historical Records of the Survey of India*, Dehra Dun.

Prakash, Gyan. 1990. "Writing Post-Orientalist Histories of the Third world: Perspectives from Indian Historiography." *Comparative Studies in Society and History* 32, 2 (April): 383–408.

Raychaudhuri, Tapan. 1988. *Europe Reconsidered: Perceptions of the West in Nineteenth Century Bengal*. Delhi: Oxford University Press.

Rennell, James. *Memoir of a Map of Hindoostan or the Moghul's Empire*. 3d ed. London: M. Brown for the author. Reprint Patna: N.Y. Publications, 1975.

Said, Edward W. 1978. *Orientalism*. New York: Pantheon Books.

———. 1984. *The World, the Text, and the Critic*. Cambridge, MA: Harvard University Press.

———. 1986. "Orientalism Reconsidered." In Francis Barker, P. Hulme, M. Iversen, and D. Loxley, eds., *Literature, Politics, and Theory: Papers from the Essex Conference, 1976–84*. London.

Sen, Surendranath. 1925. *The Administrative System of the Marathas*. Calcutta. Third edition Calcutta: K. P. Bagchi, 1976.

Sharma, Ram Sharan. 1980. *Indian Feudalism: c. 300–1200*, 2d revised ed. Delhi.

Spear, Thomas George Percival. 1978. *The Oxford History of Modern India, 1750–1975*. Second edition. Delhi/New York: Oxford University Press.

Stein, Burton. 1989. *Thomas Munro: The Origins of the Colonial State and His Vision of Empire*. Delhi/New York: Oxford University Press.

Stepan, Nancy. 1982. *The Idea of Race in Science: Great Britain, 1800–1960*. Hamden, CT: Archon Books.

Sutherland, Lucy S. 1952. *The East India Company in Eighteenth Century Politics*. Oxford.

Townsend, Joseph. 1791. *A Journey through Spain in the years 1786 and 1787, with particular attention to the agriculture, manufacture, commerce, population, taxes, and revenue of that country*. 3 vols. London: C. Dilly.

Tully, Mark and Satish Jacob. 1985. *Amritsar: Mrs. Gandhi's Last Battle*. London: Jonathan Cape.

Washbrook, David. 1981. "Law, State and Agrarian Society in Colonial India." *Modern Asian Studies* 15, 3: 649–721.

Nicholas B. Dirks

9. Colonial Histories and Native Informants: Biography of an Archive[1]

I

> Real history and chronology have hitherto been desiderata in the lit-
> erature of India, and from the genius of the people and their past
> government, as well as the little success of the inquiries hitherto made
> by Europeans, there has been a disposition to believe that the Hindus
> possess few authentic records. Lieut.-Colonel Mackenzie has certainly
> taken the most effectual way, though one of excessive labour, to ex-
> plore any evidences which may yet exist of remote eras and events.
>
> Board of Control, East India Company, February 9, 1810

Anwar Abdel Malek was perhaps the first to notice that orientalism appropriated history from the Oriental in two related senses. Orientalism took
history away by claiming the exclusive authority of history in making its
claims; and orientalism denied history to the Oriental by asserting the
essential—both metahistorical and nonhistorical—character of the Orient
and its people. As Malek wrote in 1963, "According to the traditional orientalists, an essence should exist—sometimes even clearly described in meta-
physical terms—which constitutes the inalienable and common basis of all
the beings considered; this essence is both 'historical,' since it goes back
to the dawn of history, and fundamentally a-historical, since it transfixes
the being, 'the object' of study, within its inalienable and non-evolutive
specificity, instead of defining it as all other beings, states, nations,
peoples, and cultures—as a product, a resultant of the vection of the forces
operating in the field of historical evolution." More recently, Edward Said
has developed and extended this argument, demonstrating the myriad
ways in which orientalism has constituted peoples and territories as ontological essences rather than historical entities.[2]

Said has argued that orientalism itself deploys a kind of "mythic dis-

course " that "conceals its own origins as well as those of what it describes." In this discourse, "Arabs [as the most salient example of Said's
book] are presented in the imagery of static, almost ideal types, and neither as creatures with a potential in the process of being realized nor as
history being made."[3] But in the denial of history to the Oriental, history
becomes lost altogether. Said insists on reading the history back in, seeing
the origins of orientalist discourse in colonial histories, predicated on a
past of conquest and rule. The pasts of the colonized, he writes, were
erased as soon as conquest made possible the production of new forms of
knowledge that endowed colonialism with natural legitimacy.

Nevertheless, Said no sooner makes this point than he proceeds to
read texts of high imperialism that were written after these histories of
conquest and assume, with few signs of struggle, the absence of history
for the colonized subject. In this essay I seek to examine competing histories, and historicities, before colonized histories were ensnared and silenced. I will attempt to read the ambivalences and contests within early
colonial historicities, imagined when colonial historiographies were still
dependent on native informants and colonial histories were still unsecured
by the political triumphs that made possible the "illusion of permanence."
Although the colonial project of erasing colonized histories was itself fundamental to full colonial rule, this project did not succeed, as John Seeley
argued for the actual British conquest of India, "in a fit of absentminded-
ness." Erasures were written over histories that were being actively recovered and rewritten at the same time they were being transformed into
histories of loss and subordination. Mythical discourses were constructed
out of historical encounters.

In the late eighteenth and early nineteenth centuries, a great number
of British writers—among them Dow, Elphinstone, Wilks, Malcolm, and
Mackenzie—felt compelled to write about pre-British Indian history.
These writers often engaged in more scholarly fashion a growing body of
assertion and argumentation about the fundamental nature of Indian society and its civil and political institutions, in the context of extensive debates about the colonial project of conquering and ruling India. Whether
in discussions about the permanent settlement in Bengal or modes of revenue settlement with peasants or village communities elsewhere in India,
about the aftermath of the impeachment of Warren Hastings and the Pitt
Act, or about the development of policies concerning military conquest,
degrees of social and religious intervention, or the fundamental institutions of East India Company governance, historical questions were pre-

eminent. Although most British commentators saw the eighteenth century as a decadent prelude to and justification for British rule, and although they frequently disparaged Indian historical sensibilities and traditions, they nevertheless felt the need to understand India historically.

The early period of colonial rule is of course better known for the textually and philologically trained "orientalists" than for the "historians," although there was in fact a great deal of complementation in the work of the two groups. Most writers on Indian history borrowed from the work of the orientalists when speculating about ancient (pre-Muslim) India or generalizing about the character of Indian society. Alexander Dow studied Persian while an officer in the East India Company's army and published a translation of a standard Persian history in 1768. In his introduction to the translation, he wrote about subjects such as the nature of Mughal government and the effects of British rule, and only wrote seven pages on Hindu customs and manners. Though not a Sanskritist, he relied on the tutelage of a Brahman pundit in Banaras, and adopted a textual and Brahmanic view of Indian society. Many years later, the administrator and historian Monstuart Elphinstone wrote his two-volume work on Indian history with extensive borrowings from the work of orientalists, particularly in his sections on society and ancient history. But Elphinstone based the authority of his scholarship on his own extensive perusal of historical documents, as well as—in marked and explicit contradistinction to Mill— on his own personal experience of being in India.[4] Elphinstone was clearly convinced that India could not be understood merely through its texts and grammars.

Many of the historical documents used by Elphinstone in his attempt to reconstruct the political history of the Deccan had been collected by Colin Mackenzie.[5] Mackenzie, who spent most of his long career in peninsular India as cartographer and surveyor, had spent much of his time and resources collecting every historical record and artifact he could find. By the time of his death in 1821, Mackenzie had amassed a collection that still contains the largest set of sources for the study of the early modern historical anthropology of southern India. Mackenzie's collection also represents colonial Britain's most extensive engagement with Indian history and Indian historicity. Specifically not an orientalist—Mackenzie never learned an Indian language—Mackenzie was perhaps more serious than any other official East India Company servant in his attempts to assemble a thick historical archive for peninsular India. In these attempts, Mackenzie not only relied almost exclusively on Indian assistants and informants, but he understood that the project of writing Indian history could be detached neither from the Indians who produced it nor from the politics of Britain's involvement in the establishment of colonial rule in India. This is not to say that Mackenzie did not share early colonial interests, for however idiosyncratic he was he was also deeply involved in the early project of conquest and rule. Nevertheless, Mackenzie's collection soon fell into a growing fault line between official orientalism and colonial sociology; on the one hand Mackenzie's textual materials did not meet orientalist standards for classicism and antiquity; on the other hand Mackenzie's histories seemed too peculiar, too sullied by myth and fancy, and too localist and Oriental to be of any real help in the development of administrative policy. Mackenzie's life and collection can thus be read to reveal the ambivalences in the historical encounter that produced the mythic discourses of high imperialism in British India.

II

> Colonel Colin Mackenzie achieved unique fame because he was primarily a man of action with a wide outlook. Though by birth a highlander, by breeding a European and by vocation an instrument of British Imperialism in India, he was a universal man.
>
> T. V. Mahalingam, 1972

Born in 1754, Colin Mackenzie was a Scot from the outer Hebrides who went to India at the age of twenty-nine to pursue both a military career and his interest in Hindu mathematics. Mackenzie subsequently used his mathematical aptitude to become a skilled surveyor and cartographer, and carried out a series of surveys in India that differed from all others in their broad range and scholarship. In 1810 Mackenzie became the first Surveyor General of Madras, and in 1815 he was appointed the first Surveyor General of India, a post he held until his death in 1821.

When Mackenzie first arrived in India he stayed for a time in Madura, where he was introduced to "the most distinguished of the Brahmins in the neighbourhood" who were employed in collecting mathematical information for his hosts. According to Alexander Johnston, the son of these hosts and subsequently one of Mackenzie's dearest friends, "Mr. Mackenzie, in consequence of the communication which he had with them [Brahmans], soon discovered that the most valuable materials for a history of India might be collected in different parts of the peninsula, and during his residence at Madura first formed the plan of making that collection, which afterwards became the favorite object of his pursuit for 38 years of his life. . . ."[6] Indeed, Mackenzie spent much of his life in India compiling a massive collection of documents, manuscripts, inscriptions, drawings, and other artifacts that have since been the single richest archive for the historical, literary, and anthropological study of peninsular India during the centuries immediately preceding British rule.

Looking back over his life, in his only surviving autobiographical reflections penned in a letter to Johnston in 1817, Mackenzie noted that the first thirteen years of his life in India were substantially wasted. As he wrote, "though not devoid of opportunities, yet the circumscribed means of a subaltern officer, my limited knowledge of men in power or office, and the necessity of prompt attention to military and professional duties, did not admit of that undeviating attention which is so necessary at all times to the success of any pursuit."[7] Like later anthropologists who have seen tradition literally disappear before their eyes, Mackenzie regretted that certain objects, as also "traits of customs and of institutions that [then] could have been explained," could not then be scrutinized by one in his constrained circumstances. In particular, Mackenzie lamented that he was unable to use those years to "assiduously cultivate" a knowledge of "the native languages." Mackenzie noted that these were years of military hardship and constant conquest: "Official encouragements to study the languages of the vast countries that have come under our domination since my arrival in India, were reserved for more happy times. . . ." For Mackenzie at least, orientalist knowledge had to follow colonial conquest.

Mackenzie was clear about his necessary complicity in the brute realities of colonial power. His early discoveries were all made on military campaigns, and Mackenzie himself conflated the role of the soldier and the scientist.

> That science may derive assistance, and knowledge be diffused, in the leisure moments of camps and voyages, is no new discovery; but . . . I am also desirous of proving that, in the vacant moments of an Indian sojourn and campaign in particular (for what is the life of an Indian adventurer but one continued campaign on a more extensive scale), such collected observations may be found useful, at least in directing the observation of those more highly gifted to matters of utility, if not to record facts of importance to philosophy and science.

Mackenzie's early years thus were one continuous military campaign. And Mackenzie had no doubts about the ennobling influence of British rule, at the same time that his life has subsequently served to perpetuate the story of Britain's rescue of India from its own decadent demise. As he wrote about the early years of his Indian sojourn: "From the evils of famine, penury, and war, the land was then slowly emerging; and it struggled long under the miseries of bad management, before the immediate administration of the south came under the benign influence of the British government." That Mackenzie's own influence has itself been seen as benign by subsequent generations of Indian historians can hardly obscure his full participation in the colonial conquest of India.

During Mackenzie's early years in the Army Engineers, he was frequently deputed to do survey work in those districts of the Deccan that had been ceded to the Company by Hydar Ali of Mysore and the Nizam of Hyderabad. Between 1792 and 1799, Mackenzie spent much of his time engaged in a survey of the "Nizam's Territories," the area encompassing what today are the districts of Cuddapah and Kurnool in Andhra Pradesh. In the course of this survey work, Mackenzie began to develop a comprehensive sense of what a survey should be. As he wrote about the area he was surveying: "The Dekhan was in fact then a *terra incognita*, of which no authentic account existed, excepting in some uncertain notices and mutilated sketches of the marches of Bussy, and in the travels of Tavernier and Thevenot, which by no means possess that philosophical accuracy demanded in modern times." Mackenzie sought therefore to make the land known, and to do so through a combination of strategies that included detailed mapping and description as well as the collection of as many local and authentic accounts as he could find.

During his surveying work in the Deccan, Mackenzie was recalled four times for military service, where his surveying and engineering skills were put to use to position artillery and act as technical advisor for assaults. Although other officers of the Company were aware of the "political as well as military"[8] importance of Mackenzie's surveys, the last decades of the eighteenth century were times of frequent and critical military engagement for the Company. The most dramatic of Mackenzie's military assignments and the most formidable challenge to British military ambitions in peninsular India was at Seringapatam, in the fourth and final Anglo-Mysore war that took place in 1799, where the British finally defeated a ruler who had been, with his father Hydar Ali, responsible for transforming the political and social landscape of southern India during the previous forty years. During Tipu's final stand, Mackenzie was engineer in charge of the batteries to the north of the Cauvery, "from which side the successful assault was delivered."[9]

After the defeat of Tipu, Mackenzie was commissioned to organize and conduct a survey of Mysore to fix the boundaries of the newly conquered territories and to map and gain some preliminary detailed information about an area two thirds the size of Scotland. The Great Mysore Survey, as it was called, lasted from 1799 until March 1809, during which time Mackenzie maintained nominal charge over the conclusion of the Deccan survey as well. In his appointment letter he was told that his attention was not to be confined to "mere military or geographical information, but that your enquiries are to be extended to a statistical account of the whole country."[10] Nevertheless, his impressively conceived scheme for a survey "embracing the statistics and history of the country, as well as its geography"[11] was constantly frustrated by a shortage of support from the Company, which wanted to do a survey "on the cheap" and was less convinced than Mackenzie of the need for a general plan.

Mackenzie learned that his general scheme would have to be scaled down at the end of 1801, just after he had finished his initial survey of the northern and eastern frontier of Mysore. As a result he had to discontinue his survey of the natural history of the country, had to fire a number of his principal assistants, and had his stipend and general establishment cut in half. Despite these problems, and virtually constant problems of ill health, Mackenzie conducted an extraordinarily detailed survey. In addition to preparing general maps of each district and descriptions of salient geographical features, the survey included a census of villages, forts, houses, classes of inhabitants (i.e., a breakdown of the population into its constituent castes, tribes, and occupational groups), waterworks, and so forth; historical "memoirs" of each district "illustrative of the revolutions and remarkable events of the country and of the origin and succession of the several Rajahs, Polligars, and Native Rulers for the last three centuries"; and "cursory remarks and accounts of the soil, productions, manufactures, minerals, inhabitants, etc."[12] Even though the Board of Control never gave Mackenzie adequate financial support, it is clear that some of his most influential contemporaries appreciated the extraordinary labor of the survey. John Malcolm, then the British Resident in Poona, wrote to Mackenzie in 1803 that "the work in which you are engaged and in which you have made such considerable progress will be when it is finished highly honorable to yourself and useful to the government and that it will contain a mass of information respecting the geography, history, commerce, revenue, police and population of Mysore which must prove of the greatest advantage to every officer connected with the conduct of administration."[13]

Mackenzie's survey, commissioned so soon after the fall of Seringa-patam, was necessarily limited in nature. At the outset Mackenzie in-formed Colonel Barry Close, the Resident of Mysore, that his survey would not "descend to the minutiae of measurements of the quantity of the cultivated and uncultivated lands, with details more properly belong-ing to an Agricultural Survey," concentrating rather on "full information of its [Mysore's] extent, form, and capacity in a Political and Military Light."[14] Elsewhere, Mackenzie noted that "enquiries into the Revenue were altogether avoided, as tending to create an uneasiness, and possible counteraction that would have possibly retarded the progress of the other branches, without deriving sufficient advantages."[15] Some years later, when giving advice to the British surveyor of Coorg, Mackenzie advised him against making "many minute enquiries," as such would "at first alarm their minds with friendless suspicions."[16] In any case, the East India Com-pany had restored the rule of the Wodiyar Rajas of Mysore, who forty years before was overthrown by the Mysore Sultans, and had no direct reason to assemble revenue information. Although he sought to collect information about the origins of land tenures, Mackenzie specifically avoided the facts of production.

Mackenzie was also reticent to engage in direct census activity. The population, he noted, "as far as depends on the number of villages and generally of houses I . . . form a gross calculation of"; but Mackenzie went on to observe that "to take an actual account [of population] would re-quire the immediate interposition of the management, and the aversion of the natives to these enquiries are well known."[17] Mackenzie felt that a gross calculation was in any case quite accurate and the best available means to procure reliable data. When writing to Elphinstone after the British conquest of the Maratha country, he wrote, "I would recommend to you by all means to get the accounts of the population according to the Hindoo system; it is nothing prejudicial to their ideas as in their own system of Police; the number of families and houses is always furnished; but you should not proceed to count heads nor cattle; nor employ the surveys in it; I only succeeded by conciliatory measures and by employing very discreet natives—the plan was entirely of their own and agreeable to ancient practice."[18] He went on to emphasize that: "It was by this machin-ery [i.e., the use of a native establishment] only that I was enabled to complete the geometrical details of the Mysore Survey—by means of other Bramins, Jain, and all castes formed for the purpose the other His-torical and Statistical investigations were carried through." Nevertheless, at one point the Dewan of Mysore expressed his concern that "all further enquiries respecting the number of Ryots and inhabitants of either sex in Mysore may be put a stop to. . . ."[19]

Despite Mackenzie's limited objectives, the Company was keen to know as much as possible about the extent and nature of the newly conquered territories and, in addition to commissioning Mackenzie's survey, authorized two other Company servants to engage in surveys of their own. In November 1799, after Mackenzie had received orders for the detailed survey of Mysore, Colonel William Lambton put forward his own proposals for a "Mathematical and Geographical Survey" that would extend across the peninsula from the Bay of Bengal to the Arabian Sea. The proposal was accepted by the government in February 1800, and Lambton shortly thereafter began his trigonometrical survey in Mysore, using methods and measurements slightly different from Mackenzie's. Although Mackenzie was consistently generous in his official writings about Lambton, it was clear that there was always some rivalry, and less than total cooperation, between the two.

There was also some overlap between Mackenzie's survey and the investigations of Francis Buchanan, an Edinburgh-educated surgeon who in February 1800 was commissioned to investigate "the state of agriculture, arts and commerce in the fertile and valuable dominions acquired in the recent and former war, from the late sultaun of Mysore, for the purpose of obtaining such insight in to the real state of the Country, as may be productive of future improvement and advantage."[20] Whose advantage was not entirely made clear, since the British were not in a position to collect revenue directly from the Mysorean countryside, although they did demand an annual payment of tribute from the newly reconstituted Mysore state. Buchanan's charge seemed more generally to suggest the Company's interest in the possibilities of commercialized agriculture and expanded markets. Buchanan was asked to inventory the different crops and vegetables, the types of cultivation, the variable implements of husbandry, the different breeds of cattle, the extent of local subsistence in food production, the nature of land tenures, the cost of labor and manner of its remuneration, and the extent of money use and the kinds of local markets, as well as the various natural productions of the country "in arts, manufactures, or medicine and particularly those which are objects of external commerce." Given Buchanan's background in medicine and botany, Buchanan could give the Company the desired scientific account of the area's natural resources. The efforts to survey Mysore suffered, however, from profound administrative confusion. Before Mackenzie was appointed Surveyor General of Madras in 1810, there was no central means or mechanism within India to coordinate activities of the kind engaged in by Mackenzie, Lambton, and Buchanan.

The most detailed part of Mackenzie's Mysore survey was his "Memoirs of the Northern Pargunnahs of Mysore," the product of work conducted in 1800 and 1801 before the cutbacks. In addition to the usual statistical tables, called "Caneeshamar," Mackenzie collected numerous historical memoirs of the royal families of each region. As early as July of 1800, Mackenzie wrote that he was making some progress in his enquiries into that part of the history of "this country . . . which belongs to its Hindoo rulers and collecting all the materials I can get in the several districtions of books, Inscriptions, and Traditions." He further noted that, as he did not know the local languages, he had to employ "Native Writers and Translators of the Canara, Mharatta, etc."[21] For Chitteldroog, Mackenzie's assistants collected and translated four different family histories and then correlated the recorded genealogy of the royal family with chronological information available in local inscriptions. As Mackenzie wrote in his second report, "The Historical Accounts of the Populations of Government of the Districts were compiled from creditable sources of information on the spot; sometimes traditions from registers and chequed by dates and eras, ascertained from grants and inscriptions where they could be referred to; a reciprocal correction was frequently derived from one to the other; and more satisfactory as no communication existed between the different authorities whenever a certain internal evidence arises favorable to their accuracy."[22] The royal histories, or vamcavalis, were received, so Mackenzie tells us, from "the official persons employed in the hereditary duties of Naadgoudes, Goudes, etc., in whose hands their records are kept." The vamcavalis frequently recorded why a particular group or family had settled in the place that subsequently became known as the base for their rule. Mayaconda, for example, was chosen by the Raja because when he was hunting with his dogs in its deep woods, a hare miraculously fought off the dogs and chased them back to their master. The Raja then discovered that in the days of the Vijayanagara rulers a local chief had died, and his wife Mayaca had thrown "herself into the fire of her Husband's pyre according to their law." Because of the virtue accruing to this act, and the transformation of the chief and his wife into "veerooloo" ("persons remarkable for virtue"), the site had become charged with extraordinary properties and powers. The family histories also recounted stories of the glorious exploits and courageous rule of the relevant Rajas, thus inscribing contemporary rulers and places with special legacies and powers.

The Rajas ("Polligars") of places like Chitteldroog had for the most part met their match in the military campaigns conducted by Hydar Ali and Tipu Sultan in the last decades of the eighteenth century. Hydar and Tipu had systematically attacked the forts of the Polligars, capturing the entire royal family and carting it off to their capital city of Seringapatam. Although they often made the old rulers into honorary functionaries, such as bukshi, they made sure to keep them and their heirs away from their political and social bases. In their place, Hydar and Tipu placed "amil-dars," or managers, who were charged with the task of maintaining order and collecting revenue. This administrative centralization, very different from the kind of "feudal" incorporation deployed after military conquest by the former kings of Vijayanagara, anticipated precisely the military and administrative strategies of the East India Company. If anything, Hydar and Tipu succeeded rather better than the British in dispensing with and displacing the local political elites of the Deccan, for even by the turn of the century most British officers felt the need to rule and collect revenue through local chiefs as landlords, or "zamindars." Indeed, Mackenzie's studied attempt to collect the genealogical records of these displaced chiefs was due to the East India Company's desire to sort out claims of local political legitimacy and evaluate the nature and potential resistance of these forms of local political rule. Colonialism had to ease into the forms of direct rule that the sultans of Mysore had already deployed, as it happens in relation to their own strategy of developing the administrative infrastructure to enable them to oppose the spread of British rule in India.

Despite the clear political rationale for collecting information about local chiefs, Mackenzie's enthusiasm for assembling accounts full of what many of his contemporaries felt to be ethnographic trivia and historical fable was both boundless and peculiar. Even Mackenzie often doubted the utility and veracity of many of the texts that were faithfully reproduced, commenting for example on the vamcavali of the Jerremulla Samastan Family that "the whole of this account appears to be from tradition and very doubtful if not erroneous in dates the succession of the Polligars perhaps only excepted."[23] Other accounts were given solely "by way of specimen of what are preserved in the hands of the Natives."[24] Nevertheless, even though many accounts provided fascinating perspectives on the meaning of political authority and the categories of social identity, not to mention local textual genres and sociologies of knowledge, Mackenzie was most interested in a fairly narrowly conceived historical record. His only comment in the survey records about local worship was to note that Lingum worship seemed to have at some point died out, in all probability, he conjectured, due to some as yet unknown political revolution.

However, Mackenzie clearly felt that every "traditionary account" contained some potentially useful historical information and wished to leave nothing uncollected or unexplored. Furthermore, in his 1805 annual report on the Mysore Survey, he wrote that the documents he had collected consisted "not merely of a dry chain of uninteresting facts but are connected by various illustrations of the genious and manners of the People, their several systems of Government and of Religion, and of the predominant causes that influence their sentiments and opinions to this day, lights are derived on the Tenures of Lands, the origin and variety of assessment of rents and revenues, and the condition of the People, the privileges of the different classes, and the genious and spirit of the Government prevalent generally in the south for centuries." He believed that he had successfully established that there had been a political unity under what he called the "Dominion of the Carnatic," by which he meant the rule of the Vijayanagara empire. By understanding the institutions of Hindu government that had been part of Vijayanagara rule, Mackenzie felt that the Company could gain "much useful information on many of these institutions, laws, and customs, whose influence still prevail among the various Tribes of Natives forming the general Mass of the Population at this day." Indeed, Mackenzie wrote extensively about the benefits of historical knowledge for British rule in India.

> At a moment when the attention of the Governments in India and the Legislature in Europe is turned to the amelioration of the state of the Native Subjects the means of conciliating their minds; of exciting habits of industry and cultivating the arts of peace under the security and milder influence of fixed Rules it is presumed that such Investigations cannot be viewed with indifference under the Management of the East India Company whose best interests are involved in what tends to the acquisition of a more intimate knowledge of the country and its resources and the suggestions thence arising on the means of improving its revenues and commerce and promoting the prosperity of Provinces inhabited by a Population on the most moderate computation of Ten Millions of Native Subjects. (1803 Report on the Mysore Survey)

Of particular concern to Mackenzie was his sense that much local historical knowledge had perished under the same conditions of instability that had led to a deterioration of the social and political life of the natives. Mackenzie declared that he felt it imperative to grasp "whatever opportunities existed for investigating what yet remained in the hands of the Natural Inhabitants of these countries which had escaped the general wrack and destruction of written records and more permanent monuments following the unsettled state of the country for so long a period."[25]

Mackenzie extended his efforts well beyond the Mysore area as he became increasingly convinced of the great importance of his endeavor. At his request, a memorandum was circulated to senior British officials in southern India in 1808 that began as follows:

> Major Mackenzie has for this sometime past thro the offices of his friends collected various materials that are supposed to convey considerable information on the ancient history, state, and institutions of the south of India, but he finds several parts are still doubtful, which he believes might be yet illustrated by materials of various descriptions in the hands of the natives; and which from their obscurity are liable to be neglected and lost, but might be still recovered by the interposition of the Gentlemen in the Diplomatic, Judicial, Revenue, and Medical departments particularly.

In longer detailed memos that Mackenzie circulated to officials with whom he was acquainted, he laid out in considerable detail the kinds of materials he was interested in collecting. He specified his interest in materials concerning the early history of Buddhism and Jainism in the South, as well as more generally any accounts of religious "conventions" and "establishments." He was interested in coins, antiquities of any description, drawings of ancient tombs and burial mounds, rubbings or copies of inscriptions.

Most of all, he was interested in "history." And Mackenzie had a critical sense of how history was constructed in relation both to cultural genre and political context. For example, he noted that "regular historical narrations and tracts are seldom found among the Natives, and such notices as exist, are generally preserved in the form of religious legends and popular poems and stories." Mackenzie went on the note that there were exceptions, listing:

> Vumshavelly, or genealogies of the several dynasties and considerable families; Dunda Cavelly, or chronological registers and records, sometimes preserved by official persons; Calliganums, literally prophecies, but sometimes really conveying under that assumed disguise, Historical information with more apparent freedom than could be addressed to Oriental Sovereigns; Cheritra and Cudha, frequently applied to tales and popular stories, but sometimes containing correct information of remarkable characters and events ap-

proaching to the nature of our memoirs; and Rakas, financial records and registers of the ancient revenues and resources of the country.[26]

Thus Mackenzie justified and explained his eclectic interests and procedures, aware all the while of the problems of authenticity, as he wrote to Connor: "If during the Survey you can get any notices of the History of the Country in Canara, it would be preferable to a made up Persian account as being more original."[27] And, rather than despair over the ahistoricism of the oriental mind, he assumed that non- or quasi-historical genres, such as prophecies and popular stories, were less historical than they might otherwise have been in order to disguise their political and therefore dangerous nature.

One of the reasons that Mackenzie had a much clearer sense of the politics of knowledge than most of his colonial compatriots was that he was deeply involved in the actual collection of historical information. He assumed neither that he could conduct his work without the myriad efforts of native assistants nor that this work would constitute only a set of technical problems. Mackenzie seems to have been unique not only in the degree to which he trusted his native assistants but also in the extent of his involvement in their own struggles to procure historical knowledge in the context of the complex politics of early colonial conquest and rule in India.

III

The connexion than formed with one person, a native and a Bramin, was the first step of my introduction into the portal of Indian knowledge; devoid of any knowledge of the languages myself, I owe to the happy genius of this individual, the encouragement and the means of obtaining what I so long sought. . . . From the moment the talents of the lamented Boria were applied, a new avenue to Hindoo knowledge was opened. . . .

Colin Mackenzie, 1817

Mackenzie's concern to ameliorate the state of native subjects and to collect historical information concerning them did not rest on the kinds of characterizations of India and Indians engaged in by many of his assistants. Benjamin Heyne, a naturalist and friend of Mackenzie's who accompanied him on the Mysore survey, was a particularly outspoken critic of Indian character: "In general it may be said of the Mysoreans that they are exactly like the other Hindoos, no better nor worse; They have the same propensities of lying, cheating, domineering. They are equally perfidious, fickle, dissembling, inconstant, treacherous, adulterous, as their Eastern and Northern neighbors. They are on the other hand courteous, polite, resigned, and endowed with most passive virtues."[28] Thus anticipating Macauley's remarks about Bengalees in his essay on Warren Hastings by some forty years, Heyne made clear what must have been a prevailing attitude among many of Mackenzie's early colonial associates. Heyne differed substantially from Mackenzie in his assessment of the state of Indian knowledge. He wrote that he found virtually no learned men among the Hindus and that all local knowledge—whether concerning medicine or that embodied in local texts, songs, and dramas—was either quackery or a "mere travesty" of classical Sanskrit sources. But if Heyne highlights Mackenzie's particular commitment to engaging local knowledge, he also anticipates the kind of view that shortly thereafter became enshrined as official colonial knowledge about India.

What distinguished Mackenzie and his general project most from his colonial contemporaries was his respect for and reliance on local Indians for information and scholarly assistance. The pages of the Mysore survey betray in particular the ubiquitous and pervasive presence of Mackenzie's chief interpreter, a man by the name of Kavelli Venkata Boria. Mackenzie met Boria in 1796, and quickly recognized the young man's brilliance, as well as his potential importance to his own project of discovering India. Mackenzie wrote that Boria, "of the quickest genius and disposition," possessed "that conciliatory turn of mind that soon reconciled all sects and all tribes to the course of inquiry followed with these surveys." Boria was, as Mackenzie said, "the first step of my introduction into the portal of Indian knowledge."

Mackenzie's first concern was his own lack of linguistic skills, and also the appalling lack of official British competence in southern India's languages. He noted that on the reduction of Seringapatam in 1799 "not one of our people could translate form the Kanarese alone." For the Mysore Survey, Mackenzie noted that he confronted a situation where "no less than 5 Provincial Languages are used by so many different distinctions of natives constituting the great mass of population exclusive of four others that are occasionally requisite in more literary inquiries." As he noted, "a Satisfactory Investigation and access to the Sentiments of the people as well as to that knowledge derived from a ready intercourse would be a matter of serious difficulty and concern."[29] Mackenzie made it clear he had to have an extremely talented establishment of linguists.

Mackenzie went on to say, however, that the requisite skills for the work of his survey and associated antiquarian pursuits were combined in the person of Boria himself, "whose industry and perseverence were not more useful to my Geographical pursuits than his integrity and conciliatory spirit were instrumental to the rapid progress and favorable reception of these Enquiries in the minds of the Natives."[30] Boria had formidable linguistic skills, with command of Tamil, Telugu, Kanarese, and Sanskrit, as well as considerable skill in deciphering medieval inscriptional scripts and grammars. As Mackenzie's chief interpreter, he worked to collect texts, traditions, and materials of diverse kinds and also to explain and translate their contents. He also prepared most of the papers on the Northern Purgunnahs, including an extensive "Memoir on the mode of management observed in the Ballaghaat," in addition to his collections and translations "confirmed by such other evidence as leaves little room of doubt." After Boria's death, Mackenzie assembled a testimonial about Boria's extraordinary linguistic skills and scholarly credentials from a Madras orientalist by the name of A. Falconar, Persian Translator to Government.[31] Although Boria died in 1803, still a young man who had been only seven years in Mackenzie's service, he recruited and trained an establishment of learned Brahmans, including two brothers and various relations and acquaintances, thereby institutionalizing what became Mackenzie's lifelong project of "collecting" India. Time after time Mackenzie professed that it was only through the merits and assiduity of his "native establishment" that he was able "to engage in those Researches into the nature and state of the country which have enabled me to collect the materials on this undertaking."[32]

Though many of these declarations took place in letters to the government pleading for further support for his establishment, it was on his own initiative and largely with his own resources that Mackenzie hired and trained his group of Brahman assistants. Beginning in 1796, with efforts intensifying after 1799, Mackenzie's establishment helped him collect epigraphical evidence and local histories of kingly dynasties, chiefly families, castes, villages, temples, and monasteries, as well as other local traditions and religious and philosophical texts in Sanskrit, Persian, Arabic, Tamil, Telugu, Kanarese, Malayalam, and Hindi. Mackenzie went far beyond even the ambitious scheme he had proposed for a proper survey, employing additional staff as his circumstances permitted to travel around peninsular India, first with him and then on their own, collecting every "traditionary account" they could find. When Mackenzie died in 1821, he had amassed a collection of 3,000 stone and copper plate inscriptions, 1,568 literary manuscripts, 2,070 local tracts, and large portfolios and collections of drawings, plans, images, and antiquities. As Alexander Johnston wrote in 1832, Mackenzie's was "the most extensive and the most valuable collection of historical documents relative to India that was ever made by any individual in Europe or in Asia."

It was during the Mysore survey that Mackenzie's own collection of materials really escalated. As Mackenzie wrote, while the survey work was being conducted, "the collection of materials on the history, antiquities, and statistics of the country was going on throughout the whole of the provinces, under the presidency of Fort St. George, on the basis of the information originally obtained on the Mysore survey, by natives trained and instructed by me for this purpose." Mackenzie stressed that this process had cost the government little, since "all the purchases have been entirely at my private expense, as well as the collection of MSS. Throughout the Karnatik Malabar, the southern provinces, the Cirkars, and the Dekhan." Clearly Mackenzie felt that the British government should take more active interest in his endeavors; "the success of these investigations," he wrote, "justifies the hope, that considerable advantage may be derived from following up the same plan of research wherever the influence of the British government affords the same facilities, in the intervals of military occupation."[33]

During the Mysore Survey, Mackenzie realized not only that his native staff was indispensible for the task of collecting and translating historical, geographical, and ethnographical materials but that his native assistants were in a position to mediate a complex sociology of local knowledge, one in which, as noted above, indigenous inhabitants often greeted British curiosity with "friendless suspicion." Mackenzie was particularly concerned not to use the kind of intimidation that apparently accompanied most attempts—whether by British officials or the amildars of Tipu Sultan—to collect local knowledge, writing that "The persons and properties of the Inhabitants have been protected from all violence of any kind with me, and I have particularly attended to conciliate their minds, which was indeed necessary for easier obtaining my object."[34] But the difficulties encountered in collecting survey-related information only constituted the tip of the iceberg in "friendless suspicion." Mackenzie himself was never unaware of the potential resistance to hand over information, as also of the inverse problem that if he did not exercise scrupulous caution he would get only the kind of information that his informants thought he desired. As he wrote to P. Connor in 1816, "I presume you are yourself sufficiently aware of the Native character in general, to know that expressing any extraordinary anxiety or solicitude for any particular object is the sure way to excite suspicion, delay, and sometimes opposition—Some apparent indifference is useful and necessary and I want to recommend your abstaining from taking notes of your remarks on their answers to questions in their presence."[35] Questions of authority, and of the myriad relations between power and knowledge, were raised over and over again in the accumulation of Mackenzie's archive.

During the first two decades of the nineteenth century, Mackenzie's assistants traveled widely throughout peninsular India, collecting, copying, and translating materials, all the while corresponding regularly with Letchmia, who had replaced his brother Boria as Mackenzie's chief assistant after Boria's death. Letters to Letchmia often included lists of material, long synopses of particular traditions and histories, and extensive itineraries and accounts of the successes and failures of individual attempts to collect material. Frequently the letters, written in ungrammatical English, sought additional authority to enable the assistants to persuade local people to allow them access to various forms of knowledge. In areas not under direct British rule, such as Travancore, Mackenzie's men had to use their wits. According to C. Appavoo: "Mr. Ward told Mr. Turnbull that he cannot get any order to procure the histories etc. in this country. Coll. Munro told him he cannot give order to the country people to furnish any informations, but the servants may make friendships with the country people and get the old accounts of the Rajahs."[36] But in adjacent parts of British India, Munro, a good friend of Mackenzie's and a constant supporter of the latter's antiquarian efforts, gave written orders to the surveyors for the managers of each district, requesting their assistance. In other areas, Mackenzie's men had frequently to turn to the local British Collector. When Seenevassiah journeyed to Matorantakum and Chittamoorjee in 1809, he began copying temple inscriptions, only to be told by the temple priest that he must stop: "then the Bramin of the Pagoda they prevented me and told me that they want order of the Circar, therefore next day I went to the Cachary at Caroong Cooly and acquainted with the Collector Mr. Hide, who told me now you may go, they do not prevent you, accordingly I went afternoon to the pagoda and seen all the inscriptions." Most assistants reported that before they copied inscriptions or local texts, they attempted to use their own letters from Mackenzie to procure letters from the local Collector. Mackenzie only was known in some places, and only he could have authority attached to his name through the confirmation of locally known British officials.

Mackenzie's assistants were mostly Brahmans, although he employed a number of Christians and at least one Jain. When they first went to a village to begin their enquiries, they typically asked to be taken to the learned Brahmans of the place. At times the approaches were made directly, as when Nitala Naina "privately made friendship with one of the learned Bramin there named Soobausaustry who had a large library of holy and pious books. . . . I gave him a one rupee present." In most cases the Brahmans who were contacted deployed local networks to assist the task. Sooba Row recorded in 1807 that "I was acquainted that a learned Shastry had preserved some ancient Pooranums therefore I went to his house made friendship with him and asked him that he had any ancient Pooranums etc., he told that he will examine all his books and give me a list of the books that I may take copy of. I also told him to enquire if any learned Bramin got any records of the ancient kings and any inscriptions of copper plates." In this case the Shastry recommended that Soobarow talk with his father, who was a repository of the ancient customs of the kingdom, and the letter reports an extensive interview with him. Other Brahmans were also sent for, so that by the time Sooba Row was ready to leave town he had talked with half a dozen learned Brahmans of the locality. On other occasions a local headman was asked to collect the learned Brahmans. For example. Appavoo wrote in a report of 1817: "Today many Brahmans and learned people were collected by the Head Hicharadaur at Caspa in Arcot agreeable to the directions of the Collector's people. They gave me many informations respecting Arcot." In another report, C. V. Ram wrote: "I was enquiring for the history of Cacati Rajaloo, who are ruled at Aunomacondah, and Vorungale, I understand there was a aged learned Bramin at Aunomacondah, who knows the History of the ancient kings of the Cacatirajaloo, who has a library of cadjan books, as it is impossible to appear myself to him at his house, I was intending to make friendship with him thro the means of his acquaintance. . . . I requested him to order the old Bramin to give me any information of the former kings of the country, and explain me the difficult inscriptions." The subsequent information in the report was then based almost exclusively on the words of this old Bramin.

Knowledge was never imparted without suspicion and the direct invocation of some British authority. When British authority was not absolute, as mentioned above, there were frequent difficulties such as those encountered by C. V. Ram, who wrote that when he was in the zamin of Calastry, he was copying certain inscriptions in the large temple, but "after we copied three inscriptions the Rajah sent for us and directed us not to copy any more stone inscriptions with an intention of exposing the secrets of their samasthanam [kingdom]." Narrain Row wrote of similar difficulties in his visit to Gudwall. In this case he went directly to the local zamindar to present his credentials: a Persian letter from Mackenzie. The Dewan, Narrain Row reports, "enquired of me what is the use of this books Tarraureeks and Vumshavaley [chronicles and genealogies], I replied him, My Master is very desirous of knowing the curious history of the old king for that I came here." The Raja responded by preparing a letter for Mackenzie and offering Narrain Row the customary honor of betel nut. He then escorted him out of the kingdom.

Perhaps the most extraordinary story of this kind was related by Nitala Naina about his attempts to procure information about the history of the ruling Tondaiman family of Pudukkottai. Upon presenting himself and his certificate to the "Tondamaun Palagar," he was told that he had "no reason to enquire the informations." Dispirited by this interview, he turned to Sivaraumia, one of the local Brahmans he had employed to help him copy manuscripts, for advice. Sivaraumia promised that he would be able to give him two hundred books about the history of the Tondamaun country. Sivaraumia also spoke disparagingly about the Raja, saying that he was a "little Palagar in the crowd of 72 Palagars." It soon became clear, however, that Sivaraumia had done something to displease the Tondaiman court and was less than forthcoming with the materials he kept promising. As time went on, Nitala Naina got further and further imbricated in a web of intrigue centering on this man, who used every trick in the book to excuse himself for delays while making Naina increasingly dependent on him. A sample of Naina's report goes like this: "On the next day, the Sivaraumia brought up two books, Mallopooranum, and the book of Tondamaun Genealogy, it is composed in the Telenga language. I then asked him to get the particular account of Tondamaun with the dates, he answered me he would go and enquire and bring it to me. I told you did not get any complete accounts since these five months; he says he would show his progress of ten years in a day. I am told then the Sivaraumia is consulting with Teroomul Nayudoo without enquiring any informations. One day he told me he want to go soon to Tondamaun for the books, and will require some bullocks for them." In the end, this was all that was produced. Meanwhile Naina's association with Sivaraumia made him suspect in the eyes of the Tondaiman court, which came to believe the claims of another man that that man in fact was the true representative of Mackenzie, Nitala Naina having been dismissed. When Naina finally turned in despair to one of Sivaraumia's sworn enemies for help, he found that he had to promise that he would recommend employment for him in Mackenzie's service to induce him to hand over some books. Naina soon left in some disgrace, finding that he had to persuade Mackenzie that he had been conscientiously employed over a period of six months with little to show for it.

Mackenzie's assistants typically reported material they collected with little editorial comment, so relieved perhaps were they to be able to document their own productive labor. Although the assistants distinguished material on the basis of whether it was copied from a book, told by a local Brahman, or written down from the remarks of a village headman or chief, only rarely did they make the kinds of comments made by British observers regarding the promiscuous admixture of "historical" and "fabulous" materials. Sooba Row was an exception, writing that a tradition about the capture of the idol at Srirangam by Sri Lankan forces "is founded on real historical facts tho disguised by the fancy of the poet and the clouds of religious prejudice." More frequently, moral tales, extraordinary stories of the exploits of kings and heros, and attempts to date dynasties were strung together in single narratives, with occasional asides about the difficulty of collecting information. Editorial comments reflecting modern concerns about textual genre and empirical truth were made more often at the point that certain texts were copied and translated, for example when the rough translations and texts from the field were put together in a set of bound volumes during the final years of Mackenzie's life under his direct supervision. Perhaps the most extraordinary example of this is seen in the preface of a text titled by Mackenzie *Mootiah's Chronological and Historical Accounts of the Modern Kings of Madura*. It begins like this:

> I turned my thoughts towards the Chronological and Historical Accounts of the Gentoo Kings of Madura written upon Palmyra leaves in a vulgar style of the Tamil language which I found to be satisfactory but the same being in a confused order and full of tautologies and repetitions which, if I proceed to translate literally into the English, it would prove absurd in the sight of the learned, I have therefore, in my following version of the said account, omitted the tautological and repeated expressions and set aside prolixity but following laconism, digested the Chronicles into eleven chapters and preamble prefixed thereto.[37]

Here, the rectification of the text was clearly being done for British, or what were perceived as British, textual and historical sensibilities. But in the reports from the field, there are few traces of this kind of rectification. Nevertheless, the texts that were being collected and produced in the field were hardly authentic survivals of a pre-British sociology of knowledge, even as they participated in complex power-knowledge relations well outside the purview of specific colonial concerns. Appavoo, one of Mackenzie's Christian assistants, was at times forthcoming about attempts by Brahmans to suppress certain kinds of local traditions: "Here, by the Brahmins, the history of Jainas and Cooroombers are much concealed. As there is not a single learned Jaina and Cooroomber in the Jaghere, their written histories are very rare with the exception of some informations concerning them. . . . As Brahmans and other nations bear a great enmity at them, many refuse to give me such information in my route." Subsequently, he found an excellent Coorumber informant, who told him that "they were the most ancient nation derived from the Bedars and first had the entire sovereignty of the Carnata and Dravida Desums." He took it to be natural that such claims were suppressed by the Brahmans. Unsurprisingly, Mackenzie's Brahman assistants never made comments of this kind.

Some of the texts collected by Mackenzie's assistants were directly intended for British consumption. For example, a number of chieftains whose kingdoms had been defeated and/or expropriated by the Sultans of Mysore or the representatives of the East India Company produced texts that read more like petitions than either myths or histories. For example, one text reads as follows: "I am a descendant of the family of Teroomaly Naick the most famous of the Gentoo kings of Madura and Trichinopology. . . . Yet to the reverse of my misfortune, General MacDowal, who commanded Tanjore, having been informed of the chronicles of the said kings and also of my being their surviving Rajah, living incognito at Sevaganga, was pleased to signify his anxiety to have an interview with me . . . this gentleman received me with all marks of joy and honour and having enquired me about my welfare and also about the historical accounts of my ancestors, advised me to wait upon your Lordship [Mackenzie]." And it is likely that all texts were fashioned in relation to a variety of interests and concerns. Mackenzie's concerns to avoid direct enquiries about production and revenue did not mean that the revenue implications of any knowledge about local tenures or lineages might not be used by an imperial power that was at this very time establishing itself as a revenue state. Virtually all of the information collected by Mackenzie turned out to concern the rights and privileges of kings, chiefs, headmen, Brahmans, and religious institutions. There was good reason for "friendless suspicion."

But the collection of information meant the appropriation of knowledge in more than just a revenue-related sense. When local documents were collected, authority and authorship were transferred from local to colonial contexts. The different voices, agencies, and modes of authorization that were implicated in the production of the archive got lost once they inhabited the archive. Distinctions between types of texts (e.g., texts that derived from ancient authorship or the hastily transcribed remarks from a local source) and concerns about the use-value of knowledge (how textual knowledge might be used to de-authorize and de-legitimate), became blurred and increasingly dissolved at each stage of the collection, transcription, textualization, translation, and canonization of the archive. And the role of Mackenzie's native assistants became relegated to the position of technical mediation, the diaries and letters rarely if ever recopied and collated with the documents they discuss. Indeed, the East India Company saw little reason other than a respect for Mackenzie's oft-expressed concerns for the welfare of his staff to maintain any of his native assistants after the master's death. A number of Mackenzie's assistants had been pensioned off after Mackenzie moved from Madras to Calcutta in 1818. Letchmia was kept on, in charge of a small residual staff, but his role was significantly diminished after Mackenzie died.

IV

> A collection was formed at a considerable cost of time, labour and expence, which no individual exertions have ever before accumulated, or probably will again assemble. Its composition is of course very miscellaneous, and its value with respect to Indian history and statistics remains to be ascertained, the collector himself having done little or nothing towards a verification of its results.
>
> H. H. Wilson, 1828

Despite Mackenzie's enthusiasm, it is clear that the British government was always somewhat reserved about the value of his endeavors. As we already noted, allowances for the Mackenzie Survey had been drastically cut in 1801, with deleterious consequences not only for implementation of the survey but also for more extensive researches. Although at various points Company and government officials expressed their approbation, Mackenzie's career prospered chiefly because of his abundantly evident surveying and administrative skills, and also because he was among the most dedicated and hard working Company servants of his time. As the Chief Secretary of Government in Madras wrote in October of 1807, "in the zealous execution of the duties of the arduous undertaking in which he has been so long engaged . . . and in honourable disinterestedness, I do not believe that Major Mackenzie is surpassed by any Publick Officer in India."[38]

There was never any doubt about Mackenzie's surveying and cartographic talent. James Rennell, the architect of the Bengal Survey and the senior cartographer of the early Raj, wrote about the "masterly manner" of Mackenzie's Survey: "The discrimination of the different objects is such as to render an idea of the nature of the country, perfectly clear on inspection. And I doubt not but the accuracy is equal to the execution. It is also a work of great magnitude in respect to its superficial extent; being, if I mistake not, considerably larger than the kingdom of Ireland."[39] And the Board of Directors in London received the materials of the Mysore Survey with evident admiration. In their dispatch dated February 9, 1810, they noted that

> it is a great pleasure to us to bestow our unqualified and warm commendation upon his long-continued, indefatigable, and zealous exertions in the arduous pursuits in which he was employed, and upon the works which those exertions have produced. . . . The actual survey, upon geometrical principles, of a region containing above 40,000 square miles, generally of an extremely difficult surface, full of hills and wilderness, presenting few facilities or accommodations for such a work, and never before explored by European science, in a climate very insalubrious, is itself no common performance; and the minute divisions and details of places of every description given in the memoirs of the survey, with the masterly execution, upon a large scale, of the general map, and its striking discrimination of different objects, rarely equalled by any thing of the same nature that has come under our observation,—form altogether an achievement of extraordinary merit, adding most materially to the stores of Indian geography, and of information useful for military, financial, and commercial purposes.

So impressed were the members of the Board of the potential utility of Mackenzie's maps and memoirs that they declared that the survey was not to be published, that "no copy of his map, or of the division of it, further than for the public offices just mentioned, ought to be permitted to be taken."[40]

The Board also expressed its appreciation of Mackenzie's "superadded inquiries into the history, the religion, and the antiquities of the country" that, admittedly, Mackenzie's "other fatiguing avocations might have been pleaded as an excuse for not attending." Although casting some doubt on the actual "authenticity" of the records collected, as also on the general wisdom of an enterprise that seemed to require such "excessive labour," the Board allowed "that this effort promises the fairest of any which has yet been made to bring from obscurity any scattered fragments of true history which exist, and undoubtedly encourages the expectation of ultimately obtaining both considerable insight into the state of the country and its governments in more modern periods, and some satisfactory indications of its original institutions and earlier revolutions." Mackenzie himself responded quite insistently to the doubts about the authenticity of the grants to Brahmans, which made up the subject of most of the inscriptions as well as many of the manuscripts, noting that "not an instance of forgery has been discovered or even suspected, save one, (and that rather assists history)." Of particular interest in the Board's comment about Mackenzie's historical labors was that the lack of "real history and chronology" in India was taken as evidence not of the lack of historical consciousness but rather of the "commotions and changes" that had been so "unfavourable to the preservation of political records." India's lack of history—and of a sense of history—had not yet become colonial orthodoxy.

The Board's evaluation of Mackenzie's collection was based largely on earlier correspondence by Bentinck, Governor of Madras, Mark Wilks, British Resident in Mysore, and John Malcolm, Resident of Poona, in response to widespread recognition in Madras that Mackenzie was not being adequately supported and encouraged by the government. Bentinck observed that "the valuable collection of manuscripts and other documents of the highest antiquity which that officer has been enabled to procure, may be expected to throw useful light on the dark ages of Oriental history, and to be equally valuable as a guide in the pursuit of literary knowledge, as in the attainment of correct information with regard to the former tenures of property and the laws of the ancient dynasties of the peninsula of India."[41] Bentinck seemed fully aware of the importance of his collection for the general project of British rule, and he feared that only Mackenzie would be able to make sense of these manuscripts, for no one else had his experience and expertise. "The object will be accomplished by him, or it will probably never be accomplished, even if his materials in their present state were to fall into other hands, they might be considered as lost. . . ." He strongly recommended that London realize the importance of both the manuscripts and the man, and at the very least reimburse him for his actual expenditures.

Although Mark Wilks, who in 1817 published his three-volume work *Historical Sketches of the South of India* with extensive references to Mackenzie's collection, was perhaps the most enthusiastic advocate of Mackenzie's historical labors, he was in fact highly doubtful of the historical value of anything other than the inscriptions. "The Department of history in this country," he wrote, "is so deformed by fable and anachronism, that it may be considered as an absolute blank in Indian literature." Wilks went on to suggest what most Indian historians since then have thought, namely that Indian "historical" texts and chronicles are so sullied by myth and fancy that they would be useful only to trace developments in Indian literature in late medieval and early modern times. Wilks turned, however, to the inscriptional record for southern India, to which Mackenzie had contributed so much by making rubbings of thousands of stone and copper plate inscriptions. He opined that

> There is but one mode which appears to afford the most distant hope of supplying this important defect. The grants generally of a religious nature inscribed on stone and copper plates which are to be found in every part of the south of India are documents of a singularly curious texture, they almost always fix the chronology, and frequently unfold the genealogy and military history of the Donor and his ancestors, with all that is remarkable in their civil institutions or religious reforms.

Thus anticipating the procedures of most subsequent Indian historiography, Wilks assumed that, since history is predicated on chronology, inscriptions are preferable to other texts. Inscriptions could be used to date kings, reigns, wars, and other events; whereas Mackenzie's texts—loose composites of oral and literary tradition that could rarely be definitively dated or trusted—seemed to constitute their own internal set of time referents, events, and structures and did not succumb easily to master historical narratives and appropriations.

Wilks also shared Bentinck's official view of the value of any reliable historical information about the nature of landed property. As he wrote, "If it should be found practicable to trace by a series of authentic documents the history of landed property in the south of India, I imagine that no subject of superior interest and importance can be presented to the attention of a British Government." Wilks was "certain that the research would unfold the most useful information on many important points connected with the political economy and good Government of India." Indeed, no other subject so exercised British official opinion in the early years of the nineteenth century, particularly in southern India where the debate between advocates of the Permanent Settlement with landlords (zamindars) and those, following Munro, who favored direct (or ryotwari) settlement with the "cultivators" was raging. Although Wilks was less interested in religion, he did note that Mackenzie had opened important new windows on the understanding of the history of Hinduism. Noting that the religion of the Hindus "is usually represented as unchanged and unchangeable," he remarked that "the religious history of Europe is scarcely less pregnant with revolutions" and that "everything in short that is usually considered most interesting and instructive in general history may be traced and illustrated," by Mackenzie's texts.

Although Bentinck had clearly regretted for some years that his hands had been tied by the Board of Control from remunerating Mackenzie properly for his efforts, the final result of this correspondence was that the Company recognized Mackenzie's contribution, increased his salary by 50 percent, gave him a monthly stipend to rent a house to maintain his establishment, and endowed him with an account for at least some of his research expenses, "trusting that it will not amount to any large sum." The Board also expressed its hope that Mackenzie's new position of "Barrack-master" in Mysore, to which he was appointed at the conclusion of the Mysore Survey, would afford him the necessary leisure to "digest and improve the materials he has collected." But just a few months later, at the end of 1810, the government of Madras created a position Mackenzie had long (for fourteen years) advocated, Surveyor-General of Madras, and appointed him to it. As Mackenzie put it, the government suddenly responded both to the increased costs of its surveys and the "unconnected confused manner in which these works were executed, without any general fixed system." However, Mackenzie's recognition and elevation made it even more difficult for him to find the time to work on his historical interests, and that too at the very moment he was to be supported to do precisely this. No sooner did Mackenzie settle down to his new administrative position than he was engaged as Chief Engineer[42] for a British expeditionary force that captured Java from the French in 1811. As before, he made an extensive collection of materials, including both descriptive maps and charts and extensive collections and translations of Dutch, Javanese, and Malay manuscripts.[43] Also as before, Mackenzie spent a good deal of his energy looking into the "history and antiquities of the island," for which he seems to have been accorded more ready interest, as well as financial support, than had ever been the case in India. Mackenzie himself, interestingly, lamented only that "the powerful aid of the penetrating acute genius of the Brahmans which had been of such importance in India, was here wanting."[44]

When, after a short sojourn in Calcutta, Mackenzie finally returned to Madras in 1815, he arrived just in time to learn that his office of Surveyor-General at Madras was to be abolished. His disappointment was tempered by the fact that he learned simultaneously that he was to be appointed Surveyor-General of India, the first occupant of this prestigious post. By this time, however, Mackenzie's health was fragile and his age told heavily on his energy. He wrote that after learning of his new appointment, his attention had, "in consequence been chiefly turned to that object ever since, with the view of fulfilling the Honourable Court's intentions in an appointment which I must ever consider an honourable mark of their distinction, that justly demands efforts that I had no longer in contemplation." It soon became clear that he had to move his base from Madras to Calcutta, the capital of British rule in India, and in 1817, after completing the memoirs for the survey of the Ceded Districts along the same lines as he done for Mysore, he left Madras for the last time.

Mackenzie's new administrative responsibilities, and his move to Calcutta, seriously retarded his historical research. In particular, he found that it was difficult to move his establishment out of southern India: "The individuals reared by me for several years being natives of the Coast or the Southern provinces and almost as great strangers to Bengal and Hindostan as Europeans, their removal to Calcutta is either impracticable, or where a few from personal and long attachment (as my head Brahmin, Jain translator, and others), are willing to give this last proof of their fidelity, yet still it is attended with considerable expence." Without his full establishment, Mackenzie correctly worried that "most of what I had proposed to condense and translate from the originals in the languages of their country could not be conveniently, or at all, effected in Calcutta."

Nevertheless, Mackenzie was determined to attempt it, planning, "in this last stage, preparatory to my return to Europe, to effect a condensed view of the whole collection and a catalogue raisonnée of the native manuscripts and books etc. and to give the translated materials such form as may at least facilitate the production of some parts, should they ever appear to the public by persons better qualified, if the grateful task be not permitted to my years or to my state of health." Mackenzie went on to suggest to Johnston that it would, he hoped, "appear to all considerate men, that some leisure and tranquil exclusive application of an arrangement of these [materials] would be at least necessary to one who has now resided thirty-four years in this climate, without the benefits of once going to Europe."

Even at this stage, Mackenzie received little support or sympathy from Company officials, who never gave any indication of their genuine commitment to Mackenzie's historical labors. In the meanwhile, Johnston advocated his friend's cause, calling on Charles Grant, the former Chairman of the Court of Directors, to attempt to persuade him of "the great advantage it would secure for Oriental history and literature, were Col. Mackenzie to be allowed by the Directors to come to England upon leave, in order that he might, with the assistance of the different literary characters in Europe, arrange his valuable collection of materials." Grant apparently responded favorably, but did nothing before Johnston learned that Mackenzie had died in Calcutta in 1821, still "without having had leisure to engage in the preparation of any condensed view of his collections."[45]

V

> Archaeology describes discourses as practices specified in the element of the archive.
>
> Michel Foucault, *The Archaeology of Knowledge*, 131

We are left with silence. For not only did Mackenzie fail to prepare a "condensed view" or a "Catalogue Raisonné," he wrote little about either the collection itself or his sense of its significance beyond what I have already recorded. Most of his publications were in fact nothing more than annotated editions of texts translated by his assistants. The only exceptions were a couple of papers on the significance of Jainism in the history of southern India, as well as a long paper submitted at a meeting of the Royal Asiatic Society in April of 1815, entitled: "View of the principal Political Events that occurred in the Carnatic, from the dissolution of the Ancient Hindoo Government in 1564 till the Mogul Government was established in 1687, on the Conquest of the Capitals of Beejapoor and Golconda; compiled from various authentic Memoirs and Original MSS., collected chiefly within the last ten years, and referred to in the Notes at the bottom of each page." The title alone reveals the emphasis on sources, specifically on their authenticity and originality, as well as his concentration on establishing the chronology and circumstances of the principal political events of southern India's history.

Aside from these few traces, Mackenzie leaves the weight of a voluminous, detailed, and dry official correspondence, which demonstrates his attention to duty and confirms the judgment of the Company in elevating him to positions of seniority in the surveying of colonial India. And he leaves us his collection. Since Mackenzie so rarely spoke for the collection, we must let the collection speak for him—but not for him in the sense that we might wish to use the collection to trace the originary voice of an author or the guiding presence of a master orientalist. Although Mackenzie had clear ideas about what kinds of materials and texts he wanted, and communicated these ideas in both direct and indirect ways to the people who collected things for him, he was so obsessive a collector that his principal interest sometimes seemed to be sheer accumulation. The collection—its texts, drawings, marginalia, antiquities, and diaries—is a sedimentation of myriad voices. Some of the most prominent voices are those of the "native establishment" itself, not just Boria and Letchmia but also Nitala Naina, Wedhanayagam Siromony, and Babu Rao, among others. Other voices can be heard in the texts themselves, sometimes ascribed to a village Brahman, an ancient sage, or a regional ruler. As we have seen, Mackenzie's historiographical concerns and modes of collection opened his archive to voices that were rarely heard.

The collection of these voices in a colonial archive, however, undermined both Mackenzie's idiosyncratic project and our capacity to hear the voices themselves any longer. In the catalogs assembled by Wilson and then Taylor, and even more in the official administrative uses of and references to the Mackenzie Collection later in the century, the voices become anonymous footnotes for a new kind of colonial knowledge.[46] Our attempt to specify and sort these voices is further frustrated by the fact that the textual traditions represented in the archive have, despite Mackenzie's own eclectic historiographical sensibility, been seen as subversive of the standards of authority, authorship, and authenticity that have motivated the last two hundred years of western textual scholarship. The archive now known as the Mackenzie Collection sediments far more than the original voices I have tried to uncover in this chapter; it has also been the deposi-

tory for Wilson's disinterest, more generalized orientalist contempt, and
the monumental incompetence of the Reverend William Taylor, the man
who was appointed to succeed Wilson. Colonized voices have been written over even where they were most deeply inscribed in the early archives
of colonial knowledge.

As much as Mackenzie was clearly an instrument of British imperialism in India, as Mahalingam so succinctly put it, his life and his collection
stand at a bit of an angle to many aspects of early colonial rule. Mackenzie
was not alone in his historical interests—they were certainly shared by
Wilks, Malcolm, Elphinstone, Raffles, and myriad other British officials of
the late eighteenth and early nineteenth centuries. Unlike these other men,
however, Mackenzie was unable to produce a master historical narrative
of his own, and he set up an apparatus of collection that turned up works
even most colonial historians found difficult to esteem. The collection's
first and most eminent bibliographer, H. H. Wilson, became progressively
less interested in Mackenzie's project the more he worked on it, casting
doubt on the historical value of many of the texts. Bentinck's fears were
almost realized when Wilson came close to abandoning the project before its completion. And the Company Directors complained that they
had been presented with the collection as a fait accompli on payment of
10,000 pounds to Mackenzie's widow shortly after the colonel's death.
They noted also that the portion of materials they had seen "does not lead
us to form any very favourable opinion of the value of the remainder."[47]
The maps remained as proud documents of British conquest, and it is no
accident that Mackenzie's name receives its fullest and most unambiguous
praise in the histories of the survey of India. But the texts, the fabulous
myths, confused chronicles, and chaotic epistles from his collectors, with
all that they tell us about the collisions of context and meaning, power,
and knowledge, have gathered far more dust than ink.

Concerns by men such as Bentinck and Johnston about Mackenzie's
silence had progressively fewer echoes in the subsequent history of his
collection. Wilson's catalog was, as we have seen, ambivalent about the
worth of the collection. As soon as Wilson completed his initial catalog,
published in 1828, he dropped the project completely. When Mackenzie's
chief assistant, Cavelly Venkata Letchmia, applied to the Madras division
of the Asiatic Society to carry on Mackenzie's work of collection and cata-
loging after the master's death, the society rejected the application on the
grounds that no oriental would be able to do the managerial and critical

work necessary to oversee such a project. According to the head of the Asiatic Society of Bengal, James Prinsep, "Such an extensive scheme would need the control of a master head, accustomed to generalization, and capable of estimating the value of drift of inscriptional and literary evidence. The qualifications of Cavelly Venkata for such an office, judging of them by his 'abstract,' *or indeed of any native* [my emphasis], could hardly be pronounced equal to such a task, however useful they may prove as auxillaries in such a train of research."[48] Instead, they hired Taylor, a missionary in Madras and self-professed orientalist, who can only be judged, even in nineteenth-century colonial terms, as at best a poor scholar, and more accurately as an eccentric and somewhat deranged antiquarian.

The history of the Mackenzie collection thus demonstrates the consolidation of a new epistemic regime, in which the progress of textual scholarship became progressively linked to the conventions and certainties of a British colonial sociology of India. This history of silence also tells the story of the dramatic appropriation of native voices, meanings, and histories by colonial forms and logics of knowledge. Even Mackenzie's impressive reticence to gloss and catalog his own collection became the pretext for the marginalization of the native scholars Mackenzie had himself seen as so instrumental in his project. Natives could only be informants; native knowledge only the stuff of anthropological curiosity. In the late nineteenth century, when Mackenzie's collection was referred to at all it was as a reference for the origin stories of local castes in the proliferation of manuals and gazetteers produced by District level administrators. Fragments of Mackenzie's obsessive but uncritical collection were salvaged by a colonial science that gave new order to the decadent profusion of texts and histories of early colonial encounter.

Walter Benjamin wrote that "Every passion borders on the chaotic, but the collector's passion borders on the chaos of memories."[49] For Mackenzie, steeped in Enlightenment convictions about truth rather than modernist concerns about experience, the chaos was rooted in the unknown rather than the unremembered. But because Mackenzie's unknown kept obscuring what he did know, about the character of collection and the struggles of history, we know far less about the practices of Mackenzie's archive than we might like. Again to quote Benjamin, "For what else is this collection but a disorder to which habit has accommodated itself to such an extent that it can appear as order."[50] With Mackenzie's silence, there was nothing but disorder.

As colonial rule in India became more secure, and the histories of conquest were rewritten as epics of imperial entitlement, Mackenzie's silence dissolved into the silencing of India, the suppression both of the history and the historicity of India. Said's story can now be told, that of a colonialist mythic discourse untroubled either by other voices or any awareness of its own genealogy of historical process and struggle, of its own violence and violation.

Notes

1. This paper is based on research supported by the Social Science Research Council, the American Institute of Indian Studies, the Institute for Advanced Study, and the John S. Guggenheim Foundation. I am particularly grateful to the staff of the India Office Library (IOL), London, where I was permitted the use of uncataloged material in the Mackenzie papers. I am also grateful to helpful readings by Carol A. Breckenridge, David Ludden, and Thomas Trautmann.

2. Said quotes the passage from Malek in his *Orientalism* (New York: Pantheon, 1978), 97. See Anwar Abdel Malek, "Orientalism in Crisis," *Diogenes* 44 (Winter 1963): 107–8.

3. Said, *Orientalism*, 321. For a critical appreciation of Said, see my introduction to Nicholas B. Dirks, ed., *Colonialism and Culture* (Ann Arbor: University of Michigan Press, 1992).

4. Montstuart Elphinstone, *The History of India: The Hindu and Mahometan Periods* (London: J. Murray, 1841). Mill's eight-volume history of India seemed to have been the last word on the subject, and Elphinstone clearly felt the need to apologize for his own work so soon after Mill's. Mill had, as Elphinstone pointed out, never been in India. See James Mill, *The History of British India* (London: Baldwin, Cradock, and Joy, 1820; repr. New York: Chelsea House, 1968).

5. For further musings on Mackenzie, see my "Glorious Spoliations: Picturesque Beauty, Colonial Knowledge, and Colin Mackenzie's Survey of India," in Catherine Asher and Thomas Metcalf, eds., *Perceptions of India's Visual Past*, forthcoming.

6. Excerpted in William Taylor, *Catalogue Raisonné of Oriental Manuscripts in the Library of the (Late) College of Fort Saint George* (Madras, 1857), ii, iii.

7. "Biographical Sketch of the Literary Career of the Late Colin Mackenzie, Surveyor-General of India; comprising some particulars of his collection of manuscripts, plans, coins, drawings, sculptures, etc., illustrative of the antiquities, history, geography, laws, institutions, and manners of the ancient Hindus; contained in a letter addressed by him to the Right Hon. Sir Alexander Johnston, V.P.R.A.S., etc. etc.," *Madras Journal of Science and Literature* (1835).

8. W. C. Mackenzie, *Colonel Colin Mackenzie: First Surveyor-General of India* (Edinburgh and London: W & R Chambers Ltd., 1952), 53.

9. Colonel R. H. Phillimore, *The Historical Records of the Survey of India* (Dehra Dun, 1945), I, 351.

10. Survey of India Records (SIR), National Archives of India (NAI), vol. 68.

11. Mackenzie, *Colonel Colin Mackenzie*, 269.

12. Ibid., p. 79.

13. SIR, vol. 68, letter dated November 13, 1803.

14. SIR, vol. 41, letter dated November 9, 1799.

15. SIR, vol. 44, letter dated January 10, 1803.

16. SIR, vol. 44, letter dated January 11, 1816.

17. SIR, vol. 41, letter from Mackenzie to Mysore Resident, dated November 24, 1800.

18. SIR (Misc), letter from Mackenzie to Elphinstone, September 7, 1818.

19. Phillimore, *Historical Records* II, 367.

20. Home Miscellaneous, IOR, vol. 256, extract of Bengal Public Consultation, 14 March 1800, letter February 24, to Governor-General.

21. SIR, vol. 41, letter from Mackenzie to Colonel Montresor, dated July 28, 1800.

22. SIR, vol. 42, letter dated Madras July 12, 1803.

23. Foreign Miscellaneous, NAI, vol. 92, 180.

24. Ibid., 247.

25. SIR, vol. 42, Second Report on the Mysore Survey, Letter from Mackenzie to Close, July 12, 1803.

26. "Memorandum of the Means of procuring historical materials regarding the south of India," doc. no. 65, Box 3, Mackenzie uncataloged miscellaneous papers, IOL.

27. SIR, vol. 42, 1816.

28. Foreign Miscellaneous Series, NAI, vol. 94.

29. SIR, Report on Mysore Survey, July 1803.

30. Ibid.

31. SIR, vol. 41, letter to Mackenzie dated June 25, 1803.

32. SIR, Letter to Gov't, Madras, July 29, 1808.

33. Mackenzie, *Colonel Colin Mackenzie*, 274, 275.

34. SIR, vol. 41, letter to Close, dt. May 29, 1801.

35. SIR, vol. 156.

36. The subsequent quotes and references are to the Mackenzie Collection, Unbound translations, Class XII, housed in the India Office Library, London. The volume and book numbers are idiosyncratic and sometimes contradictory. For the only index to this collection, see the appendix to H. H. Wilson, *Catalogue of Oriental Mss. of Col. Mackenzie* (Calcutta: 1828).

37. Mackenzie General Collection, IOL, vol. 2.

38. Board's Collection, IOL, no. 6426.

39. Ft. St. George Public Consultation, August 16, 1808.

40. Mackenzie, *Colonel Colin Mackenzie*, 366.

41. Board's Collection, IOL, no. 6426, letter dated March 14, 1807.

42. Mackenzie, *Colonel Colin Mackenzie*, 122.

43. C. O. Blagden, *Catalogue of Manuscripts in European Languages Belonging to the Library of the India Office* (London: Oxford University Press, 1916).

44. Ibid., p. 358.

45. Taylor, *Catalogue* (note 6), ix, x.

46. See my "Castes of Mind," *Representations* (Winter 1992).

47. Phillimore, *Historical Records* (note 9), 483.

48. *Madras Journal of Literature and Science* (October 1836): 44.

49. Walter Benjamin, "Unpacking my Library," in *Illuminations* (New York: 1969), 60.

50. Ibid.

Arjun Appadurai

10. Number in the Colonial Imagination

In the latter part of 1990, in the last months of the regime of V. P. Singh and in the turbulent transition to the rule of the country by S. Chandrasekhar, India (especially the Hindi-speaking North) was rocked by two major social explosions. The first, associated with the Mandal Commission Report, pitted members of different castes against each other in a manner that many feared would destroy the polity. The second, associated with the holy city of Ayodhya, pitted Hindus and Muslims against each other over the control of a sacred site. These crosscutting issues, whose interrelationship has been noted and analyzed a great deal in recent months, both involved questions of entitlement (what are your rights?) and of classification (what group do you belong to and where does it fit in the political landscape?). This chapter explores the colonial roots of one dimension of the volatile politics of community and classification in contemporary India. In so doing, it follows the lead of many recent authors who have traced caste and communitarian politics to the politics of group representation in the twentieth century (Kothari 1989a, 1989b; Shah 1989) as well as to the role of the colonial census (Thapar 1989). But the precise and distinctive links between enumeration and classification in colonial India have not been specified, and that is what this essay proposes to do.

Edward Said's famous book (1978) is centrally concerned with the forms of knowledge that constitute what he defined as orientalism, but he does not specify how exactly the orientalist knowledge project and the colonial project of domination and extraction were connected. Nevertheless, in two ways he does set the stage for the argument of this chapter. Discussing the various ways the discourse of orientalism created a vista of exoticism, strangeness, and difference, he says that: "Rhetorically speaking, Orientalism is absolutely anatomical and *enumerative*; to use its vocabulary is to engage in the particularizing and dividing of things Oriental into manageable parts." (Said 1978: 72; emphasis mine). A little later in the book he suggests that in exhuming dead Oriental languages, orientalists were involved in a process in which "reconstructive precision, science, even *imagination* could prepare the way for what armies, administrations, and bureaucracies would later do on the ground, in the Orient " (Said: 123; emphasis mine).

I want in this essay to show that the exercise of bureaucratic power itself involved the colonial imagination and that in this imagination number played a crucial role. My general argument is that exoticization and enumeration were complicated strands of a single colonial project and that in their interaction lies a crucial part of the explanation of group violence and communal terror in contemporary India. In making this argument, it might be noted that I build on Ludden's concern with "orientalist empiricism" (in this volume).

My central question is simple. Is there any special force to the systematic counting of bodies under colonial states in India, Africa, and Southeast Asia, or is it simply a logical extension of the preoccupation with numbers in the metropolis, that is, in Europe in the sixteenth and seventeenth centuries? In asking this question, and in seeking to answer it, I have been inspired by two essays: one by Benedict Anderson (1991) and one by Sudipta Kaviraj (1989), which together suggest an important new agenda for a critique of European colonial rule. Taking the Indian colonial experience as my case, I shall try to elaborate the idea that we have paid a good deal of attention to the classificatory logic of colonial regimes, but less attention to the ways in which they employ quantification, in censuses as well as in various other instruments like maps, agrarian surveys, racial studies, and a variety of other productions of the colonial archive.

Let me briefly anticipate my argument. I believe that the British colonial state did employ quantification in its rule of the Indian subcontinent in a way that was different from its domestic counterpart in the eighteenth century (Brewer 1989) and from its predecessor states in India, including the Mughals, who certainly had elaborate apparatuses for counting, classifying, and controlling the large populations under their control. To make this case, I make two arguments and raise a number of questions for further research. The first, more extensive, argument will seek to identify the place of quantification and enumeration in British classification activities in colonial India. The second, only briefly adumbrated here, will suggest why, contrary to appearance, this variety of "dynamic nominalism" (Hacking 1986) was different from earlier state-supported numerical exercises both in the metropolis and in the colonies.

Enumerative Strategies

Much has been written about the virtual obsession of the British state in India with classifying its Indian population. The *locus classicus* of this literature is Bernard Cohn's essay "The Census and Objectification in South Asia" (1987; original 1984; original manuscript version 1970), where he shows that the Indian census, rather than being a passive instrument of data-gathering, creates, by its practical logic and form, a new sense of category-identity in India, which in turn creates the conditions for new strategies of mobility, status politics, and electoral struggle in India. The classificatory dimension of Cohn's work has been carried forward by many scholars, including Nicholas Dirks (1987), David Ludden (this volume), Gyan Prakash (1990), and several historians of the subaltern school, including Guha (1983), Arnold (1988), and Chakrabarty (1983). It has also recently been resituated in a major study of the orientalist imagination in India (Inden 1990). Cohn's concern with the census has also been carried forth in an important edited collection (Barrier 1981). All these historians have shown, in various ways, that colonial classifications had the effect of redirecting important indigenous practices in new directions, by putting different weights and values on existing conceptions of group-identity, bodily distinctions, and agrarian productivity. But less attention has been paid to the issue of numbers, of measurement, and of quantification in this enterprise.

The vast ocean of numbers, regarding land, fields, crops, forests, castes, tribes, and so forth, collected under colonial rule from very early in the nineteenth century, was not a utilitarian enterprise in a simple, referential manner. Its utilitarianism was part of a complex including informational, justificatory, and pedagogical techniques. Particular functionaries at particular levels of the system filling bureaucratic forms designed to provide raw numerical data did see their tasks as utilitarian in a commonsense, bureaucratic way. State-generated numbers were often put to important pragmatic uses, including setting agrarian tax levels, resolving land disputes, assessing various military options, and, later in the century, trying to adjudicate indigenous claims for political representation and policy change. Numbers surely were useful in all these ways. But the less obvious point is that statistics were generated in amounts that far defeated any unified bureaucratic purpose, and agrarian statistics, for example, were not only filled with classificatory and technical errors; they also encouraged new forms of agrarian practice and self-representation (Smith 1985).

Thus, though early colonial policies of quantification were utilitarian in design, I would suggest that numbers gradually became more importantly part of the illusion of bureaucratic control and a key to a colonial *imaginaire* in which countable abstractions, both of people and of resources, at every imaginable level and for every conceivable purpose, created the sense of a controllable indigenous reality. Numbers were part of the recent historical experience of literacy for the colonial elite (Money 1989; Thomas 1987), who had thus come to believe that quantification was socially useful. There is ample evidence that the significance of these numbers was often either nonexistent or self-fulfilling, rather than principally referential with regard to a complex reality external to the activities of the colonial state. In the long run, these enumerative strategies helped to ignite communitarian and nationalist identities that in fact undermined colonial rule. One must therefore ask how the idea of number as an instrument of colonial control might have entered the imagination of the state?

In regard to England, the answer to this question must go back to the story of numeracy, literacy, state fiscalism, and actuarial thinking in the seventeenth and eighteenth centuries (Hacking 1975; chap. 12; 1982; 1986; Brewer 1989). This is a very complex story indeed, but by the end of the eighteenth century, "number," like "landscape," "heritage," and the "people," had become part of the language of the British political imagination (Ludden: this volume), and the idea had become firmly implanted that a powerful state could not survive without making enumeration a central technique of social control. Thus the census in Britain made rapid technical strides throughout the nineteenth century and doubtless provided the broad scaffolding for the late-nineteenth-century census in India. A recent overview of material on the nineteenth-century census in Britain (Lawton 1978) suggests that, operating as it did within a framework of commonsense classifications, shared by officialdom with ordinary people, the British census did not have the refractive and generative effects that it did in India.

While I cannot decisively show here that the operations of the British census "at home" were different from those in India, there are three sound reasons to suppose that there were important differences. First, the basis of the British census was overwhelmingly territorial and occupational rather than ethnic or racial.[1] Second, insofar as its concerns were sociological in England, the census tended to be directly tied to the politics of representation, as in the issue of "rotten boroughs." Finally, and most important, both British and French census projects (as well as the embryonic social sciences with which they were associated), tended to reserve their most invasive investigations for their social margins: the poor, the sexually profligate, the lunatic, and the criminal. In the colonies, by contrast, the *entire* population was seen as "different" in problematic ways, this shift lying at the very heart of orientalism (Nigam 1990: 287). Furthermore, in India, this orientalist inclination was preordained to meet its indigenous counterpart in the apparent cardinality of difference in the indigenous ideology of caste, as it appeared to western eyes. The similarities and differences between the British and French colonial projects in this regard have yet to be worked out, but it is clear that the concern with deviance and marginality at home was extended to the management of entire populations in the Orient (Armstrong 1990; Rabinow 1989). While there were clear and important connections between the enterprises of classification, science, photography, criminology, and so on, in the metropolis and in the colonies, it does not appear that enumerative activities had the same cultural form in England and in India, if nothing else because the English did not see themselves as a vast edifice of exotic communities, devoid of a polity worth the name.

In a colonial setting, such as the Indian one, the encounter with a highly differentiated, religiously "other" set of groups must have built on the metropolitan concern with occupation, class, and religion, all of which were a prominent part of the British census in the nineteenth century. This created a situation, part of what David Ludden has, in this volume, called "orientalist empiricism," in which the hunt for information and for archivizing this information took on enormous proportions, and numerical data became crucial to this empiricist drive. By this time, statistical thinking had become allied to the project of civic control, both in England and in France (Canguilheim 1989; Ewald 1986; Hacking 1972, 1982, 1986), in projects of sanitation, urban planning, criminal law, and demography. It would thus have been tempting for European bureaucrats to imagine that good numerical data would make it easier to embark on projects of social control or reform in the colonies.

This argument raises two separate but related issues. Was India a *special* case or a *limiting* case in regard to the role of enumeration, exoticization, and domination in the techniques of the modern nation-state? I would argue that it was a special case, because in India the orientalist gaze encountered an indigenous system of classification that seemed virtually invented by some earlier, indigenous form of orientalism. I do not subscribe to the view that early Hindu texts constitute a simple variation on later orientalist texts, thus justifying the exoticizing tendencies of, for example, the colonial legal digests. Making this case fully would take me too far afield in this context, but let me simply note that essentialism too is a matter of context, and that the relationship between Hindu stereotyping and British essentialism in the matter of caste cannot be considered apart from a thoroughgoing comparison of state formations and religious formations in very different historical contexts.

Nevertheless, it would be foolish to pretend that British orientalism did not encounter in India as indigenous social *imaginaire* that appeared to valorize group difference in a remarkable way. Caste in India, even if it was itself a very complicated part of the Indian social imaginary, and was refracted and reified in many ways through British techniques of observation and control, was nevertheless not a figment of the British political imagination. In this regard, Oriental essentializing in India carried a social force that can come only when two theories of difference share a critical assumption: that the bodies of certain groups are the bearers of social difference and of moral status. This is where India is a *special* case. But looked at from the vantage point of the present, India may also be regarded as a *limiting*[2] case of the tendency of the modern nation-state to draw on existing ideas of linguistic, religious, and territorial difference to "produce the people" (Balibar 1990).

The role of numbers in complex information-gathering apparatuses such as the colonial one in India had two sides that, in retrospect, need to be distinguished. The one side may be described as *justificatory*, the other as *disciplinary*. A very large part of the statistical information gathered by British functionaries in India did not just facilitate *learning or discovery*, in regard to ruling Indian territories. This statistical information also assisted in arguing and teaching, in the context of bureaucratic discourse and practice, first between the East India Company and the English parliament and later between the officials of the Crown in India and their bosses in London (Smith 1985 is a classic statement of the general logic that knits together reports, manuals, and records in nineteenth-century India). Numbers were a critical part of the discourse of the colonial state, because the metropolitan interlocutors of the colonial state had come to depend on numerical data, however dubious their accuracy and relevance, for major social or resource-related policy initiatives. This justificatory dimension of the use of numbers in colonial policy, of course, also relates to the different levels of the British state in India, where numbers were the fuel for a series of nested struggles between Indian officials at the lowest levels of the bureaucracy, up the system to the governor-general of India, through a series of crosscutting committees, boards and individual office-holders, who conducted a constant internal debate about the plausibility and relevance of various classifications and the numbers attached to them (Dirks 1987: chap. 10 and 11; Hutchins 1967: 181; Presler 1987: chap. 2).

Numbers regarding castes, villages, religious groups, yields, distances, and wells were part of a language of policy debate, in which their referential status quickly became far less important than their discursive importance in supporting or subverting various classificatory moves and the policy arguments based on them. It is important to note here that numbers permitted comparison between kinds of places and people that were otherwise different, that they were concise ways of conveying large bodies of information, and that they served as a short-form for capturing and appropriating otherwise recalcitrant features of the social and human landscape of India. It is not so much that numbers did not serve a straightforward referential purpose in colonial pragmatics, serving to indicate features of the Indian social world to bureaucrats and politicians, but that this referential purpose was often not so important as the rhetorical purpose. This is in part due to the fact that the sheer vastness of the numbers involved in major policy debates in the nineteenth century often made their strictly referential or "informational" dimension unmanageable.

Yet the justificatory functions of these numerical strategies seem to have been no more important than their pedagogical and disciplinary ones. With regard to this latter function, Foucault's ideas about biopolitics certainly are most relevant, since the colonial state saw itself as part of the Indian body politic while it was simultaneously engaged in reinscribing the politics of the Indian body, especially in its involvement with sati, hook-swinging, possession rites, and other forms of body-manipulation (Dirks 1989; Mani 1990). I will return to this point later. But the numerical issue complicates matters somewhat. For what is involved here are not simply the logistical needs of the state but also its discursive needs, construed centrally as statistical needs.

What is more, this was not just a matter of providing the numerical grist for a policy apparatus whose discursive form had been constructed through a complex European development involving probabilistic thinking and civic policy. It was also a matter of disciplining the vast officialdom of the colonial state (see also Smith 1985 and Cohn 1987), as well as the population that these officials wished to control and reform, so that numbers could become an indispensable part of its bureaucratic practices and style.

Number and Cadastral Politics

The moment of rupture between the empiricist and disciplinary moments of colonial numerology can be seen in the many technical documents produced in the middle of the nineteenth century. There are many ways in which this shift can be conceptualized, including the one that sees it as a "transformation of the census as an instrument of taxes to an instrument of knowledge," in the words of Richard Smith (1985), who identifies this shift as occurring in the Punjab around 1850. In the discussion that follows, I use a document from roughly the same period, from western India, to illustrate the formation of the new sort of numerical gaze of the colonial state in the middle of the nineteenth century.

This document, published under the title *The Joint Report of 1847*, was actually published as a book in 1975 by the Land Records Department of the state of Maharashtra in western India. Its subtitle is *Measurement and Classification Rules of the Deccan, Gujarat, Konkan and Kanara Surveys*. It belongs to a class of document that shows the East India Company seeking to standardize its land-revenue practices across the full extent of its territories and to rationalize practices generated in the latter part of the eighteenth and in the early part of the nineteenth century, in the heat of conquest. It is, par excellence, a document of bureaucratic rationalization, which seeks to create and standardize revenue rules for all the land under East India Company jurisdiction in the Deccan region. But it also contains a series of letters and reports from the early part of the 1840s, which reveal a serious debate between local and central officialdom about the minutiae of mapping the agricultural terrain of western India, and its larger purposes, such as assessment and dispute-settlement. It is a quintessential document of cadastral politics.

Following Ranajit Guha's characterization of "the prose of counter-insurgency" (Guha 1983), we may call the *Joint Report* a classic example of *the prose of cadastral domination*. This is a prose, composed partly of rules, partly of orders, partly of appendices, and partly of letters and petitions, which must be read together. In this prose, the internal debates of the revenue bureaucracy, the pragmatics of rule-formation, and the rhetoric of utility always accompanied the final recommendations, by authorities at various levels, of new technical practices. These are documents whose manifest rhetoric is technical (i.e., positivist, transparent, and neutral), but whose subtext is contestatory (in regard to superiors) and disciplinary (in regard to inferiors).

The bulk of the document, like most others of its ilk, is truly Borgesian, struggling to find textual methods and representations adequate to capturing both the scope and the minutiae of the Indian agri-terrain. The analogy to Borges's classic story of the map that had to be as large as the domain it iconicized is not fanciful, as is evidenced by the following complaint by one official about an earlier technique of mapping:

> At the time of Mr. Pringle's survey of the Deccan there were some very detailed and intricate records prepared, under the name of kaifiats, which we have also found it expedient to do away with as useless, and tending by their great length and complexity to involve in obscurity, rather than elucidate, the subjects of which they treat, and by their very bulk to render the detection of errors a matter of impossibility (1975 footnote: the kaifiats prepared for many of the villages assessed by Mr. Pringle were upwards of 300 yards in length). (*Joint Report*: 55)

Notwithstanding this complaint in 1840 about the Borgesian absurdities of earlier mapping efforts, the tension between representational economy and detail does not disappear. Throughout the 1840s, a battle continues between the survey authorities of the Deccan and the Board of Revenue, which has somewhat more synoptic and panoptic aspirations for its surveys. There is, *first* of all, the relationship between measurement and classification, which is itself an explicit subject of discussion in many of the letters and reports leading up to the *Joint Report of 1847*, which fixed the basic rules of survey for this region for several subsequent decades. As regards measurement, the British officials directly responsible for the assessment regarded it as a problem of adapting existing trigonometric, topographic, and protraction methods to create maps that they saw as both accurate and functional. They were concerned to "multiply copies of these maps in the most economical and accurate manner, as well as to guard against any future fraudulent attempt at alteration," and therefore these officers suggested that "they should be lithographed" (*Joint Report*: 9–10). The concern for accuracy in measurement already incorporated existing statistical ideas about percentages of error, and of "average error," which they wanted to reduce.

These officers recognized that classification was a much trickier issue than measurement; regarding measurement, however, they were naively positivist ("these results are of an absolute and invariable character, capable of being arrived at with equal certainty by many modes": p. 10). The classification of fields for purposes of a fair assessment posed a host of problems involving the typification of variation for purposes of classification, so that the classification could be general enough to apply to a large region, yet specific enough to accommodate important variations on the ground. The resulting solution was complex and involved a ninefold classification of soils, a complex system of notation for field assessors, and a complex algorithm for translating such qualitative variation into quantitative values relevant to revenue assessment.

Put another way, the detailed disciplines of measurement and classification (the one relying on the iconic practices of trigonometry and surveying in general and the other on numerical and statistical ideas of "average" and of percentage error), were the twin techniques through which an equitable policy of revenue was envisioned, based on principles of the most general applicability that would simultaneously be as sensitive as possible to local variation. This mentality—generality of application and sensitivity to minute variations—was the central tension not just of cadastral surveys but of all the informational aspirations of the colonial state. As I explain below, this mentality is also the crucial link between the cadastral logic of the first half of the century and the human censuses of the latter part of the century, as regards enumeration and exoticization.

The exchanges surrounding the 1847 report also reveal the emergent tension between the varieties of knowledge that constituted "orientalist empiricism." It should not be very surprising that officials more closely concerned with local variation and on-the-ground accuracy and fairness were resentful of the obsessive panoptical needs of the higher levels of the bureaucracy. Illustrating literally the power of the textual "supplement" (in the deconstructionist usage), numerical tables, figures, and charts allowed the contingency, the sheer narrative clutter of prose descriptions of the colonial landscape, to be domesticated into the abstract, precise, complete, and cool idiom of number. Of course, numbers could be fought over, but this battle had a instrumental quality, far removed from the heat of the novel, the light of the camera, and the colonial realism of administrative ethnographies.

These properties were of particular value to those who sought to tame the very diversities of the land and the people that other aspects of the Oriental episteme such as photography, travelogues, engravings, and exhibitions did so much to create. In 1840, Lieutenant Wingate, the official most responsible for translating the assessment needs of the colonial state into locally feasible technical and bureaucratic practices in the Deccan, wrote to the Revenue Commissioner in Poona, his immediate superior, clearly expressing frustration with the changing interests of the central bureaucracy: "The present survey, moreover, was instituted for purely revenue purposes, and the question of rendering it subservient to those of Geography and Topography is now mooted for the first time. It can hardly therefore be in fairness objected to the plan of operations that it does not include the accomplishment of objects that were not contemplated at the time of its formation" (p. 69).

The official at the next level up in the revenue bureaucracy, though less forthright than Wingate, nevertheless makes it clear that he is puzzled by the relation between the revenue needs and the "scientific" needs of his superiors. He adds, at the conclusion of an important letter, mediating between two important levels of the bureaucracy, that "for every purpose for which a Revenue Officer can desire a map, those already furnished by the late survey under Major Jopp, and those now making out [sic] by the Deccan Revenue Surveys, of which a specimen is annexed, seem to me amply sufficient; and if anything more accurate or detailed be required, it must be, I conclude for some purpose of speculative science, on the necessity or otherwise of which I am not required to express an opinion" (pp. 81–82).

Documents such as the *Joint Report of 1847* were crucial in the disciplining of lower-level, especially native functionaries in the empiricist practices of colonial rule. In the collection of maps, measures, and statistics of every sort, these documents, and the rules contained and debated within them, show that lower-level European officials were critically concerned with making sure that the standards of colonial administrative practice were drilled into the minutest bodily techniques of these measurers. These techniques could be seen as disciplinary techniques applied both to lower-level European officialdom and to their Indian subordinates. But there was an important difference. Whereas the former might not recognize their own subjection to the regime of number in the idioms of science, patriotism, and imperial hegemony (with which they were racially identified), for Indian officialdom, these practices were a direct inscription onto their bodies and minds of practices associated with the power and foreignness of their rulers. In this, as in other aspects of the control of colonial labor and resources, not all subalternities are identical.

The vast apparatus of revenue-assessment was in fact part of a complex apparatus of discipline and surveillance in and through which native functionaries were instilled with a whole series of numerical habits, (tied to other habits of description, iconography, and distinction), in which number played a complex set of roles, including those of classification, ordering, approximation, and identification. The political arithmetic of colonialism was taught, quite literally, on the ground and translated into algorithms that could make future numerical activities habitual and instill bureaucratic description with a numerological infrastructure.

In each of these important ways, the prose of cadastral control set the grounds, and constituted a rehearsal, for later discourse concerning human communities and their enumeration. This rehearsal had three components: it set the stage for the widespread use of standardizing enumerative techniques to control on-the-ground material variations; it treated the physical features of the landscape, as well as its productivity and ecological variability, as separable (to some extent) from the complex social rights involved in its use and meaning for rural Indians; and it constituted a pedagogical preparation for the kind of disciplinary regime that would later be required for human census enumerators and tabulators at all levels.

Number (and the statistical ideology underlying number) was the "ligature" of these cadastral texts and provided the key links between these texts and the debates that they reported and the practices they were designed to discipline. Thus, through a careful reading of these apparently simply technical documents, one can unearth ideological tensions and fractures as well as practices of teaching and of surveillance, in which it is not only the case that "land is to rule" (Neale 1969). Colonial rule had a pedagogical and disciplinary function, so that "land is to teach": the measurement and classification of land was the training ground for the culture of number in which statistics became the authorizing discourse of the appendix (giving indirect weight to the verbal portion of the text) at the same time that it gave higher level officials a pedagogical and disciplinary sense of controlling not just the territory over which they sought to rule, but also the native functionaries through which such rule needed to be effected. As far as the native is concerned, the regime of number, as every page of such documents makes clear, is partly there to counteract the mendacity that is seen as constitutional to most natives, both farmers and "measurers."

We thus have one part of an answer to the question with which we began, namely: what special role does the enumeration of bodies have under colonial rule? I have suggested that numbers were a changing part of the colonial *imaginaire* and function in justificatory and pedagogical ways as well as in more narrowly referential ones. The history of British rule in the nineteenth century may be read in part as a shift from a more functional use of number in what has been called the fiscal militarism of the British state at home (Brewer 1989) to a more pedagogical and disciplinary role. Indian bodies were gradually not only categorized but given quantitative values (Bayly 1988: 88–89), increasingly associated with what Hacking has called "dynamic nominalism" (Hacking 1986), that is, the creation of new kinds of self by officially enforced labeling activities.

Number played a critical role in such dynamic nominalism in the colonial setting, partly because it provided a shared language for information-transfer, disputation, and linguistic commensuration between center and periphery and for debates among a huge army of mediating bureaucrats in India. Number, thus, was part of the enterprise of *translating* the colonial experience into terms graspable in the metropolis, terms that could encompass the ethnological peculiarities that various orientalist discourses provided. Numerical glosses constituted a kind of metalanguage for colonial bureaucratic discourse within which more exotic understandings could be packaged, at a time when the relation between enumerating populations and controlling and reforming society had come together in Europe. These numerical glosses that appear as accompanying data for discursive descriptions and recommendations are best regarded as a normalizing frame for the stranger discursive realities that the verbal portions of many colonial texts needed to construct. This normalizing frame functions at two of the levels discussed by Foucault, those of knowledge and power, text and practice, reading and ruling. Following Richard Smith's distinction (1985) between rule-by-record and rule-by-report, it can be seen that numbers in *records* provided the empirical ballast for the descriptivist thrust of the colonial gaze, whereas numbers in *reports* provided more of a normalizing frame, balancing the contestatory and polyphonic aspects of the narrative portions of these reports, which shared some of the tensions of what Guha has called the "prose of counter-insurgency."

Colonial Body Counts

These enumerative practices, in the setting of a largely agricultural society already to a large degree practically prepared for cadastral control by the Mughal state, had another major consequence. They were not merely a rehearsal for the enumerative practices of the Indian national census after 1870. They also accomplished a major and hitherto largely unnoticed task. The huge apparatus of revenue settlements, land surveys, and legal-bureaucratic changes in the first half of the nineteenth century did something beyond commoditizing land (Cohn 1969); transforming "lords into landlords" and peasants into tenants (Prakash 1990); and changing reciprocal structures of gift and honor into saleable titles, which were semiotically fractured and were rendered saleable, while retaining some of the metonymic force that tied them to named persons. They also unyoked social groups from the complex and localized group-structures and agrarian practices in which they had previously been embedded, whether in the context of the "silent settlement" of *inams* in South India (Frykenberg 1977; Dirks 1987), of *inams* in Maharashtra (Preston 1989), of "bonded" laborers in Bihar (Prakash 1990), or of Julahas in Uttar Pradesh (Pandey 1990). The huge diversity of castes, sects, tribes, and other practical groupings of the Indian landscape were thus rendered into a vast categorial landscape untethered to the specificities of the agrarian landscape.

This unyoking occurs in two major steps, one associated with the period before 1870, in which issues of land settlement and taxation are dominant colonial projects, and the other with the period from 1870 to 1931, the period of the great All-India census, in which the enumeration of human populations is the dominant project. The period from about 1840 to 1870 is the period of transition from one major orientation to the other. The first period sets the stage for the second in that it is dominated by a concern for the physical and ecological basis of land productivity and revenue, and (as I have already suggested) to some extent unyokes this variability from the social and human world associated with it, in the context of efforts to wage a battle of standardization against on-the-ground variation. In the second period, so usefully explored by Rashmi Pant (1987) in the context of the North-West Provinces and Oudh, the reverse move occurs, and human groups (castes) are treated to a considerable extent as abstractable from the regional and territorial contexts in which they function. It is of course important to note that these colonial projects were concurrently plagued by internal contradictions (the urge to specificity and to generalizability in the All-India Census names of castes, for example), by contradictions between different colonial projects, and by, most important, the fact the colonial bureaucratic operations did not necessarily transform practices or mentalities on the ground. I shall return to this issue toward the end of this chapter, in a discussion of the colonial subject.

Pant's seminal essay discusses the way in which caste came to become a crucial "site" for the activities of the national censuses after 1870, against *other* alternative sites. Along with the essay by Smith (1985) referred to already, Pant's argument allows us to see that colonial bureaucratic practice, as a contingent and historically shaped locus of agency in its own right, helped to create a special and powerful relationship between essentialization, discipline, surveillance, objectification, and group-consciousness, by the last decades of the nineteenth century.

Numbers played a crucial role in this conjuncture, and the earlier statistical panopticon was a crucial factor in the gravitation of the census toward caste as a key site of social classification, since caste appeared to be the key at once to Indian social variability as well as to the Indian mentality. Pant, who builds on the earlier work of Smith, points out that the use of caste for "differentiating a stream of data" was first applied in the realm of sex statistics from this region. Specifically, it was argued in the 1872 *Report* of the All-India Census for the North-West Provinces and Oudh that certain hypotheses about sex ratios in relation to female infanticide could only be explained by reference to caste. This concern with explaining and controlling "exotic" behaviors is a crucial piece of evidence that empiricism and exoticization were not disconnected aspects of the colonial imaginary in India. This linkage of empirical statistics and the management of the exotic was the basis for a more general policy orientation to the effect that much of what needed to be known about the Indian population would become intelligible only by the detailed enumeration of the population *in terms of caste*.

Although the subsequent history of the All-India Census shows that, in practice, there were enormous difficulties and anomalies involved with the effort to construct an all-India grid of named and enumerated "castes," the principle was not abandoned until the 1930s. As Pant shows, "by the turn of the century, the epistemological status of caste as a locale for recognizing qualified and socially effective units of the Indian population was well established—as our Census Reports of 1911–1931 confirm" (Pant 1987: 149). But it is also worth noting that since the hunt for data about caste created a huge and unmanageable flow of information, even as early as the 1860s, only "numerical majorities" were given prominence in the census reports. Thus, the concern with numerical majorities emerged as a principle for organizing census information. This apparently innocuous bureaucratic principle, of course, is a logical basis for the ideas of "majority" and "minority" groups that subsequently affected Hindu-Muslim politics in colonial India and caste politics in India during the twentieth century, up to the present.

While it is true that caste as *the* master-trope with which to taxonomize the Indian landscape is a relatively late product of colonial rule (Pant 1987), the more general essentialization of Indian groups goes back at least to the beginnings of the nineteenth century, if not earlier, as Gyan Pandey has shown with regard to the weaving castes of Uttar Pradesh (Pandey 1990). Until the last decades of the nineteenth century, however, the "essentialization" of groups in orientalist and administrative discourse was largely separate from the enumerative practices of the state, except insofar as they were directly linked to localized revenue purposes. A recent analysis of an 1823 colonial census in South India (Ludden 1988) shows that the later nineteenth-century preoccupation with social classification and enumeration is anticipated very early. But this early census seems, on the whole, pragmatic, localistic, and relational in its treatment of groups, rather than abstract, uniformitarian, or encyclopaedic in its aspirations. This was still a census oriented to taxation rather than to knowledge, in Smith's terms.

After 1870, however, not only had numbers become an integral part of the colonial *imaginaire* and of the practical ideologies of its low-level functionaries (as I have suggested), but Indian social groups had become both functionally and discursively unyoked from local agrarian landscapes and set adrift in a vast pan-Indian social encyclopaedia. This unyoking was a function of the growing sense that the social morphology of caste could provide an overall grid, through the census, for organizing knowledge about the Indian population. These are the conditions for the special force of the Indian census after 1870, which was intended to quantify previously set classifications but in fact had just the reverse effect, which was to stimulate the self-mobilization of these groups into a variety of larger translocal political forms.

Here also is the place to note the key difference between the British and their Mughal predecessors: while the Mughals did a great deal to map and measure the land under their control for revenue purposes (Habib 1963), thus generating a large part of the revenue vocabulary alive in India and Pakistan even today, they conducted no known census of persons, a fact noted by Habib as the central reason why it is difficult to estimate the population of Mughal India (Habib 1982: 163). Enumeration of various things was certainly part of the Mughal state *imaginaire* as was the acknowledgment of group identities, *but not the enumeration of group identities*. As for the other major precolonial political formations of the subcontinent, such as the Vijayanagara kingdom, they do not appear to have shared the linear, centralizing, record-keeping modes of the Mughals, and were oriented to number as a far more subtle cosmopolitics of names, territories, honors, shares, and relations (Breckenridge 1983). In this regard, non-Mughal states in the Indian subcontinent before colonial rule (including those like the Marathas who ran elaborately monetized political domains: Perlin 1987) do not seem to have been concerned with number as a direct instrument of social control. Enumerative activities were tied, in these precolonial regimes, to taxation, to accounting, and to land revenue, but the linkage of enumeration to group identity seems very weak indeed. Where it did exist it seems to have been tied to very specific social formations, such as *akharas* (wrestling/gymnastic sodalities), and not to the enumeration of the population at large.[3]

For this last, *totalizing* thrust to enter the *imaginaire* of the state, the crucial intervening step was the essentializing and taxonomizing gaze of early orientalism (of the European variety), followed by the enumerative habit applied to the land in the first half of the nineteenth century, and finally the idea of political representation as tied, not to essentially similar citizens/individuals, but to communities conceived as inherently "special." The essentializing and exoticizing gaze of orientalism in India, in the eighteenth and nineteenth centuries, provides the crucial link between census classifications and "caste and community politics." Here we are finally at the heart of the argument both as regards the differences between the colonial regime in India (and its metropolitan counterparts as well as its indigenous predecessors) and the link between colonial classificatory politics and contemporary democratic politics. The enumeration of the social body, conceived as aggregations of individuals whose bodies were inherently both collective and exotic, sets the ground for group difference to be the central principle of politics. Linking the idea of representation to the idea of "communities" characterized by bio-racial commonalities (internally) and bio-racial differences (externally) seems to be the critical marker of the colonial twist in the politics of the modern nation-state.

What occurred in the colony was a conjuncture that never occurred at home: the idea that techniques of measurement were a crucial way to normalize the variation in soil and land conjoined with the idea that numerical representation was a key to normalizing the pathology of difference through which the Indian social body was represented. Thus, the idea of the "average man" ("l'homme moyen" of Quetelet), smuggled in through statistics (as its epistemological underbelly), was brought into the domain of group difference. This sets up an orientalist extension of the metropolitan idea of the numerical representation of groups (conceived as composed of "average individuals") and the idea of "separate" electorates, which is a natural outgrowth of the sense that India was a land of groups (both for civil and political purposes) *and* that Indian social groupings were inherently "special." Thus, under colonial rule, at least in British India, the numerical dimension of classification carries the seeds of a special contradiction since it was brought to bear on a world conceived as a world of incommensurable *group* differences.

Nationalism, Representation, and Number

The "communitarian" approach, which later (in the first part of the twentieth century) has its most dramatic manifestation in separate electorates for Hindus and Muslims (Hasan 1979; Pandey 1990; Robinson 1974), was by no means restricted to them. It was built on earlier ideas about caste as the critical principal of a general morphology of the Indian population (as known through the census) and still earlier ideas about the powers of enumeration in grasping the variability and the tractability of India's land and resources. This communitarian approach was also crucial in defining the dynamics of ideas of majority and minority as culturally coded terms for dominant and disenfranchised groups in South India (Frykenberg 1987; Saraswathi 1974; Washbrook 1976: chap. 6) and elsewhere. It is thus very plausible to argue, as Rajni Kothari (1989a, 1989b) and others have done, that the very fabric of Indian democracy remains adversely affected by the idea of numerically dominated bloc-voting, as opposed to more classically liberal ideas of the bourgeois individual casting his vote as a democratic citizen.

Although it is beyond the scope of this chapter to show in a detailed way how the cognitive importance of caste in the census of India in the 1870s sets the ground for the communitarian politics of this century, it should be noted that even after 1931, when caste ceased to be a central concern of the Indian census, the idea of politics as the contest of essentialized *and* "enumerated" communities (the latter being a concept I owe to Kaviraj 1989) had already taken firm hold of local and regional politics and thus no longer required the stimulation of the census to maintain its hold on Indian politics. As Shah (1989) has recently noted, there has been a steady (and successful) effort in the last few decades to reverse the post-1931 policy of eliminating caste counts from the census.

Hannah Pitkin (1967) and others have written eloquently about the complex relationships between representation in its moral, aesthetic, and political senses. I need not repeat this western genealogy here, except to note that fairly early in the history of the Enlightenment the idea of democracy became tied to an idea of the representative sovereignty of subjects. Thus, as Frykenberg (1987) has pointed out for the Indian context, electoral politics became both a politics of *representation* (of the people to the people—a game of mirrors in which the state is made virtually invisible) and a politics of *representativeness*, that is, a politics of statistics, in which some bodies could be held to stand for other bodies because of the numerical principle of metonymy rather than the varied cosmopolitical principles of representation that had characterized ideas of divine rule in many premodern polities.

During the nineteenth and early twentieth century, the colonial state found itself in an interesting contradiction in India, as it sought to use ideas of representation and representativeness (numerical at their base) at lower levels of India's political order, with paternalist, monarchic, and qualitative principles at the top. The story of Indian self-government (which was confined to a variety of village and district level bodies during the bulk of the second half of the nineteenth century) became transformed steadily into the logic of Indian nationalism, which co-opted the colonial logic of representativeness and used it to annex the democratic idea of representation as self-representation.

Thus, the counting of bodies that had served the purposes of colonial rule at lower levels in the last half of the nineteenth century turned gradually into the idea of the representation of Indian selves (self-rule) as nationalism became a mass movement. Of course, in hindsight, as Partha Chatterjee has helped us see, nationalism suffered from sharing the basic thematic of colonialist thought and thus could not generate a thoroughgoing critique of it (Chatterjee 1986). So, the politics of numbers, especially in regard to caste and community, is not only the bane of democratic politics in India, but these older identities have become politicized in ways that are radically different from other local conceptions of the relationship between the order of jatis and the logic of the state. The process by which separate Hindu and Muslim identities were constructed at a macro-level, and transformed not just into imagined communities but also into "enumerated communities," is only the most visible pathology of the transfer of the politics of numerical representation to a society in which representation and group-identity had no special *numerical* relationship to the polity.

But it could still be said that colonial rule, either of the British in India, or of other European regimes elsewhere in the world, was not alone in generating enumerated communities. Many large non-European states, including the Ottomans, the Mughals, and various Chinese dynasties, had numerical concerns. Where lies the *colonial* difference? For the mature colonial state, numbers were part of a complex *imaginaire* in which the utilitarian needs of fiscal militarism in the world-system, the classificatory logics of orientalist ethnology, the shadow presence of western democratic ideas of numerical representation, and the general shift from a classificatory to a numerical bio-politics created an evolving logic that reached a critical conjunctural point in the last three decades of the nineteenth century and the first two decades of the twentieth.

The net result was something critically different from all other complex state-apparatuses in regard to the politics of the body and the construction of communities as bodies. Put very simply, other regimes may have had numerical concerns and they may also have had classificatory concerns. But these remained largely separate, and it was only in the complex conjuncture of variables that constituted the project of the mature colonial state that these two forms of "dynamic nominalism" came together, to create a polity centered around self-consciously enumerated communities. When these communities were also embedded in a wider official discourses of space, time, resources, and relations that was also numerical in critical ways, what was generated was a specifically colonial political arithmetic, in which essentializing and enumerating human communities became not only concurrent activities but unimaginable without one another.

This arithmetic is a critical part of colonial bio-politics (at least as regards the British in India) not only because it involved abstractions of number whereas other state regimes had more concrete numerical purposes (such as taxes, corvée labor, and the like). The modern colonial state brings together the exoticizing vision of orientalism with the familiarizing discourse of statistics. In the process, the body of the colonial subject is made simultaneously strange and docile. Its strangeness lies in the fact that it comes to be seen as the site of cruel and unusual practices and bizarre subjectivities. But colonial body-counts create not only types and classes (the first move toward domesticating differences) but also homogeneous bodies (within categories), because number, by its nature, flattens idiosyncrasies and creates boundaries around these homogeneous bodies, since it performatively limits their extent. In this latter regard, statistics are to bodies and social types what maps are to territories: they flatten and enclose. The link between colonialism and orientalism, therefore, is most strongly reinforced not at the loci of classification and typification (as has often been suggested) but at the loci of enumeration, where bodies are counted, homogenized, and bounded in their extent. Thus the unruly body of the colonial subject (fasting, feasting, hook-swinging, abluting, burning, and bleeding) is recuperated through the language of numbers that allows these very bodies to be brought back, now counted and accounted, for the humdrum projects of taxation, sanitation, education, warfare, and loyalty.

My argument thus far might be read as implying that the colonial project of essentializing, enumerating, and appropriating the social land-scape was wholly successful. In fact, that is not the case, and there is ample evidence from a variety of sources that the projects of the colonial state were by no means wholly successful, especially in regard to the colonizing of the Indian consciousness. In various kinds of peasant and urban revolt, in various kinds of autobiographic and fictional writing, in many different sorts of domestic formation and expression, and in various kinds of bodily and religious practices Indians of many classes continued practices and reproduced understandings which far predated colonial rule. What is more, Indian men and women deliberately recast their conceptions of body, society, country, and destiny in movements of protest, internal critique, and outright revolt against colonial authorities. It is indeed from these various sources that the energies of local resistance were drawn, energies and spaces (ranging from prayer groups and athletic associations to ascetic orders and mercantile orders) that provided the social basis of the nationalist movement. It was these energies that permitted someone like Gandhi, and many other lesser-known figures, to recapture social and moral ground from the British (and from the discourse of orientalism itself). These reflections bring us back to a problem raised earlier, that of the colonial subject, in relation to the enumerative and classificatory projects of the state.

There is of course no easy generalization to be made about the degree to which the effort to organize the colonial project around the idea of essentialized and enumerated communities made inroads into the practical consciousness of colonial subjects in India. It is easy enough, however, to say that the results must have varied according to various dimensions of the position of the colonial subject: her gender, her closeness to or distance from the colonial gaze, her involvement with or detachment from colonial politics, her participation in or distance from the bureaucratic apparatus itself. It is also true that various Indian persons and groups did remain (in memory if not in empirical reality) tied to locality, whatever the panopticon saw, or said. Also, while certain components of the colonial state were active propagators of the discourses of group identity, others, such as those involved with education, law, and moral reform, were implicated in the creation of what might be called a colonial bourgeois subject, conceived as an "individual." This problem is not resolvable here, but it needs to be remarked as an important issue that any interpretation of enumerated communities will eventually have to engage.

But even if various spaces remained free of the colonial panopticon (whether through the agency of resisting colonial subjects or the incapacities and contradictions of the colonial juggernaut), the fact is that the colonial gaze, and its associated techniques, have left an indelible mark on Indian political consciousness. Part of this indelible heritage is to be seen in the matter of numbers.

It is enumeration, in association with new forms of categorization, that creates the link between the orientalizing thrust of the British state, which saw India as a museum or zoo of difference and of differences, and the project of reform, which involved cleaning up the sleazy, flabby, frail, feminine, obsequious bodies of natives into clean, virile, muscular, moral, and loyal bodies that could be moved into the subjectivities proper to colonialism (Arnold: 1988). With Gandhi, we have a revolt of the Indian body, a reawakening of Indian selves, and a reconstitution of the loyal body into the unruly and sign-ridden body of mass nationalist protest (Amin 1984; Bondurant 1958). But the fact that Gandhi had to die after watching bodies defined as "Hindu" and "Muslim" burn and defile one another reminds us that his success against the colonial project of enumeration, and its idea of the body politic, was not, and is not, complete.

The Postcolonial Heritage

The burning body of Roop Kanwar (associated with the renascent Rajput consciousness of urban males in small-town Rajasthan), the self-immolations of young, middle-class men and women after the Mandal Commission Report was revitalized, and the bodies of the *kar sewak*s in Ayodhya and of Muslims in Lucknow and elsewhere suggest that indigenous ideas of difference have become transformed into a deadly politics of community, a process that has many historical sources. But this cultural and historical tinder would not burn with the intensity we now see, but for contact with the techniques of the modern nation-state, especially those having to do with number. The kinds of subjectivity that Indians owe to the contradictions of colonialism remain both obscure and dangerous.

This essay was conceived and written while the author was a MacArthur Foundation Fellow in the School of Social Sciences, Institute for Advanced Study, Princeton, during 1989–90. I am grateful to the staff of the Institute for all manner of support. This essay was first presented at a panel on "Bodies and States" at the 112th Annual Meeting of the American Ethnological Society, Atlanta, Georgia, April 26–28, 1990. I am grateful for comments and questions from that audience and for the comments of the two discussants, Talal Asad and Roy Porter. This version reflects my debts to suggestions and criticisms from the editors of this volume (Carol A. Breckenridge and Peter van der Veer) as well as from: Dipesh Chakrabarty, Joshua Cole, Nicholas Dirks, Sandria Freitag, David Ludden, and Gyanendra Pandey. I would like to dedicate this essay to my mentor, Bernard Cohn (University of Chicago), who presented me with an early version of his pathbreaking paper on the census when I arrived in his office as a graduate student in 1970. I hope he will treat it as a modest testimony to his stimulation.

Notes

1. Territorial, that is, in its concern with boroughs, counties, and regions. David Ludden: personal communication.
2. I owe this contrast to Dipesh Chakrabarty, to whom I also owe the reminder that this problem is critical to my argument.
3. Sandria Freitag: personal communication.

References

Government of Maharashtra. 1975. Selections from the Records of the Bombay Government of Papers of *The Joint Report of 1847: Measurement and Classification Rules of the Deccan, Gujarat, Konkan and Kanara Surveys*. Nagpur: Government Press.

Amin, Shahid. 1984. "Gandhi as Mahatma: Gorakhpur District, Eastern UP,

1921–2." In Ranajit Guha, ed., *Subaltern Studies: Writings on South Asian History and Society*, III. Delhi/London: Oxford University Press.

Anderson, Benedict R. 1991. "Census, Map, Museum." In *Imagined Communities* (revised edition; original 1983). New York and London: Verso.

Armstrong, Nancy. 1990. "The Occidental Alice." *Differences: A Journal of Feminist Cultural Studies* 2, 2: 3–40.

Arnold, David. 1988. "Touching the Body: Perspectives on the Indian Plague." In Guha and Spivak, *Selected Subaltern Studies*.

Balibar, Étienne. 1990. "The Nation Form: History and Ideology." *Review* (Fernand Braudel Center) 13, 3 (Summer): 329–61.

Barrier, N. Gerald, ed. 1981. *The Census in British India: New Perspectives*. New Delhi: Manohar.

Bayly, Christopher A. 1988. *Indian Society and the Making of the British Empire*. New Cambridge History of India, II, 1. Cambridge: Cambridge University Press.

Bondurant, Joan V. 1958. *Conquest of Violence: The Gandhian Philosophy of Conflict*. Princeton, NJ: Princeton University Press.

Breckenridge, Carol A. 1983. "Number Use in the Vijayanagara Era." Conference on the Kingdom of Vijayanagar, The South Asia Institute, University of Heidelberg, Heidelberg, July 14–17, 1983. Manuscript.

Brewer, John. 1989. *The Sinews of Power: War, Money, and the English State, 1688–1783*. New York: Alfred A. Knopf.

Canguilheim, Georges. 1989. *The Normal and the Pathological*. New York: Zone Books.

Chakrabarty, Dipesh. 1983. "Conditions for Knowledge of Working-Class Conditions: Employers, Government and the Jute Workers of Calcutta, 1890–1940." In Guha and Spivak, *Selected Subaltern Studies*. Oxford.

Chatterjee, Partha. 1986. *Nationalist Thought and the Colonial World: A Derivative Discourse?* London: Zed Books for the United Nations University.

Cohn, Bernard S. 1969. "Structural Change in Indian Rural Society." In Robert E. Frykenberg, ed., *Land Control and Social Structure in Indian History*. Madison: University of Wisconsin Press.

———. 1987. "The Census, Social Structure and Objectification in South Asia." In *An Anthropologist Among the Historians and Other Essays*. Delhi and London: Oxford University Press.

Dirks, Nicholas B. 1987. *The Hollow Crown: Ethnohistory of an Indian Kingdom*. Cambridge: Cambridge University Press.

———. 1989. "The Policing of Tradition in Colonial South India." Presented at the Ethnohistory Workshop, University of Pennsylvania.

Ewald, François. 1986. *L'État Providence*. Paris: B. Grasset.

Frykenberg, Robert E. 1977. "The Silent Settlement in South India, 1793–1853: An Analysis of the Role of Inams in the Rise of the Indian Imperial System." In Robert E. Frykenberg, ed., *Land Tenure and Peasant in South Asia*. New Delhi: Orient Longman.

———. 1987. "The Concept of 'Majority' as a Devilish Force in the Politics of Modern India: A Historiographic Comment." *Journal of the Commonwealth History and Comparative Politics* 25, 3 (November): 267–74.

Guha, Ranajit. 1983. "The Prose of Counter-Insurgency." In Ranajit Guha, ed. *Subaltern Studies: Writings on South Asian History and Society*, II. New Delhi and London: Oxford University Press.

Guha, Ranajit and Gayatri Chakravorty Spivak, eds. 1988. *Selected Subaltern Studies*. New York and Oxford: Oxford University Press.

Habib, Irfan. 1963. *The Agrarian System of Mughal India (1556–1707)*. Bombay and London: published for the Department of History, Aligarh Muslim University by Asia Publishing House.

———. 1982. *An Atlas of the Mughal Empire: Political and Economic Maps*. Centre of Advanced Study in History, Aligarh Muslim University. Delhi and New York: Oxford University Press.

Hacking, Ian. 1975. *The Emergence of Probability: A Philosophical Study of Early Ideas About Probability, Induction and Statistical Inference*. Cambridge and New York: Cambridge University Press.

———. 1982. "Biopower and the Avalanche of Printed Numbers." *Humanities in Society* 5, 3–4 (Summer and Fall): 279–95.

———. 1986. "Making Up People." In Thomas C. Heller, Morton Sosna, and David E. Wellbery, eds., *Reconstructing Individualism: Autonomy, Individuality, and the Self in Western Thought*. Stanford, CA: Stanford University Press.

Hasan, Mushirul. 1979. *Nationalism and Communal Politics in India, 1916–1928*. New Delhi: Manohar.

Hutchins, Francis G. 1967. *The Illusion of Permanence: British Imperialism in India*. Princeton, NJ: Princeton University Press.

Inden, Ronald B. 1990. *Imagining India*. Oxford and Cambridge, MA: Basil Blackwell.

Kaviraj, Sudipta. 1989. "On the Construction of Colonial Power: Structure, Discourse, Hegemony." Presented to a conference on Imperial Hegemony, Berlin. Manuscript.

Kothari, Rajni. 1989a. "Communalism: The New Face of Indian Democracy." In *State Against Democracy: In Search of Humane Governance*. Delhi: Ajanta Publications; New York: New Horizon Press.

———. 1989b. "Ethnicity." In *Rethinking Development: In Search of Humane Alternatives*. Delhi: Ajanta Publications; New York: New Horizon Press.

Lawton, Richard, ed. 1978. *The Census and Social Structure: An Interpretative Guide to Nineteenth Century Censuses for England and Wales*. London and Totowa, NJ: F. Cass.

Ludden, David E. 1988. Caste Landscapes in Southern Tamil Nadu and the 1823 Tirunelveli Census. Forthcoming in Arjun Appadurai, ed., *Caste in Practice*.

Mani, Lata. 1990. "Contentious Traditions: The Debate on *Sati* in Colonial India." In Kumkum Sangari and Sudesh Vaid, eds., *Recasting Women: Essays in Indian Colonial History*. New Brunswick, NJ: Rutgers University Press.

Money, John. 1989. Teaching in the Marketplace, or Caesar Adsum Jam Forte: Pompey Aderat: The Retailing of Knowledge in Provincial England. Clark Library, UCLA, March 4, 1989. Manuscript.

Neale, Walter C. 1969. "Land is to Rule." In Robert E. Frykenberg, ed., *Land*

Control and Social Structure in Indian History. Madison: University of Wisconsin Press.

Nigam, Sanjay. 1990. "Disciplining and Policing the 'Criminals by Birth,' Part 2: The Development of a Disciplinary System, 1871–1900." *Indian Economic and Social History Review* 27, 3 (July–Sept.): 257–87.

Pandey, Gyanendra. 1990. *The Construction of Communalism in Colonial North India*. New Delhi and London: Oxford University Press.

Pant, Rashmi. 1987. "The Cognitive Status of Caste in Colonial Ethnography: A Review of Some Literature of the North West Provinces and Oudh." *Indian Economic and Social History Review* 24, 2: 145–62.

Perlin, Frank. 1987. "Money-Use in Late Pre-Colonial India and the International Trade in Currency Media." In John F. Richards, ed., *The Imperial Monetary System of Mughal India*. Delhi: Oxford University Press.

Pitkin, Hanna F. 1967. *The Concept of Representation*. Berkeley and Los Angeles: University of California Press.

Prakash, Gyan. 1990. *Bonded Histories: Genealogies of Labor Servitude in Colonial India*. South Asian Studies 44. Cambridge and New York: Cambridge University Press.

Presler, Franklin A. 1987. *Religion Under Bureaucracy: Policy and Administration for Hindu Temples in South India*. Cambridge and New York: Cambridge University Press.

Preston, Laurence W. 1989. *The Devs of Cincvad: A Lineage and the State in Maharashtra*. Cambridge/New York: Cambridge University Press.

Rabinow, Paul. 1989. *French Modern: Norms and Forms of the Social Environment*. Cambridge/London: MIT Press.

Robinson, Francis. 1974. *Separatism Among Indian Muslims: The Politics of the United Provinces' Muslims, 1860–1923*. London and New York: Cambridge University Press.

Said, Edward W. 1978. *Orientalism*. New York: Vintage Books.

Saraswathi, S. 1974. *Minorities in Madras State: Group Interest in Modern Politics*. Delhi: Impex India.

Shah, Arvind M. 1989. "Caste and the Intelligentsia." *Hindustan Times*. March 24.

Smith, Richard S. 1985. "Rule-By-Records and Rule-By-Reports: Complementary Aspects of the British Imperial Rule of Law." *Contributions to Indian Sociology* 19, 1: 153–76.

Thapar, Romila. "Imagined Religious Communities? Ancient History and the Modern Search for a Hindu Identity." *Modern Asian Studies* 23(1989): 209–32.

Thomas, K. 1987. "Numeracy in Early Modern England." *Transactions of the Royal Historical Society* 5th series 37: 103–32.

Washbrook, David A. 1976. *The Emergence of Provincial Politics: The Madras Presidency, 1870–1920*. Cambridge and New York: Cambridge University Press.

Contributors

Arjun Appadurai is Director of the Humanities Institute and Barbara E. and Richard J. Franke Professor in the Humanities at the University of Chicago. His previous books include *Worship and Conflict Under Colonial Rule* (1981), *The Social Life of Things* (editor, 1984) and *Gender, Genre, and Power in South Asian Expressive Traditions* (co-editor, University of Pennsylvania Press, 1991). He is associate editor of the journal *Public Culture*.

Carol A. Breckenridge is the editor of the comparative cultural studies journal *Public Culture* and teaches at the University of Chicago. She has published on colonialism, religion, and cosmopolitan forms in India. She is the editor of *Modern Sites: Public Culture in Modern India* (forthcoming 1993).

Vinay Dharwadker currently teaches English, American, and non-Western Literatures in the Department of English, University of Oklahoma. His first book of poems, *Sunday at the Lodi Gardens*, will be published in July 1993. He is the co-editor, with A. K. Ramanujan, of *Modern Indian Poetry: An Anthology* and, with Barbara Stoler Miller and A. K. Ramanujan, of *The Columbia Book of Indian Poetry*, both forthcoming. He is working at present on a two-volume anthology of his translations of modern Hindi and Marathi poetry, some of which appeared in a book-length feature in *TriQuarterly*.

Nicholas B. Dirks is Professor of History and Anthropology and Director of the Center for South and Southeast Asian Studies at the University of Michigan. He is the author of *The Hollow Crown: Ethnohistory of an Indian Kingdom* (1987) and editor of *Colonialism and Culture* (1992). In addition to current work on the colonial archive of Colin Mackenzie, he is doing research on colonial constructions of caste in India and postcolonial political culture in southern India.

Jayant Lele is Professor in the Departments of Political Studies and Sociology, Queen's University, Kingston, Canada, and teaches critical social theory, comparative politics of developing societies, and political sociology. After pursuing post-graduate education at Poona University, he received his Ph.D. from Cornell. He has been a visiting Professor at both Universities, and has held Senior Fellowships from the Shastri Indo-Canadian Institute. His publications include *Tradition and Modernity in Bhakti Movements* (1981), *Elite Pluralism and Class Rule* (1981), *Language and Society* (1988) and *State and Society in India* (1990).

David Lelyveld, an historian of modern India, is the author of *Aligarh's First Generation: Muslim Solidarity in British India* (1988) and South Asia editor of the *Encyclopedia of Asian History* (1988). He has taught at the University of Minnesota, Columbia University, and the University of Washington. His current research deals with the social history of the Urdu language.

David Ludden is Associate Professor of History and Chairman of the Department of South Asia Regional Studies at the University of Pennsylvania. His first monograph, *Peasant History in South India*, was reissued in paperback in 1989. He is currently completing a volume entitled *Agriculture and Indian History* for *The New Cambridge History of India*.

Sheldon Pollock studied classics and Sanskrit at Harvard Univesity (AB 1971, Ph.D. 1975), and Sanskrit poetry and philosophy in Pune, Banaras, and Andhra Pradesh. He is George V. Bobrinskoy Professor of Sanskrit and Indic Studies, and Chairman, Department of South Asian Languages and Civilizations, University of Chicago. His most recent book is Vol. III of the *Ramayana of Valmiki: An Epic of Ancient India* (1991). He is currently working on the historical imagination of premodern India and on the cultural politics of old Kannada.

Rosane Rocher is Professor of South Asian Studies and a former director of the National Resource Center for South Asia at the University of Pennsylvania. She is the author of several works dealing with the history of linguistics and of Indian studies, including two biographies of eighteenth-century British orientalists: *Alexander Hamilton (1762–1824): A Chapter in the Early History of a Sanskrit Philology* (1968) and *Orientalism, Poetry, and the Millennium: The Checkered Life of Nathaniel Brassey Halhed, 1751–1830* (1983). Much of her current research focuses on the dynamics of intercultural communication and on patterns of life in internationally oriented societies.

Gayatri Chakravorty Spivak is Professor of English and Comparative Literature at Columbia University. She has published *Myself Must I Remake: The Life and Poetry of W. B. Yeats* (1974) and *In Other Worlds:*

Essays in Cultural Politics (1987). She has translated and introduced Jacques Derrida's *Of Grammatology* (1976) and edited, with Ranajit Guha, *Selected Subaltern Studies* (1987). She is currently working on reading narrative as ethical instantiation; her new book *Outside in the Teaching Machine* is in press.

Peter van der Veer is Professor of Comparative Religion and Director of the Centre for the Comparative Study of Religion and Society at the University of Amsterdam. Previously he taught cultural anthropology at the University of Pennsylvania. He is the author of *Gods on Earth: The Management of Religious Experience and Identity in a North Indian Pilgrimage Centre* (1988) and *Religious Nationalism: Hindus and Muslims in India* (forthcoming 1993).

Index

SOUTH ASIA SEMINAR SERIES

PUBLISHED BY THE UNIVERSITY OF PENNSYLVANIA PRESS

Orientalism and the Postcolonial Predicament: Perspectives on South Asia, edited by
Carol Breckenridge and Peter van der Veer. 1992.
Gender, Genre and Power in South Asian Expressive Traditions, edited by Arjun
Appadurai, Frank J. Korom, and Margaret A. Mills. 1991.

PUBLISHED BY THE SOUTH ASIA REGIONAL STUDIES DEPARTMENT,
UNIVERSITY OF PENNSYLVANIA

Making Things in South Asia: The Role of the Craftsman, edited by Michael W.
Meister. 1988.
The Countries of South Asia: Boundaries, Extensions, and Interrelations, edited by
Peter Gaeffke and David Utz. 1988.
Science and Technology in South Asia, edited by Peter Gaeffke and David Utz. 1988.
Identity and Division in Cults and Sects in South Asia, edited by Peter Gaeffke. 1984.

University of Pennsylvania Press
NEW CULTURAL STUDIES
*Joan DeJean, Carroll Smith-Rosenberg,
and Peter Stallybrass, Editors*

Jonathan Arac and Harriet Ritvo, editors. *Macropolitics of Nineteenth-Century Literature: Nationalism, Exoticism, Imperialism.* 1991

John Barrell. *The Birth of Pandora and the Division of Knowledge.* 1992.

Bruce Thomas Boehrer. *Monarchy and Incest in Renaissance England: Literature, Culture, Kinship, and Kingship.* 1992

Carol Breckenridge and Peter van der Veer, editors. *Orientalism and the Postcolonial Predicament: Perspectives on South Asia.* 1993

E. Jane Burns. *Bodytalk: When Women Speak in Old French Literature.* 1993

Julia V. Douthwaite. *Exotic Women: Literary Heroines and Cultural Strategies in Ancien Régime France.* 1992

Barbara J. Eckstein. *The Language of Fiction in a World of Pain: Reading Politics as Paradox.* 1990

Katherine Gravdal. *Ravishing Maidens: Writing Rape in Medieval French Literature and Law.* 1991

Jayne Ann Krentz, editor. *Dangerous Men and Adventurous Women: Romance Writers on the Appeal of the Romance.* 1992

Linda Lomperis and Sarah Stanbury, editors. *Feminist Approaches to the Body in Medieval Literature.* 1993

Karma Lochrie. *Margery Kempe and Translations of the Flesh.* 1991

Alex Owen. *The Darkened Room: Women, Power and Spiritualism in Late Victorian England.* 1990

Jacqueline Rose. *The Case of Peter Pan, or The Impossibility of Children's Fiction.* 1992

This book has been set in Linotron Galliard. Galliard was designed for Mergenthaler in 1978 by Matthew Carter. Galliard retains many of the features of a sixteenth-century typeface cut by Robert Grajon but has some modifications that give it a more contemporary look.

Printed on acid-free paper.